Records of Old Macon County, N.C.

Records of Old Macon County, N.C.

1829-1850

compiled by

Barbara Sears McRae

CLEARFIELD

Printed for
Clearfield Company, Inc. by
Genealogical Publishing Co., Inc.
Baltimore, Maryland
1991

Reprinted for
Clearfield Company, Inc. by
Genealogical Publishing Co., Inc.
Baltimore, Maryland
2000, 2006

International Standard Book Number: 0-8063-1302-1

Made in the United States of America

Table of Contents

Foreword

Old Macon County, North Carolina, was a large territory that at one time included all the land from the Blue Ridge on the east to the state boundaries of South Carolina, Georgia and Tennessee—an area that now encompasses all or part of seven western North Carolina counties and half of the Great Smoky Mountains National Park.

The region opened for settlement after the Cherokee Nation, by the Treaty of 1817 & 1819, ceded the land between the previous boundary (the "Meigs & Freeman" line), and the ridge of the Nantahala Mountains. A few white settlers, including several men who had married Cherokee women, lived in the area before the treaty was signed. Except in the case of white men claiming land in right of their Indian wives, legal ownership awaited the surveying and platting of the territory by the state.

In 1820, a survey party led by Capt. Robert Love mapped the new territory and laid it out in districts and tracts. The state displayed the resulting map, known as the Love Survey, in the Haywood County courthouse, in Waynesville. The first land sale took place there Sept. 20, 1820. Deeds from this sale and other early transactions were registered in Haywood County.

The Love survey divided the new territory into 18 districts, and set off tracts of land within each district in 50 to 300-acre sections. The survey party chose the site of Franklin, the future county seat, and laid it off in town lots. The town was named for Jesse Franklin, one of the commissioners responsible for organizing the new territory.

The 1817-19 treaty excluded a number of 640-acre reservations granted to individual Cherokee heads of household who wished to remain as citizens of North Carolina. These reservations became a cause of dispute among the settlers, and the Cherokees eventually lost them. However, the State paid the heads of the households, or their heirs, for their property rights. The reservations themselves were broken up into tracts and made available for land grants. Several later deeds mention reservation boundaries or Indian improvements.

The new territory remained part of Haywood until its population increased enough to warrant establishment of a new county. Settlement was rapid. Within 10 years of the first land sale the population had reached 5,333. The state legislature established Macon County in 1828, and the first county court met in Franklin in March 1829. John Dobson, the new county register, recorded his first deed on June 19, 1829.

The original territory of Macon County included all or part of the present counties of Macon, Jackson (est. 1851), Swain (est. 1871) and Transylvania (est. 1861). In 1835, the Cherokees gave up their remaining lands in North Carolina—what are now the counties of Cherokee (est. 1839), Clay (est. 1861) and Graham (est. 1872), and the land along the Nantahala River in present Macon County. Until the establishment of Cherokee County, the entire territory was administered as part of Macon.

Many of the documents registered in Macon's early record books were land grants. Despite the businesslike way in which the Love survey party undertook its job, and the orderly way in which the state proceeded with land sales, property ownership was not without confusion. As early as 1798, Buncombe County (Haywood's "mother" county) had issued land grants in part of this territory. Though these grants were later voided, some of the grantees pursued their legal rights through the courts and some appear to have retained ownership. Other legal disputes arose over land held or claimed by Cherokees.

The Love party graded the land according to its value, the price ranging from $4 per acre for the top grade, to 50 cents per acre for the poorest grade. Grantees were to pay down one-eighth of the purchase price, with the balance due in four annual payments. Often the original grantee failed to complete payment and sold or assigned his or her rights to someone else.

Land that was not platted in the Love survey could be obtained by entry and claim after 1835; the land was offered at lower prices than the Love plats, to make it more widely available. A would-be owner began the process by surveying the tract and marking a corner, and then either filing a plat or listing the location and acreage in the Entry-taker's office in Franklin. The grantee was required to make some improvement to the property. If no disputes arose within 12 months, he or she followed the established procedure for obtaining a state grant. Depending on its value, entered land went for either $5 or $10 per 100 acres.

During its early settlement years, "old" Macon County was a frontier land. For many American families, it was a stop on the trail leading west. Settlers seeking land and opportunity came here primarily from adjoining areas of North Carolina, the South Carolina upstate, and parts of Georgia and Tennessee. Some of these settlers, and many of their descendants, moved on as newer frontiers beckoned. The most recent migration took place among loggers and their families, who moved to the Pacific northwest in large numbers during the early 20th Century, after heavy timbering took its toll on the Southern Appalachian forests.

Because of its terrain, Macon was not well suited for the large plantation-style farming of other parts of the South. Slavery was never as important in the mountains as it was elsewhere, and slaves made up only about 8-9% of the population during much of the ante-bellum period. Nevertheless, a number of transactions involving slaves appear in the register books. Most of these were mortgages, reflecting the economic value of slaves in a cash-poor society where land was as cheap as a nickel an acre, and the mainstays of the economy were subsistence farming and barter.

There were no banks in Macon County until early in the 20th Century. Some early settlers obtained financing from the Bank of the State of North Carolina, at Morganton. The bank had an agent, Isaac Avery, who represented its interests in Macon County. Some local businessmen also used the Branch of the Bank of Cape Fear, in Asheville, after it opened. Most "banking," however, was more personal. Local merchants often loaned money or provided goods on credit, sometimes holding mortgages on real or personal property as security. Besides revealing economic activities and living conditions of the period, these chattel mortgages are sometimes the only official record left of an individual.

This book is based on abstracts of original documents kept by the Register of Deeds in the Macon County Courthouse, Books A - E, covering years 1829 through most of 1849.

Though every effort has been made to create an accurate abstract of the original manuscripts, researchers should realize that accuracy cannot be guaranteed. The original records are often difficult to read, and themselves contain errors. For example, names of individuals and locations may be spelled three or four different ways within a single document. When this occurred, all variations of personal names are given.

The original register books are in generally excellent condition; they are kept in the Register of Deeds office, Macon County Courthouse, Franklin NC 28734. Microfilm copies are available in the N.C. Division of Archives, Raleigh, NC, and in other repositories.

Barbara Sears McRae

Franklin, N.C.

April 30, 1990

Records of Old Macon County, N.C.

Macon County Deed Book A

1A SG 115, JOHN LEATHERWOOD, $502.50, 167.5 ac., Sec. 3, Dis. 14, on Tennessee R. Granted Dec. 31, 1828; registered June 18, 1829.

1B JOSEPH WELCH and GEORGE RUSEL to JOHN SHULAR, all of Macon, 277 ac., Dis. 10, E. side of Tennessee R., for $620 paid to Rusel. June 16, 1829, *Joseph___, George ___*. Wit: ____ *WELCH, ___ WELCH Jr*. Record is torn.

1B ENNIS SHEP(HERD) to JAMES BRISON, 54 ac. Sec. 49, Dis. __, bought at land sales in 1820; Brison to pay am't due state. Sep. 25, 1829, *Enos Shep____*. Wit: *JOHN TATHAM, THOMAS TATHAM*. Record is torn.

2A Mortgage: JOSEPH WELCH of Macon to THOS. W.P. POINDEXTER, 55 ac. on N. side & conjunction of Tennessee & Tuckasege R., Sec. 1, Dis. 1; also, at forks of rivers, Sec. 38, Dis. 8. Condition: Welch to repay 2 notes to Poindexter. 1829. (Torn)

2B PARCHCORN FLOWER to THOS. W.P. POINDEXTER of Haywood Co. NC, for $300, 1 sq. mile reservation, both sides Tessenty Cr. near mouth of creek. Feb. 13, 1826, *Parchcorn (his X mark) Flower*. Wit: *JAMES POINDEXTER, REBECCA C. POINDEX-TER, QURAT (his X mark), INDIAN (his X mark) SAM*. Proven by James Poindexter, Mar. 1829 court. Registered July 29, 1829.

3 THOMAS WELCH, Sr of Haywood Co. conveyed to ASAPH ENLOW, JOSEPH WELCH & ABRAHAM ENLOW, ESQ., all of Haywood Co., the tract where I now live, Sec. 18, Dis. 8, known as Stecoah old Fields, on July 5, 1826, taking a conditional bond. He now (1828) sells this tract to DILLARD LOVE for $500. Oct. 15, 1829, *Thomas Welch Senior*. Wit: *WM. WELCH, Jr., THOMAS WELCH Jr*. Proven by Wm. Welch, June 1829 court. Registered July 29, 1829.

4 THOMAS WELCH, Sr., for $1725, now conveys to ASAPH ENLOW, JOSEPH WELCH & ABRAHAM ENLOW 300 ac. on Tuckasege R. July 5, 1827, *Thomas Welch Sr*. Wit: *ANDREW WELCH, WILLIAM WELCH, Jr*. Reg. July 29, 1829.

5 SG 116, JESSE BERRY, $106, 53 ac., Sec. 11, Dis. 1, NE bank of Tuckasege R. below plantation occupied by DAVID SHULAR, on Shulars Cr. Granted Jan. 2, 1829; registered Aug. 15, 1829.

6 SG 119, JOHN GIBBS, $230, 98.25 ac., Sec. 15, Dis. 8, W. bank of "Tuckaseag" (Tuck-asege) R. Granted Jan. 9, 1828; registered Aug. 15, 1829.

7 SG 127, MARMADUKE KIMBROUGH, $237, 158 ac., Sec. 77, Dis. 15. Granted Jan. 10, 1829; registered Aug. 16, 1829.

8 BENJAMIN HOWARD of Haywood Co. NC to ASAPH ENLOW, for $1725, land on W. side of Tennessee R. & "Roashes" (Rish's?) Branch, Sec. 70, Dis. 15. Feb 28, 1827, *B. Howard*. Wit: *JOSHUA ROBERTS, M. PATTON*. Proven by M. Patton, Jun. 1829 court. Registered Sept. 28, 1829.

9 DAVID PEAKE to JOHN LAMM, both of Haywood Co. NC, 70 ac. Sec. 32, Dis. 12, which Peake purch. at Franklin, 1822. Sep. 24, 1828. *David Peak*. Wit: *WILLIAM BRISON, Senr., GRAY CROWE*. Proven by Wm Brison, Sep. 1829. Reg. Nov. 2, 1829.

9 JONATHAN PHILIPS, heir of ROBERT PHILLIPS, dec'd, to THOMAS AMMONS, 50 ac., Sec. 30, Dis. 12, purch. at Waynesville, 1820. Sept. 25, 1829, *Jonathan Phillips*. Wit: *JEREMIAH R. PACE, JOHN AMMONS*. Reg. Nov. 2, 1829.

10 SG 120, GEORGE HUGHS, $200, Sec. 46, Dis. 10 on "Ioley" (Iotla) Creek. Granted Jan. 9, 1829; registered Nov. 24, 1829.

11 LUKE BARNARD to ANDREW BARNARD, for $1,000, land on "Catugajay" (Car-toogechaye) Cr.; mention of Andrew Barnard's Spring Branch. Feb. 1829, *Luke Barnard*. Wit: *THOS. LOVE, E. AMMONS*. Ack. in Sep. 1829 court. Reg. Nov. 24, 1829.

12 JOSEPH WELCH to JESSEY R. SILAR, both of Macon, for $400, a Negro boy named
    CEASOR, about 21 years of age, healthy and sensible. Jan. 31, 1829. *Joseph Welch*. Wit:
    JOHN ALLMAN, B. BRITTON. Ack. in court, Sep. 1829. Reg. Nov. 24, 1829.

12 GIDEON F. MORRIS to JESSEE R. SILAR, both of Macon, for $350, a Negro girl
    named SALLEY, 22 years of age. Sep. 23, 1821. Wit: *JAMES ROBINSON*. Ack. in Sept.
    1829 court. Registered Nov. 24, 1829.

12 JAMES MARTIN of Rabun Co., Ga. & WILLIAM MCCLURE of Haywood Co., NC
    agree McClure to hold the negro MERIER girl now in his possession until Martin pay
    $150. Oct. 1, 1828, *James Martin, William McClure*. Wit: *JAMES VERMILIAN*.
    Registered Nov. 24, 1829.

13 Came before J.R. SILAR, acting J.P. of Macon Co., GEORGE H. KIMBROUGH, who
    swore he held note for $462.50 on M.D. KIMBRUGH due abt July 7, 1829; note was
    lost. Oct. 12, 1829. Ack. in Dec. 1829. court. Registered 22 Dec. 1829.

13 WILLIAM MINGUS of Rockingham Co., NC to EPHRAIM AMMONS of Haywood
    Co. NC, for $387.50, a Negro woman, PATIENCE, 22 yrs old & her child SEILAR. May
    11, 1827. *William J. Mingus*. Wit: *PETER (his X mark) LEDFORD, Jr., POLLY (her X
    mark) CONLEY*. Registered Feb. 8, 1830.

14 SG 111, WILLIAM ANGEL, assignee of SAMUEL JOHNSTON for $621, 192+ ac,
    Sec. 13, Dis. 12, Sugar Town fork, Tenn. R. Granted Nov. 26, 1828; reg. Jan. 29, 1830.

15 THOMAS W. POINDEXTER of Macon relinquishes to N.C. his right in 640 ac. purch.
    from PARCH CORN FLOWER, a reservee. Oct. 8, 1829. *Thomas W.P. Poindexter*. Wit:
    HUMPHREY POSEY, who proved in court, Dec. 1829. Reg. Feb. 8, 1830.

15 SAM AN (his X mark) JUNESTUKIE rec'd from JOSEPH WELCH $50 for reservation;
    empower Welch to assign my name to the deed of conveyance to the state. Dec. 14,
    1829. Wit: *ED. L. POINDEXTER*, who proved Dec. 24, 1829. Reg. Feb. 9, 1830.

16 SG 121, RICHARD WILSON, $460, 159 ac. Sec. 11, Dis. 7, crossing Savannah Cr.
    Granted Jan. 9, 1829; registered Jan. 8, 1830.

17 WILLIAM BERRY to DILLARD LOVE, both of Macon, for $60, 1/2 ac. lot (No. 23) in
    Waynesville, Haywood Co. NC. Apr. 10, 1823, *William Berrey*. Wit: *DAVID
    COLEMAN, JNO. CLINE*. Proven by John Cline, Apr. 10, 1829. Reg. Feb. 9, 1830.

No page 18 or 19.

20 ROMULUS M. SAUNDERS and HUMPHREY POSEY, Commissioners app'ted by the
    Pres. of U.S. in behalf of N.C., to undersigned Cherokee claimants to Reservations by vir-
    tue of Treaty between Chiefs & Headmen of Cherokee tribe & the U.S.A. in 1817 &
    1819, sums following the name of claimants, which they ack., to wit: (Names in brackets
    are as they appear in the signature section, if spelled differently than in the reserve list)

    • CA,TA TEE HEE for his reservation, $ 600
    • PANTHOR , $ 320
    • CULSOWEE, $ 250
    • CO A LEACH [*Cooleeke*], $ 250
    • TOM and WAKEY, children and heirs of TRO,LINERS TA LUURED, $ 100
    • SIX KILLER, $ 250-----? (550?)
    • SUAGA, $ 250
    • PARCH CORN FLOWER, $ 750
    • OO,SANTEE TAKE, $ 100
    • THE CAT [*Cate*], $ 750
    • OU,SATTA, only son & heir of CIULAH [*Hinstah?*], dec'd, $1,050
    • KARHALLA [*Kirkulla*] or THIGH, $ 950
    • WALLACEE, $ 200
    • WHIPPERWILL, $ 150
    • TARRAPIN, $ 150
    • ARKELUKE [*AR HA LEE HE*], $ 300
    • BIG TOM, $ 400
    • CHIULA [*Cheiule*], $ 400
    • AR,TAW OR [Artower], $ 250

• TOM, CHAW,CAW HEE & TANNAGAHA [*Tannagahee*], children of OLD MOUSE, dec'd, $ 100
• TOM; NI,TWO AH [*NInitwah*]; ROMAN NOSE; DICKEY WESSER [*Wesson*]; CATEY GIRKY [*Catagirha*]; MUS(*K*)RAT; ARSENA [*Arcena*]; CHIULA; SHELL; SNAIL; BACKWATER, son & heir of OLD JUNALUSKEY, dec'd; SALLY, widow of STANDING TURKEY, dec'd, each $100.
• JUNALUSKEY; AXE; CHIMISTEESTEE or SAM; CATIM or BUFFELOW; CEALY, a widow; BIG GEORGE; STUNASTAH or KEY; EDWARD WELCH; BETTEY [*Betsey*], a widow; TAMOOAK [*Tanooah*]; WAKEE, widow of WILLIAM JONES; JOHN COLSTON; TOUCHASTASTAKE [*Toachastashee*], each $50.
• JOHNSTON, NINA-NA-TATE [*Ninanatah*], CHI-IS-U [*Cehecace*] & NAGA, children of TUSTACAHA or SHAVE HEAD, dec'd, $200.

Aforesaid sell N.C. their 640-ac. reservations, surveys as filed w. Cherokee agent. Wit: *MARSHALL T. POLK, J.K. GRAY.* Proven by James K. Gray. Reg. Mar. 10, 1830.

23 Same as previous document. Settlements made with:
• YONAGUSKA; WILLNOTA; LONG TOM; TARRAPIN; CATATEEHEE & wife, NANCY; JUNALUSKA & wife WALLEE; MASASUTTA [*Wesagutta?*] & wife, CHERANAR children & heirs of JENCY, dec'd, $350.
• NANCY & OUNULA, wid.; WHIPPORWILL; NAGAHUNSORLUN; NIRCHO,LEE; WALLER; NANNY, NAULY & FAKEA(?) ch. & heirs of YELLOW BEAR, $300
• SALLY, wid. of LITTLE DEER, dec'd & her present husband WALLOSEE, $200
• GIDIAN F. MORRIS, guardian of the 3 children of LITTLE DEER, $800.
• LITTLE GEORGE; CAT & wife, JENNY [*Jamey*]; JIM; CHAW,UI CA [*Chau Cui*], children & heirs of WALLEE, dec'd, $550.
• JOHN DAVIDSON; TOM CONNAUGHT; TE CA NIR HEE and his wife GO-CHACEE [*Eschamca*]; STA-COII & wife CAN HIR NA [*Can Hee Nee*] children & heirs of CA HEE CA, dec'd, $400.
• SARAH, wid. of MEGGY HARTTEN, dec'd; ALL BURNS [*All Bones*] & NAHA [*Noka*], children of deceased, $400.
• JOHN WALKER, $250.

Wit: *MARSHAL T. POLK, J.K. GRAY, N.B. HYATT, DILLARD LOVE.* Proven by James K. Gray except for John Walker who ack. in court. Reg. Mar.13, 1830.

25 GIDEON F. MORRIS and wife, NAHA, to R.M. SAUNDERS and HUMPHREY POSEY, Commissioners, for $3,000, 640 ac. reserve on Tennessee R. on which THOMAS LOVE resides. Dec. 12, 1829, *G.F. Morris, Naka (her X mark)*. Wit: *MARSHALL POLK, J.K. GRAY, JOSHUA ROBERTS.* Ack. Dec. ct, 1829. Reg, Mar. 13, 1830.

26 ROMULUS M. SAUNDERS and HUMPHREY POSEY, Commissioners, to JOHN WELCH, a Cherokee Indian, $1250, & commissioners to pay cost of a suit against BENJAMIN S. BRITTAIN for recovery of 640 ac. reservation on "Ioley" (Iotla) Creek, where Benjamin S. Brittain lives. Welch had the land surveyed. Dec. 5, 1829, *John (his X mark) Welch.* Wit: *MARSHALL T. POLK, J.K. GRAY.* Reg. March 13, 1830.

27 JOHN WELCH to BENJAMIN S. BRITTAIN, 640 ac. reservation, on which suit now pending in Lincoln Superior Ct. by Welch vs. Brittain for recovery. Brittain releases claim to facilitate settlement w. the Indians. Wit: MARSHAL T. POLK, JOSHUA ROBERTS. Suit dismissed, Brittain to pay costs of suit in Lincoln Co. except for plaintiff's attorney. *B.S. Brittain.* Ack. in Dec. court, 1829. Reg. Mar. 13, 1830.

28 G.F. MORRIS, N.S. JARRETT, JOHN HALL, NATHAN B. HYATT and GEORGE DICKEY pledged sec. of $800 for the 3 children of LITTLE DEAR, to pay them $800 when of age, and they sign their share of his reservation to the state; or else $800 and interest to the state, if they refuse. R.M. SAUNDERS & HUMPHREY POSEY contracted with SALLY, widow of Little Deer for $200 for her dower & $800 for children. Dec. 10, 1829, *G.F. Morris, N.S. Jaratt, John Hall, N.B. Hyatt, George Dicky.* Wit: *J.K. GRAY, M.T. POLK.* Registered Mar. 13, 1830.

29 SG 131, JOHN WATSON assignee of G. FALLS, for $178, Sec. 15, Dis. 7, 89 acres on K Creek. Granted Nov. 30, 1829; registered Mar. 24, 1830.

30 DAVID LAIRD to WEST TRUET, both of Macon, for $250, 127+ ac. on Tennessee R.,
    Dis. 10, Sec. 46. Oct. 27, 1829, *David Laird*. Wit: *JN. DOBSON, PEREGRINE
    ROBERTS*. Registered April 13, 1830.

31 SG 137, IRAD HIGHTOWER assignee of WILLIAM CASADA, for $71, town lot #10,
    one acre on the maine street. Granted Dec. 29, 1829; registered May 23, 1830.

32 SG 141, JOHN CRIESMAN, for $75, 50 acres, Sec. 51, Dis. 10, lying upon the Grate
    Road. Granted Dec. 29, 1829; registered May 23, 1830.

33 SG 67, GEORGE DICKEY, 320 acres, Sec. 18, Dis. 11, on Tennessee R. Granted Feb. 9,
    1827; registered May 23, 1830.

33 SG 148, GEORGE RODGERS, for $89.50, 61 acres, Sec. 72, Dis. 15 on W. bank of Ten-
    nessee R. Granted Dec. 31, 1829; registered May 23, 1830.

34 MILTON BERRY to MILTON BERRY, son of WILLIAM BERRY, for nat'l love & af-
    fection of sd Milton Berry toward sd nephew, a white cow & calf of darkis colour. Nov.
    13, 1826. *Milton Berry*. Wit: *YONG (his Y mark) AMMONS, JAMES (his X mark) CUL-
    VERE*. Registered June 7, 1830.

35 IRAD S. HIGHTOWER to NIMROD S. JARRETT, both of Macon., for $600, one ac. in
    town of Franklin, lot #10 on the main street. Mar. 24, 1830. *Irad S. Hightower*. Wit: *B.S.
    BRITTON*. Registered June 7, 1830.

35 MARY ELIZE TRUSTEE, for love, etc. towards loving children, WILLIAM ANDREW
    JACKSON TRUSTEE, WILBY JOHN WESLEY TRUSTEE, HANNA ELIZ. MATIL-
    DY TRUSTEE, LUCINDY PAROLEE MAIDY(?) TRUSTEE, give each: one cow &
    calf & their incr., feather bed & furniture when they come of age, sow & pigs, wheal to
    ea. girl, to all & single, goods & chattels in my dwelling house. June 12, 1829. *Mary
    Elize (her X mark) Trustee*. Wit: *IRAD S. HIGHTOWER, JAMES WHITTAKER*. Proven
    by Irad S. Hightower, Mar. 1830 court. Registered Jun. 7, 1830.

36 NIMROD S. JARRITT to GIDIAN F. MORRIS, both of Macon, for $1600, lot #10 in
    Franklin, on the main street, with all houses, outhouses etc. Mar. 24, 1830. *N.S. Jarritt*.
    Wit: B.S. BRITTON. Registered June 7, 1830

37 SG 150, THOMAS KIMSEY, LUKE BARNETT, JAMES WHITAKER, trustees of the
    Baptist Congregation now instituted contiguous to Town of Franklin, for $10, 3+ ac., part
    of 400 ac. on which Franklin situated. Granted Jan. 6, 1830; reg. Jun. 9, 1830.

38 JESSE R. SILAR to JAMES K. GRAY, both of Macon, for $200, Lot No. 8 in Town of
    Franklin, one acre on main street. May 12, 1829, *J.R. Siler*. Wit: *JOSHUA ROBERTS,
    WILLIAM SILAR*. Proven by Joshua Roberts. Registered June 10, 1830.

38 JAMES MOORE to ASAPH ENLOE for $360, 84 ac., Sec. 71, Dis. 15, on W. side Ten-
    nessee R. Jan. 28, 1830, *James Moore*. Wit: *JNO. D. CARNE, J.K. GRAY*. Proven by
    James K. Gray. Registered June 10, 1830.

39 SG 136, JAMES MOORE, for $126, 84 ac., Sec. 71, Dis. 15 on W. side Tennessee R.
    Granted 29 Dec. 1829; registered June 11, 1830.

40 SG 138, GEORGE WIKEL, for $805, 259+ ac., Sec. 3, Dis. 8, NW side of Tuckasejah
    R., crossing Little Savannah. Granted Dec. 29, 1829; registered June 11, 1830.

41 SG 153, JOHN BRISON, Sr., for $1175, 272+ ac., Sec. 7, Dis. 7, on River Tuckasejah.
    Granted May 19, 1830; registered June 22, 1830.

42 SG 102, WILLIAM MCCONNELL, for $65, 65+ ac., Sec. 1, Dis. 15, on Tennessee
    R.Granted Jan. 12, 1828; registered July 7, 1830.

42 SG 129, WILLIAM SILAR, for $126, 84 ac., Sec. 42, Dis. 15. Granted 13 Jan. 1829;
    registered July 7, 1830.

43 SG 147, ZEBULON I. THOMAS, for $376, 188 ac., Sec. 5, Dis. 14, crossing "Coweter
    Creak" (Coweeta). Granted Dec. 31, 1829; registered July 7, 1830.

44 SG 132, SAMUEL WIKEL, for $257, 85+ ac., Sec. 7, Dis. 8, Big Savannah Cr. Granted
    Nov. 31, 1829; registered July 7, 1830.

45 WILLIAM CARPENTER to GEORGE RISH, both of Macon, for $50, half of Sec. 91, Dis. 15. June 22, 1830. Ack. by *Wm. Carpenter.* (No witness) Reg. June 20, 1830.

46 GEORGE RISH to WILLIAM CARPENTER, both of Macon, for $50, half of No. 91, Dis. 15. June 22, 1830. *George (his X mark) Rish.* Wit: *MOSES JARRETT, J. HOWARD.* Registered July 20, 1830.

46 TOBIAS GUTTERY to WILLIAM H. THOMAS, both of Macon Co. for $93, a certain Negro girl named HANNAH, six years old. Jan. 4, 1830. *Boys Guttery.* Wit: *WILLIAM CABE, JNO. T. DOBSON.* Registered July 20, 1830.

47 SAMUEL LOVINGGOOD of Haywood Co., NC to SAMUEL ROSE of Macon, for $250, Sec. 33, Dis. 17. Mar. 17, 1830, *Samuel Lovinggood.* Wit: *JAMES SHEARER Junr., JAMES A. (his X mark) SHEARER.* Registered July 23, 1830.

48 GEORGE DICKEY to JAMES WHITAKER, both of Macon, for $400, 170 (120?) ac., Sec. 18, Dis. 11 on Tennessee R. Mar. 25, 1829. *George Dickey.* Wit: *BERTON DICKEY, GEORGE DICKEY Jnr.* Registered July 23, 1830.

48 SG 152, SAMUEL LOVINGGOOD, $156, 78 ac., Sec. 33, Dis. 17. Granted Jan. 8, 1830; registered July 23, 1830.

49 JAMES RUDDELL to MICHAEL WIKEL, in consideration of a covenant bet. Wikel & Ruddle in 1821, Wikel's covenant being under seal & said Ruddle not complying, Ruddle relinquishes for $95, 100+ ac., Sec. 2, Dis. 4, Big Savannah Cr. June 10, 1830*James Ruddell.* Wit: *J.* PHILLIPS, H.B. TRAMMELL. Registered Jul. 27, 1830.

50 Mortgage: NOAH PEARSON to JOHN SHULAR, both of Macon, for $525, 3 young Negroe boys, PETER, abt. 12 yrs, FRANK, 11 on the 12 Oct. next & HARRY, 5 yrs. last Christmas day, clear of all impediments relative to Health. Condition: John Shular holds note on me to WM. F. MCKEE, 28 Mar.1829 for $400, wit. by REUBEN MOODY & $100 judgment in favor of McKee & $75 cash pd now. Mar. 23, 1830. *Noah Pearson.* Wit: *WM. WELCH, BENNETT SMITH.* Registered Aug. 16, 1830.

50 JOAB L. MOORE to JANE BRADLY's her Hears for $125 pd by Jane Bradly, 113+ ac., Sec. 92, Dis. 15. Jun. 23, 1830. *Joab L. Moore.* Wit: *M. PATTON, B.W. BELL.* Ack. in June 1830 court. Registered Aug. 16, 1830.

51 TOM, a native of the Cherokee nation of Indians to ROMULUS M. SAUNDERS & HUMPHREY POSEY, Commissioners, for $100, gives up his right to 640 ac. claimed by him as a Reservation on Sugartown Forke of Tennessee River. Apr. 28, 1830. *Tom (his X mark).* Wit: *JOSHUA ROBERTS, J.R. ALMON.* Reg. Sep. 6, 1830.

52 TOM, a Cherokee, to ROMULUS M. SAUNDERS & HUMPHREY POSEY, Commissioners, for $50, all rights in mother JINNY'S 640-ac. reservation. Apr. 29, 1830. *Tom (his X mark).* Wit: *JOSHUA ROBERTS, J.R. ALLMAN.* Reg. Sep. 6, 1830.

52 JESSE R. SILAR of Macon to DAVID B. COMMING, JEREMIAH HARRISON, WILLIAM SILAR, WILLIAM A. BRITTON, JACOB SILAR, JOHN DOBSON, JAMES K. GRAY, trustees & successors, for good will & affection for Methodist Denomination, acre on line of No. 25; they to keep in repair a house & place of worship. June 21, 1830. *J.R. Silar.* Wit: *JOSHUA ROBERTS, JAMES ROBINSON.* Reg. Sep. 19, 1830.

55 MARMADUKE KIMBROUG to JOHN MCCONNELL, both of Macon, for $237, 158 acres, Sec. 17, Dis. 15. June 18, 1830. *M.D. Kimbrouh.* Wit: *ASA ENLOW, GEO. K. KIMBRUH.* Registered Oct. 19, 1830.

56 SG 22, JOSIAH KIRBY, for $208.25, 119 acres in Haywood County, Sec. 56, Dis. 11, on "Elijaks" Creek (Ellijay). Granted Dec. 30, 1824; reg. Oct. 20, 1830.

56 Bond: $10,000 for NATHAN B. HYATT, appt'd clerk of Court of Pleas & Qtr Sessions—by Hyatt, DILLARD LOVE, WM. WELCH, ASOPH ENLOW, L. POINDEXTER, HENRY DRYMAN, JOHN HOWARD, all of Macon. Mar. 25, 1829. Wit: *JOHN MOORE,* Chrman, *JOHN B. LOVE.* Reg. Oct. 25, 1830.

57 Bond: $2,000 for NATHAN B. HYATT, clerk of court—by Hyatt, JAMES R. LOVE, EDWARD L. POINDEXTER, DILLARD LOVE, JAS. ANGEL, JOHN HOWARD. Mar. 25, 1829. Wit: *JOHN MOORE*. Registered Oct. 25, 1830.

57 Bond: $10,000 for NATHAN B. HYATT, clerk of court—by Hyatt, DILLARD LC·VE, N.S. JARRETT. Mar. 23, 1830. Wit: *JOHN HALL*. Reg. Oct. 25, 1830.

58 Bond: $2,000 for NATHAN B. HYATT, clerk of court—by Hyatt, DILLARD LOVE, NIMROD S. JARRETT. Mar. 23, 1830. Wit: *JOHN HALL*. Reg. Oct. 25, 1830.

58 JAMES D. HUSE to JOB THOMAS of Macon, for val. rec'd, 57+ ac. Sec. 53, Dis. 10, purch. at 1822 sale. Sep. 28, 1830. *James D. Huse*. Wit: *J. PHILLIPS, JOHN TATOM*. (Barely legible.)

59 JAMES D. HUSE to JOBE THOMAS, for val. rec'd, Sec. 49, Dis. 10, purch.1822. Sept. 23, 1830, *James D. Huse*. Wit: *J. PHILLIPS, JOHN TATHAM*. Reg. Oct. 25, 1830.

59 JOHN L. SMITH of Haywood Co. NC to JAMES W. GUINN of Macon for $100, part of 640-ac survey, S. of "Coulewhee" (Cullowhee) Mtn, 310 ac. Jun. 25, 1829. *J.L. Smith*. Reg. Oct. 9, 1830 in Haywood; registered in Macon Nov. 4, 1830.

60 JAMES D. HUGHS to PETER NOLEN, both of Haywood Co. NC, for $200, Sec. 48, Dis. 10, granted Hughs Feb. 9, 1827. Crosses Watauga Cr., 66+ ac. Sep. 5, 1827. *James D. Hughs*.Wit: *J.R. SILAR, JOBE (his X mark) BROUGTON*. Reg. Nov. 5, 1830.

61 JOHN GILLESPIE to JONATHAN H. WHITESIDES, both of Macon, for $175, 40 ac., Gerges Cr. of "Catoojay" (Cartoogechaye), part of Sec. 19, Dis. 16. Jan. 21, 1830. *John Gillespie*. Wit: *HIRAM DIMSDALE, DAVID (his O mark) JOHNSTON*. Reg. Nov. 5, 1830.

61 SG 146, SAMUEL SMITH, $226, 97 acres, Sec. 7, Dis. 14, Tennessee River. Granted Dec. 31, 1829; registered Nov. 13, 1830.

62 GEORGE ROGERS to ASEPH ENLOE, both of Macon, for $275, 61 ac., Sec. 72, Dis. 15, W. bank Tennessee R., incl. millseat on Standridge's Cr. Feb. 3, 1830. *George Rogers*. Wit: *M. RUSSEL, SAMUEL KELLEY*. Reg. Nov. 13, 1830.

63 SG 118, MATTHEW DAVISE, for $192, 96 acres, Sec. 54, Dis. 11, crossing "Elijy" (Ellijay Creek). Granted Jan. 9, 1829; registered Feb. 9, 1831.

64 JACOB HISE to GEORGE W. HISE for $1500, 127+ ac., Sec. 2, Dis. 8, "Tuckesegoh" (Tuckasegee) R. opposite island (SG #113). Sep. 30, 1830. *Jacob Hise*. Wit: *W.P. POTEET, JOHN R. (his X mark) HISE*. Registered Dec. 24, 1830.

65 Bond: $2,000 for NATHAN B. HYATT, elected clerk of court—by Nathan B. Hyatt, DILLARD LOVE, MIKAEL WIKEL, BENJAMIN S. BRITTON, JACOB F.P. TRAMMELL, JOHN HALL. Mar. 21, 1831. Wit: *SAUL SMITH*. Registered June 14, 1831.

66 Bond: $10,000 for NATHAN B. HYATT, elected clerk of court—by Hyatt, DILLARD LOVE, MICHEL WIKEL, BENJ. S. BRITTON, JACOB F.P. TRAMMELL, JOHN HALL. March 21, 1831. Wit: *SAUL SMITH*. Reg. June 14, 1831.

66 JAMES BRISON, Jr. to JAMES KNOWLEN, both of Macon., for $500, 208 ac., Sec. 54, Dis. 10, crossing the Grate Road, then Rabbits Cr. Feb. 17, 1831. *James Brison*. Wit: *WILLIAM RODGERS*. Registered June 14, 1831.

67 JOHN WIKE to JOHN WIKE, Junr., both of Macon, for $100, 50+ ac. on Tuckaseegee R. March 23, 1831. *John (his X mark) Wike*. Wit: *J. HOWARD, SAMUEL LOVE*. Registered June 15, 1831.

68 HENRY ADDINGTON to GEORGE RISH, both of Macon, for $11, part of Sec. 102, Dis. 15, corner made by Rish & STANDRIDGE, near JONATHAN WOODY's house, 11 ac. Nov. 4, 1830. *Henry Addington*. Wit: *JOSHUA ROBERTS, D.B. BURNET*. Registered June 15, 1831.

69 JAMES B. LOVE, DORCAS G. WELCH & JOHN M. WELCH her husband, of
Madison Co. TN; JOHN D. LOVE of Ray Co., TN; THOMAS B. LOVE of Macon Co.
NC; SARY COLMON & husband DAVID COLMON, of Macon; MARY CONNER &
SAMUEL CONNER, her husband, of Monroe Co., TN; SAMUEL C. LOVE, JOSEPH
B. LOVE, MARTHA & ALBERT G. LOVE of Macon—only heirs of ROBERT LOVE
Jr, dec'd, for $250, convey to THOMAS LOVE of Macon, 250 ac. in Madison, TN, 9th
Surv. Dis., range 182, Sec. 10, granted by State of TN to Robert Love, Jr. by grant #__
for $500. Land bd. John M. Welch. *James B. Love* signed May 23, 1829. Wit: *MARTIN
HEFLEY & LIN BRADFORD. Thomas B. Love, Samuel C. Love & Joseph B. Love*
signed Aug. 31, 1829. Wit: *DILLARD LOVE & JOSEPH YONG.* N.B. HYATT, clerk, by
JOHN HALL, D.C., certified that Salley Colmon was questioned apart from her husband,
David Colmon. Signed: *James B. Love, Thomas B. Love, Samuel C. Love, Jos. B. Love,
David Colman, Salley Colman.* Reg. Jun. 16, 1831.

71 SG 165, THOMAS RODGERS, for $55, 55 ac., Sec. 12, Dis. 7. Granted Jan. 1, 1831;
registered June 16, 1831.

72 THOMAS RODGERS to HUGH ROGERS, both of Macon , for $200, 55 ac. Mar. 23,
1831, *Thomas Rodgers.* Wit: *SAMUEL C. LOVE.* Reg. June 17, 1831.

72 JESSE R. SILAR to JOHN GILLASPEY Senr., both of Macon, for $300, land on "War-
rior or Wolf Forke" (Wayah) of "Cautagejoy" (Cartoogechaye), Sec. 35, Dis. 15. Aug.
25, 1829. *Jesse R. Silar.* Wit: *JAMES ROBINSON, J.R. ALMON.* Reg. Jun. 17, 1831.

73 MARY SHULAR, widow of GEORGE SHULAR, dec'd, GEORGE SHULAR, JOHN
SHULAR, DAVID SHULAR, EMANUEL SHULAR, legal heirs of George Shular, to
EBENEZER HUTON for $200, 61 ac. in Haywood Co. NC, both sides Shulars Cr., Sec.
12, Dis. 1, on NE side of the Tuckasegee R. June 21, 1830, *Mary (her X mark) Shular,
Emannuel (his X mark) Shular, John (his X mark) Shular, David (his X mark) Shular.*
Wit: *WM. W. BAIRD(?), JAMES WIGGINS, MARKE COLMON.* Just as to G. Shular &
D. Shular, ack. by E. Shular. Registered June 17, 1831.

74 SAMUEL HOLLAND of Columbia Co., OH, inventor of a new & useful improvement
on the griss & manufacturing mill, for $20 & other considerations, conveys exclusive
rights in Macon & Haywood Co. to N.S. JARRETT & WILLIAM WHITTICAR of
Macon Co. Mar. 13, 1831. *Samuel Holland.* Wit: *E.S. IRVIN, J.B. TRAMMELL.*
Registered June 7, 1831.

75 GIDIAN F. MORRIS of Macon to N.S. JARRETT, JOHN HALL, N.B. HYATT,
GEORGE DICKEY, who are bound with him on a bond of $1,600 in his guardianship of
the 3 children of SALLY, widow of LITTLE DEER, dec'd. Her dowry in his reservation
was $200 for self, plus $800 for her 3 children. Commissioners R.M. SAUNDERS &
HUMPHREY POSEY pd $800 to Morris as lawful guardian. He to pay them their shares
as they come of age; if they refuse to make title of reservation to state, he to pay state
$800 less expense of educating and maintaining children. July 29, 1830. *G.F. Morriss,
N.S. Jarritt, John Hall, N.B. Hyatt, George Dickey.* Wit: *J.K. GRAY, M.T. POLK.* Further, Morris deeds lot 10 in Franklin to them for $1 as security for this bond; lot includes
large dwelling house, store house & kitchen. *Gidian F. Morris.* Wit: *D.W. JARRITT.*
Registered June 20, 1831.

78 SG 144, JOHN KIMSEY, $196.84, 131+ ac., Sec. 87, Dis. 15. Granted Dec. 29, 1829;
registered Aug. 30, 1831.

78 SG 164, JACOB CALER, $163.50, 105 ac., Sec. 28, Dis. 10, crossing main fork of
Cowee Creek. Granted Dec. 29, 1830; registered Aug. 30, 1831.

79 SG 122, SAMUEL BRISON, $239, 153 ac., Sec. 33, Dis. 10 in Haywood Co. NC.
Granted Jan. 9, 1829; registered Aug. 31, 1831.

80 SG 156, PETER COWARD, $600, 190 ac., Sec. 17, Dis. 16, crossing "Coutoogajoy"
(Cartoogechaye) Cr. Granted Sep. 20, 1830; reg. Sep. 1, 1831.

80 SG 158, GEORGE PENLAND, $146, 53 ac. Sec. 8, Dis. 13. Granted Dec. 21, 1830;
    registered Sep. 1, 1831.

81 SG 159, GEORGE PENLAND, $658, 164 ac. Sec. 16, Dis. 13 on Tennessee R. Granted
    Dec. 21, 1830; registered Sep. 1, 1831.

82 HENRY ADDINGTON to JOHN ADDINGTON, both of Macon, for $1,000, three par-
    cels: 125 ac. crossing Standridges Creek, Sec. 96, Dis. 15; , 71+ ac., adj. first, crossing
    Standridges Cr., part of Sec. 85, Dis. 15; and 49 ac. adj. No. 96 on west, part of No. 97,
    Dis. 15. March 5, 1831. *Henry Addington.* Wit: *AMOS CURTIS, JACOB (his X mark)
    CATHAY.* Acknowledged in court, June 1831. Registered Sep. 3, 1831.

83 GEORGE WIKEL to JOSHUA HALL, Jr., both of Macon, for $1,950, 259+ ac. on Little
    Savannah Cr. June ___, 1831. *George Wikel.* Wit: *MOSES HALL, ALFRED HALL.*
    Proved by Moses Hall, June 1831 court. Registered Sep. 3, 1831.

83 JOSEPH WELCH to JOSHUA HALL, both of Macon, for $2,000, three tracts: 116 ac.,
    Sec. 36, Dis. 17; 108 ac., Sec. 37, Dis. 17; 61 Ac., Sec. 72, Dis. 16. All joining & lying
    on the Tennessee R. including the old Town House (of Cowee). Hall to pay am't due
    state. No date. *Joseph Welch.* Wit: *JAMES WHITTICAR.* Reg. Sep. 13, 1831.

84 RUBEN MOODY, Junr. and MARY, his wife, to JOHN LEATHERWOOD, Jr., for
    $300, a slave woman named PHILLIS and her 3 children, to wit: FANNY, abt 4 yrs,
    LEVI, 2 yrs, BOB, 6 mos. June 10, 1831. *Ruben Moody, Polly Moody.* Wit: *WM.
    MCCONNEL, WM. BERRY.* Registered Oct. 8, 1831.

84 Mortgage: ALLEN ELLIS to DRURY WEEKS my cattle—cow & calf, 2-yr old heifer—
    my interest in standing crop of corn, household furniture, 2 feather beds & furniture, 2
    pots, skillet, dresser ware(?) for $64 prin. due DAVIDSON, HALL & FOSTER in Iredell
    Co. N.C. June 30, 1831. *Allen Ellis.* Wit: *FRANCES JOHNSTON.* Reg. Oct. 8, 1831.

85 WILLIAM MCCONNEL to DAVID MCCONNEL, both of Macon, for $65, 65+ ac.,
    Sec. 1, Dis. 15 on Tennessee R. Jul. 27, 1830. *William McConnel.* Wit: *JOHN STEVEN-
    SON, JACOB (his X mark) CATHEY.* Ack. Sept. 25, 1831. Registered Oct. 8, 1831.

86 Mortgage: THOMAS J. RONE, for $250, to WILLIAM ROANE a Negro girl, MINER-
    VA, abt 10 or 12 yrs of age. Condition: Roane to pay note due Wm. Roane for $250.
    Aug. 1, 1831. Wit: *R.J. CHEEK, J.H. ROAN.* Sept. 25, 1821, came Richard J. Cheek
    before me, JOSEPH JOHN DANIEL, judge of Sup. Ct. of Law & Equity, to prove sig. of
    Thomas J. Rone—*J.J. Daniel.* Registered Oct. 25, 1831.

86 Sheriff's sale: BINUM W. BELL, Sh'ff of Macon, to JAMES MORRISON, in judgment
    of June 1831 co. court in Morrison's favor against JAMES RUDDELL, who was ordered
    to pay $300 + int. to Morrison. Morrison had high bid of $12 for property, Sec. 154, Dis.
    8, including dwelling. Sep. 11, 1831. *B.W. Bell, Sh'ff.* Wit: *WILLIAM ROANE, G.F.
    MORRISS.* Registered Dec. 15, 1831.

87 SG 149, JOHN REDMOND, $88, 59 ac. Sec. 28, Dis. 11. Granted 4 Jan. 1830;
    registered Feb. 2, 1832.

88 Bond: $10,000 for JOHN HALL, clerk & master in equity—by Hall, SILAS
    MCDOWEL, MONTREVILLE PATTON, all of Macon. Registered Oct. 12, 1831.

88 SG 183, JOHN BRYSON Jr., $249, 83 ac., Sec. 16, Dis. 7. Granted Jan. 14, 1832;
    registered Apr. 3, 1832.

89 HENRY ADDINGTON to DAVID LEDFORD for $300, 50 ac. on "Shop"(Shope)
    branch of Skeener Cr., bd. JOHN KIMZEY, EPHRAIM AMMONS. Nov. 5, 1831.
    Henry Addington. Wit: *JNO. COOK, HENDERSON SAUNDERS.* Acknowledged in
    April 1832 court. Registered May 2, 1832.

89 HENRY ADDINGTON to JESSE STANDRIDGE, for $200, 80 ac. on Standridge's
    Creek, Sec. 97, Dis. 15. Mar. 10, 1830. *Henry Addington.* Wit: *JNO. COOK, JNO. W.
    WEEK(?).* Proven by Cook in April 1832 court. Registered May 2, 1832.

90 JESSE STANDRIDGE to JESSE SAUNDERS for $250, 80 ac. on Standridge Creek, Sec. 79, Dis. 15. Feb. 15, 1832. *Jesse Standridge.* Wit: *GEO. MCCLURE, M. FRANCIS.* Michael Francis proved before JNO. HALL, Clk., April 1832. Reg. May 2, 1832.

91 JESSE SAUNDERS to JESSE LEDFORD for $150, 62+ ac., corner of No. 89 & 86. Feb. 22, 1832. *Jesse Saunders.* Wit: *HUMPHREY POSEY, M. FRANCIS.* Proven by oath of Michael Francis in April 1832 court. Registered May 2, 1832.

91 JAMES K. GRAY to JESSE R. SILER, both of Macon, for $1050, Lot #8 in Franklin, one ac. on main street. Jan. 19, 1831. *James K. Gray.* Wit: *JOHN SILER, ROBERT HUGANS.* Hugans made oath in April Session. Registered May 2, 1832.

92 JOHN BROADAWAY to J.R. SILER, both of Macon, for $250, 128 ac. on Tennessee R., Sec. 21, Dis. 14, purchased Nov. 1, 1822 from State Commissioners. Oct. 18, 1830. *John Broadaway.* Wit: *JAMES ROBINSON, SAMUEL ROBISON.* Proven by Samuel Robison, April 1832 session. Registered May 2, 1832.

92 EDWARD L. POINDEXTER to JESSE R. SILER, both of Macon, for $500, 60 ac. on E. side of Tennessee R. Feb. 1, 1830. *E.L. Poindexter.* Wit: Proven by JOHN TATHAM in April 1832 court. Registered May 3, 1832.

93 Security for bond: EDWARD L. POINDEXTER, prosecutor of 5.5 shares of Tenn. R. Turnpike Rd., pledges security to JESSE R. SILER, for $10—Negro boy ISAAC, abt 15 yrs, & all interest Poindexter has in real estate of JOHN BARKER, dec'd, in Rutherford Co. NC. Poindexter, principal, & JOSEPH WELCH, JOSHUA PARSONS, BENJAMIN S. BRITTAIN, ISAAC TRUIT, DRURY WEEKS, ASAPH ENLOW secure $2,000 bond, payable in 5 years w. interest. April 12, 1832. *E.L. Poindexter.* Wit: *THOMAS DEWS, Jr., JOHN R. ALLMAN.* Registered May 3, 1832.

94 JOSEPH WELCH, JOSHUA PARSONS & EDWARD L. POINDEXTER to THOMAS DEWS, Jr., for $10, all their interest in Tennessee R. Turnpike Rd. BENJAMIN S. BRITTAIN, ASEPH ENLOE, GIDEON F. MORRIS, ISAAC TRUIT, DREWRY WEEKS have been bound with said parties. Apr. 12, 1832. *Joseph Welch, Joshua Parson, E.L. Poindexter.* Wit: *JAMES WHITIKER.* Proven by James Whitiker in April 1832 court. Registered May 3, 1832.

95 SG 174, JOHN STANDRIDGE, for $120.50, 62 ac., Sec. 90, Dis. 15. Granted Dec. 31, 1831; registered May 3, 1832.

96 HUMPHREY POSEY to ELIAS MOORHEAD, both of Macon, for $510, 50 ac., part of Sec. 63, Dis. 16 on mouth of "Iole" (Iotla) Cr., W. bank of Tennessee R., incl. mill pond & mill. Sep. 9, 1831. *Humphrey Posey.* Wit: *JOSEPH H. EARLEY,* who proved in April 1832 court. Registered June 11, 1832.

97 On Apr. 3, 1797, State of N.C. granted JOHN HOLDEMAN and JACOB ESHLEMAN 200,960 ac. in Buncombe Co. on the Tennessee, Tuckasegee and "Nantahele" (Nantahala) rivers. State issued letters patent. I, John Haldeman of Columbia, Lancaster Co., Penn., deputed JOHN BROWN, late of Penn., now of N.C., my attorney to ascertain, trace boundary and take possession of land. Aug. __ 1830. *Jno. Holdermen.* Wit: *N.W. SAMPLES, Junr., HENRY CARPENTER* before MOLTON C. ROGERS, justice of superior court (Penn.). On Oct. 7, 1831, J.J. DANIEL, judge of Superior Court, (Macon Co.) ordered document to be registered. Registered June 21, 1832.

99 8th day March 1797, by virtue of warrants to me delivered by JOSEPH HENRY, entry officer of Buncombe Co., I have surveyed for JOHN HOLDERMAN & JACOB ESHLEMAN assignee of WILLIAM PATE, 200,960 ac. of land on waters of Tennessee, Tuckasegee and "Nantyalee" (Nantahala) Rivers, joining Elicott's true, crossing Tennessee R. along ANDREW BAIRD's lands. May 8, 1797. *J. BOYD, D. Surv., DAVID MCPEETERS & DAVID NELSON,* chairmen. Registered June 11, 1832.

99 JAMES MCDANNEL & REBECAH MCDANNEL of Macon, to ANDREW MCDAN-
NIEL, for valuable services rendered & labour bestowed & natural affection & high
regard, and $100, land in Burke Co. NC, both sides of Davidson's Mill Cr., branch of
Catawba R., two parcels, 100 ac. & 50 ac. April 11, 1832. *James McDannel, Rebecah
McDannel*. They acknowledged before J.D. DONNELL, judge of superior court, April
11, 1832. Registered July 2, 1832.

100 JAMES MCDANNEL & REBECAH MCDANNEL to ANDREW MCDANNEL, all of
Macon, for services & affection and $500, 96 ac. in Burke Co. NC on Catawba R. Apr.
11, 1832. *James McDannel, Rebecah McDannel*, who acknowledged the deed in court.
Registered July 2, 1832.

101 SG 169, WILLIAM BUCKHANNON, $294, 196 ac., Sec. 3, Dis. 12, E. bank of Ten-
nessee R. Granted Dec. 22, 1831; registered July 3, 1832.

102 SG 145, MICHEL WATERS, $214, 140 ac. Sec. 60, Dis. 16. Granted Dec. 31, 1829;
registered July 17, 1832.

103 SG 180, JOSHUA HALL, assignee of JOSEPH WELCH, $187 pd by Welch, 116 ac.
Sec. 36, Dis. 17, bank of Tennessee R. Granted Jan. 7, 1832; registered July 17, 1832.

104 SG 181, JOSHUA HALL, assignee of JOSEPH WELCH, $93 paid by Welch, 61 ac.,
Sec. 72, Dis. 15. Granted Jan. 7, 1832; registered July 17, 1832.

104 SAMUEL SMITH to NATHON SMITH, both of Macon, for $226, 97 ac. on Tennessee
R., Sec. 7, Dis. 14. July 23, 1831. Wit: *L.G. SMITH, ROBIN (ROLAN?) WATERS*.
Proven by L.G. Smith, Aug. 1832 session of court. Registered Aug. 3, 1832.

105 THOS. CATHY to THOMAS BROWN, both of Macon, for $250, land, on S. side of
Tennessee R., to a line equal distance between the Dwelling of OSANTATOGA and
SKEKENNA, crossing Telico Cr.; 640 ac, the same more or less granted to one Indian by
the name of Skikinna. June 19, 1832. *Thomas Cathey*.Wit: *JOSEPH WELCH, JOHN
WESLEY BROWN*. Registered Aug. 3, 1832.

106 ELIAS MOREHEAD to HUMPHREY POSEY of Macon Co., for $500, part of Sec. 63,
Dis. 16, 50 ac. on W. bank of the Tennessee R., across mouth of "Iolee" (Iotla) Cr., land
& mill. June 13, 1832. *Elias Moorhead*. Wit: *JOHN STARNS, SAMUEL BURNS*. Proven
by John Sterns. Registered Aug. 4, 1832.

106 ALFORD BROWN to THOMAS BROWN, Junr., both of Macon, for $450, Sec. 2, Dis.
9, 152 ac. on E. side of Tennessee R., crossing Georges Creek. June 18, 1832. *Alfred
Brown*. Wit: *B.S. BRITTON, ROBERT HALL*. Registered Aug. 4, 1832.

107 THOMAS BROWN, Junr. to MOSES HALL, both of Macon Co., for $450, Sec. 2, Dis.
9, 152 ac. on E. side of Tennessee River. Jun. 19, 1832. *Thomas Brown*. Wit: *B.S. BRIT-
TON, ROBERT HALL*. Registered Aug. 4, 1832.

108 MATTHEW RUSSELL of Macon to JOHN MCDOWELL of Haywood Co. NC, for
$800, 124 ac. granted Matthew Russell Dec. 30, 1825; on W. bank of Tennessee R., Sec.
69, Dis. 15. *Matthew Russel*. Wit: *WATSON SHIRRELL, JNO. DOBSON*. Proven by
John Dobson in June 1832 session. Registered Aug. 4, 1832.

108 JOHN ADDINGTON to MOSES ADDINGTON, both of Macon, for $725, 153 ac., Sec.
13, Dis. 15, passing the Cartoogechaye. Sep. 15, 1830. *John Adington*. Wit: *JACOB
SILAR, WILLIAM SILAR*. Proven by Jacob Siler, June 1832 court. Registered Aug. 4,
1832.

109 WILLIAM ANGEL to THOMAS M. ANGEL, both of Macon, for $300, town lot #4 in
Franklin. June ___, 1830. *William (his X mark) Angel*. Wit: *SAMUEL C. LOVE, B.W.
BELL, Sheriff*. Registered Aug. 4, 1832.

110 Bond: SILAS MCDOWELL, JESSE R. SYLER, WILLIAM ROANE, pledge bond of
$10,000 for Silas McDowell, clerk of Sup. Ct. Oct. 11, 1831. Registered Aug. 4, 1832.

110 Bond: SILAS MCDOWELL, JESSE R. SILER, WILLIAM ROANE, pledge bond of
$10,000 for McDowell. Oct. 11, 1831. Registered Aug. 4, 1932.

111 PETER NOLAN to JOSEPH R. JOHNSTON/JOHNSON both of Macon, for $300, 66
ac., Sec. 48, Dis. 10, crossing Watauga Creek. Oct. 29, 1830. *Peter Nolan.* Wit: *B.S.
BRITTAIN, WM. F. MCKEE.* Registered Aug. 4, 1832.

112 SG 185, JOSHUA ROBERTS, for $131, one acre in Franklin, town lot #12 on the main
street. Granted May 17, 1832; registered Aug. 4, 1832.

112 SG 184, JOSHUA ROBERTS, for $311, 152 ac. Sec. 33, Dis. 16. Granted May 17, 1832;
registered Aug. 4, 1832.

113 JOSHUA ROBERTS to JESSE R. SILER, for $400, 65 ac., Sec. 33, Dis. 16. June 20,
1832. *Joshua Roberts.* Wit: *J.W. KILLIAN, JAMES L. ERWIN.* Acknowledged in June
1832 court. Registered Aug. 4, 1832.

114 Sheriff's sale: JAMES MCKEE, Esq., sheriff for Haywood Co. to HUMPHREY POSEY
of Macon, to satisfy judgment of Court of Pleas & Qtr. Sessions in favor of JACOB
SHULER against JOHN POSEY, 231 ac. on the W. bank of the Tennessee R., Sec. 43,
Dis. 16. At public sale Sep. 27, 1824, Humphrey Posey had high bid of $44. June 8,
1832. Wit: *J.R. WILLIAMSON, HILT(?) ASBURY, N.S. JARRETT.* Proven by John R.
Williamson in Jun. 1832 court. Registered Aug. 4, 1832.

115 MARGARET WELCH, widow & adm. of estate of WM. WELCH Senr., dec'd, and
SAMUEL BURNS & ELIZABETH BURNS, legal heirs of dec'd, to JESSE R. SILER
for $400, 113 ac. on N.E. bank of Tuckasegee R., Sec. 4, Dis. 1, on THE BEAR's line, to
a Rattlebox on the River Bank. Dec. 29 1831. *Margaret (her X mark) Welch, Samuel
Burns, Elizabeth (her X mark) Burns.* JOSEPH WELCH & B.S. BRITTON took ex-
amination of Elizabeth Burns, feme covert, separate & apart from her husband. Wit: *WIL-
LIAM THOMAS.* Reg. Aug. 4, 1832.

117 Mortgage: JOSEPH WELCH of Macon to JOSEPH CALLAWAY of Monroe Co. TN,
for $5; to indemnify MATTHEW MCGHEE & JOHN MCGHEE of Monroe Co. for
$1200 in two notes of hand, one to John McGhee for $1000, the other to John McGhee or
$200. For security, Welch pledged 2 tracts: one, 53+ ac. in fork of Tennessee & Tuck-
asegee R., Sec. 32, Dis. 8; second, 50 ac. opposite the first, across the Tuckasegee, Sec.
1, Dis. 1, on N. bank of Tennessee R. at the lower end of an old Indian field, the place sd
Joseph Welch now lives. Also, six Negroes, a man, DANIELS, abt 36 yrs old; a boy
TOM abt 18; a boy WALLACE, abt 13; a girl SUSE abt 10; a boy about 6 (no name
given); a boy MONROE abt 3. Jan. 10, 1832. *Joseph Welch, Joseph Callaway, Mathew
W. McGhee, John McGhee.* Wit: *S.S. GLEN & MAJOR WIMBERLY* of Monroe Co. TN.
Maj. Wimberly proved in court; Squire S. Glen's oath admitted to record, JOHN B. TIP-
TON, clerk; ordered to be certified to Macon County, NC by ERSKIN H. WEAR.
Registered in Macon Co., Aug. 24, 1832.

(The original book has pages 111B-118B inserted here)

111B Bond: JOHN R. WILLIAMSON & JESSE R. SILAR, for John R. Williamson, appt'd
clerk & master in equity. Apr. 11, 1832. *J.R. Williamson, J.R. Silar.* Ack. before SILAS
MCDOWELL. Reg Aug. 20, 1832.

111B Bond: JOHN HALL, BENJAMIN S. BRITTON, JAMES K. GRAY, GEORGE DICK-
EY, $10,000 bond for John Hall, Clerk of Ct. of Pleas & Quarter Sessions. Dec. 23, 1832
(sic). Registered Aug. 26, 1832.

112B Bond: JOHN HALL, BENJAMIN S. BRITTON, JAMES K. GRAY, GEORGE DICK-
EY, $2,000 bond for John Hall. Dec. 23, 1831. Wit: *H. DRYMAN.* Reg. Aug. 26, 1832.

112B Mortgage: NOAH PERSON to JAMES W. GUINN, WM. H. STEALMAN, THOMAS
DEWS, for $200, Negro boy, HARRY. Person owes Guinn $75 & Stedman $65 plus $20
more if I am not convicted of the perjury alledged against me, & Dews $30 plus $30
more if not convicted; due 6 mos. from now. Oct. 11, 1832. *Noah Person.* Wit: *J.R.
SILAR.* Proven by Jesse R. Silar, Oct. 1832 court. Reg. Oct. 27, 1832.

113B Mortgage: NOAH PERSON to NIMROD S. JARRITT, ROBERT HALL, JAMES W. GUINN, for $700: 6 horses, 9 cattle, hogs & sheep, waggon & gering, my right of the claim of Negrow boy HARRY mortgaged to WM. H. STEALMON, THOMAS DUES, JAMES W. GUINN; also redemsion of Negrow boy mortgaged to ROBERT HALL. Condition: Jarritt, Hall & Guynn went bail for Noah. If he appears at Apr. court & indemnifies them, mortgage void. Oct. 12, 1832. *Noah Person.* Wit: *JOHN HALL.* Reg. Oct. 28, 1932.

113B Mortgage: NOAH PERSON for $500 paid by ROBERT HALL have delivered to him one Negroe boy named FRANK if Person save Hall harmless on a bond this day given of $400 payable to JS. WELCH, then mortgage to revert to Person. Oct. 7, 1832. *Noah Person.* Wit: *W.H. STEALMON.* Reg. Oct. 28, 1832.

114B SG 173, JOHN BRYSON, assignee of JOHN BRYSON JR., $270 for 135 ac., Sec. 68, Dis. 16. Later says JOHN QUEEN is grantee. Grant Dec. 31, 1831; reg. Dec. 17, 1832.

115B SG 179, JOHN WATSON, $157, Sec. 31, Dis. 11. Gr. Jan. 7, 1832; reg. Dec. 17, 1832.

115B Bond: SILAS MCDOWELL, JAMES K. GRAY, JESSE R. SILER, post $2,000 bond for Silas Mcdowell, Clerk of Superior Court of Law. Appeared before me, DAVID L. SWAIN, Judge of Superior Court, Oct. 12, 1832. Reg. Dec. 17, 1832.

116B JAMES CATHOR to JAMES N. BRYSON, both of Haywood Co. NC, for $300, Sec. 5, Dis. 7. July 29, 1831. *James (his X mark) Cathor.* Wit: *N. EDMONSTON, WM. WELCH.* Registered Dec. 18, 1832.

117B JAMES N. BRYSON of Haywood Co. NC to WILLIAM H. BRYSON of Macon for $400, 82 1/2 ac., Sec. 5, Dis. 7 on the river. July 30, 1831. *James N. Bryson.* Wit: *THOMAS ROGERS, HUGH ROGERS.* Registered Dec. 1832.

118B GILBERT FALLS to GEORGE LONG, both of Macon, for $200, 50 ac., Sec. 19, Dis. 7. Oct. 8, 1831. *G. Falls.* Wit: *MARY (her X mark) CUNNINGHAM, ELIZABETH (her X mark) CUNNINGHAM,* who swore bef. MARTIN RODGERS, JP. Reg. Dec. 24, 1832.

119 SG 186, WILLIAM KIMSEY, $261, 174 ac. Sec. 5, Dis. 15. Granted May 17, 1832; registered Dec. 2, 1832.

120 Mortgage: GIDEON F. MORRIS of Macon for $2658.25 to THOMAS FLEMMING of Charleston, SC, Franklin town lot #10, S. side Main St., W. end of street, one ac., incl. dwelling, store house & out houses where J.R. ALMON & CO. does business in store & publick House. J.R. Almon & Co. execute note to Thomas Flemming for $2,658.25 due Jan. 15, 1834. If J.R. Almon & Co. pay full amt, mortgage to be void. *G.F. Morris.* Wit: *J.R. SILAR, M. KILLIAN.* Proven by Milas Killian, Dec. 1832 court, JOHN HALL, clerk, for himself, NATHAN B. HYATT, NIMROD S. JARRETT & GEORGE DICKEY objected to deed being recorded on ground lot No. 10 was previously mortgaged to them (Book A, p. 75). Court overruled & ordered recorded. Reg. Jan. 5, 1833.

121 SG #___, MARMADUKE KIMBROUGH, $280, 150 ac. Sec. 84, Dis. 15. Granted Dec. 31, 1831; Registered Jan. 22, 1833.

121 JAMES W. GUINN bound to JOHN DOBSON for $700, Jan. 11, 1833. Condition: James W. Guinn this day sold John Dobson 100 ac. between land of JOHN LEDFORD, John Dobson & EPHRAIM AMONS on Tennessee R. Guinn to surrender land within 24 hr of demand, then obligation will be void. Jan. 11, 1833. *J.W. Guinn.* Wit: *BALDON H. TAYLOR.* Registered Jan. 22, 1833.

122 M.D. KIMBROUGH of Anderson Dist. SC, to ELIJAY KIMSEY, for $102, part of 52+ ac., Sec. 84, Dis. 15 on AMOS CURTIS line and State road. Nov. 15, 1832. *M.D. Kimbrough.* Wit: *THOMAS KIMSEY, JAMES KIMSEY.* Registered Feb. 11, 1833.

123 JOSHUA ROBERTS of Buncombe Co. NC to NIMROD S. JARRET of Macon for $400, Lot 12 in Franklin, on Main St., one acre. Dec. 29, 1832. *Joshua Roberts.* Wit: *GEORGE MCCLURE, WILLIAM GREGG.* Registered Mar. 12, 1833.

124 JOSHUA ROBERTS of Buncombe Co. NC to NIMROD S. JARRET of Macon, for
$350, 88+ ac., part of Sec. 33, Dis. 16. June 23, 1832. *Joshua Roberts.* Wit: *DAVID KIM-
ZEY, GEORGE MCCLURE.* Registered Mar. 13, 1833.

124 M.D. KIMBROUGH of Anderson Dist. SC, to DAVID KIMZEY of Macon, for $190,
87+ ac. Sec. 84, Dis. 15. Nov. 15, 1832. *M.D. Kimbrough.* Wit: *THOMAS KIMZEY,
JAMES KIMZEY.* Registered Mar. 13, 1833.

125 E. ELIJAH JOHNSTON Sr. of Macon to JAMES WITHROE of Macon, for val. rec'd,
105+ ac., Sec. 50, Dis. 10 purch. at land sale Nov. 2, 1822 in Franklin. Aug. 10, 1832.
Elijah Johnston. Wit: *JOHN TATHAM, JOS. R. JOHNSON.* Reg. Mar. 13, 1833.

126 JAMES WILLSON to AGNES RUDDLE, both of Macon, for natural love & affection, a
2-yr-old heifer. *James Willson.* Wit: *JOHN WILLSON, MARY RUDDELL.* Registered
Mar. 13, 1833.

126 WILLIAM BUCKANAN to ENOS SCROGGS, both of Macon, for $250, 65+ ac., part
of Sec. 3, Dis. 12, E. side Tennessee River. Feb. 8, 1832 *William R. Buchanan.* Wit:
JOHN CABE, JONATHAN DENTON. Registered Mar. 13, 1833.

127 SG 177, GEORGE LOUDERMILK, $75, 50 ac., Sec. 32, Dis. 10, S. fork of Cowee
Creek. Granted Jan. 7, 1832; registered Mar. 14, 1833.

128 SG 176, GEORGE LOUDERMILK, $50.25, 50+ ac. Sec. 29, Dis. 10, S. fork of Cane
Creek. Granted Jan. 7, 1832; registered Mar 14, 1833.

129 WILLIAM R. BUCHANNON to JONATHAN DENTON, both of Macon, for $295, 123
ac. on E. side of Tennessee R., bd. WILLIAM LEDFORD's survey. Feb. 28, 1832. *William R. Buchannan.* Wit: *JOHN CABE, ENOS SCROGGS.* Registered Mar. 14, 1833.

129 THOMAS SHEPHERD to JOHN WOOD, both of Macon, for $250, 116 ac., Sec. 28,
Dis. 16. Dec. 25, 1831. *Thomas (his X mark) Shepherd.* Wit: *ASA ENLOW, JNO.
HOWARD.* Registered Mar. 15, 1833.

130 THOMAS SHEPHERD to JOHN MCCLURE, both of Macon, for $450, 170 ac. Sec. 6,
Dis. 16. Dec. 25, 1831. *Thomas (his X mark) Shepherd.* Wit: *ASA ENLOW, JN.
HOWARD.* Registered Mar. 15, 1833.

131 SG 195, DAVID RODGERS, $309, 103 ac. Sec. 14, Dis. 7. Granted Dec. 27, 1832;
registered April 8, 1833.

**Concludes section of JOHN DOBSON, April 11, 1833. JOHN HOWARD, register from the present day for
Macon County.**

133 SG 191, THEOPHILUS JOHNSTON, $227, 150 ac. Sec. 7, Dis. 16, crossing "Car-
tooyachaye" (Cartoogechaye) Cr. Granted Dec. 24, 1832; registered May 1, 1833.

134 SG 184, GEORGE PENLAND, $261, 134 ac. Sec. 30, Dis. 16. Granted Dec. 8, 1832;
registered May 1, 1833.

135 SG 187, for $10 to THOMAS LOVE Sr., GEORGE PENLAND, JESSE R. SILER,
JOHN HALL, JAMES WHITAKER, trustees of Franklin Academy, 10 ac., part of 400
ac. reserved for Town of Franklin, corner of land conveyed to Baptist Congregation.
Granted Dec. 3, 1832; registered June 1, 1833.

136 SG 77, ANDREW HEMPHILL, $858.74, 286+ ac., Sec. 2, Dis. 15. Granted Jan. 4, 1828;
registered June 4, 1833.

137 Mortgage: JOHN BATES to SILAS MCDOWELL both of Macon, for $40, a bay mare
in his possession. Mar. 9, 1833. *John Bates.* Wit: *JOHN HALL.* Reg. June 4, 1833.

137 GIDEON F. MORRISS of Macon to N.S. JARRETT, JOHN HALL, NATHAN B.
HYATT, GEORGE DICKEY Sr. They were bound with him Dec. 10, 1829 for $1600,
in guardianship of children of LITTLE DEER, dec'd. Morris, as guardian, rec'd $800
from R.M. SAUNDERS & HUMPHREY POSEY, commissioners, in consideration that
he would give bond. Commissioners contracted with SALLY, widow of Little Deer, for
her dower at $200, plus $800 for right of her 3 children. Morris gives Lot 10 in Franklin
as security, Jun. 29, 1830. 1st document signed: *G.F. Morris, N.S. Jarrett, John Hall,
N.B. Hyatt, George Dickey Senr.* Wit: *J.K. GRAY, M.T. POLK.* 2nd signed: *G.F. Morris.*
Wit: *JOHN S. WATERS, D.H. JARRETT.* ROBERT HUGGINS, Ch'man, testified to
court's decision to register doc. Reg. June 5, 1833.

141 SG 78, WILLIAM UNDERWOOD, 52 ac., Sec. 21, Dis. 7, on Tuckasegee R. Granted
Dec. 31, 1832; registered June 21, 1833.

141 Mortgage: JOHN MURRY to GEORGE WYKEL, both of Macon, for $230, 100 ac.,
Sec. 25, Dis. 11. Wikel to release sec. for payment of 2 sums, a note for $142 due next
Christmas, which may be discharged in horses; another for $117.50, due Sep. 1834.
Murry conveys to Wykel, 7 cattle, 6 sheep, mare & colt, 3 beds & furniture, 5 hogs, one
bran(?) house & their furniture, household & kitchen furniture. Sep. 13, 1833. *Jno.
Murry.* Wit: *J.W. GUIN.* Reg. Sep. 16, 1833.

143 DANIEL JOHNSTON to G.W. LOVINGGOOD, both of Macon, for $49, improvement
on head of "I.Ola" (Iotla) Creek formerly occ. by D. WEEKS, also 2 cows, bay colt, 3
beds & furniture, 2 trunks, kitchen furniture. April 17, 1833. *Daniel (his X mark)
Johnston.* Wit: *JAMES ALLEN, MARTHA (her X mark) ALLEN.* Reg. Sep. 25, 1833.

144 GEORGE PENLAND to JAMES POTEET, both of Macon, for $350, 174 ac., Tenn. R,
Sec. 30, Dis. 16. Jun. 22, 1833. *George Penland.* Wit: *JAS. TRUET, JN. GUIN.* Reg.
Sep. 27, 1833.

145 Sheriff's sale: by court order in N.S. JARRETT vs. ABNER STATE, sh'ff sold State's
land on Big Branch, Dis. 15, Sec. 92, the same conveyed by JOAB MOORE to JANE
BRADLY, now State's wife. WM. CARPENTER had high bid, Apr. 8, 1833, $10. June
15, 1833. *JAMES TRUET, Shf.,* by *THOMAS LONG, Dep.* Wit: *WM. H. STEELMAN, N.
WM. KERR.* Reg. Sep. 27, 1833.

145 JOHN WILKINS to WILLIAM CARPENTER, both of Macon, for $600, 165 ac., Sec. 2,
Dis. 14. Aug. 13, 1831. *John Wilkins.* Wit: *HUMPHREY POSEY, SAMUEL KELLY.*
Reg. Sep. 27, 1833.

146 ZEBULON J. THOMAS to STEPHEN GRAY, both of Macon, for $700, 90 ac., part of
Sec. 72, Dist. 15, Tennessee R., near State Road. June 18, 1833. *Zebulon J. Thomas.* Wit:
L. VANDYKE. Registered Sep. 28, 1833.

147 GEORGE LONG to GEORGE CUNNINGHAM & JACOB SHULAR, all of Haywood
Co. NC, for $130, 50 ac. on Cullowhee Cr. May 4, 1833. *George (his X mark) Long.*
Wit: *JOS. KEENER, WM. H. BRYSON.* Registered Sep. 28, 1833.

148 ENOS SHIELDS for val. rec'd, to JAMES POTEET, WILLIAM POTEET & BAR-
NARD POTEET, all of Macon, 2 tracts, one, 88 ac., Sec. 1, Dis. 11; the other, 112 ac.,
Sec. 47, Dis. 10, purch. at 1822 land sale at Franklin. May 20, 1833. *Enos Shields.* Wit:
J. PHILLIPS, JOHN TATHAM. Jonathan Phillips proved deed. Reg. Sep. 30, 1833.

149 Mortgage: GEORGE LEDFORD to ROBERT S. BRYSON, both of Macon, for $8.62,
speckled cow & calf. Condition: note due by April 13 next. *George Ledford.* Wit:
DANIEL BRYSON. Registered Sep. 30, 1833.

150 SG 300, to AMOS CURTIS, JOHN DOBSON, JOHN OBELL, GEORGE K. HUGHS,
WILLIAM BRITTAIN, ROBERT HUGGINS, JESSE R. SILER, for $20, 20 ac., part of
Sec. 35, Dis. 16. Granted Jan. 10, 1833; registered Sep. 30, 1833.

151 Sheriff's sale: JAMES TRUETT, Sheriff, to GEORGE MCCLURE, assignee of JOHN
R. ALLMAN & CO., on judgment of Macon court, Dec. 1833, against MILTON
BERRY, commanding sale of land & improvements consisting of field houses & apper-
tainances, on Rabit Cr., adj. an improvement where DAVID COLEMAN formerly lived
& a part of said improvement, which levy was made Oct. 15, 1832 by E. DOWDLE &
CO. At public sale, Apr. 9, 1833, McClure had high bid of $5.50. *James Truet, shff*. Ack.
by E. DOWDLE. Wit: *THOS. LONG*. Reg. Oct. 2, 1833.

152 DAVID SHULAR of Haywood Co. NC, to WM. H. THOMAS of Macon, for $1200, 173
ac. on Tuckasegee R., Sec. 27, Dis. 8. July 18, 1829. *David (his X mark) Shular*. Wit:
JOS. BRADSHAW, THOS. BRADSHAW, Z.J. THOMAS. Registered Oct. 2, 1833.

153 SG 139, NIMROD JARRETT, for $150, 75 ac. on Tessentee Cr., Sec. 19, Dis. 13.
Granted Dec. 29, 1829; registered Oct. 2, 1833.

154 ELIZABETH SELVY to ROBERT R. DUCKWORTH, both of Macon, for $50, land on
Wards Cr., Rutherford Co., owned by my father ALEXANDER DUCKWORTH in his
lifetime, in which I hold equitable share by heirship of 100 acs. May 21, 1833. *Elizabeth
(her X mark) Selvey*. Wit: *WM. F. MCKEE, LINDSEY FORTUNE*. Reg. Oct. 3, 1833.

155 SG #140, NIMROD JARRETT, $102, 51 ac., where Morrase trace crosses Tessentee
Creek, Sec. 20, Dis. 13. Granted Dec. 29, 1829; registered Oct. 2, 1833.

156 Power of Attorney: JETHRO THOMPSON of Macon appoint trusty friend SAMUEL
SMITH of Macon my lawful attn'y to sell my draw in State Lottery of GA, lot No. 171,
14 Dis., 4th Sec. Oct. 11, 1833. *Jethro (his x mark) Thompson*. Wit: *S.G. SMITH, J.H.
SMITH*. Registered Oct. 12, 1833.

157 WILLIAM BROWN to ABSOLOM HOOPER, Jr., both of Macon, for val. rec'd, 51 ac.,
Sec. 6, Dis. 6, purchased at 1822 land sale in Franklin. Feb. 21, 1832. *William Brown*.
Wit: *WILLIAM HOOPER*. Registered Nov. 1, 1833.

157 JOHN WILES to MICHEL WATTERS, both of Macon, for $200, 74 ac., Sec. 25, Dis. 7.
Apr. 10, 1832. *John Wiles*. Wit: *A. CATHEY, HUMPHREY POSEY*. Reg. Nov. 4, 1833.

158 ZEBULON J. THOMAS & ISAAC MAUNEY, of Macon, adm. of GEORGE RUSH,
dec'd, for $500, to JOHN SELLARS of Macon, two tracts. The first, 11 ac., part of Sec.
102, Dis. 15, on Rush's line, corner of Rush & Standridge; the second, 145+ ac. tract
granted to George Rush, corner of No. 72. June 30, 1833. *Isaac Mauney, Zebulon J.
Thomas*. Wit: *JN. HOWARD*. Registered Nov. 29, 1833.

159 THOMAS HAYNE of Haywood Co. NC, to LEWIS VANDYKE of Macon, for $200, 75
ac. on Tennessee R. where old line crosses river, Sec. 10, Dis. 14. Sep. 15, 1828. *Thomas
Hayne*. Wit: *J.M. BRYSON, BENNETT SMITH*. Reg. Nov. 29, 1833.

160 LEWIS VANDYKE to NIMROD S. JARRETT, both of Macon, for $200, part of tract
granted to JOHN WILKINS on Tennessee R. Sept. 15, 1828. *Lewis Vandyke*. Wit: *JNO.
HOWARD, GEORGE MCCLURE*. Registered Nov. 29, 1833.

161 SG 125, GEORGE RUSH, for $_____, 140+ ac., Sec. 94, Dis. 15. Granted Jan. 10, 1828;
registered Dec. 3, 1833.

162 Sheriff's sale: JAMES TRUETT, Sh'ff of Macon, to JOHN HALL, to satisfy judgment
of county ct. against JOHN JONES for $8.20, land or improvement on which John Jones
& JOSIAH JONES now live, adj. line of ROBERT HALL & land on which HUGH
QUEEN now lives. John Hall had high bid of $9.15. Dec. 25, 1832. *JAmes Truett,
Sheriff*. Registered Dec. 3, 1833.

163 SG 190, SAMUEL SMITH, $206, 103 ac., Sec. 16, Dis. 13, on Tennessee R., crossing
Middle Cr. at a mill shoal. Granted Dec. 20, 1832; reg. Dec. 16, 1833.

164 SG #___, MOSES HALL, assignee of ALFRED BROWN, for $228 pd by Brown, 152
ac., Sec. 2, Dis. 9, Georges Cr. Granted Dec. 29, 1832; reg. Dec. 23, 1833.

165 Mortgage: JOHN R. ALLMAN & CO. to NIMROD S. JARRETT, both of Macon, for $500, 3 Negroes: JENNY, MATILDA & MARY ANN. Condition: Allman & Co. to pay exec. of WILLIAM ANGEL, Sr., dec'd, $500 note—Jarrett, security. Dec. 24, 1833. *J.R. Allmon & CO., N.S. Jarrett.* Wit: *GEORGE MCCLURE.* Reg. Mar. 10, 1834.

165 WILLNALA, an Indian chief, brother of YOUNAGUSKA or DROWNDED BEAR, of Haywood Co. NC, in 1830 sold to WILLIAM H. THOMAS of Haywood Co. for $143, a Negro girl named HANNAH, 9 yrs. of age, purchased of JOHN DOBSON; now give bill of sale to be agreeable to law of the white people. Aug. 30, 1833. *Willnala, (his X mark).* Wit: *EBENEZER NEWTON.* Registered Mar. 10, 1834.

166 AMOS BROWN for $250 to ISAAC TRUET, both of Macon, 640 ac., Tennessee R., beg. in old field on the UNAKELLAH'S line, to AMARCHER's line. Dec. 27, 1833. *Amos Brown.* Wit: *THOMAS SHEPHERD, DREWRY WEEKS.* Reg. Mar. 10, 1834.

167 JAMES M. BRYSON for val. rec'd, to JOHN TATHAM, both of Macon, 52 ac., Sec. 33, Dis. 11, which Tatham conveyed to my wife MARGARET, by the name Margaret Murry. Tatham purchased tract at 1822 sale in Franklin. Dec. 20, 1833. *James M. Bryson.* Wit: *WM. F. MCKEE, WM. SORRELS.* Registered Mar. 10,

167 Mortgage: JESSE A. JAMES to ISAAC MAUNEY, both of Macon, wool carding machine in Mauney's mill. Condition: Mauney paid $40 to NIMROD S. JARRETT for James; James to repay loan. 1833. *J.A. James.* Wit: *JOHN HALL.* Reg. Mar. 10, 1834.

168 ISAAC TRUET to JOSEPH WELCH, JAMES WHITAKER & JAMES TRUET, all of Macon, for $500, 640 ac. on Tennessee R., the OLD MOUSE's Reservation, beg. in old field on TOONAUGHHEALL's line. Dec. 28, 1833. *Isaac Truit.* Wit: *JAS. M.W. THOMASSON.* Registered Mar. 11, 1834.

169 JOHN SHULAR to JOSEPH WELCH, both of Macon, for $900, 277 ac., Sec. 9, Dis. 10, NE bank of Tennessee R., mouth of Cowee Cr., near site of old Cabbin. Nov. 9, 1833. *John Shular.* Wit: *HUMPHREY POSEY, JAS. H. WIGGINS.* Reg. Mar. 11, 1834.

170 PETER LEDFORD to THOMAS HAYNE, both of Haywood Co. NC, for $200, 25 ac., Tennessee R. Sep. 1, 1828. *Peter Ledford.* Wit: *JN. HOWARD, JACOB CRONE.* Registered Mar. 11, 1834.

171 SAMUEL BRODWAY to JOHN HOWARD, both of Macon, for val. rec'd, 55+ ac., Sec. 19, Dis. 14, Tennessee R. Apr. 1, 1833. *Samuel Broadway.* Wit: *A. PINSON, MARLAN NORTON.* Registered Mar. 12, 1834.

172 JOSEPH WELCH to HUMPHREY POSEY, both of Macon, for $2,000, 277 ac., Sec. 9, Dis. 10, E. bank Tennessee R. above mouth of Cowee Cr., near site of old cabin. Purchased 1821, at Waynesville. Nov. 9, 1833. *Joseph Welch.* Wit: *JOHN SHULAR, JAS. H. WIGGINS.* Registered Mar. 18, 1834.

173 SAMUEL BROADWAY to JOHN HOWARD, both of Macon, for val. rec;d, 52+ ac., Sec. 22, Dis. 14, Commissioners Cr. Dec. 18, 1833. *Samuel Broadway.* Wit: *A. PINSON, MARLAN NORTON.* Registered Mar. 18, 1834.

174 PETER COWARD of Rutherford Co. NC to JONATHAN H. WHITESIDES of Macon, for $1,000, 190 ac., Sec. 17, Dis. 16, on the "Cautoogajay" (Cartoogechaye). Oct. 20, 1830. *Peter Coward.* Wit: *BENJAMIN D. COWARD, OLIVER COWARD, HIRAM DOMESDALE.* Registered Mar. 19, 1834.

175 ISAAC TRUET to JOSEPH WELCH, JAMES WHITAKER and JAMES TRUET, all of Macon, for $100, 50 ac., Sec. 8, Dis. 10, incl. improvement where ISAAC TRUET now lives. Dec. 28, 1833. *Isaac Truet.* Wit: *JS. WM. THOMASSON.* Registered Mar. 19, 1834.

176 OLD MOUSE to ISAAC TRUET, both of Haywood Co. NC, for $60, 640 ac. on Tennessee R., bd. TOONAUGHEALL's line, ARMACHER's line. July 4, 1825. *Old Mouse (his X mark).* Wit: *SAMUEL R. WOODFIN, CHARLES L. DORYLY.* Signature of "S.WF" proven by THOMAS BROWN. Registered Mar. 29, 1834.

176 AUSTIN BANISTER to JOHN HOWARD, both of Macon, for $250, 89 ac. on Tennessee R., crossing Commissioners Cr., Sec. 20, Dis. 14. Dec. 21, 1832. *Austin (his X mark) Banister.* Wit: *LABAN LONG, JOHN H. CHANDLER, A. SMITH.* Registered Mar. 29, 1834.

178 Sheriff's sale: JAMES TRUET, sheriff of Macon County, on order of Sup. Ct. against ARCHABALD READ and JOHN READ for $49.53 recovered by JAMES BRYSON, seized Sec. 45, Dis. 11, on Sugartown fork, containing 78 ac.,& sold at public auction to JAMES POTEET, agent for WM. W. PERSEY/PURSEY, who had high bid of $10. April 8, 1834. *Jas. Truet, Sh'ff.* Wit: *S. MCDOWELL, WM. ROGERS.* Registered May 7, 1834.

179 W.D. SMITH to THOMAS GENENS (Jennings?) for $218, Negro girl, FRANCIS, abt 7 yrs old, sound & healthy. Apr. 12, 1832. *W.D. Smith by HENRY GRADY.* Wit: *DILLARD LOVE.* Proven by Love, Apr. 1834 court. Registered May 8, 1834.

180 DAVID COLEMAN to MARKE COLEMAN, both of Macon, for $348.75, a negro boy named TOM, aged 19 years. Nov. 27, 1833. *David Coleman.* Wit: *GEORGE COLEMAN, ANDREW COLARD.* Andrew Colard proved in April court. Registered May 8, 1834.

180 AMOS CURTIS of Macon for nat'l love & affection for beloved son, WATSON CURTIS, 4 horses, 20 cattle, 30 sheep, 40 hogs, also all my household & kitchen furniture & working tools. Feb. 28, 1834. *Amos Curtis.* Wit: *JOHN MCDOWEL, JOHN SELLARS.* John McDowel proved Mar. 29, 1834. Registered May 8, 1834.

181 AMOS CURTIS to WATSON CURTIS, his son, for maintenance of Amos Curtis, etc., tract of land where I now live, 146 ac. Feb. 28, 1834. *Amos Curtis.* Wit: *JOHN MCDOWEL, JOHN SELLARS.* Proven by McDowel. Registered May 8, 1834.

182 EUCHELLA, JOHN MOUSE, ARICK MOUSE, MOWMOUTH, TOM (may be one person, Mowmouth Tom), the widow NANLY, and PEGY BHOBKHIU NANLEY (or NOBLEY?), to AMOS BROWN, all of Haywood County NC, for $150, 640 ac. on waters of Tennessee R., the OLD MOUSE Reservation, on TOONAUGHEALL's line, AREMACKER's line. Sep. 5, 1826. *Euchella (his X mark), John Mouse (his X mark), Nanley (her X mark), Arick Mouse (his X mark), Indian Pegy (her X mark).* Wit: *ALFRED BROWN, SAMUEL B. WOODFIN.* THOMAS BROWN proved signature of Alfred Brown. On Dec. 27, 1833, Amos Brown assigned the deed over to ISAAC TRUETT for val. rec'd. *Amos Brown.* Wit: *THOMAS SHEPHERD, DREWRY WEEKS.* Registered May 9, 1834.

183 Mortgage: WM. CUNNINGHAM to JESSE R. SILER, tract lying where COL. JOHN STEPHENSON now lives, being a part of Sec. 4, Dis. 16, all that part of tract lying W. of "Cartoogagay" (Cartoogechaye) excepting about one acre adj. MOONEY's Mill, containing 137 ac. Condition: Cunningham to pay $300 to state for John Stephenson, and also to Jesse Siler a note of hand he executed to him this day, due Feb. 1, 1835, for $500. Mar. 14, 1834. *Wm. Cunningham.* Wit: *J.K. GRAY, M. KILLON.* Reg. May 15, 1834.

184 JAMES POTEET to JESSE R. SILER, for $400, Negro, DANIEL, abt 41 yrs. Feb. 22, 1830. *James Poteet.* Wit: *JOHN TATHAM.* Ack. April 1834 ct. Reg. May 15, 1834.

184 Mortgage: WILLIAM CUNNINGHAM to JESSE R. SILER, both of Macon, Negro girl, SALLY, abt 26 yrs of age, security for 2 notes, each for $100. Sep. 20, 1833. *William Cunningham.* Wit: *JAMES ROBINSON.* Registered May 16, 1834.

185 JOHN WOODY of Habersham Co. GA for val. consideration, to JOHN STEPHENSON of Haywood Co. NC, 116 ac. Oct. 9, 1824. *John Woody.* Wit: *JAMES MOORE,* who proved in April 1834 court. Registered May 16, 1834.

185 JOHN STEPHENSON of Macon for val. consideration, to J.R. SILER, 116 acres, Sec. 5, Dis. 16, purch. 1824 from JOHN WOODY, who purchased in 1821. *John Stephenson.* Wit: *M. KELLON, J.K. GRAY.* Proven by James K. Gray. Reg. May 16, 1834.

185 JAMES NOLEN, Senr. to JOSEPH BRENDLE, both of Macon, for $550, 208 ac., Sec.
    54, Dis. 10, on the Rabbit's Creek. Aug. __, 1833. *James Nowlin*. Wit: *MOSES HALL,
    J.R. NOWLIN*. J.R. Nowlin proved in April 1834 court. Reg. May 16, 1834.

186 Power of Attorney: EMANUEL SETSER & JOHN SETSER, of Macon, app't CHRIS-
    TOPHER SETSER of Macon our att'y in business of estate of JACOB SETSER, dec'd,
    of Franklin Co., GA, to sign any & all conveyances, to purchasing of low land lying in
    county of Franklin, etc. June 28, 1834. *Emmanuel Setser, John Setser*. Wit: *J.W. GUINN*.
    Registered Aug. 20, 1834.

187 Power of Attorney: ANN KENNEDY of Macon, formerly of York Dist., S.C., appoint
    ASAPH/ASA ENLOE of Macon my attn'y to collect money & sue for possession of tract
    in York District, on Bullock's Cr. The tract was devised to me by a mortgage given by
    JOHN KENNEDY & NATHAN P. KENNEDY. They were to conserve the possession
    of said tract for her natural life, with comfortable maintenance, or, if Ann moved, or at
    her choice, to pay $85 per year. She moved from York to Macon in Jan. 1831. Feb. 1,
    1834. *Ann (her X mark) Kennedy*. Wit: *E. DOWDLE*. Proved by Dowdle in July 1834
    court. Registered Aug. 27, 1834.

189 Mortgage: BENJAMIN S. BRITTAIN of Haywood Co. NC owed $1439.12 to ROBERT
    B. VANCE, dec'd, by bond. As security, he deeds to DAVID VANCE & DAVID L.
    SWAIN, executors of Robert B. Vance, dec'd, 4 Negroes—ESTHER & her 3 children,
    BOSTON, WILL & RANSOM. If Brittain pays $1439.12 by July 1, 1830, this deed
    void. June 25, 1828. Reg. in Haywood Co. July 14, 1828. Signature of Brittain proven by
    JOHN HALL. Registered in Macon County Aug. 27, 1834.

190 JOHN MOORE of Macon to the heirs of ROBERT LOVE, Junr., dec'd: JAMES B.
    LOVE; JOHN M. WELCH & DORCAS, his wife; JOHN D. LOVE; THOMAS B.
    LOVE; DAVID COLEMAN & SARAH, his wife; SAMUEL CONNER & MARY, his
    wife; SAMUEL C. LOVE; GEORGE W. PROCTER & MARTHA, his wife; and AL-
    BERT G. LOVE, 2 tracts, one, 275 ac., Sec. 32, Dis. 11, jcn. of Sugar Town Fork & Ten-
    nessee R.; other, 178 ac., Sec. 14, Dis. 11. Moore had rec'd of Robert Love Junr. in his
    lifetime full value & confirms sale to the heirs. April 11, 1832. Moore ack. in July 1834
    court. Wit: *RICHARD P. FORTUNE, J. PHILLIPS*. Reg. Aug. 29, 1834.

192 WILLIAM MCCONNELL to THOMAS KIMSEY, both of Macon, for $48, 8 ac., Sec.
    3, Dis. 15, on the River. April 17, 1834. *William McConnell*. Wit: *WM. CABE, DAVID
    KIMZEY*. Wm. Cabe proved in July 1834 court. Reg.Aug. 29, 1834.

192 MICHAEL WATERS to SAMUEL WATERS, both of Macon, for $200, 75 ac., Sec. 25,
    Dis. 17 on Burningtown Cr. Jan. 20, 1834. *Michael (his X mark) Waters*. Wit: *B.S. BRIT-
    TAIN, JAMES TRUET*. Proven by Truet in July 1834 court. Registered Aug. 30, 1834.

194 SG 163, JACOB PALMER, $99, 66 acres, Sec. 23, Dis. 13. Granted Dec. 29, 1830;
    registered Sep. 2, 1834.

195 SG 162, JACOB PALMER, $232, 86.5 acres, Sec. 22, Dis. 13. Granted Dec. 29, 1830;
    registered Sep. 2, 1834.

196 SG 199, BENJAMIN DUVALL, assignee of THOMAS BROWN, for $5 pd by Thomas
    Brown, 57 ac., Sec. 7, Dis. 10, E. bank of Tennessee R. Granted Jan. 8, 1834; registered
    Sep. 2, 1834.

197 SG 62, HENRY ADDINGTON, $174.78, 116+ ac., Sec. 97, Dis. 15, on Standridge's Cr.
    Granted Feb. 9, 1827; registered Sep. 2, 1834.

198 SG 87, HENRY ADDINGTON, $195, 130 ac., Sec. 85, Dis. 15 on Standridge's Cr.
    Granted Jan. 2, 1828; registered Sep. 3, 1834.

199 SG 89, HENRY ADDINGTON, assignee of JOHN STANDRIDGE, for $911 pd by John
    Standridge, Sec. 81, Dis. 15, crossing Standridge's Cr. Granted Jan. 12, 1828; registered
    Sep. 3, 1834.

200 SG 123, HENRY ADDINGTON, assignee of JOHN STANDRIDGE, for $55 pd by John
    Standridge, 55 ac., Sec. 102, Dis. 15. Granted Jan. 9, 1829; registered Sep. 3, 1834.

201 SG 143, to HENRY ADDINGTON, assignee of JOHN STANDRIDGE, for $131.25 pd by John Standridge, 131+ ac., Sec. 86, Dis. 15. Granted Dec. 29, 1829; reg. Sep. 3, 1834.

202 WILLIAM UNDERWOOD of Haywood County NC, to PETER LONG of Macon for $200, land on Tuckasegee R. Jan. 4, 1834. *William (his X mark) Underwood*. Wit: *ELIJAH UNDERWOOD, JAMES B. LONG*. Registered Sep. 4, 1834.

203 Bond: $2,000 for JOHN D. CARNS, elected Clerk & Master in Equity, pledged by Carns, JESSE R. SILER & Esq. MCCLURE, all of Macon. Apr. 13, 1833. *Jno. D. Carns, J.R. Siler, E.W. McClure*. Wit: *JOSHUA ROBERTS*. Reg. Oct. 3, 1834.

204 Bond: $10,000 for JOHN TATHAM, Clerk of Court, pledged by Tatham, RICHARD WILSON Snr., THOMAS TATHAM Snr., JOHN WILSON, WM. BRYSON Snr., JOHN DOBSON, JOHN DILLARD, ZACHARIAH CABE, JAMES POTEET, CHRISTOPHER SETSER. Oct. 8, 1833. Wit: *J. PHILLIPS*. Registered Oct. 3, 1834.

205 Bond: $10,000 for JOHN TATHAM, Clerk of Court, pledged by Tatham, RICHARD WILSON Senr., THOMAS TATHAM Senr., JOHN WILSON, WILLIAM BRYSON Senr., JOHN DOBSON, JOHN DILLARD, ZACHARIAH CABE, JAMES POTEET, CHRISTOPHER SETSER. Oct. 8, 1833. Wit: *J. PHILLIPS*. Registered Oct. 4, 1834.

205 ANDREW WELCH to NOAH BURCHFIELD, both of Macon, for $235, 67+ ac., Sec. 28, Dis. 8 on Tuckasegee R. Oct. 6, 1834. *Andrew Welch*. Wit: *MARK COLMAN*, who proved deed in court. Registered Nov. 6, 1834.

206 JOHN RISH to ANDREW WELCH, both of Macon, for $112, 67+ ac., Sec. 28, Dis. 8, on Tuckasegee R. Mar 5, 1832. *John (his X mark) Rish*. Wit: *ANDREW COLARD, JOHN WELCH, MARK COLMAN*. Proved by Mark Colman. Registered Nov. 6, 1834.

207 Bond: $10,000 for SILAS MCDOWELL, elected Clerk of Sup. Ct. Pledged by McDowell, JESSE R. SILER, JAMES K. GRAY. Oct. 10, 1834. Reg. Nov. 28, 1834.

208 Bond: $4,000 for SILAS MCDOWELL, elected Clerk of Sup. Ct. Pledged by McDowell, JESSE R. SILER, JAMES K. GRAY. Oct. 10, 1834. Reg. Nov. 28, 1834.

208 Bond: $10,000 for SILAS MCDOWELL, elected Clerk of Sup. Ct. Pledged by McDowell, JESSE R. SILER, JAMES K. GRAY. Oct. 8, 1833. Reg. Nov. 28, 1834.

209 Bond: $2,000 for SILAS MCDOWELL, elected Clerk of Sup. Court. Pledged by McDowell, JESSE R. SILER, JAMES K. GRAY. Oct. 8, 1833. Reg. Nov. 28, 1834.

210 SG 208, ZACHARIAH CABE, $1,196, 299 ac., Sec. 5, Dis. 12, on Tennessee R. Granted Dec. 26, 1833; registered Nov. 28, 1834.

211 SG 207, THOMAS JENNINGS, assignee of JAMES MURRY, for $240 paid by Murry, 160 ac., Sec. 24, Dis. 11. Granted Dec. 21, 1833; registered Nov. 29, 1834.

212 THOMAS BROWN of Macon to WILLIAM MORRISSON, late of Burke, Co, NC, for $2,000, 2 tracts on NE side of Tennessee R., Sec. 1, Dis. 9 and Sec. 1, Dis. 10. Dec. 4, 1832. *Thos. Brown*. Wit: *MOSES HALL, HENSON QUEEN*. Proved by Hall in Oct. 1834 court. Registered Feb. 10, 1835.

213 TAVNER B. MOORE of Haywood bound to JOHN P. MOORE by $500 note to convey 111 ac. on Ellagee Cr., Sec. 55, Dis. 11. Aug. 8, 1821. *Tavner B. Moore*. Wit: *ZACHARIAH PEAK*. Peak proving in court, Oct. 1834. Registered Feb. 16, 1835.

213 WILLIAM GILLISPEE to ENOS CRAWFORD, both of Macon, for $156, 54 ac., Sec. 36, Dis. 15. June 25, 1834. *W.M. Gallespie*. Wit: *JACOB SILER, HARRIAT SILER*. Proved by Jacob Siler in court, Feb. 1835. Registered Apr. 3, 1835.

214 JESSE CORNWELL to JOHN WEST, for $375, a Negro girl, VARIEL(?), aged 15 years. July 14, 1832. *Jesse Cornwell*. Wit: *JOSEPH LONG*. Registered Apr. 3, 1835.

214 MARTAIN ANGEL to JAMES ANGEL, both of Macon, for $324, 179 ac. Sec. 2, Dis. 11, on Tennessee R., crossing Mill Cr. Feb. 11, 1835. *Martin Angel*. Wit: *JAMES W. GUIN*. Proven by Guin in Feb. 1835 court. Registered Apr. 3, 1835.

215 JAMES WHITAKER to JAMES ANGEL, both of Macon, for $800, 120 ac., Sec. 18,
     Dis. 11, on Tennessee R. Sep. 17, 1834. *James Whitaker*. Wit: *M. WIKLE, STEPHEN
     WHITAKER*. Registered Apr. 3, 1835.

216 ABRAM PICKLESIMER, for val. rec'd, to JOHN HOOPER, of Macon, 83 ac., Sec. 4,
     Dis. 6, which Picklesimer purchased at the land sale at Franklin, Oct. 30, 1822. Feb. 7,
     1835. Acknowledged A. P___?. Wit: *W.H. POTEAT, JOEL LINARD*. Registered Apr. 3,
     1835.

217 SG 205, EDWARD CHASTAIN, $224, 112.25 ac. on W. bank of Tuckasegee R., Sec. 2,
     Dis. 5. Granted Dec. 21, 1833; registered April 3, 1835.

218 SG 206, ABSALOM HOOPER, assignee of MELLON BROWN, for $76.54 paid by
     Mellon Brown, 51 ac., Sec. 6, Dis. 6, on bank of the River. Granted Dec. 21, 1833;
     registered April 3, 1835.

219 SG 204, for $75 paid by MICHAEL WATERS, assignee of JOHN WILES, of JAMES
     BRYMEN, 75 acres, Sec. 25, Dis. 17. Granted Dec. 5, 1833; registered April 3, 1835.

220 JOAB L. MOORE to ENOS CRAFFORD, both of Macon, for $190, 54.25 ac., Sec. 39,
     Dis. 15, crossing Wolf Cr. (Wayah Cr.). *Joab L. Moore*. Wit: *J.W. GUIN, JOHN CUN-
     NINGHAM*. Proved by James W. Guin, Feb. 1835 court. Registered April 4, 1835.

221 Mortgage: MILES CARROLL to JAMES PEAK & LOGAN BERRY, one improvement
     and corn growing near JOHN STRAIN's known as the HILEND improvement, 5 horses
     & improvement where DAVID ROGERS now lives. Oct. 17, 1834. Wit: *W.F. MCFEE*.
     Condition: Carroll is to appear before the Superior Court of Law in Franklin in April next
     in two cases served on him and bear him clear of all demands or charges whatsoever.
     Proven by W.F. McFee, Feb. 1835 court. Registered April 4, 1835.

222 SAMUEL SMITH to ARON SMITH, both of Macon, for $400, tract of land, Sec. 16,
     Dis. 13, crossing Middle Creek at a mill shoal. July 31, 1834. *Samuel Smith*. Wit: *S.G.
     SMITH, WM. LEDFORD*. Proven by William Ledford, Oct. 1834 court. Registered Apr.
     4, 1835.

223 Mortgage: FELAX AXLEY of Macon to JAMES AXLEY of Monroe Co., TN, for
     $1,797.27, 136 vol. of books, 2 feather beds & furniture, 3 trunks, clock, man's saddle,
     kitchen furniture & cupboard ware, 2 cooking ___, cupboard now in Tennessee in posses-
     sion of JON'N P.H. PARTAIN(?) Senr., gig & horses, 60 ac. on Gist Creek, 80 ac. on lit-
     tle east fork of the Pigeon River, 102+ ac. on Clear Street(?) Sumner(?). Oct. 10, 1834.
     Felax Axley. Wit: *JESSE R. SILER, ROBERT K. KIRKPATRICK*. Reg. Apr. 4, 1835.

224 Mortgage: BENJAMIN S. BRITTAIN of Haywood Co. NC for $1439.20 paid by
     DAVID VANCE & DAVID L. SWAIN, executors of ROBERT B. VANCE, dec'd, have
     mortgaged four negroes, to wit, ESTHER and her three children, BOSTON, WILL &
     RANSOME. Also, Brittain assigns all interest as a legatee under the will of Doctor(?)
     Robert B. Vance, dec'd, in his estate. June 25, 1828. *B.S. Brittain*. Wit: *JOSHUA
     ROBERTS*. Recorded by R. LOVE, Clerk, in Haywood Co.; registered in Haywood by
     WILLIAM WELCH, July 14, 1828. Proved by Joshua Roberts in Macon, Feb. 1835
     court. Registered in Macon County April 4, 1835.

225 ABRAHAM PICKLESIMER of Macon, for natural love & affection I bear my children
     WATSON WILSON & BENSON PICKLESIMER, all goods, chattels, personal estate,
     etc. Watson Wilson & Benson to provide sufficient maintenance to Abraham during his
     life, and give their sisters & half brothers when they become of age the following: one
     good cow & calf to POLLY, one ditto ditto to CLOE ANNA & a young horse beast to
     each of their half-brothers, viz. GEORGE & ABRAHAM PICKLESIMER Jr. I have put
     Watson Wilson & Benson in full possession by delivering to them one certain gelding.
     Feb. 19, 1834. Ack.: *Abraham Picklesimer*. Wit: *J.D. BROWN, BENJAMIN HOOPER,
     JEFFERSON MIGS(?)*. Registered April 4, 1835.

226 SG 171, GEORGE F. CALER, $224, 122 acres, Sec. 20, Dis. 10, "Coweetey" (Cowee)
     Cr. Granted Dec. 35, 1831; registered April 4, 1835.

227 LINDSEY FORTUNE to NATHAN DEHART, both of Macon County, for $360, 74+
ac., "Kowee" (Cowee) Cr., Sec. 20. Dis. 10. Oct. 15, 1833. *Lindsey Fortune*. Wit: *M.
KELLION, JS. TRUET*. Proved by Milas Killeon, Feb. 1835 ct. Reg. April 6, 1835.

227 Mortgage: JOSEPH YOUNG to THOMAS BROWN, both of Macon, Sorrel Poney,
brendle bull, brendle steer, 2 black bulls, all 3 yrs old, 3 feather beds & furniture, 2
ovens, skillet, pot, table(?). Condition: There are 2 judgements against Young, one in
favor of JAMES AIVINELL(?), $39.87, dated July 7, 1834, one in favor of ANDREW
BRADLEY, $2.45, plus cost on each. July 12, 1834. *Joseph Young*. Wit: *JOEL
MCCRARRY, JOHN HALL, ISAAC TRUET*. Registered May 2, 1835.

228 Sheriff's sale: THOMAS LONG, Sheriff, sold at public sale an improvement on Middle
Cr. in Macon, sold as the property of JAMES WHITE at suit of ZACHARIAH PEAK for
$2.75 to WILLIAM CARPENTER. Apr. 9, 1833. *Thos. Long*. Wit: *B.S. BRITAIN*.
Registered June 20, 1835.

229 SAMUEL WOODFIN to FEREBEE BELK, both of Macon, for $50, one negro man
named SQUASH and 2 horse calfs, a gray and sorrel. April 8, 1833. *Samuel Woodfin*.
Wit: *JAMES ALLIN*. Registered June 25, 1835.

229 SAMUEL VERMILLIAN of Macon for natural friendship & love for my granddaughter,
SIDNEY ELLENDER STUART, a daughter of SEMENTER(?) and ESTER STUART.
Now Ester is dead & the child being an orphan, I wish that a cow & calf that said Stuart
has use of that is mine should go to use of sd child, & for that purpose I have the cow &
earling (sic) in Stuart's hands so long as he takes care of them for use of the child, but if
he sells or otherwise uses them, then I leave them to my next friend, JAMES VERMIL-
LIAN to go & take them & sell them & put the money to interest for the use of the child.
The cattle I leave with Stuart are the cow & calf my son JAMES got of WILLIAM
MCCLURE. Nov. 5, 1834. *Samuel (his X mark) Vermillian*. Wit: *J. HOWARD*. Proved
by John Howard. Reg. June 25, 1835.

230 Bond: SAUL SMITH, HENRY ADDINGTON & WILLIAM W. PEARSEY pledge
$4,000 bond Oct. 11, 1834 for Smith, who has been appointed Clerk & Master of the
Court of Equity of Macon County. Oct. 11, 1834. Registered July 20, 1835.

230 Bond: SAUL SMITH, HENRY ADDINGTON & WILLIAM W. PEARSEY pledge
$10,000 bond for Smith, appointed Clerk & Master of the Court of Equity of Macon
County. Oct. 11, 1834. Registered July 20, 1835.

231 ABNER STATE/SLATE & his wife, JANE, to WILLIAM CARPENTER, all of Macon,
for $57, part of a tract on Bridge Branch, running through GEORGE RUSH's plantation,
beginningon conditional line between JOSEPH BRADLEY & WILLIAM CAR-
PENTER, containing 30 acres, part of Sec. 92, Dis. 15. Jan. 2, 1832. Ack. by *Abner
Slate, Jane Slate*. Wit: *ASA ENLOE, H. DRYMAN*. Jane Slate was questioned separately
by JONATHAN PHILLIPS, JAMES RUSSEL & JOHN HOWARD, judges of the Court
of Pleas & Quarter Sessions, Oct. 1833 session. Registered July 20, 1835.

233 SG 250, HUMPHREY POSEY, $630, 146.5 ac., Sec. 65, Dis. 16, on Tennessee R.
Granted Dec. 27, 1834; registered July 20, 1835.

234 SG 202, WILLIAM SWEATMAN, $60.96, 50 ac., Sec. 38, Dis. 13, N. side of Tennessee
R. where state line crosses the same. Granted Nov. 29, 1833; registered July 20, 1835.

235 SG 207, for $3 pd by ch'man of Macon Co. Ct., 377+ ac. in trust for suitable situation for
male & female academies convenient to the Town of Franklin, also for other objects of
public improvement; JACOB SILER made plat. Granted Apr. 15, 1835; registered July
20, 1835.

236 SG 203, GOLDMAN INGRAM, $100, 50 ac., Sec. 38 Dis. 10, NE bank of Tennessee R.
Granted Dec. 5, 1833; registered Jul. 20, 1835.

237 SG 214, JOHN STRAIN, assignee of JOSEPH BELL, for $208 paid by Joseph Bell; 105
ac., Sec. 91, Dis. 11. Granted Jan. 5, 1834; registered Jul. 20, 1835.

238 Sheriff's sale: JAMES TRUET, high sheriff of Macon, to DILLARD LOVE, property of
WILLIAM WELCH & THOMAS WELCH Senr., on which they now live, tract called
Sticoyee old fields, 300 ac. on Tuckasegee R., which Thomas Welch bought of the State
at the Oct. 1820 sale, Sec. 18, Dis. 8, adj. lands of JOHN GIBBS, HUGH GIBBS, WIL-
LIAM COCKERAM & others, to satisfy judgment in favor of WILLIAM ROANE for
$34.90 with $6.75 interest, & a $1.20 case against William Welch & Thomas Welch Sr.
At sale July 13, 1834, William Roane had high bid of $40; Dillard Love satisfied Wil-
liam Roane for said bid. July 30, 1834. *James Truet, Sh'ff.* Wit: *WM. ROANE, D.
MCCLOUD.* Registered July 22, 1835.

239 Mortgage: JAMES POTEAT, WILLIAM P. POTEAT, BARNET POTEAT & JOSIAH
COOK of 1st part, SILAS MCDOWELL of 2nd part. McDowell agrees to endorse as
security a note to agency of state of N.C. at Morganton for $600. The Poteats & Cook
agree to sell the following: 50 ac. where Cook now lives, ref. deed of conveyance from
JONATHAN PARKER to Cook; 100 ac. belonging to Barnet Poteat, ref. a deed of conveyance to Poteat from ENOS SHIELDS - 100 ac. conveyed by Shields to W.P. Poteat;
& 174 ac. of James Poteat. April 11, 1835. *Josiah Cook, B.M. Poteat, W.P. Poteat,
James Poteat.* Wit: *FELAX AXLEY.* Reg. July 22, 1835.

240 Bond: JOHN TATHAM, THOMAS TATHAM, THOMAS ROANE, JAMES BRYSON,
JAMES POTEAT, C. SETSER & ROBERT HALL pledge $10,000 bond for John
Tatham, Clerk of Court. Oct. 10, 1834. Wit.: *J. PHILLIPS.* Reg. July 22, 1835.

241 Bond: JOHN TATHAM, THOMAS TATHAM, THOMAS ROANE, JAMES BRYSON,
JAMES POTEAT, C. SETSER and ROBERT HALL pledge $2,000 bond. for John
Tatham, Clerk of Court. Oct. 10, 1834. Wit.: *J. PHILLIPS.* Reg. July 22, 1835.

242 JAMES BARNES of Lawrence? Co., TN obtained letters patent Oct. 14, 1830 to an improvement in washing, the Revolving Steam Washer. BENJAMIN DEMMMANE?
patented a machine to destroy bed bugs, June 22, 1832. MATTHEW HUGHS & CO.
purch. exclusive rts to making, using & selling these machines in Macon, Haywood and
Buncombe Co. from the patentees. Matthew Hughs & Co., for $1,000 paid by THOMAS
W.P. POINDEXTER, JOHN HALL, EDWARD L. POINDEXTER & FRANCIS POIN-
DEXTER, all of Macon, grants them exclusive rights to use the steam washer churn and
bug killer in Macon, Haywood and Buncombe Counties. Oct. 11, 1833. Ack., *Matthew
Hughs & Co.* Registered July 22, 1835 by deputy clerk M. FRANCIS.

242 Mortgage: ARON PINSON to BYNUM W. BELL, BENJAMIN S. BRITTAIN &
SAMUEL SMITH, all of Macon, for $151, tract on E. side of Tennessee R., Sec. 37, Dis.
12, incl. the place where I now live. Condition: Pinson to pay JOHN HOWARD, guardian of the heirs of GIDEON NORTON, dec'd, 2 notes for $151. Feb. 17, 1835. *A. Pin-
son.* Wit: *JACOB PALMER.* Proved by Palmer, July 1835 court. Registered Aug. 3, 1835.

242 HUMPHREY POSEY to JOHN WEST, both of Macon, for $200, tract on N.E. bank of
Tennessee R., Sec. 9, Dis. 10. April 6, 1835. *Humphrey Posey.* Wit: *DANIEL MCCOY,
DANIEL WEST.* Proved by West, July 1835 court. Reg. Aug. 31, 1835.

244 Mortgage: B.W. BELL & B.S. BRITTAIN gave $700 security of THOS. WELCH to
DAVID ENGLAND. Welch conveys tracts lying on both sides of the Tuckasegee and
Tennessee R. & in the forks, formerly owned by THOS. W.P. POINDEXTER and by
him sold to JOSEPH WELCH. Condition: Welch to pay $700 to David England. Mar.
14, 1835. *Thomas Welch.* Wit: *JOSEPH WELCH.* Registered Aug. 31, 1835.

245 Power of Attorney: JOHN PASSMORE of Macon appoints WILLIAM F. PASSMORE
of Macon his lawful attorney to sign a deed to 300 ac. in Ashe Co., NC on Brushy fork of
Little R. adj. lands of JOSEPH SHOAT. Oct. 13, 1835. *John Passmore.* Wit: *DAVID
PASSMORE, JOHN TATHAM.* Registered Oct. 17, 1835.

246 JOHN CUTCHER of Union Co. GA to MICHAEL WATERS of Macon, for $71, a tract,
Sec. 26, Dis. 17. Oct. 1, 1835. *John (his X mark) Cutcher.* Wit: *JOHN S. WATERS,
JOHN WOODY.* Proved by John S. Waters in Oct. 1835 court. Reg. Oct. 17, 1835.

247 NIMROD S. JARRETT to JAMES ROBERTSON & JACOB SILER, for $6, part of No. 19 in 400-ac. town tract, between town lots & Seminary land. to NE corner of Methodist Church land, abt. 91 poles. July 15, 1835. *N.S. Jarrett.* Wit: *MATHEW RUSSEL.* Ack. in July 1835 court. Registered Oct. 18, 1835.

248 JOHN MURRY to JOHN REDMAN, both of Macon, for val. rec'd, 100 ac., Sec. 26, Dis. 11 which Murry purchased Oct. 31, 1822 at Franklin sale. Dec. 19, 1834. *John Murry.* Wit: *DANIEL COOK, JOHN F. BRYSON.* Registered Oct. 20, 1835.

248 LEWIS TILLY of Rabun Co. GA to JOHN AMMONS of Macon, tract, Sec. 31, Dis. 12, purchased Oct. 1820 at land sale in Waynesville. Nov. 5, 1829. *Lewis Tilly.* Wit: *THOMAS RAY.* Proved by Ray, July 1835 court. Reg. Oct. 20, 1835.

249 JOHN AMMONS to JOSHUA AMMONS, both of Macon, for val. rec'd, tract, Sec. 9, Dis. 11, which I purchased in 1822 at the land sale at Franklin. Oct. 17, 1835. Acknowleged *John Ammons.* Wit: *JOSHUA ROBERTS, JOHN TATHAM.* Reg. Oct. 20, 1835.

250 NATHAN DEHART to THOMAS WEST, both of Macon, for $250, 14+ ac., Cowee Cr., Sec. 20, Dis. 10, which Nathan Dehart purch.of LINDSEY FORTUNE. Oct. 13, 1835. Ack. *Nathan Dehart.* Wit: *B.S. BRITTAIN, D. MCCOY.* Reg. Nov. 26, 1835.

251 SG 218, HUMPHREY POSEY assignee of JOSEPH WELCH, for $701 pd by Welch, 277 ac., Sec. 9, Dis. 10, NE bank of Tennessee R. near site of old cabbin. Granted June 12, 1835; registered Dec. 10, 1835.

252 NIMROD S. JARRETT to JESSE R. SILER, for $5, part of town lot No. 19, bet. lower lots & Seminary land. Aug. 1, 1835. *N.S. Jarrett.* Wit: *J.W. KILLIAN, JACOB SILER.* Proven by Jacob Siler, Oct. 1835 court. Registered Dec. 15, 1835.

253 JOHN BRYSON of Union Co. GA to WILLIAM H. BRYSON of Macon, for $175, 50 ac. on Cullowhee Cr., Sec. 20, Dis. 7. Sep. 1, 1835. *John Bryson.* Wit: *THOS. ROGERS, J.B. ALLISON.* Ack. at Oct. 1835 court. Registered Dec. 15, 1835.

254 JOHN BRYSON JR. of Union Co. GA to WILLIAM H. BRYSON of Macon, for $525, 83 ac. on Cullowhee Cr., Sec. 16, Dis. 7. Sep. 1, 1835. *John Bryson.* Wit: *THOS. ROGERS, J.B. ALLISON.* Ack. in Oct. 1835 court. Registered Dec. 15, 1835.

255 SG #219, MICHAEL WIKEL, $319, 166 ac. on W. bank of Tennessee R., Sec. 34, Dis. 19. Granted June 12, 1835; registered Dec. 15, 1835.

256 LUKE BARNARD & ANDREW BARNARD to REBECAH MCDANIEL, all of Macon, for $3,000: 1st, 300 ac. near old Indian improvement, near an Indian grave, on "Cautoogajay" (Cartoogechaye); granted JOHN MOORE, Jan. 1, 1825. 2nd: 3 ac. on "Cautoogajay," Sec. 12, Dis. 15 granted Luke Barnard, Feb. 9, 1827. Oct. 9, 1835. *Luke Barnard, Andrew Barnard.* Wit: *J.H. WHITESIDES, JACOB SILER.* Proven by Siler, Oct. 1835 court. Registered Dec. 15, 1835.

257 ALFRED BROWN of Macon to ANDREW CATHEY, for $300, 53+ ac. on Tennessee R., Sec. 29, Dis. 17. Sep. 6, 1831. *Alford Brown.* Wit: *ANDREW CAMPBELL, WM. (his "A" mark) PRUETT.* Proven by Pruett in Oct.1835 court. Registered Dec. 15, 1835.

258 WILLIAM WILLIAMS & wife, SALLY, JOHN H. AMMONS & wife, NANCY, LAURANCE BRADLY & wife JENNY (JENCY?), ARCHABALD VAUGHN & wife ALLIS, and PHILIP KIRBY, heirs of JOSIAH KIRBY, dec'd, all of Macon, to JESSE KIRBY of Macon, for $250, 119 ac. crossing Ellijay Cr., Sec. 56, Dis. 11, sold by state of NC to Josiah Kirby. Oct. 13, 1835. *John H. Ammons, Nancy (her X mark) Ammons, Philip Kirby, William Williams, Sary (her X mark) Williams, Archabald Vaughn, Allis (her X mark) Vaughn, L. Bradly, Jinny (her X mark) Bradly.* Wit: *MATHEW DAVIS.* In October 1835 session, J. PHILLIPS, WM. HOOD & JOHN WILD, justices of Ct. of Pleas & Qtr Sessions, separately examined Sally Williams, Nancy Ammons, Jency Bradly & Allis Vann. Registered Dec. 15, 1835.

260 Mortgage: JOHN CROW of Macon to A.B. DONALDSON. Donaldson is sec. for Crow,
staying one judgment in favor of ROBERTSON & SILER for $23.26, one in favor of
JOHN DOBSON for $9.38, one in favor of DOBSON & CO. for $7.18, one in favor of
JESSE R. SILER for $8.01 1/2. Crow mortgages to Donaldson 4-horse waggon; horse
saddle, bridle & martingale; rifle gun. Dec. 19, 1835. *John Crow*. Wit: *E. DOWDLE*.
Proven by Dowdle, Jan. 7, 1836. Registered Feb. 12, 1836.

261 BENJAMIN S. BRITTAIN to CLARK BIRD, both of Macon, for $600, 640 ac. on
Telico Cr., a reserve granted to an Indian by the name of SKEKEN by treaties of 1817
and 1819, and by Skeken conveyed to GIDEON F. MORRIS. Feb. 17, 1836. *Benjamin S.
Brittain*. Wit: *JOHN HALL*. Acknowledged in Feb. 1836 court. Registered Mar. 15, 1836.

262 THOMAS CRESSAR to THOMAS J. ROANE, both of Macon, for $200, 50 ac., Sec.
55, Dis. 16, originally granted Jan. 15, 1836 (sic). Dec. 3, 1833 (sic). *Thomas (his X
mark) Cressar*. Wit: *JAMES K. GRAY, M. KILLIAN*. Proven by James K. Gray, Feb.
1836 court. Registered Mar. 15, 1836.

263 DILLARD LOVE of Macon to JESSE R. SILER, my undivided one-half of an acre tract
of land on W. bank of Tennessee R., incl. butments of bridge which title was vested in
me by an act of N.C. Legislature. Jan. 20, 1836. *Dillard Love*. Wit: *M. KILLIAN, D.R.
LOWERY*. Proven by Milas Killian, Feb. 1836 court. Reg. Mar. 15, 1836.

263 THOMAS LOVE of Macon to JESSE R. SILER, for $5, one acre on W. bank of Ten-
nessee R. above waggon ford on state rd., the right of which was vested in Love by act of
the legislature of N.C. at last session, granting to him & DILLARD LOVE rights in but-
ment of a bridge by us to be built. He directs officers of state to issue an agreement to
Jesse R. Siler. Nov. 20, 1834. *Thomas Love*. Wit: *ROBERT HUGGINS, M. KILLIAN*.
Proven by Milas Killian in Feb. 1836 court. Reg. Mar. 15, 1836.

264 Mortgage: EDWARD L. POINDEXTER to MICKEL WIKEL & JOHN TATHAM, all
of Macon, for $200, one Negro girl named SILVA(?) abt 13 yrs old. Wikel & Tatham en-
dorsed note for me to Bank Of The State of North Carolina at Morganton for $200. May
30, 1835. *E.L. Poindexter*. Wit: *S. MCDOWELL*. Proven by McDowell, Feb. 1836 court.
Registered 15 Mar. 1836.

265 Mortgage: BENJAMIN S. BRITTAIN of Macon, for $1,439.12 due on June 25, 1828 &
other lawful interest, mortgaged to DAVID VANCE & DAVID L. SWAIN, executors of
the late ROBERT B. VANCE 5 negroes, to wit: ESTER & her 3 children, BOSTON,
WILL & RANSOM. Now Brittain mortgages to Vance & Swain the 2 youngest children
of Ester, to wit, 2 female children named SARAH & CLARISSA. Dec. 9, 1835. *B.S. Brittain*. Wit: *JACOB SILER*. Proven by Siler in Jan. 1836 ct.—recorded by ULRICH
KEENER, deputy clerk of court. Registered Mar. 15, 1836.

266 SAMUEL BYRD of Yancey County, NC to THOMAS GREEN of Burke County, NC,
for $250, land crossing Middle Cr. Feb. 2, 1836. *Samuel Byrd*. Wit: *JAMES W. GUINN,
JOHN GRAY BYNUM*. Proven by James W. Guinn, Feb. 1836 court. Registered Mar. 15,
1836.

267 BLAKE PERCY/PERCEY & MARY PERCY to EPHRIUM PERCY, all of Buncombe
Co., NC, 4 negroes, to wit, BENJAMIN, _____, WILL & SOPHIA, also 300 ac. where
BLAKE PERCEY now lives, 12 cattle & all hogs belonging to said plantation, 2 beds &
other household furniture. Ephrim Percy obliges himself in sum of $2,600 to satisfy all
debts against Blake Percy & wind up his affairs, also to support Blake Percy & Mary
Percy w. comfortable living during life. Blake & Mary agreed with their other heirs that
property at Blake & Mary's deaths shall be Ephrium's. April 14, 1829. *Ephrium Percey,
Blake (his X mark) Percey, Mary (her X mark) Percey*. Wit: *J.H. POTEAT, WM. I.
LEWIS*. Proved by James Poteat, Feb. 1836 court. Registered Mar. 15, 1836.

268 SG 225, SAMUEL BYRD, $146, 73 ac. crossing Middle Cr., Sec. 35, Dis. 13. Granted
Dec. 9, 1835; registered Mar. 16, 1836.

269 SG 101, THOMAS ROGERS, $181, 50 ac., Sec. 13, Dis. 7. Granted Nov. 29, 1833; registered Mar. 16, 1836.

270 MICHAEL WATERS to MICHAEL J. WATERS, both of Macon, for $115, 51.75 ac., Sec. 26, Dis. 17. Feb. 18, 1836. *Michael (his X mark) Waters*. Wit: *THOMAS J. ROANE, D.R. LOWRY*. Proven by Roane in Feb. 1836 court. Registered Mar. 18, 1836.

271 BENJAMIN S. BRITTAIN to JESSE R. SILER, both of Macon, for $375, land on Tennessee R. purchased at sale in Franklin, 1835 & conveyed by the Governor of N.C. to JONATHAN PHILLIPS as Chairman of the County Court of Macon in trust for future disposition of the justices (town commons): No. 50 (7 ac.); No. 56 (3+ ac.); part of No. 49 (3+ ac.); part of No. 55 (1+ ac.). All incl. in one plat beg. at corner of No. 49, to bank of the Tennessee River, to line of State(?) Bridge land, containing 15+ ac. Feb. 18, 1836. *B.S. Brittain*. Wit: *J.K. GRAY, D.R. LOWRY*. Proven by James K. Gray, Feb. 1836 court. Registered Mar. 15, 1836.

272 BENJAMIN S. BRITTAIN to JAMES W. GUINN, both of Macon, for $1,000, land on Tennessee R. purch. by Brittain at sale of town commons, adj. Franklin, conveyed to JONATHAN PHILLIPS as Chairman of the County Court of Macon in trust for future disposition: No. 40 (4 ac.); No. 41 (5 ac.); No. 44 (8+ ac.); No. 45 (5 ac.); No. 46 (5 ac.); No. 47; No. 48 (5 ac.); No. 51 (5 ac.); No. 52 (6+ ac.); No. 53 (7+ ac.); No. 54 (7 ac.); also 2+ ac. of No. 55 and 1+ ac. of No.49. All embodied in one plat beg. at the corner of lot 40 near the old Coling (sic) ground, corner of original town tract, to W. bank of Tennessee R. near Jonathan Phillips' Ford, NE corner of Town Commons tract No. 55, containing 68+ ac. Jan. 11, 1836. *B.S. Brittain*. Wit: *J.K. GRAY, D.R. LOWRY*. Proven by Gray, Feb. 1836 court. Registered Mar. 19, 1836.

273 WILLIAM SILER to JESSE R. SILER, both of Macon, for $500, 123.5 ac., Sec. 26, Dis. 16. Feb. 8, 1836. *Wm. Siler*. Wit: *A. HESTER, T.P. SILER*. Proven by Albert Hester, Feb. 1836 court. Registered Mar. 19, 1836.

274 JOHN WOOD to THOMAS J. ROANE, both of Macon, for $650, 116 ac., Sec. 28, Dis. 16. Jan. 17, 1834. *John Wood*. Wit: *J.K. GRAY, M. KILLIAN*. Proven by James K. Gray, Feb. 1836 court. Registered Mar. 19, 1836.

275 JESSE LEVASKESE to MICHAEL LONG, both of Macon, for $450, 103 ac., Sec. 4, Dis. 7. Nov. 23, 1835. Acknowledged in open court by *Jesse Levaskese*. Wit: *DAVID ROGERS, HUGH ROGERS*. Registered Mar. 19, 1836.

276 JOHN ADDINGTON to DREWRY LOGAN, for $400, 108+ ac., Sec. 17, Dis. 15. Jan. 28, 1836. *John Addington*. Wit: *JACOB SILER, HARIET SILER*. Proven by Jacob Siler, Feb. 1836 court. Registered Mar. 19, 1836.

277 JOHN ADDINGTON to AMOS LEDFORD, both of Macon, for $300, 80 ac. on Standridge Cr. Dec. 5, 1834. *John Addington*. Wit: *___ DOWDLE, JESSE SANDERS*. Proven in court by Jesse Sanders, Feb. 1836 session. Reg. Mar. 19, 1836.

278 Mortgage: JOSEPH WELCH, ROBERT HALL & JAMES TRUETT, merchants & copartners in trade, in firm of Joseph Welch & Co. in Town of Franklin, sell to JOHN HALL all stock of debts, dues and demants due said firm, for $2458. Hall has executed for the company at agency of Bank of State Of N.C. at Morganton, ISAAC T. AVERY, agent, for the amount of $11, and given security for the company to different companies of merchants, to wit: MILLER REPLY & CO., $855.54; MILLICAN & WALTON, $53.35; HANDEL WRIGHT & CO., $13.00; A.Z. WOLTAN & CO., $232.77; J. MCCARTY, $27.86; and HALET KEMBALL & CO., $160.00, all of Charlestown, SC; and GEORGE PARRATH & CO. of Hamburgh, SC, making a total of $2455.86. Dec. 25, 1835. *Joseph Welch, Robert Hall, Jas. Truett*. Wit: *DILLARD LOVE, J.K. GRAY, CASLO(?) TRUET*. Proven before justices ISAAC TRUETT & J.H. BRYSON, Esq's, on oath of James K. Gray & Dillard Love, Jan. 8, 1836, at a call court - JOHN TATHAM by ULRICH KEENER, D.Clk. Registered Mar. 21, 1836.

279 SG 213, JOHN REDMOND, $75, 50 ac., Sec. 30, Dis. 11. Granted 5 Jan. 1835; registered Mar. 20, 1836.

280 SG 229, THOMAS WEST, assignee of LINDSEY FORTUNE, for $111.40 pd by Lindsey Fortune, 74+ ac., Sec. 20, Dis. 10. Granted Dec. 16, 1835; reg. May 26, 1836.

281 SG 228, NOAH BURCHFIELD, assignee of JOHN RISH, for $101.60 pd by John Rish, 67+ ac., Sec. 28, Dis. 8, on Tennessee R. Granted Dec. 9, 1834; reg. May 26, 1836.

282 SG 200, WILLIAM SILER, $247, 123+ ac., Sec. 26, Dis. 16. Granted Dec. 17, 1834; registered May 26, 1836.

283 SG 220, JACOB PALMER, $182.875, 54 ac., Sec. 21, Dis. 13, on N. fork of Tessentee Creek. Granted Sep. 16, 1835; registered May 26, 1836.

284 SG 212, for $3 pd by JESSE R. SILER, THOMAS J. ROANE & JAMES K. GRAY, in trust for Methodist Episcopal Church at Franklin, 3 ac. for a place of publick worship & burying, bd. lands conveyed by state for seminary of learning, bd. J.R. Siler, to main road from Franklin to Georgia. Granted Jan. 10, 1835; registered May 26, 1836.

285 SG 209, WILLIAM MCCONNELL, $610, 200 ac., Sec. 3, Dis. 15, on W. bank of Tennessee R. Granted Jan. 11, 1834; registered June 9, 1836.

286 MARTIN MOSS of Pickens Dist., S.C. to JOHN HOWARD of Macon, for $20, all my part of 3 tracts lying on Tennessee R., my undiv. part of land formerly belonging to GIDEON NORTON, dec'd, 1/14 part of said land; and sell my interest in the widow's dowry after her death & all my interest as one of legatees of Gideon Norton. Nov. 7, 1834. *Martin (his X mark) Moss.* Wit: *JOHN BURNS, JOHN H. SLOAN.* Proven by Sloan, Feb. 1836 court. Registered June 7, 1836.

287 Mortgage: MILES CARROL & DANEL CARROL, to B.W. BELL, sorrel mare, bay horse, 12 hogs, 2 cows, calf, yearling, set of blacksmith tools. Bell pledges security for presentation of a suit pending in Superior Court of Macon Co., WILLIAM CARROL plaintiff and JOHN DAVIS & WILLIAM F. MCFEE defendants. Apr. 4, 1835. *Miles Carrol, Danel (his X mark) Carol.* Wit: *FELAX AXLEY.* Registered June 9, 1836.

287 Power of Attorney: MARTIN MOSS of Pickens Dist., SC, empowers JOHN HOWARD of Macon lawful attn'y to settle my estate of GIDEON NORTON, dec'd, as one of legatees, & to collect such estate, and receipt ARON PINSON & TILATHA NORTON as administrators. I have sold my whole of my part of the estate to John Howard, except what I have collected which is $15. Nov. 7, 1834. *Martin (his X mark) Moss.* Wit: *JOHN BURNS, JOHN H. SLONE.* Proven by Slone in Feb. 1836 court. Registered June 9, 1836.

288 ANDREW CATHEY to HENRY QUEEN, both of Macon, for $600, 53+ ac. on Tennessee R., Sec. 29, Dis. 17. *A. Cathey.* Wit: *JOHN QUEEN, JAMES N. BRYSON.* Proven by John Queen, October 1834 court. Registered June 9, 1836.

289 Bond: SILAS MCDOWELL, JESSE R. SILER & JAMES ROBINSON pledge $10,000 bond for McDowell as Clerk of Superior Court. Oct. 1835. Registered June 1836.

289 Bond: SILAS MCDOWELL, JESSE R. SILER and JAMES ROBINSON pledge $4,000 bond for McDowell as Clerk of Superior Court. October 1835. Registered June 1836.

290 Mortgage: JAMES W. GUINN to JESSE R. SILER, both of Macon, for $1,000, tracts on Tennessee R. purch. by J.W. Guinn from B.S. BRITTAIN, part of town commons granted to JONATHAN PHILLIPS as Ch'man of County Ct of Macon, 68+ ac., for security on payment of 3 notes, to sum of $1,000. Jan. 12, 1836. *James W. Guinn.* Wit: *D.R. LOWRY.* Ack. in February 1836 court. Reg. June 24, 1836.

292 Mortgage: JAMES POTEET, ISAIAH COOK, W.P. POTEET & BARNARD POTEET
to SILAS MCDOWELL. McDowell to endorse as sec. a note payable to Bank of the
State of NC at Morganton, for $600. Mortgaged, several tracts: 50 ac. where Cook now
lives, ref. deed from JONATHAN PARKER to Cook; 100 ac. belonging to Barnard
Poteet, last conveyed from ENOS SHIELDS to Poteet; 106 ac. conveyed from Enos
Shields to W.P. Poteet; 174 ac. where ___ Poteet now lives, on NW corner of No. 27.
Feb. 5, 1836. *James Poteat, Isaiah Cook, William P. Poteet, Barnard Poteet*. Wit:
FELAX AXLEY. Proven by Felax Axely in Feb. 1836 court. Registered June 24, 1836.

293 JOHN TATHAM, for val. rec'd, to MATTHEW N. RUSSEL of Macon, right & interest
in 52 ac., Sec. 33, Dis. 11, purch. 1822 at land sale in Haywood County. Oct. 15, 1834.
John Tatham. Wit: *M. RUSSEL, THOMAS RUSSEL*. Proven in court by M.N. Russel,
April 1836. Registered June 24, 1836.

294 WILLIAM GILLESPIE of Buncombe Co. NC to JOHN GILLESPIE of Macon, for
$233, 69 ac., part of Sec. 36, Dis. 15. Dec. 11, 1832. *Wm. Gillespie*. Wit: *JACOB SILER,
MATILDA SILER*. Proven by Jacob Siler, April 1836 ct. Reg. Jun. 24, 1836.

295 GEORGE WIKEL of Macon had a mortgage on 100 ac., Sec. 26, Dis. 11, property of
JOHN MURRY; now Wikel surrenders his right back to Murry. Jan. 6, 1834. *George
Wikel*. Wit: *S. MCDOWELL, JOHN REDMAN*. Proven by Redman, June 6, 1834,
recorded by ULRICH KEENER, deputy clerk of court. Registered June 24, 1836.

295 AMOS BROWN to JOSHUA HALL, Sr., Negro boy named PETER, abt 17 yrs of age,
for $400. Oct. 24, 1834. *Amos Brown*. Wit: *ALFORD HALL*. Ack. Apr. 1836 court.
Registered June 24, 1836.

296 HIRAM DIMSDALE to JONATHAN H. WHITESIDES, both of Macon, for $224, 190
ac., Sec. 2, Dis. 16, on fork of "Cautoogaya" (Cartoogechaye). Sep. 20, 1834. *Hiram
Dimsdale*. Wit: *JAMES (his X mark) HASTIN, GEORGE W. CARSON*. Proven by
George W. Carson, April 1836 court. Registered June 24, 1836.

297 NATHAN SMITH to JASON LEDFORD, both of Macon, for $300, land on Tennessee
R., Sec. 7, Dis. 14. Jan. 31, 1834. *Nathan Smith*. Wit: *J.J. HOWARD, THOS. LONG*.
Proven by J.J. Howard, April 1836 court. Registered June 24, 1836.

298 JAMES GALBREATH to CLARK BIRD, both of Macon, for $80, all my goods,
household stuff, implements & furniture, especially that in schedule annexed: bay horse
colt, 11 sheep, 4 sows & pigs, 2 shoats, 1 calf, 1 crib of corn, all my fodder and ruff-
ness(?), 2 beds & furniture, and sleds, poles, oven pan and all my household & kitchen
furniture, the premises standing in a certain tenement, now or late in the occupation of
James Galbreath. I have put Clark Bird in possession by delivering to him one knife at
sealing & delivering of these presents. Jan. 26, 1836. *James Galbraeth*. Wit: *JOHN (his
X mark) BRYSON*. Proven by Bryson, April 1836 court. Registered June 25, 1836.

299 Bond: JOHN TATHAM, THOMAS J. ROANE, THOMAS TATHAM, C. SETSER,
JOHN DOBSON, JOHN MCDOWELL, ZACHARIAH CABE, pledge $10,000 for John
Tatham, elected clerk of court of pleas & qtr sessions. Oct. 15, 1835. Wit: ULRICH
KEENER. Registered June 25, 1836.

299 Second entry for JOHN TATHAM's bond, same as A-298.

300 Mortgage: DILLARD LOVE to GEORGE WIKEL, for $200 due next Nov. 15, Negro
girl, MIRA(?), abt 12 or 14 yrs. Labour of slave is in discharge of interest on the $200.
June 18, 1836. *Dillard Love*. Wit: *J.W. GUINN*. Proven June 18, 1836 & recorded by
ULRICH KEENER for JOHN TATHAM. Reg. June 25, 1831.

301 SG 99, THOMAS SHEPHERD, $174, 116 ac. on Cowee Cr., Sec. 22, Dis. 10. Granted
Jan. 12, 1828; registered Aug. 15, 1836.

302 SG 234, THOMAS SHEPHERD, assignee of JOHN JOHNSTON, for $280, 140 ac. cross-
ing the three forks of Cowee Creek, Sec. 11, Dis. 10. Granted Feb. 28, 1836; registered
Aug. 15, 1836.

303   SG 235,THOMAS SHEPHERD, assignee of JOHN JOHNSTON, for $270, 125 ac., Sec. 97, Dis. 10, on south fork of Cowee Cr. Granted Feb. 20, 1836; registered Aug. 15, 1836.

304   SG 236, THOMAS SHEPHERD, $129, 86 ac., Sec. 26, Dis. 10. Granted Feb. 23, 1836; registered Aug. 15, 1836.

305   SG 238, THOMAS SHEPHERD, $208.50, 134 ac., Sec. 18, Dis. 10, crossing middle fork of Cowee Creek. Granted Feb. 23, 1836; registered Aug. 15, 1836.

306   SG 237, THOMAS SHEPHERD, for $311, 91+ ac., Sec. 27, Dis. 10, crossing middle fork of Cowee Creek. Granted Feb. 23, 1836; registered Aug. 15, 1836.

307   Mortgage: BENJAMIN S. BRITTAIN of Macon to J.R. PACE, JOHN HOWARD, THOMAS J. ROAN, WILLIAM A. BRITTAIN, for $5,500, 6 negroes: ISAM, HANDY, JIM, LAWSON, MARLBOROUGH & JANE, security for note in Bank of the State of N.C. at Morganton. Apr. 16, 1836. *B.S. Brittain.* Wit: *JASON L. HYATT.* Proven August session of court, 1836. Registered Sep. 25, 1836.

308   WILLIAM MCCONNELL, only living heir & representative of PHILIP MCCONNELL, dec'd, of Haywood Co. NC, to JESSE R. SILER of Haywood, for $1,074, land in Weakley Co., TN, N fork of Oleron/Cleron(?) R., 13th Surv. Dist., Entry #74, bd. THOMAS & ROBERT LOVE's land. Sep. 23, 1826. *William McConnell.* Wit: *JOHN D. LOVE, JOHN J. POSEY.* In Oct. 1836 court JOHN TATHAM proved handwriting of John J. Posey & that Posey was an inhabitant of state at the time. JONATHAN PHILLIPS, ch'man of court, certified John Tatham was clerk of court. Reg. Oct. 22, 1836.

308   Deed of gift: JOHN BRYSON of Macon for natural love & affection for beloved grandchildren, MARTHEY JANE GREEN & JOHN B. GREEN, give them, all & singular, a mare 3 yrs old, bridle & saddle. No date. *John Bryson.* Wit: *J. PHILLIPS.* Proven Oct. 1836 session. Registered Dec. 12, 1836.

310   JONATHAN DENTON of Macon to ENOS SCROGGS, for $300, 133 ac. E.side Tennessee R., bd. WILLIAM CALER's survey. Aug. 14, 1835. *Jonathan Denton.* Wit: *JOHN SCROGGS, ALFORD SCROGGS.* Proven by John Scroggs, October 1836 court. Registered Dec. 11, 1836.

311   GEORGE W. HISE to WILLIAM STALLCUP, both of Macon, for $1,150, 127+ ac. on Tuckasegee R., Sec. 2, Dis. 8. Dec. 8, 1835. *G.W. Hise.* Wit: *JNO. B. LOVE, ALLEN (Illegible - Foster? Setser?).* Acknowledged in court, Oct. 1836. Reg. Dec. 11, 1836.

312   JAMES POTEAT to JAMES ROBISON, both of Macon, for $1,000, 174 ac. on Tennessee R., Sec. 30, Dis. 16. Sep. 23, 1833. *James Poteat.* Wit: *J.R. SILER, J.R. LAMBERT.* Proven in Oct. 1836 court by Lambert. Registered Dec. 12, 1836.

End of first bound volume, Deed Book A

313   SG 226, JOSEPH SHEPPARD, $164, 116 ac., Sec. 28, Dis. 16. Granted Dec. 9, 1835; registered Dec. 12, 1836.

314   SG 160, JOB THOMAS, assignee of JAMES HUGH, for $57 pd by Hugh, 57 ac., Sec. 53, Dis. 10, on the Rabbits Creek. Granted Dec. 29, 1830; reg. Dec. 13, 1836.

315   SG 161, JOB THOMAS, assignee of JAMES HUGHS, for $77 pd by Hughs, Sec. 49, Dis. 10 on Watauga, crossing Publick road. Granted Dec. 24, 1830; reg. Dec. 13, 1836.

316   SG 8? JOHN WILSON, $5 per 100 ac., 50 ac. on E. side of Savannah Cr. in Dis. 8. Granted Sept. 30, 1836; registered Dec. 12, 1836.

317 Mortgage: JOSEPH WELCH of Macon to JOHN H. CHINN of Monroe County, TN of
    2nd part, JOHN MCGHEE of Monroe County TN of 3rd part, for $5 pd by Chinn to in-
    demnify McGhee for $1,670.62 note executed by Welch & JAMES M. BRYSON,
    JAMES ANGEL, EDMOND MCELDER, THOMAS WELCH, JAMES TRUET &
    ROBERT HALL, bearing interest from Oct. 27, 1836. Joseph Welch sells following
    Negro slaves for life (as security): Negro man, TOM, abt 21; Negro girl SUSAN, called
    Sue, abt 14; Negro boy ALBERT, abt 10; Negro boy MANSON, abt 7. Oct. 28, 1836.
    Joseph Welch, J.H. Chinn, John McGhee by Agent J.H. Chinn. Wit: *S. MCDOWELL,
    J.K. GRAY.* Proven in Feb. 1837 ct by Silas McDowell. Registered Feb. 20, 1837.

319 Power of attorney: JOSEPH WELCH of Macon appoints JAMES P.H. PORTER of
    Sevier Co. TN att'y to apply for & receive of Col. NIMIAN EDMONSON, commis-
    sioner appt'd to sell lands of NC in county of Macon, certificates of land purch. by me at
    land sale in Franklin, October 24, 1833: in District One, Sec. 51, 61 ac.; Sec. 55, 69 ac.;
    Sec. 56, 33 ac.; Sec. 57, 53 ac.; Sec. 58, 50 ac.; & Sec. 69, 113 ac.; also Sec. 77 in Dis. 8.
    Porter to sell same & apply proceeds toward $1,670.62 note exec. by self & others of
    JOHN MCGEE of Monroe Co. TN . Oct. 29, 1836. *Joseph Welch.* Wit: *SILAS
    MCDOWELL, J.K. GRAY.* Proved by witnesses Feb. 20, 1837. Reg. Feb. 20, 1834.

320 Bond: JACOB B. TRAMMELL, JOHN STRAIN, PHILIP CANSLER, JOHN RED-
    MOND & ROBERT HALL bond of $10,000 for Jacob B. Trammell, elected Entry Taker
    by co. ct. Feb. 18, 1835. Wit: *JOHN TATHAM,* clerk. Registered Feb. 22, 1837.

320 SG 316, JACOB SILER, $26.81, 132+ ac., Sec. 29, Dis. 15, on "Catoogach" (Car-
    toogechaye) Creek. Granted Dec. 12, 1836; registered Feb. 24, 1837.

321 Macon County Ct. of Pleas & Qtr Sessions in Feb. 1837 session, heard oath of JAMES
    TRUETT, who proved deed for tract in "Weeks" (Weakley) County TN for 515 ac., ex-
    ecuted Sep. 23, 1826 by WILLIAM MCCONNELL to JESSE R. SILER, wit. by JOHN
    D. LOVE & JOHN J. POSEY. Truett proved handwriting of John J. Posey & that Posey
    is not an inhabitant of state. Ordered to be registered & recorded, JOHN TATHAM,
    clerk. J. HOWARD certified additional probate of this deed was reg. Feb. 23, 1837.

322 DRURY LOGAN to MOSES ADDINGTON, both of Macon, for val. rec'd, 55 ac., Sec.
    153, Dis. 15, purch.1836 at Franklin sale. Feb. 23, 1837. *Drury (his X mark) Logan.* Wit:
    B.F. HAWKINS, D.R. LOWERY. Proven Feb. 1837 ct. by D.R. Lowery. Registered Mar.
    8, 1837.

323 DRURY LOGAN to MOSES ADDINGTON, for $400, No. 17, Dis. 15, containing 180
    ac. Feb. 21, 1837. *Drury (his X mark) Logan.* Wit: *D.R. LOWERY, A. HESTER.* Proven
    Feb. 1837 court by D.R. Lowery. Registered Mar. 8, 1837.

324 JOB THOMAS of Macon to MILES SANDERS of Macon, formerly of Burke Co., NC,
    for $825, 57+ ac. on "Wattaugua" & Rabbit's Creeks, Sec. 32, Dis. 10, also 51+ ac. on
    "Watagua" crossing Publick Road, Sec. 49, Dis. 10. Nov. 8, 1836. *Job Thomas.* Wit:
    J.W. GUINN, who proved in Feb. 1837 court. Registered Mar. 8, 1837.

325 WILLIAM MCCONNEL of Haywood Co. NC is bound to DAVID MCCONNEL of
    Haywood in sum of $500; William to make David a good & lawful title to 105 ac. on W.
    side of the Tennessee R., bd. HEMPHILL. July 14, 1826. *William McConnell.* Wit:
    JAMES MOORE. Hand of James Moore proven by JOHN HOWARD in February 1837
    court. Registered Mar. 8, 1837.

326 HUGH ROGERS to JOHN CORN, both of Macon, for $250, 55 ac. on "Culowhee." Jan.
    19, 1836. *Hugh Rogers.* Wit: *ADAM CORN, B. KERBEY.* Proven by Adam Corn, Feb.
    1837 session of court. Registered March 8, 1837.

327 WILLIAM P. CORMAN of Monroe Co., TN, to ROBERT HUGGINS of Macon, for
    $40, full rights for 14 years in Macon to a patent improvement in the Biersheare plough.
    July 16, 1836. *W.P. Corman.* Wit: *JAMES K. GRAY.* Proven by Gray in Feb. 1837 court.
    Registered March 8, 1837.

327 W.A. BRITTAIN, for val. consideration, to WILLIAM SILER, legal rt to within certificate when he pays balance owed the state. Feb. 20, 1837. ____. Wit: *JAMES ROBIN-
SON, B.F. HAWKINS.* Proven Feb. 1837 ct. by James Robinson. Reg. Mar. 8, 1837.

328 WM. A. BRITTAIN of Macon for val. consideration to WILLIAM SILER, 140 ac. on
Cartoogajay Cr., Dis. 15, Sec. 28, purch. of state in Oct. 1820. Nov. 12, 1836. *Wm. A.
Brittain.* Wit: *J.R. SILER, JASON L. HYATT.* Proven in Feb. 1837 court by Jason L.
Hyatt. Registered Mar. 8, 1837.

328 ROBERT HAWKINS to THOMAS J. ROANE, both of Macon, for $1,000, 42 ac. on
west bank of Thomson's fork of "Cautoogajay," Sec. 54, Dis. 15, granted Robert Hawkins by patent deed. Oct. 24, 1836. *Robert Hawkins.* Wit: *S. MCDOWELL, J.K. GRAY.*
Proven in court by Silas McDowell, Feb. 1837. Registered Mar. 8, 1837.

330 SG 269, WILLIAM COCKERHAM, $10.14, 50 ac., Sec. 106, Dis. 8, mentions Choty
Ridge. Granted Dec. 12, 1836; registered Mar. 9, 1837.

331 SG 270, WILLIAM COCKERHAM, $11.73, 58 ac., Sec. 107, Dis. 8. Granted Dec. 12,
1836; registered Mar. 9, 1837.

332 SG 279, JOHN GIBBS, for $15.18, 75 ac., Sec. 104, Dis. 8. Granted Dec. 12, 1836;
registered Mar. 9, 1837.

333 SG 154, JAMES BRYSON, assignee of ENOS SHEALDS, for $105 paid by Shealds; 54
ac., Sec. 49, Dis. 11. Granted Dec. 12, 1836; registered Mar. 9, 1837.

334 SG 301, DAVID MCCONNEL, $10.14, 50 ac., Sec. 4, Dis. 15. Granted Dec. 12, 1836;
registered Mar. 9, 1837.

335 SG 303, GEORGE PENLAND, $13.98, 69 ac., Sec. 45, Dis. 13. Granted Dec. 12, 1836;
registered Mar. 9, 1837.

336 SG 345, THOMAS GRIBBLE, $250.50, 120.25 ac., Sec. 1, Dis. 3, mouth of JAMES
BUCKANNAN's Sill (Still) house branch, south side of Tuckasegee R. Granted Dec. 28,
1836; registered Mar. 9, 1837.

337 SG 250, WILLIAM R. BUCKHANNON, $16.52, 82 ac., Sec. 154, Dis. 8. Granted Dec.
12, 1836; registered Mar. 9, 1837.

338 SG 345, JOHN LAMM, assignee of DAVID PEAK, for $105 paid by David Peak, 70
ac., Sec. 32, Dis. 12, crossing the river. Granted Dec. 28, 1836; registered Mar. 9, 1837.

339 SG 252, JAMES BUCKHANNON, $10.14, 60 ac., Sec. 156, Dis. 8, little east fork of
"Suvannana" (Savannah Creek). Granted Dec. 12, 1836; registered Mar. 9, 1837.

340 SG 274, EZEKIEL DOWDLE, $16.20, 51 ac., Sec. 161, Dis. 15. Granted Dec. 12, 1836;
registered Mar. 9, 1837.

341 SG 289, WILLIAM KIMSEY, $10.14, 50 ac., Sec. 103, Dis. 15. Granted Dec. 12, 1836;
registered Mar. 10, 1837.

342 SG 339, DANEL WEST, $27.34, 135 ac., Sec. 14, Dis. 10. Granted Dec. 12, 1836;
registered Mar. 10, 1837.

343 SG 309, JACOB SILER, $10.14, 50 ac., Sec. 27, Dis. 15. Granted Dec. 12, 1836;
registered Mar. 10, 1837.

344 SG 340, THOMAS WEST, $10.14, 50 ac., Sec. 24, Dis. 10, mill fork of Cowe Creek.
Granted Dec. 12, 1836; registered Mar. 10, 1837.

345 SG 338, JOHN WILSON, $12.96, 64 ac., Sec. 153, Dis. 8, S. side of Laurel Branch of
big Savannah. Granted Dec. 12, 1836; registered Mar. 10, 1837.

346 SG 347, ELI RICKEY, $211.50, 105.75 ac., Sec. 80, Dis. 15, on Standridges Cr. Granted
Dec. 28, 1836; registered Mar. 10, 1837.

347 SG 255, JAMES BUCKHANNON, $14.02, 67 ac., Sec. 144, Dis. 8, right hand fork of lit-
tle Savannah. Granted Dec. 12, 1836; registered Mar. 10, 1837.

348 SG 317, JESSE R. SILER, $10.14, 50 ac., Sec. 51, Dis. 8. Granted Dec. 12, 1836;
registered Mar. 11, 1837.

349 SG 235, SILAS H. MCDOWELL, $125.12, 69 ac., Sec. 29, Dis. 12, Sugar Town Fork of Tennessee R. Granted Dec. 17, 1835; registered Mar. 14, 1837.

350 SG 233, SILAS MCDOWELL, $136, one acre, beginning at stake on the Main Street. Granted Dec. 18, 1835; registered Mar. 11, 1837.

351 SG 253, JAMES BUCKHANNON Jr., $20.28, 100 ac., Sec. 155, Dis. 8, crossing the little east fork of the Suvannah. Granted Dec. 12, 1836; registered Mar. 11, 1837.

352 SG 282, NIMROD S. JARRETT, $__, 77 ac., Sec. 45, Dis. 15. Granted 1836; registered Mar. 11, 1837.

353 SG 283, NIMROD S. JARRETT, $16.13, ____ ac., Sec. 42, Dis. 13. Granted 12 Dec. 1836; registered 11 Mar. 1837.

354 SG 318, JESSE R. SILER, $10.14, 50 ac., Sec. 50, Dis. 8, in a hollow, down to the flat land at what is coled the pole bridge. Granted 12 Dec. 1836; reg. 11 Mar. 1837.

355 SG 39, JESSE R. SILER, $10, one acre, beginning at the bank of the Tennessee R. near the butment of the bridge. Granted 12 Jan. 1837; registered Mar. 11, 1837.

356 SG 319, JESSE R. SILER, $14.18, 67 ac., Sec. 56, Dis. 8. Granted 12 Dec. 1836; registered 11 Mar. 1837.

357 SG 320, JESSE R. SILER, $10.14, 50 ac., Sec. 57, Dis. 8, on bank of Tennessee R. Granted 12 Dec. 1836; registered 11 Mar. 1837.

358 SG 321, JESSE R. SILER, $13.18, 67 ac., Sec. 53, Dis. 8, east bank of Tennessee R. Granted 12 Dec. 1836; registered 13 Mar. 1837.

359 SG 322, JESSE R. SILER, $10.14, 50 ac., Sec. 65, Dis. 8. Granted 12 Dec. 1836; registered 13 Mar. 1837.

360 SG 323, JESSE R. SILER, $10.14, 50 ac. Sec. 52, Dis. 8. Granted 12 Dec. 1836; registered 13 Mar. 1837.

361 SG 40, JOHN STRAIN, $5 per 100 ac., 50 ac. near head of Love's Mill Creek, Dis. 11. Granted 21 Jan. 1837; registered Mar. 13, 1837.

362 SG 23, LEVI WILSON, $5 per 100 ac.; 50 ac. on Savannah Cr., Dis. 8. Granted Dec. 28, 1836; registered Mar. 13, 1837.

363 SG 22, RICHARD WILSON, $5 per 100 ac.; 99 ac. on Savannah Cr. Dis. 8. Granted Dec. 28, 1836; registered Mar. 13, 1837.

364 SG 7, RICHARD WILSON, $4 per 100 ac.; 99 ac. on Savannah Cr., Dis. 8. Granted Dec. 28, 1836; registered Mar. 13, 1837.

365 SG 8, JAMES WILSON, $5 per 100 ac.; 85 ac. on Savannah Cr., Dis. 8. Granted Dec. 28, 1836; registered Mar. 13, 1837.

366 SG 12, WILLIAM ROLAND, $5 per 100 ac.; 50 ac. on west side of Tennessee R., Dis. 17. Granted Sep. 30, 1836; registered Mar. 13, 1837.

367 SG 3, JOSEPH ROLAND, $5 per 100 ac.; 50 ac. on N. side of "Ioallee" (Iotla) Cr., Dis. 16. Granted Sep. 30, 1836; registered Mar. 13, 1837.

368 SG 9, JAMES BUCKHANNON, $5 per 100 ac.; 50 ac. on little Savannah Cr., Dis. 8. Granted Dec. 28, 1836; registered Mar. 13, 1837.

369 SG 10, THOMAS GRIBBLE, $5 per 100 ac.; 50 ac. on Black's Branch, Dis. 8. Granted Dec. 28, 1836; registered Mar. 13, 1837.

370 SG 12, AMOS ASH, $5 per 100 ac., 20 ac. on Tuckasegee R. Granted Dec. 28, 1836; registered Mar. 13, 1837.

371 SG 13, AMOS ASH, $5 per 100 ac.; 50 ac. on W. side Tuckasegee R. Dis. 7. Granted Dec. 28, 1836; registered Mar. 13, 1837.

372 SG 14, JOSEPH BUCKHANNON, $5 per 100 ac.; 50 ac. on Savannah Cr., Dis. 8, east fork of the creek. Granted Dec. 28, 1836; registered Mar. 13, 1837.

373 SG 15, JOSEPH BUCKHANNON, $5 per 100 ac.; 50 ac. on Savannah Cr., on RICHARD WILSON's line. Granted Dec. 28, 1836; registered Mar. 14, 1837.

374 SG 16, JAMES BUCKHANNON, $5 per 100 ac.; 50 ac. on Little Savannah Creek, Dis. 8. Granted Dec. 28, 1836; registered Mar. 14, 1837.

375 SG 17, JAMES BUCKHANNON, $5 per 100 ac.; 50 ac. on Savannah Creek. Granted Dec. 28, 1836; registered Mar. 14, 1837.

376 SG 18, EPHRAIM ASH, $5 per 100 ac.; 50 ac. on W. bank of Tuckasegee R., near SW corner of tract on which AMOS ASH has an improvement, Dis. 7. Granted Dec. 28, 1836; registered Mar. 14, 1837.

377 SG 19, FRANCIS WARD, $5 per 100 ac.; 50 ac. on Green's Fork of Savannah Creek, Dis. 8. Granted Dec. 28, 1836; registered Mar. 14, 1837.

378 SG 20, JOHN WEST Senr., $5 per 100 ac.; 100 ac., on Cowee Cr., NE corner of SAMUEL BRYSON's land. Granted Dec. 28, 1836; registered Mar. 14, 1837.

379 SG 21, THOMAS WEST, $5 per 100; 80 ac. on Mill fork of Cowee Cr., Dis. 10. Granted Dec. 28, 1836; registered Mar. 14, 1837

380 SG 311, ELIJAH SHEPHERD, $11.19; 56 ac., Sec. 89, Dis. 10. Granted Dec. 12, 1836; registered Mar. 15, 1837.

381 SG 27, THOMAS MONTIETH, $5 per 100 ac.; 100 ac. on Tuckasegee R., Dis. 7. Granted Dec. 28, 1836; registered Mar. 15, 1837.

382 SG 24, WILLIAM TATHAM, $10 per 100 ac.; 80 ac. on Savannah Cr., Dis. 8. Granted Dec. 28, 1836; registered Mar. 15, 1837.

383 SG 37, ELIJAH CLURE, $4 per 100 ac.; 50 ac. on Cartoogechay Cr., Dis. 15, embracing the improvement formerly occ. by Clure. Granted Dec. 28, 1836; reg. Mar. 15, 1837.

384 SG 312, ELIJAH SHEPHERD, $11.14; 55 ac., Sec. 76, Dis. 10, crossing Cowee Creek. Granted Dec. 12, 1836; registered Mar. 15, 1837.

385 SG 313, ELIJAH SHEPHERD, $10.14; 50 ac., Sec. 77, Dis. 10, crossing middle fork of Cowee. Granted Dec. 12, 1836; registered Mar. 16, 1837.

386 SG 314, ELIJAH SHEPHERD, $10.14; 50 ac., Sec. 87, Dis. 10, middle fork of Cowee. Granted Dec. 12, 1836; registered Mar. 16, 1837.

387 SG 315, ELIJAH SHEPHERD, $10.14; 50 ac., Sec. 86, Dis. 10. Granted Dec. 12, 1836; registered Mar. 16, 1837.

388 SG 320, THOMAS SHEPHERD Jr., $10.14; 50 ac., Sec. 87, Dis. 10, on W. bank of "Harts" (Hurst's?) fork of Cowee. Granted Dec. 12, 1836; registered Mar. 16, 1837.

389 SG 326, THOMAS SHEPHERD Jr., #10.14; 50 ac., Sec. 82, Dis. 10, on "Husks" (Hurst's?) fork of Cowee, crossing the upper corner of cabin hut by SHEPPARD & MASON. Granted Dec. 12, 1836; registered Mar. 16, 1837.

390 SG 327, THOMAS SHEPHERD Jr., $10.14; 50 ac., Sec. 19, Dis. 10. Granted Dec. 12, 1836; registered Mar. 16, 1837.

391 SG 328, THOMAS SHEPHERD Jr., $10.21; 51 ac., Sec. 84, Dis. 10, on "Husks" (Hurst's?) Creek. Granted Dec. 12, 1836; registered Mar. 16, 1837.

392 SG 330, THOMAS SHEPHERD Jr., $10.14; 50 ac., Sec. 13, Dis. 10. Granted Dec. 12, 1836; registered Mar. 16, 1837.

393 SG 329, THOMAS SHEPHERD Jr., $10.21; 51 ac., Sec. 83, Dis. 10. Granted Dec. 12, 1836; registered Mar. 16, 1837.

394 SG 335, THOMAS SHEPHERD Jr., $10.61; 52 ac., Sec. 88, Dis. 10. Granted Dec. 12, 1836; registered Mar. 16, 1837.

395 SG 332, THOMAS SHEPHERD Jr., $21.28; 100 ac., Sec. 13, Dis. 10. Granted Dec. 12, 1836; registered Mar. 17, 1837.

396 SG 333, THOMAS SHEPHERD Jr., $10.14; 50 ac., Sec. 70, Dis. 10, on S. side of piney mountain between S. & middle forks of Cowee Creek. Granted Dec. 12, 1836; registered Mar. 17, 1837.

397 SG 334, THOMAS SHEPHERD Jr., #11.14; 55 ac., Sec. 16, Dis. 10. Granted Dec. 12, 1836; registered Mar. 17, 1837.

398 SG 258, BENJAMIN S. BRITTON, $23.16; 117 ac., Sec. 96, Dis. 16. Granted Dec. 12, 1836; registered Mar. 17, 1837.

399 SG 259, BENJAMIN S. BRITTON, $37; 170 ac., Sec. 57, Dis. 16. Granted Dec. 12, 1836; registered Mar. 17, 1837.

400 SG 260, BENJAMIN S. BRITTAIN & JOHN HALL, $25.92; 54 ac., Sec. 41, Dis. 8, on Tennessee R., Turkey Creek. Granted Dec. 12, 1836; reg. Mar. 17, 1837.

401 SG 261, BENJAMIN S. BRITTAIN & JOHN HALL, $21.43; 50 ac., Sec. 42, Dis. 8, on Turkey Cr. of Tennessee R. Granted Dec. 12, 1836; registered Mar. 18, 1837.

402 SG 262, BENJAMIN S. BRITTON & JOHN HALL, for $32.48; 60 ac., Sec. 44, Dis. 8, crossing Turkey Cr. Granted Dec. 12, 1836; registered Mar. 18, 1837.

403 SG 263, BENJAMIN S. BRITTON & JOHN HALL, $14.93, 72 ac., Sec. 43, Dis. 8, on Turkey Cr. of Tennessee R. Granted Dec. 12, 1836; registered Mar. 18, 1837.

404 SG 264, BENJAMIN S. BRITTON & JOHN HALL, $14.59; 71 ac., Sec. 40, Dis. 8, on SE bank of Tennessee R. Granted Dec. 12, 1836; registered Mar. 18, 1837.

405 SG 265, BENJAMIN S. BRITTON & JOHN HALL, $12.81; 59 ac., Sec. 49, Dis. 8, crossing Turkey Cr. Granted Dec. 12, 1836; registered Mar. 18, 1837.

406 SG 310, HENDERSON SANDERS, $14.00; 50 ac., Sec. 99, Dis. 15, on "Standage" (Standridge) Creek. Granted Dec. 12, 1836; registered Mar. 27, 1837.

407 SG 25, HENDERSON SANDERS, $5 per 100 ac.; 50 ac. on waters of "Skenner" (Skeenah) Cr. Granted Dec. 12, 1836; registered Mar. 27, 1837.

408 SG 266, NATHANIEL CARROLL, $10.14; 50 ac., Sec. 107, Dis. 15. Granted Dec. 12, 1836; registered Mar. 27, 1837.

409 SG 33, B.W. BELL, $5 per 100 ac.; 50 ac. on Tennessee R., Dis. 11. Granted Dec. 28, 1836; registered Mar. 27, 1837.

410 SG 304, JAMES RUSSEL, $28.57; 141+ ac., Sec. 11, Dis. 12. Granted Dec. 12, 1836; registered Mar. 27, 1837.

411 SG 292, JAMES LEDFORD, $10.14; 50 ac., Sec. 119, Dis. 15. Granted Dec. 12, 1836; registered Mar. 27, 1837.

412 SG 296, JACOB MASON, $14.75, 73 ac., Sec. 148, Dis. 8, Greens Fork of Big Savannah Cr. Granted Dec. 12, 1836; registered Mar. 27, 1837.

413 SG 276, TRAVIS ELMORE, $10.14, 50 ac., Sec. 66, Dis. 11. Granted Dec. 12, 1836; registered Mar. 27, 1837.

414 SG 271, MATHEW DAVIS, $24.51, 121 ac., Sec. 89, Dis. 11. Granted Dec. 12, 1836; registered Mar. 28, 1837.

415 SG 275, TRAVES ELMORE, $13.78, 68 ac., Sec. 10, Dis. 11. Granted Dec. 12, 1836; registered Mar. 29, 1837.

416 SG 38, TRAVIS ELMORE, $5 per 100 ac., 50 ac. on waters of Rabits Creek of Tennessee R. Granted Dec. 28, 1836; registered Mar. 29, 1837.

417 SG 5, DAVID GUYER, $5 per 100, 100 ac. on Tennessee R., Dis. 10. Granted Dec. 28, 1836; registered Mar. 31, 1837.

418 SG 298, THOMAS MONTEATH, $10.19, 53 ac., Sec. 141 Dis. 8 on E. side of little Savannah Creek. Granted Mar. 12, 1836; registered Mar. 30, 1837.

419 SG 6, PHILLIP GUYER, $5 per 100, 100 ac. on Teathey Creek. Granted Dec. 28, 1836; registered Mar. 31, 1837.

420 SG 34, JESSE GRIGG, $5 per 100 ac., 50 ac. on Cartoogechaye Creek, Dis. 15. Granted Dec. 28, 1836; registered Mar. 30, 1837.

421 ABNER STATE (Slate?) & JANE, his wife, to heirs of WILLIAM CARPENTER, all of
Macon, for $125, 66 ac., part of Sec. 92, Dis. 15, near the bridge branch. Oct. 15, 1836.
Abner State, Jane (her X mark) State. Wit: *THOS. LONG, LABAN LONG.* Proven by
Laban Long in Mar.1837 court. Registered May 10, 1837.

422 SG 284, DAVID JOHNSON, $10.99, 52+ ac., Sec. 21, Dis. 16. Granted Dec. 12, 1836;
registered Mar. 30, 1837.

423 SAMUEL ROSE to JOHN JOHNSTON (JOHNSON) ROSE, both of Macon, for $250,
78 ac., Sec. 33, Dis. 17. Jan. 13, 1837. *Samuel (his X mark) Rose.* Wit: *ALFORD HALL,
JOHN INGRAM.* Registered May 10, 1837.

424 Haywood County, NC: TAVENER B. MOORE to GEORGE T. LEDFORD, for $700,
58 ac. on E. side of Sugartown R., crossing mill pond, bd. Moore. Grantee also called G.
Towery Ledford. Mar. 7, 1826. *Tavner B. Moore.* Wit: *MAT DAVIS, HIRAM LEDFORD.*
Proven on oath of Mathew Davis, March 1837 court. Registered May 10, 1837.

425 WILLIAM CARPENTER to JACOB CARPENTER, both of Macon, for $100, 113 ac.,
Sec. 92, Dis. 15. Feb. 1, 1834. *Wm. Carpenter.* JOHN HOWARD proved. Reg. May 10,
1837.

426 J.B. TRAMMEL of Macon for val. rec'd, to JOHN BRYSON SR., interest in 168 ac.,
Sec. 8, Dis. 7, purch. & div. by ADAM CORN & J.B. TRAMMELL at 1822 sale in
Franklin. Mar. 17, 1837. *J.B. Trammell.* Wit: *FELAX AXLY.* Reg. May 10, 1837.

426 WM. WITMEIR of Pickens Co. SC, to JOHN W. DAVIS of Buncombe Co. NC, for
$525, 126 ac., Toxaway R., one tract & part of another granted JOHN COB. Mar. 5,
1834. *William Whitmire.* Wit: *JESSE READ, JOSEPH MOORE.* Proven in Mar. 1837
court by Joseph Moore. Registered May 10, 1837.

428 WILLIAM ANGEL to THOMAS M. ANGEL, both of Macon, for $826.14, 192 ac., Sec.
13, Dis. 12, Sugartown R.; also half of 113 ac., Sec. 15, Dis. 12, except Dower of
ELIZABETH ANGEL, wife of WILLIAM ANGEL, Dec'd., granted her by ct. of pleas
& qtr sessions. Feb. 24, 1837. *William Angel.* Wit: *WM. H. PEARCEY, ALEXANDER
ANGEL.* Alexander Angel proved, Mar. 1837 ct. Reg. May 10, 1837.

429 JACOB CARPENTER to DAVID CARPENTER, both of Macon, for $100, 113 ac., Sec.
92, Dis. 15. Dec. 19, 1836. *Jacob Carpenter.* Wit: *JACOB PALMER, J. HOWARD.*
Proven in March 1837 court by J. Howard. Registered May 10, 1839.

430 JESSE SANDERS to HENDERSON SANDERS for $40, 15 ac. on "Standeridge" Cr.,
corner of Sec. 97, Dis. 15. No date. Ack. in March 1837 court by *Jesse Sanders.* Wit:
JOHN MCDOWELL, WILLIAM MCGEE. Registered May 10, 1837.

431 WILLIAM A. BRITTAIN to JOHN MOORE, both of Macon, for $1,087.60, 271 ac., on
"Cautuga" (Cartoogechaye) Cr., passing the Poplar Cove. Feb. 25, 1837. *William A. Brit-
tain.* Wit: *WILLIAM SILER, J.W. GUINN.* Proven in March 1837 court by William Siler.
Registered May 10, 1837.

432 GIDEON F. MORRIS to JOHN R. ALLMAN, both of Macon, for $2,500, Franklin town
lot #10, on Main Street. Oct. 23, 1834. *G.F. M.(?) Morris.* Wit: *FELAX AXLY.* Proven in
March 1837 court by Felax Axly. Registered May 10, 1837.

433 JONATHAN M. BRYSON to JOHN R. ALLMAN of Macon, for $125, 160 ac. crossing
county rd., Sec. 19, Dis. 11. May 27, 1837. *J.M. Bryson.* Wit: *JACOB B. TRAMMEL,
SAMUEL STANFORD.* Proven by Jacob B. Trammel before JOHN TATHAM, May 29,
1837. Registered June 25, 1837.

434 Mortgage: ROBERT HALL to WILLIAM MORRISSON & SAMUEL BRYSON, as
sec. on note they endorsed for JOSEPH WELCH, JAMES TRUET & Robert Hall of
$2,000, drawn on the bank at Morganton: land where I now live in Dis. 16, known by the
INGRAM tract, containing 135 ac. May 30, 1837. *Robert Hall.* Wit: *MOSES HALL,
RILEY MARTIN.* Robert Hall acknowledged in June 1837 court. Registered June 26,
1837.

435 Mortgage: JAMES TRUET to WILLIAM MORRISSON & SAMUEL BRYSON as sec. on $2,000 loan they obtained from the bank of Morganton for ROBERT HALL, James Truett & JOSEPH WELCH, the following tracts: Dis. 9, No. 14 (104 ac.); Dis. 9, No. 28 (103 1/2 ac.); Dis. 9, No. 29 (59 ac.); Dis. 9, No. 30 (87 ac.); Dis. 9, No. 31 (56 ac.); Dis. 9, No. 32 (57+ ac.); Dis. 9, No. 37 (54 ac.); Dis. 10, No. 3 (166 ac.); Dis. 10, No. 4 (83 ac.); Dis. 10, No. 5 (110 ac.); Dis. 10, No. 8 (52 ac.), also the tole bridge on the Tennessee R. called ISAAC TRUET's Bridge. May 29, 1837. *James Truet.* Wit: *MOSES HALL, RILEY MARTIN.* James Truet ack. in court, June 12, 1837. Registered June 26, 1837.

436 Mortgage: ROBERT HALL to BENJAMIN S. BRITTAIN, both of Macon, 135 ac. where I now live on S. side of Tennessee R., Sec. 81, Dis. 16, to secure a note of JOSEPH WELCH & CO., which Brittain endorsed in the bank of Morganton for $1,500.June 3, 1837. *Robert Hall.* Wit: *H.G. WOODFIN, JOHN HALL.* Registered June 26, 1837.

437 Mortgage: JAMES TRUET to BENJAMIN S. BRITTAIN, both of Macon, to secure Brittain's $1,500 note at the bank at Morganton, the following tracts: Dis. 10, Sec. 8 (52 ac.); Dis. 10, Sec. 5 (110 ac.); Dis. 10, Sec. 3 (166 ac.); Dis. 10, Sec. 4 (83 ac.); one Indian Reservation called the MOUSE tract in Dis. 10, 640 ac.; Dis. 9, Sec. 14 (104 ac.); Dis. 10 (sic - probably should be Dis. 9), Sec. 29 (50 ac.); Dis. 9, Sec. 28 (103 ac.); Dis. 9, Sec. 30 (87 ac.); Dis. 9, Sec. 31 (56 ac.); Dis. 9, Sec. 37 (54 ac.); also, my right and title to my bridge on the Tennessee R. known as Truett's Bridge. June __, 1837. *James Truett.* Wit: *H.G. WOODFIN, JOHN HALL.* Registered June 26, 1837.

438 Mortgage: JOSEPH WELCH, JAMES TRUET & ROBERT HALL of Macon, for BENJAMIN S. BRITTAIN having endorsed to James Truet a note of $1,500 in the bank at Morganton, the following tracts purchased by Joseph Welch and now the property of Joseph Welch & Co.: Lot No. 15 (150 poles) in the Town of Franklin; one lot near town in the lower tract, No. 5 (5+ ac.); Lot No. 34 (6+ ac.). June __, 1837. *James Truett, Joseph Welch, Robert Hall.* Wit: *JOHN HALL.* Registered June 26, 1837.

439 SG 291, GEORGE T. LEDFORD, $10.41, 50 ac., Sec. 90, Dis. 11, on Sugar Town fork of Tennessee R. Granted Dec. 12, 1836; registered June 30, a837.

440 SG 336, WILLIAM WEST, $10.14, 54 ac., Sec. 69, Dis. 10, west side of Brooke's Cr. Granted Dec. 12, 1836; registered July 1, 1837.

441 SG 241, THOMAS AMMONS, for $11.81, 59 ac., Sec. 54, Dis. 12. Granted Dec. 12, 1836; registered July 1, 1837.

442 SG 4, BENJAMIN S. BRITTAIN, $10 per 100 ac., 640 ac. on Teathey Creek, corner Sec. 96, Dis. 16. Granted Dec. 16, 1836; registered July 1, 1837.

443 SG 11, JAMES L. JOHNSTON, $5 per 100 ac., 50 ac. on "Skeener" (Skeenah) Creek, on line of Sec. 97, Dis. 15. Granted Dec. 18, 1836; registered July 1, 1837.

444 SG 272, POLLY DAVES, $13.98, 69 ac., Sec. 98, Dis. 11. Granted Dec. 12, 1836; registered July 1, 1837.

445 SG 35, GEORGE HAMPTON, $5 per 100 ac., 50 ac. near N. end of ELIJAH JOHNSTON'S improvement on Savannah Cr, Dis. 8. Granted Dec. 28, 1836; registered July 1, 1837.

446 SG 337, ABRAHAM WIGGINS Jr., $___, 68 ac., Sec. 32, Dis. 8, on east bank of "Chunoluska" (Junaluska) Creek. Granted Dec. 12, 1836; registered July 1, 1837.

447 SG 28, DAVID LEDFORD, $5 per 100 ac., 50 ac. on "Skeener" (Skeenah) Creek, corner of Sec. 90, Dis. 15. Granted Dec. 28, 1836; registered July 1, 1837.

448 SG 269, JOHN CORBIN, $10.10, 50 ac., Sec. 81, Dis. 11. Granted Dec. 12, 1836; registered July 1, 1837.

449 SG 449, JOHN CORBIN, $11.14, 55 ac., Sec. 80, Dis. 11. Granted Dec. 12, 1836; registered July 1, 1837.

450 SG 3, B.S. BRITTAIN, $10 per 100 ac., 640 ac. in Dis. 16, corner of Sec. 80, Sec. 98.
     Granted Dec. 16, 1836; registered July 1, 1837.

451 SG 285, SAMUEL Y. JAMESON, $14.24, 60 ac., Sec. 74, Dis. 17, on N. bank of Ten-
     nessee R. Granted Dec. 12, 1836; registered July 1, 1837.

452 SG 286, SAMUEL Y. JAMESON, $16.14, 79+ ac., Sec. 9, Dis. 17. Granted Dec. 12,
     1836; registered July 1, 1837.

453 SG 287, SAMUEL Y. JAMESON, $16.29, 84 ac., Sec. 75, Dis. 17, on Tennessee R.
     Granted Dec. 12, 1836; registered July 1, 1837.

454 SG 288, SAMUEL Y. JAMESON, $11.11, 53 ac., Sec. 18, Dis. 18, on Toxaway R.
     Granted Dec. 12, 1836; registered July 1, 1837.

455 SG 341, THOMAS WELCH, $10.43, 51 ac., Sec. 45, Dis. 17. Granted Dec. 12, 1836;
     registered July 3, 1837.

456 SG 342, THOMAS WELCH, $14.18, 75 ac., Sec. 19, Dis. 17. Granted Dec. 12, 1836;
     registered July 3, 1837.

457 SG 344, THOMAS WELCH, $46, 75 ac., Sec. 18, Dis. 17, crossing Burning town Creek.
     Granted Dec. 12, 1836; registered July 3, 1837.

458 SG 254, JESSE BURRELL, $14.18, 72 ac., Sec. 8, Dis. 18, on east side of Big Creek.
     Granted Dec. 12, 1836; registered July 3, 1837.

459 SG 459, WILLIAM BARNS, $19.96, 67 ac., Sec. 4, Dis. 18, SW of a branch of Challuga
     (Chatooga) R. Granted Dec. 12, 1836; registered July 3, 1837.

460 SG 257, WILLIAM BARNS, $17.39, 55 ac., Sec. 6, Dis. 18. Granted Dec. 12, 1836;
     registered July 3, 1837.

461 GEORGE PATTON to JOAB L. MOORE, both of Macon, for $732, 168+ ac., Sec. 8,
     Dis. 16. April 25, 1837. *Geo. Patton.* Wit: *A.J. PATTON, WILLIAM ANGEL.* Proven by
     William Angel, June 1837 court. Registered July 10, 1837.

462 GEORGE PATTON to JOAB L. MOORE, both of Macon, for $575, 132+ ac., Sec. 9,
     Dis. 16. April 25, 1837. *Geo. Patton.* Wit: *A.J. PATTON, WILLIAM ANGEL.* Proven by
     William Angel in June 1837 court. Registered July 10, 1837.

463 GEORGE PATTON to JOAB L. MOORE, both of Macon, for $488, 120+ ac., Sec. 10,
     Dis. 16. April 25, 1837. *Geo. Patton.* Wit: *A.J. PATTON, WILLIAM ANGEL.* Proven by
     William Angel, June 1837 court. Registered July 10, 1837.

464 GEORGE PATTON to WILLIAM ANGEL, both of Macon, for $544, 141 3/4 ac., Sec.
     6, Dis. 15, crossing "Cautoogachaye" (Cartoogechaye) Cr. May 1, 1837. *Geo. Patton.*
     Wit: *A.J. PATTON, J.L. MOORE.* Proven by Joab L. Moore, June 1837 court. Registered
     July 10, 1837.

465 GEORGE PATTON to WILLIAM ANGEL, both of Macon, for $240, 90 ac., Sec. 7,
     Dis. 18. April 25, 1837. *Geo. Patton.* Wit: *A.J. PATTON, J.L. MOORE.* Proven by Joab
     L. Moore, June 1837 court. Registered July 10, 1837.

466 GEORGE PATTON to WILLIAM ANGEL, both of Macon, for $675, 178 3/4 ac., Sec.
     8, Dis. 15. April 25, 1837. *Geo. Patton.* Wit: *A.J. PATTON, J.L. MOORE.* Proven by
     Joab L. Moore, June 1837 session. Registered July 10, 1837.

467 JONATHAN PHILLIPS, Ch'man of County Ct of Macon, to JESSE R. SILER, for $348,
     parcel on N. side of Main Rd. leading from Franklin to bridge across Tennessee R., part
     of 400 ac. on which town is situated: town land lots #17, 18 and 24, and of the lower
     tract, #54, all adjoining, 23+ ac. in all. Apr. 12, 1837. *J. Phillips.* Wit: *B.F. HAWKINS,
     JCB TRAMMELL.* Proven by Jacob B. Trammell, June 1837 court. Registered July 10,
     1837.

468 JONATHAN PHILLIPS, Ch'man of County Court of Macon, to JESSE R. SILER, for $125, part of 400 ac. on which town of Franklin is situated, including lots #27 and 28 and one town lot, #25 on NW end of Main Street, containing 10+ ac. Apr. 12, 1837. *Jonathan Phillips.* Wit: *B.F. HAWKINS, JCB TRAMMELL.* Proven by Jacob B. Trammel, June 1837 court. Registered July 10, 1837.

469 JONATHAN PHILLIPS, Ch'man of County Court of Macon, to JESSE R. SILER, for $56, lot #43 in Franklin, at stake on big road, containing 7+ ac. Apr. 12, 1837. *Jonathan Phillips.* Wit: *B.F. HAWKINS, JCB TRAMMELL.* Proven in June 1837 court by Jacob B. Trammell. Registered July 10, 1837.

470 JONATHAN PHILLIPS, Ch'man of County Court of Macon, to RUDDS MORGAN, for $20, tract in town containing 150 poles (no description). April 12, 1837. *Jonathan Phillips.* Wit: *B.F. HAWKINS, J.B. TRAMMELL.* Ack. in June 1837 court. Registered July 10, 1837.

471 Sheriff's sale: JAMES TRUETT, Esq., High Sheriff of Macon County, to THOMAS WELCH of Macon for $501, land of JOSEPH WELCH and GIDEON F. MORRIS to satisfy judgement of court for $424. Sum recovered by THOS. W.P. POINDEXTER. Court commanded sheriff sell 53+ ac. to satisfy judgment. Advertised & sold the tract, on the north bank of the Tennessee R. to where the Tennessee and Tuckasegee intersect, then up the Tuckasegee. At sale, Feb. 18, 1835, Thomas Welch by his friend, DAVID ENGLAND, had high bid of $501 for tracts. Feb. 18, 1835. *James Truett.* Wit: *MOSES ADDINGTON.* Truett ack. in June 1837 court. Registered July 10, 1837.

472 THOMAS W.P. POINDEXTER to GEORGE N. HUGHS, both of Macon, for $600, 103+ ac. on Tennessee R., Sec. 39, Dis. 8, which I purchased in land sale, October 1836. June 11, 1837. *Thos. W.P. Poindexter.* Wit: *JOHN HALL, MILLAN T. HUGHS.* Proved by John Hall, June 1837 court. Registered July 14, 1837.

473 JAMES ANGEL to JAMES ROBISON & EZEKIEL DOWDLE, all of Macon, for $600, 3 tracts: 161 ac. on Tennessee R., Sec. 91, Dis. 15; 247 ac. on Tennessee R., Sec. 14, Dis. 11; 148 ac., Sec. 123, Dis. 10. May 29, 1837. *James Angel.* Wit: *J.R. ALLMAN, H.G. WOODFIN.* Proven by H.G. Woodfin. Registered July 14, 1837.

475 ELI RICKEY to JOHN SELLARS & ESTHER BATY, exec. of JAMES BATY, dec'd, for $300, 105+ ac., on Standridges Creek, Sec. 80, Dis. 15. Mar. 11, 1837. *Eli (his X mark) Rickey.* Wit: *J.H. HOWARD.* Proven by J.H. Howard, June 1837 court. Registered July 14, 1837.

476 JESSE R. SILER to SILAS MCDOWELL, both of Macon, for $165, 27+ ac., part of Sections 25, 26 and 27 in Dis. 16, on the S. side of Big Road leading up "Cautoegajoy" (Cartoogechaye) Cr., bet. 3/4 and one mile from Franklin, on corner of HECHE's land. May 19, 1837. *J.R. Siler.* Wit: *J.K. GRAY, M.T. HUGHS.* Proven by Gray in June 1837 court. Registered July 14, 1837.

477 ARON PINSON to JOHN HOWARD, both of Macon, for $400, 85 ac. on Tennessee R., Sec. 37, Dis. 13, purchased at the Oct. 20, 1820 land sale. Mar. 1, 1836. *A. Pinson.* Wit: *JAMES WHITE, MARY M. HOWARD.* Proven James White, June 1837 court. Registered July 14, 1837.

478 Deed of Trust: MILAS CARROLL and WM. CARROLL to JOHN SETZER for $34, our claim to Sec. 70, Dis. 11 on Rabits Cr. May 31, 1837. *Milas Carroll, Wm (his X mark) Carroll.* Wit: *WM. WELCH.* Proven by Wm. Welch, June 1837 court. Registered July 4, 1837.

478 Land entry: Dis. 8, on Tennessee R., near corner of No. 36, containing 100+ ac. Oct. 27, 1836. *N. EDMONSON,* Commissioner. Assign certificate to GEORGE N. HUGHS. *THOS. W.P. POINDEXTER.* Wit: *JOHN HALL, MILLAN T. HUGHS.* Proven by John Hall in June 1837 court. Registered July 14, 1837.

479 Mortgage: JOSEPH WELCH to JESSE R. SILER; NIMROD S. JARRETT; JAMES
     ROBINSON & JACOB SILER, merchants trading under name of Robinson & Siler; and
     THOMAS WELCH, all of Macon, for $160.83:
     • District 1: Sec. 49, 62 ac.; Sec. 54, 61 ac.; Sec. 55, 69 ac., Sec. 58, 50 ac., Sec. 57, 53
       ac., Sec. 140, 50 ac., Sec. 69, 113 ac.
     • District 8: Sec. 77, 130 ac.; Sec. 78, 75 ac.
     • also, dower of life estate of SALLY BELK, widow of DARLING BELK, in tract on
       Tuckasegee R., commonly called BIG BEAR's Reservation, 640 ac.
     • also, undiv. share of sd land which descended to SOPHIA MIRANEY? (MCRANEY?),
       formerly SOPHIA BELK, one of heirs at law of Darling Belk dec'd.
     Condition: if Joseph Welch's mother's executors pay to Jesse R. Siler $101.93 + int.
     from June 3, 1837, & to Nimrod S. Jarrett $117.53 + int., & to Robinson & Siler $76.87
     + int., & to Thomas Welch $300 + int., then sale is void. June 9, 1837. *Joseph Welch.*
     Wit: *FELAX AXLY.* Proved in court by Felax Axly, June 1837 court. Reg. July 4, 1837.

481 Sheriff's sale: JAMES TRUETT, Esq., High Sheriff of Macon, to THOMAS WELCH of
     Macon. Judgment against JOSEPH WELCH & GIDEON F. MORRIS for $400,
     recovered by THOS. W.P. POINDEXTER. Sheriff ordered to sell 54 ac. to satisfy Poin-
     dexter: Sec. 1, Dis. 1, N. bank of Tenn. R. to Tuckaseege R. Thomas Welch by his friend
     DAVID ENGLAND had high bid of $501 for two tracts. Feb. 14, 1835. *James Truett.*
     Wit: *MOSES ADDINGTON.* Ack. in June 1837 court. Reg. July 14, 1837.

483 SG 45, CHRISTOPHER SETSER, $5 per 100 ac., 50 ac. on "Elija" (Ellijay) Creek in
     Dis. 11, near what is called First Gap, incl. improvement made by JAMES CLARK.
     Granted June 12, 1837; registered Aug. 3, 1837.

484 SG 484, SILAS LITTLE JOHN, $5 per 100 ac., 50 ac. on the "Tuckseejah" (Tuckasegee)
     R. in Dis. 7, on corner of Sec. 30. Granted Sep. 14, 1837; registered Oct. 3, 1837.

485 Deed of trust: ANDREW COLVERT of Macon to WILLIAM H. THOMAS, for $65,
     grey mare. Sep. 14, 1837. *Andrew Colvert.* Wit: John Tatham Reg. Oct. 20, 1837.

486 SG 82, THOMAS C. FORD, $5 per 100 ac., 50 ac. on head waters of "Elija" (Ellijay)
     Cr., Dis. 11, NE of Sec. 119. Granted Sep. 16, 1837; registered Oct. 5, 1837.

487 SG 83, THOMAS C. FORD, $5 per 100 ac., 50 ac. on waters of "Elijah" (Ellijay) Cr.,
     Dis. 11, lower line of Sec. 119. Granted Sep. 15, 1837; registered Oct. 5, 1837.

488 SG 51, THOMAS CABE, $5 per 100 ac., 100 ac. in Dis. 13 on upper line of Sec. 41.
     Granted Sep. 15, 1837; registered Oct. 5, 1837.

489 SG 52, JAMES CABE, $5 per 100 ac., 100 ac. on Turtle Pond Cr., waters of "Shager"
     Town R., Dist. 12, on west side of Turtle Pond Cr. Granted Sep. 15, 1837; registered Oct.
     5, 1837.

490 SG 53, WILLIAM CABE, $5 per 100 ac., 100 ac. on head waters of Sugar Town (Cul-
     lasaja) R., Dis. 12, near BARNES Cabbin on Blue Ridge. Granted Sep. 15, 1837;
     registered Oct. 5, 1837.

491. SG 54, ZACHARIAH CABE, $5 per 100 ac., 100 ac. on Turtle Pond Cr., being waters of
     Shager Town Creek (Cullasaja River), Dis. 12, bounded JAMES CABE's land. Granted
     Sep. 15, 1837; registered Oct. 5, 1837.

492 SG 55, JOHN CABE, $5 per 100 ac., 50 ac. on the N. side of Tennessee R. in Dis. 12, N.
     line of #9, corner of #10. Granted Sep. 15, 1837; registered Oct. 5, 1837.

493 SG 57, JOHN LEDFORD, $5 per 100 ac., 50 ac. on "Tesenty" (Tessentee) Cr., Dis. 13,
     on line of No. 33. Granted Sep. 15, 1837; registered Oct. 5, 1837.

494 SG 63, SAMUEL REYNOLDS, $5 per 100 ac., 75 ac. on Vandyke's fork of "Coweter"
     (Coweeta) Cr., on line of No. 37, Dis. 14. Granted Sep. 15, 1837; registered Oct. 5, 1837.

495 SG 62, WILLIAM PATTON, $5 per 100 ac., 50 ac. on "Cartoochaga" (Cartoogechaye)
     Creek, Dis. 15. Granted Sep. 15, 1837; registered Oct. 5, 1837.

496 SG 69, WILLIAM YOUNG, $5 per 100 ac., 25 ac. on "Wautauga" (Watauga) Cr., Dis.
     10, on line of Sec. 124. Granted Sep. 15, 1837; registered Oct. 6, 1837.

497 SG 70, WILLIAM YOUNG, $5 per 100 ac., 50 ac. near head of "Wautauga" (Watauga) Cr., Dis. 10, on corner of Sec. 124. Granted Sep. 15, 1837; registered Oct. 6, 1837.

498 SG 71, MATTHEW RUSSEL Jr., $5 per 100 ac., 18+ ac., E. side Tenn. R., Dis. 11, bd. BELL, on W. line of the CAT's Mountain. Granted Sep. 15, 1837; reg. Oct. 6, 1837.

499 SG 49, WILLIAM A. BRITTAIN, $5 per 100 ac., 100 ac. on Cartoogechaye, Dis. 15, corner of Sec. 28. Granted Sep. 15, 1837; registered Oct. 6, 1837.

500 SG 73, REBECAH MCDANIEL, $5 per 100 ac., 49 3/4 ac. on "Cartoogechaja" (Cartoogechaye) Cr., Dis. 15, adj. DIMSDALE line, JOHNSTON's entry. Granted Sep. 15, 1837; registered Oct. 6, 1837.

501 SG 74, REBECCA MCDANIEL, $10 per 100 ac., 200 ac. on "Cautoogechaje" (Cartoogechaye) Cr., Dis. 15, on line of #30, on corner of GILLISPIE's grant of No. 23. Granted Sep. 15, 1837; registered Oct. 6, 1837.

502 SG 50, JAMES BUCKHANNON, $5 per 100 ac., 100 ac. on little Savannah Cr., in Dis. 8, on line of No. 142. Granted Sep. 25, 1837; registered Oct. 6, 1837.

503 SG 81, J.B. BROOKS, $5 per 100 ac., 50 ac., S. side of Tuckasegee R, near Shepherd's Cr. below where AMOS SHEPHERD lives. Granted Sep. 15, 1837; reg. Oct. 6, 1837.

504 SG 77, JOHN REDMAN, $10 per 100 ac., 200 ac. on Cats Creek, being waters of Tennessee R., in Dis. 11, on corner of Sec. 174. Granted Sep. 15, 1837; reg. Oct. 6, 1837.

505 SG 60, JOHN MOORE Sr., $5 per 100 ac., 50 ac. on "Cartoogeehaje" (Cartoogechaye) Cr., Dis. 15. Granted Sep. 11, 1837; registered Oct. 6, 1838.

506 SG 61, JOHN MOORE Sr., $5 per 100 ac., 50 ac. on "Cartoogeehaje" (Cartoogechaye) Cr., Dis. 15. Granted Sep. 15, 1837; registered Oct. 6, 1837.

507 SG 75, JEREMIAH R. PACE, $5 per 100 ac., 150 ac. on Savannah Cr. waters of Tuckasegee R., in Dis. 8, on W. corner of No. 161. Granted Sep. 15, 1837; reg. Oct. 6, 1837.

508 SG 324, CHARLES STILES, $16.20, 80 ac., Sec. 159, Dis. 8, on W. side of main Savanna (Savannah Cr.), crossing the creek, crossing "Bets" (Betsy?) Branch. Granted Dec. 12, 1836; registered Oct. 6, 1837.

509 SG 36, JOHN COCKRAM, $5 per 100 ac., 50 ac. on the Tennessee R., Dis. 10, on N. line of Sec. 65. Granted Dec. 28, 1836; registered Oct. 11, 1837.

510 SG 55, DAVID MOOREHEAD, $420, 97+ ac., Sec. 53, Dis. 15, crossing "Cautoogajoy" (Cartoogechaye) Cr. Granted Sep. 20, 1826; registered Oct. 7, 1837.

511 SG 29, BENJAMIN JOHNSTON, $5 per 100, 50 ac. on "Cautoogechaje" (Cartoogechaye) Cr., Dis. 15, W. corner of Sec. 53. Granted Dec. 28, 1836; reg. Oct. 7, 1837.

512 SG 26, WILLIAM P. POTEET, $5 per 100 ac., 76+ ac. on E. side of "Wautauga" (Watauga) Creek, on SE corner of Sec. 47, Dis. 10, with JOHNSTON's line. Granted Dec. 28, 1836; registered Oct. 7, 1837.

513 SG 182, BYNUM W. BELL, $73, one acre in Franklin, town lot #2, on Main Street. Granted June 14, 1832; registered Oct. 7, 1837.

514 SG 64, BENJAMIN STILES, $5 per 100 ac., 25 ac. on N. side of Tennessee R., Dis. 13, on line of Sec. 9. Granted Sep. 15, 1837; registered Oct. 7, 1837.

515 SG 78, BENJAMIN STILES, $5 per 100 ac., 50 ac. on Turtle Pond Cr., Dis. 12. Granted Sep. 15, 1837; registered Oct. 7, 1837.

516 SG 58, JASON LEDFORD, $5 per 100 ac., 53 ac., on south side of Tennessee R., Dis. 14. Granted Sep. 15, 1837; registered Oct. 12, 1837.

517 SG 76, GEORGE PENLAND, $5 per 100 ac., 50 ac. on N. side of Tennessee R. Dis. 13, on SW corner of Sec. 8. Granted Sep. 15, 1837; registered Oct. 17, 1837.

518 SG 59, JACOB MASON, $5 per 100 ac., 50 ac. on Savannah Cr., Dis. 8, on corner of Sec. 149. Granted Sep. 15, 1837; registered Oct. 12, 1837.

519 SG 79, JAMES WEBSTER, $5 per 100 ac., 100 ac., Dis. 6, on Mill Creek of "Tuck-asegah" (Tuckasegee) R. on WIKE's line. Granted Sep. 15, 1837; registered Oct. 19, 1837.

520 SG 66, LEVI WILSON, $5 per 100 ac., 75 ac. on Savannah Cr. of Tuckasegee R. Granted Sep. 15, 1837; registered Oct. 19, 1837.

521 SG 56, ROBERT FOX, $5 per 100, 50 ac. on W. side of Tuckasegee R., Dis. 6, on corner of Sec. 11. Granted Sep. 15, 1837; registered Oct. 19, 1837.

522 SG 65, LEWIS VANDYKE, $5 per 100, 50 ac. on Vandyke fork of Coweeter (Coweeta Creek), with boundary of Sec. 36, Dis. 14. Granted Sep. 15, 1837; registered Oct. 19, 1837.

523 SG 375, DAVID ROGERS, $243, 143 ac., Sec. 11, Dis. 7, crossing K Creek. Granted Sep. 15, 1837; registered Oct. 19, 1837.

524 SG 68, MATHIAS WIKE, $5 per 100 ac., 50 ac. on W. side of Tuckasegee R. in Dis. 6, near WEBSTER's improvement. Granted Sep. 15, 1837; registered Oct. 20, 1837.

525 SG 67, MATHIAS WIKE, $5 per 100, 24 1/2 ac. on W. side of Tuckasegee R. below POTS ford, corner of Sec. 22. Granted Sep. 15, 1837; registered Oct. 20, 1837.

526 SG 363, JACOB DEATS, $16.17, 75 ac., Sec. 23, Dis. 7. Granted Sep. 15, 1837; registered Oct. 20, 1837.

527 SG 362, MILAS ASHE, $12.25, 56 ac., Sec. 27, Dis. 7. Granted Sep. 15, 1837; registered Oct. 20, 1837.

528 SG 361, JESSE R. SILER, assignee of EDWARD L. POINDEXTER, for $90.14, 60 ac., Sec. 37, Dis. 8, on bank of Tennessee R. Granted Sep. 15, 1837; registered Oct. 20, 1837.

529 SG 359, GIDEON NORTON, $76, 76 ac., Sec. 16, Dis. 14, crossing Mulberry Cr. Granted Sep. 15, 1837; registered Oct. 20, 1837.

530 JOSEPH WELCH, JAMES TRUET & ROBERT HALL of Macon, to serve to WM. M. MORTON, Agent of Georgia Railroad & Banking Company, payment of $2,500 note, release to Wm. M. Morton all debts, etc.of firm of Joseph Welch & Co. now in the hands of JOHN HALL for settlement. Hall to release amt sufficient for sd firm of Welch & Co. & debt in the hands of J.W. GUINN, not exceeding $800. Money Morton collects after satisfying claims to be applied to described, not given bank. Signed J.M. BERGSON, en-dorsed by James Truet, Joseph Welch, Robert Hall & JAMES ANGEL, now in suit in hands of J.W. Guinn, att'y of Ga. RR & Banking Co. Sep. 26, 1837. *Robert Hall, Joseph Welch, James Truet.* J.R. PACE test. as to R. Hall; J.S. ROBERTSON as to Welch & Truet. Reg Oct. 21, 1837.

531 JACOB SILER of Macon to REBECCA MCDANIEL, for $715.17, a parcel on Car-toogechaye, Sec. 29, Dis. 15. July 8, 1837. *Jacob Siler.* Wit: *A. MCDANIEL, THOS. MCDANIEL.* Ack. in court, Sept. 1837 session. Registered Oct. 21, 1837.

532 JOHN STRAIN of Macon to LOGAN BERRY, for $5, seven ac. of Sec. 40. May 22, 1837. *John Strain.* Wit: *J.K. GRAY, M.B. STRAIN.* Ack. in court, Sept. 1837 session. Registered Oct. 21, 1837.

533 JOHN STRAIN of Macon to MERRIT B. STRAIN for $400, 105 ac., Sec. 11, Dis. 11. July 4, 1836. *John Strain.* Wit: *JOHN TATHAM, J.K. GRAY.* Ack. in court, Sept. 1837 session. Registered Oct. 21, 1837.

534 DAVID MOREHEAD to BENJAMIN JOHNSON, for $500, 97+ ac., Sec. 53, Dis. 15, on "Cartoogajay" (Cartoogechaye) Creek, granted to Moorehead by SG #55. Jan. 1, 1827. *David Morehead.* Wit: *JAMES H.(?) SMITH, WILLIAMSON FORTUNE.* The writ-ing of Williamson Fortune was proven on oath of ROBERT JOHNSON, Sep. 28, 1837. Registered Oct. 21, 1837.

535   JOHN H. CHINN, by virtue of deed of trust invested in me by JOSEPH WELCH, to service to JOHN MCGHEE, amount $1,670.72, dated Oct. 28, 1836, have exposed to public sale in the town of Franklin the four Negroes mentioned and described in that deed. John McGhee had high bid of $1,600. The four were TOM, aged 21, SUSAN, aged 14, ALBERT, aged 10, and MANNAE (MANSON?) aged 7. Sep. 25, 1837. *John H. Chinn, trustee.* Wit: *FELAX AXLY.* Ack. in court, Sept. 1837 session. Registered Oct. 23, 1837.

536   JOSEPH MORE of Macon to WILLIAM DUCKWORTH of Buncombe Co., NC, for $200, 50 ac. on Toxaway R., on E. side of Flat Creek. Feb. 20, 1836. *Joseph More.* Wit: *JAS. ERWIN Junr., JONATHAN LENARD.* Ack. in court, Sept. 1837 session. Registered Oct. 23, 1837.

537   JOSEPH Y. LOVE to D. LOVE, both of Macon, for $4,800, tract of land whereon my father, SAMUEL B. LOVE, now dec'd, formerly lived, in Washington Co., TN, on road between Jonesborough in Washington Co. & Elizabeth Court house in Cartier Co., E. Tenn., agreeable to commissioners appt'd to divide the tract between my brother, ROBERT C. LOVE & my sister, LOUISIA M. JOHNSTON, wife of H. JOHNSTON; also, my undiv. part of 3 other tracts in Greesy Cove & on Indian Creek of Washington Co., & my undiv. part of 7 Negroes now living on tract near Jonesborough. Feb. 22, 1837. *J.Y. Love.* Wit: *J.P.R. LOVE, DAVID MCCOY(?).* Ack. in court, Sept. 1837 session. Registered Oct. 23, 1837.

538   JOHN HIDE of Haywood Co., NC, to WILLIS GUY of Macon, for $250, two tracts: Sec. 19, Dis. 12 on Sugartown Fork of Tennessee R., 59 ac.; Sec. 20, Dis. 12, 117 ac. Aug. 7, 1839. *John Hide.* Wit: *R.D. CLARK,* who proved in Sept. 1837 court. Registered Oct. 23, 1837.

539   HENRY DRYMAN to JOHN LEDFORD, both of Macon, for $240, Sec. 13, Dis. 14, on the Tennessee R. Nov. 5, 1833. *H. Dryman.* Wit: *J.W. GUINN,* who proved in court, Sep. 1837. Registered Oct. 23, 1837.

540   SG 293, AMOS LEDFORD, $12.65, 62+ ac., Sec. 98, Dis. 15. Granted Dec. 12, 1836; registered Nov. 6, 1837.

541   CLEMMONS HOOPER to JOHN HOWARD, both of Macon, 55 ac. on Tennessee R. Sec. 18, Dis. 14. May 13, 1837. *C. Hooper.* Wit: *JOSEPH HICKS,* who proved Dec. 9, 1837. Registered Dec. 9, 1837.

542   SG 31?, JOSEPH R. JOHNSTON, $5 per 100 ac., 75 ac. on Watauga Cr., Dis. 10, on line of No. 47. Granted Dec. 28, 1836; registered Dec. 28, 1837.

543   Bond: SAUL SMITH, JAMES W. GUINN, JOHN R. ALLMAN, pledge $10,000 bond for Saul Smith, app'ted Clerk & Master in Equity. Oct. 14, 1836. Registered Dec. 29, 1837.

543   Bond: JOHN HALL, JOHN R. ALLMAN, SAUL SMITH, MARK COLEMAN pledge $2,000 for John Hall as Clerk of Macon County. Sep. 26, 1837. Registered Dec. 29, 1837.

544   Bond: JOHN HALL, JOHN R. ALLMAN, SAUL SMITH, MARK COLEMAN pledge $10,000 for John Hall as Clerk of Macon County. Sep. 26, 1837. Registered Dec. 30, 1937.

545   Bond: SILAS MCDOWELL, JESSE R. SILER, JAMES ROBISON pledge $10,000 bond for Silas McDOwell as Clerk of Superior Court. Sep. 26, 1837. Registered Dec. 30, 1837.

546   Bond: SILAS MCDOWELL, JESSE R. SILER, JAMES ROBISON pledge $4,000 bond for Silas McDowell as Clerk of Superior Court. Sep. 26, 1837. Registered Dec. 30, 1837.

547   SG 30, B.S. JOHNSTON, $5 per 100 ac., 50 ac., Dis. 16, NW corner of Sec. 21. Granted Dec. 28, 1836; registered Jan. 16?, 1836.

548   SG 32, B.S. JOHNSTON, $5 per 100 ac., 50 ac. on "Cartogeehege" (Cartoogechaye) Cr., Dis. 16, corner of Sec. 22. Granted Dec. 28, 1838; registered Jan. 10?, 1838.

549 SG 1, JACOB SHOPE, $5 per 100 ac., 100 ac. on Burning Town Cr. Granted Dec. 16, 1836; registered Jan. 29, 1838.

550 SG 308, JACOB SHOPE, $19.28, 98+ ac., Sec. 13, Dis. 17, crossing Burning Town Creek. Granted Dec. 12, 1836; registered Jan. 29, 1838.

551 SG 2, JOSEPH DAVES, $5 per 100 ac., 50 ac. on Burning Town Creek, Dis. 17, on corner of Sec. 22. Granted Dec. 16, 1836; registered Jan. 29, 1838.

552 SG 273, JOSEPH DAVIS, $13.19, 67+ ac., Sec. 22, Dis. 17. Granted Dec. 12, 1836; registered Jan. 29, 1838.

553 SG 343, MICHEL WATERS, $11.14, 55 ac., Sec. 83, Dis. 16. Granted Dec. 12, 1836; registered Jan. 29, 1838.

554 SG 80, JOHN WIKE, $5 per 100 ac., 100 ac. on west side of Tuckasegee R. Dis. 6, on corner of Sec. 1. Granted Sep. 15, 1837; registered Jan. 29, 1838.

555 SG 46, BINUM W. BELL, $5 per 100 ac., 50 ac. on Wautauga Cr., Dis. 10, on line of Sec. 123, on line of AMMONS entered land. Granted July 29, 1837; reg. Jan. 29, 1838.

556 JAMES L. JOHNSTON to AMOS LEDFORD, both of Macon, for $25, a tract on the N. fork of "Skenner" (Skeenah Cr.), Dis. 15, borders Sec. 57. Mar. 11, 1837. *James L. Johnston.* Wit: *ROBERT CALER, JAMES W. GUINN.* Registered Jan. 29, 1838.

557 NIMROD S. JARRETT to JOHN HOWARD, both of Macon, for $150, 25 ac. on Tennessee R., part of tract granted JOHN WILKINS, Sec. 13, Dis. 14, to a Rattlebox on bank of river. Oct. 9, 1836. *N.S. Jarrett.* Wit: *ROBERT HUGGINS, G.W. MOORE.* Proven in court by G.W. Moore, Jan. 1838. Registered Jan. 29, 1838.

558 HUMPHREY POSEY to MATHEW MASHBURN for $300, 122 ac., W. side of Tennessee R. Sec. 39, Dis. 16. Sep. 6, 1836. *Humphrey Posey.* Wit: *J.R. SILER, M. KILLIAN.* Registered Jan. 29, 1838.

559 JAMES SHEARER to MATHEW MASHBURN, both of Macon, for $300, 76 ac., W. side Tennessee R., Sec. 44, Dis. 16. Oct. 12, 1836. *James Sherer.* Wit: *J.R. PACE, BENJAMIN F. HAWKINS.* Registered Jan. 29, 1838.

560 ENOS SHEALD to JESSE R. SILER, both of Macon, for val. rec'd, my right & interest in 53 ac., Sec. 44, Dis. 11. Jan. 26, 1838. *Enos Shields.* Wit: *WM. MULL, SAUL SMITH.* Registered Jan. 29, 1838.

560 Bond: SAUL SMITH, JAMES W. GUIN, JOHN R. ALLMAN, pledge $4,000 for Saul Smith, Clerk & Master in Equity. Oct. 17, 1836. Registered Jan. 29, 1838.

561 JOHN ADDINGTON to JESSE LEDFORD, for $700, 191 ac., part of Sec. 96, Dis. 15; part of Sec. 97, part of another tract, both sides Skeener Cr., corner of land purch. from HENRY ADDINGTON. Dec. 22, 1837. *John Addington.* Wit: *AMOS LEDFORD, HENDERSON SANDERS.* Registered Jan. 31, 1838.

563 AMOS LEDFORD to JESSE LEDFORD, for $8, 32 ac., Sec. 98, Dis. 15. Aug. 17, 1837. *Amos Ledford.* Wit: *BRYANT GIBBS, JOHN MCDOWELL.* Registered Feb. 9, 1838.

564 PETER MATHIS of Macon to WILLIAM H. BRYSON, for $34, 57 ac., Sec. 57, Dis. 7, purch. at the 1836 land sale in Franklin. Dec. 29, 1837. *Peter (his X mark) Mathis.* Wit: *ADAM CORN, G. FALLS.* Registered Feb. 10, 1838.

564 JOSEPH Y. LOVE to DILLARD LOVE, for $2,400, my rt. in 8 slaves: JOE, NANIE, ELBERT, LEM, CAROLINE, HARRIATT, SAM & MARTHA, my interest being 1/2. Feb. 22, 1837. *J.Y. Love.* Wit: *M. FRANCIS, JNO. B. LOVE.* Reg. Feb. 11, 1838.

565 Mortgage: WEST TRUET of the one part, SILAS MCDOWELL of the second part, JAMES K. GRAY of the third part. Truet mortgaged following tracts to James K. Gray, all in Dis. 10: 127+ ac. on Tennessee R., Sec. 46, beginning at the Rattlebox on upper corner of No. 45; 97 ac., Sec. 44; 50 ac., Sec. 103; 50 ac., Sec. 107; 55 ac., Sec. 111. Truet to pay $120 to McDowell, or Gray to sell land to highest bidder and pay $120 to McDowell from the proceeds. Sep. 4, 1838. *West (his X mark) Truet, J.K. Gray.* Wit: *M. FRANCIS, MILTON L. HUGHS.* Registered Feb. 11, 1838.

566 T.W.P. POINDEXTER to JAMES POINDEXTER & EVIN POINDEXTER, all of Macon, for $500, 217 ac. on Tennessee R. known as PARCHCORN place, Sec. 36, Dis. 8, on "Chunoslaskees" (Junaluska) or Alarka (Yalaka) Cr. Jan. 11, 1838. *Thos. W.P. Poindexter*. Wit: *J.R. SILER, MARK COLEMAN*. Registered Feb. 12, 1838.

567 Mortgage: JAMES POINDEXTER & EVIN POINDEXTER to THOMAS W.P. POINDEXTER, all of Macon, for $500, 217 ac., Sec. 36, Dis. 8. James & Evin contracted with Thomas W.P. to pay installments due at the Treasury in Raleigh, amounting to $700 plus interest. Jan. 11, 1838. *James (his X mark) Poindexter, Evens Poindexter*. Wit: *J.R. SILER, MARK COLMAN*. Registered Feb. 12, 1838.

568 Mortgage: JAMES POINDEXTER to THOMAS W.P. POINDEXTER, both of Macon, to sec. payment of promissory note of $1,100 dated Jan. 10, 1838, mortgage to him two Negro girls, SALLY, ten years old and ELIZA, eight years old. Jan. 11, 1838. *James Poindexter*. Wit: *JUDY POINDEXTER, RACHEL (her X mark) KIRKLIN*. Registered Jan. 29, 1838.

569 THOMAS W.P. POINDEXTER to JAMES POINDEXTER, both of Macon, for $1,100, two black or colored girls: SALLY, a black girl 10 yrs old, ELIZA, a yellow or mulatto girl 8 yrs old. Jan. 10, 1838. *Thos. W.P. Poindexter*. Wit: *JUDY POINDEXTER, RACHEL (her X mark) KIRKLIN*. Registered Feb. 12, 1838.

570 HENRY MOSS to JOHN LOUDERMILK, both of Macon, for $15, land on N. side Elijah Cr., on line of No. 118, Dis. 11. Sep. 27, 1837. *Henry Moss*. Wit: *HENRY? HIRVEY? HAGIN, JOHN KIMSEY*. Registered Feb. 23, 1838.

571 SG 253, WILLIAM ROGERS, $15.18, 75 ac., Sec. 42, Dis. 11. Granted Dec. 12, 1836; registered Feb. 24, 1838.

572 SG 86, LOGAN BURY, $5/100 ac., 50 ac. on head waters of "Rabits" Cr., Dis. 11, on line of Sec. 7; on STRAIN's corner. Granted Feb. 26, 1838; registered Mar. 29, 1838.

573 Mortgage: BENJAMIN S. BRITTEN to THOMAS J. ROANE for $5,000, the following Negroes: ISAM, BOSTON, WILSON, RANSOM, ESTHER, LAWSON, DICK, JANE, SARY, CLARY. Also, several tracts of land in Dis. 16: Sec. 47 (300 ac.); Sec. 48 (300 ac.); Sec. 49 (233 ac.). Jan. 27, 1838. *B.S. Brittian*. Condition: Roane is security for Brittian in sum of $4,000 plus interest drawn on Bank of State of North Carolina, now in suit in Superior Court of Burke (County). JEREMIAH R. PACE stood as principal & Benjamin S. Brittian, Thomas J. Roane & others as security. Benjamin S. Brittain is the man who ought to pay the judgment that may be obtained as he received the money. *B.S. Brittian*. Wit: *E. DOWDLE*. Registered Mar. 28, 1838.

574 WEST TRUETT to JOHN HALL Senr., both of Macon, for $100, 100 ac., Sec. 50, Dis. 13, sold at land sale in Franklin, Oct. 1836 by E.N. EDMONSON, commissioner, & purchased by DANIEL GARLAND. Hall is to pay amount due state. Jan. 24, 1838. *West (his X mark) Truet*. Wit: *JAMES ROBISON, J.K. GRAY*. Registered Mar. 28, 1838.

575 SG 107, JOHN SUTTON, $5/100 ac., 100 ac. on Savannah Cr., Dis. 8. Granted Feb. 26, 1838; registered Mar. 28, 1838.

576 SG 373, JOHN SUTTON, for $____, 51 ac., Sec. 149, Dis. 8, N. side of MASON's Branch. Granted Mar. 1, 1838; registered Mar. 29, 1838.

577 SG 370, JOHN CONNELLY, for $490.10, 248 ac., Sec. 14, Dis. 8, on Tennessee R. Granted Mar. 1, 1838; registered Mar. 29, 1838.

578 SG 381, JAMES RUDDLE, for $259, 100+ ac., Sec. 8, Dis. 8, crossing big Savannah. Granted Mar. 1, 1838; registered Mar. 29, 1838.

579 SG 101, THOMAS LONG, $5 per 100, 100 ac. on "Coweteer" (Coweta) Cr., Dis. 14, on corner of No. 55. Granted Feb. 26, 1838; registered Mar. 29, 1838.

580 SG 109, ENOS D. SHEALD, $5/100 ac., 50 ac. on "Iolee" Cr., Dis. 11, on corner of Sec. 93. Granted Feb. 26, 1838; registered Mar. 30, 1838.

581 SG 103, JAMES PEAK, $5/100 ac., 100 ac. in Dis. 11, on line of Sec. 11. Granted Feb.
     26, 1838; registered May 25, 1838.

582 SG 374, JAMES TRUITT, for $____, 52 ac., Sec. 3, Dis. 10, on NE bank of Tennessee
     R. Granted Mar. 1, 1838; registered May 25, 1838.

583 SG 100, WILLIAM KINSLAND, $5/100 ac., 95 ac., Dis. 10, S. bank of Watauga Cr., on
     JOHNSTON's line. Granted Feb. 26, 1838; registered May 25, 1838.

584 SG 358, ROBERT LOVE, Jr. & JOHN MOORE, for $534, 178 ac., Sec. 34, Dis. 11.
     Granted Sep. 15, 1837; registered May 25, 1838.

585 SG 382, WILLIAM A. BRITTAIN, $420, 140 ac. on "Cartoogech" (Cartoogechaye) Cr.,
     Sec. 28, Dis. 15. Granted Mar. 1, 1838; registered May 25, 1838.

586 SG 385, WILLIAM SILER, for $____, 83 1/2 ac., Sec. 45, Dis. 15. Granted Mar. 1, 1838;
     registered May 25, 1838.

587 SG 387, WILLIAM SILER, for $____, 52 ac., Sec. 47, Dis. 15. Granted Mar. 1, 1838;
     registered May 25, 1838.

588 SG 386, WILLIAM SILER, for $____, 65 ac., Sec. 46, Dis. 15. Granted Mar. 1, 1838;
     registered May 25, 1838.

589 JAMES DILLARD of Rabun Co. GA, to G.W. ANGEL of Macon, for $410, 120 ac.,
     Sec. 18, Dis. 11, on the river. Oct. 18, 1837. *James Dillard.* Wit: *THOS. ANGEL, E.
     DOWDLE.* Registered May 26, 1838.

590 PETER LEDFORD to JAMES BRADLEY, both of Macon, for $225, 30 ac. on Ten-
     nessee R., part of a grant in Dis. 14, on original line of No. 10. Aug. 3, 1837. *Peter (his X
     mark) Ledford.* Wit: *J. HOWARD, MARY M. HOWARD.* Registered May 26, 1838.

591 PETER LEDFORD to JAMES BRADLEY, both of Macon, for $75, 95 ac. on the Ten-
     nessee R., Sec. 29, Dis. 14, which Ledford purchased at 1836 land sale in Franklin. Brad-
     ley to pay the amount due the state. Aug. 5, 1837. *Peter (his X mark) Ledford.* Wit: *J.
     HOWARD, J.W. DOWDLE.* Registered May 26, 1838.

592 JAMES TRUETT to WILLIAM MORRISON & SAMUEL BRYSON, all of Macon, for
     $50, 52 ac. on NE bank of Tennessee R., on corner of No. 5 (no District given). Mar. 30,
     1838. *J.L(?) Truett.* Wit: *J. HOWARD, M. WIKLE.* Registered May 26, 1838.

593 WILLIAM MORRISON & SAMUEL BRYSON to DANIEL WEST, all of Macon, for
     $350, 52 ac. on the NE bank of Tennessee River, including the "tole bridge that ISAAC
     TRUITT built and known as Truitt's Bridge." Mar. 31, 1838. *William Morrison, Samuel
     (his X mark) Bryson.* Wit: *J. HOWARD, T.S. CLINGMAN.* Howard proved in Apr. 1838
     court. Registered May 26, 1838.

594 State of North Carolina to AVE OLA & SUSANNAH, children & heirs of LITTLE
     DEER, deceased, a Cherokee Indian, for $800 paid by commissioners ROMULUS M.
     SANDERS & HUMPHREY POSEY, a tract on Burning Town Creek containing 640 ac.,
     acquired as a reservation by Little Deer under the treaty of 1817. Mar. 25, 1837. *Ava
     Ollah (her X mark), Susan (her X mark).* Wit: *JWO (Cherokee letters), AVE (her? X
     mark), JOHN WINN (his X mark).* JOHN TATHAM & ANDREW CALVERT—
     balance(?).

595 MASON MCLEOD of Macon to E. MCLEOD of Buncombe Co., NC, for $100, 52 ac.
     on Middle Cr., Sec. 60, Dis. 13, bought Oct. 24, 1836 at land sale in Franklin. E. Mc-
     Leod to pay state the amount due. Jan. 11, 1838. *Mason McLeod.* Wit: *J. HOWARD.*
     Registered May 26, 1838.

595 MOSES WHITESIDES to JOHN HALL of Macon, for $400, 218 ac., Sec. 40, Dis. 16.
     Oct. 21, 1837. *Moses Whitesides.* Wit: *B.F. HAWKINS, W.T. COLEMAN.* Registered
     May 26, 1838.

596 WILLIAM INGRAM to B.S. BRITTIAN, both of Macon, for $150, two tracts in Dis.
     16—Sec. 86 (52 ac.) & Sec. 80, (60 ac.). Nov. 5, 1837. *W. Ingram.* Wit: *P.W. ED-
     WARDS.* Registered May 26, 1838.

597 ELIJAH CLURE to JACOB PALMER, both of Macon, for $50, 50 ac. in Dist. 15, north of the fence "imbrasing" the improvement formerly occupied by Clure. Mar. 30, 1838. *Elijah (his X mark) Clure.* Wit: *JOHN HALL.* Registered May 29, 1838.

598 HUMPHREY POSEY, formerly of Macon, to JOHN HALL of Macon, for $129, part of the Watauga plains, being in Dis. 16, part of Sec. 43, containing 43 ac. Nov. 16, 1837. *Humphrey Posey.* Wit: *JAS. ROBISON, G.W.J. MOORE.* Registered May 29, 1838.

598 THOMAS LOVE Senr. of Tennessee to JESSE R. SILER of Macon, for $1,500, 178 ac. on E. side of Tennessee R., nearly opposite town of Franklin, Sec. 34, Dis. 11, purchased by ROBERT LOVE Jr. & JOHN MOORE at the land sale in October 1820 and granted to them Sep. 15, 1837. Thomas Love, Senr. being the legal representative of Robert Love, Jr. Oct. 23, 1837. *Thos. Love.* Wit: *JAMES WATS, S.H. WATERS.* Registered May 29, 1838.

600 Sheriff's sale: JAMES TRUET, Esq., High Sheriff of Macon, to BENJAMIN S. BRITTEN of Macon, three lots in town of Franklin, to satisfy judgment of Superior Court of Burke Co. against JOSEPH WELCH in favor of JOHN CARSON for $169.16, recovered by Carson. The lots were: one on which JACOB D. WELCH now lives, being No. 15 of survey & containing 150 poles; one on town commons, joing lines with JOHN HALL & others, being No. 5 of survey, containing 5 ac.; one other, lot #34, joining lines with JACOB B. TRAMMEL & others, containing 6+ ac. The Court ordered James Truet to recover the sum from Welch of $104 principle with interest from May 18, 1837, plus $9.70 for costs. Benjamin S. Brittian was last & highest bidder with bid of $16 at public sale on 3rd day of Sept. court. Dec. 20, 1837. *James Truet per E. DOWDLE, dep. sheriff.* Wit: *J.S.L. MOORE.* Ack. by E. Dowdle in court, April 1838. Registered May 29, 1838.

602 BENJAMIN S. BRITTEN to THOMAS P. MOORE of Macon, for $225, 59 ac. on "Ioly" (Iotla) Cr., part of Sec. 51, Dis. 16. Mar. 1, 1838. *B.S. Brittian.* Wit: *H.G. WOODFIN, T.V. ROGERS.* Registered May 29, 1838.

603 ALFORD ANGEL & WILLIAM PERSEY, both of Macon, are bound in the sum of $500. Angel to bid off a certain tract of land in District 12: Sec. 35 (51 ac.) & Sec. 40 (51 ac.) N.B., the first has an improvement made on it by Wm. Persey. Angel is to pay for the labor. If they cannot agree, each is to choose a man, and if they cannot agree, each to choose another man. N.B. the branch running through Sec. 35 to be the line up to the fork, etc. dividing the land equally. Oct. 27, 1836. *A. Angel, W.H. Persey.* Wit: *E. AMMONS, JAMES RUSSEL.* Registered May 29, 1838.

604 MARK BURRELL of Union Co., Ga. to CHARLES WOODRING, for val. rec'd, my right etc. in 55 ac., Sec. 12, Dis. 6, which Burrell purchased at sale at Franklin Oct. 24, 1836. Feb. 1, 1838. *Mark (his X mark) Burrell.* Wit: *ABSOLOM (his X mark) HOOPER, JOHN (his X mark) HOOPER.* Registered May 29, 1838.

604 JOHN REDMAN to HOWELL MOSS, Jr., both of Macon, for $____, 100 ac., Sec. 26, Dis. 11, which Redman purchased of JOHN MURRY and which Murry purchased at the Oct. 31, 1822 land sale in Franklin. Apr. 15, 1837. *John Redman.* Wit: *H.G. WOODFIN, W. CUNNINGHAM.* Registerd May 29, 1838.

605 B.S. BRITTIAN to PHILIP GUYER, both of Macon, for $750, tract on "Ioly" (Iotla) Cr., Sec. 57, Dis. 16. Mar. 20, 1838. *B.S. Brittian.* Wit: *J.W. GUINN.* Registered May 29, 1838.

606 THOMAS J. ROAN to J.K. GRAY, both of Macon, for $1,000, 242 ac. on Cartoogajay Cr., Sec. 54, Dis. 15. Nov. 7, 1837. *Thos. J. Roan.* Wit: *JOHN HALL, W. CUNNINGHAM.* Registered May 30, 1838.

607 Mortgage: THOS. J. ROANE to JAMES K. GRAY for performance of securing payment of debt of $530 to ROBERT HAWKINS, of which $280 was due Dec. 25, 1837, & $250 due Dec. 25, 1838; Roane appointed Gray trustee & conveyed to him a certain Negro girl named MINERVA, aged about 14, a brown horse 4 or 5 years old, a sorrel mare, a bay filly, one waggon & gare, 5 head of milch cattle, 12 head of young cattle, 3 work oxen, 25 head of sheep, 30 head of stock hogs, ___ & furniture. Nov. 7, 1837. *Thos. J. Roane.* Wit: *JOHN HALL, WM. CUNNINGHAM.* Registered May 30, 1838.

608 ANDREW MCDANIEL, THOMAS MCDANIEL, MARTHA MCDANIEL, THOMAS MCCLURE & MARY, his wife, and BARNARD WILSON & ELIZABETH, his wife, to REBECAH MCDANIEL for $1,000, tracts we have as legatees of JAMES MCDANIEL, dec'd: in Dis. 15, Sec. 31 (200 ac.) on "Cartoagusay" (Cartoogechaye) Cr., and Sec. 30 (150 ac.) on "Cartoogaya." Mar. 7, 1838. *Andrew McDaniel, Thomas McDaniel, Martha McDaniel, Thomas McClure, Mary McClure.* Wit: *A.J. PATTON, J. HOWARD.* Registered June 8, 1838.

609 THOMAS J. ROANE to JOHN MOORE, both of Macon, for $20, 50 ac., Sec. 55, Dis. 16, originally granted Jan. 15, 1826. Dec. 5, 1836. *Thos. J. Roan.* Wit: *J.K. GRAY, JOHN HANNAH.* Proven in court, Mar. 1838 by James K. Gray. Registered June 8, 1838.

610 JAMES VERMILLION of Macon to JOHN HOWARD for $75, 60+ ac. on head waters of Commissioners Cr., Dis. 14, Sec. 40, also 60 ac., Sec. 45; Howard to pay the state the amount due. Oct. 9, 1837. *James Vermillion.* Wit: *C.M. STILES, J.M.(?) DOWDLE.* Registered June 8, 1838.

611 WILLIAM ROGERS to JESSE R. SILER, both of Macon, for $50, 32 ac., part of Sec. 42, Dis. 11. Feb. 7, 1838. *Wm. F. Rogers.* Wit: *J.R. ALLMAN, NATHAN ALLMAN.* Proven by Nathan Allman, Jun. 8, 1838. Registered Jun. 8, 1838.

612 SG 92, GEORGE CUNNINGHAM, $5/100 ac., 50 ac. on "Watagau" (Watauga) Cr., at foot of Cowee Mtn, on 4th corner of Sec. 123, Dis. 10. Granted Feb. 26, 1838; registered June 13, 1838.

613 SG 47, JOSEPH YOUNG, $5/100 ac., 50 ac. at head of Watauga Cr., Dis. 10, east of DILLARD LOVE's improvement at edge of State Rd, running with line of Sec. 123. Granted July 29, 1837; registered June 15, 1838.

614 SG 91, TRAVIS CARPENTER, $5/100 ac., 50 ac. on Savannah Cr., corner of SUTTEN's land. Granted Feb. 26, 1838; registered June 15, 1838.

615 CATHERINE MOORE, widow of TAVENER MOORE, dec'd, JOHN MOORE, POLLY MOORE, ANERSON MOORE & JACOB MOORE, heirs of Tavener B. Moore, all of Macon except John Moore of Rabun Co. GA, for val. rec'd, to GEORGE T. LEDFORD of Macon, 77 ac., Dis. ___ (Dis. 11?—torn), Sec. 51, which Tavner B. Moore purchased at sale in Franklin, 1832. No date. *John Moore, JERAMIAH BARTAN, Catherine (her X mark) Moore, Polly (her X mark) Moore, NATHAN A. (his X mark) MOORE, Jacob (his X mark) Moore.* Wit: *ISAAC MOORE.* Registered June 15, 1838 by J.F. GRANT, Dep. Clerk.

616 Mortgage: BENJAMIN S. BRITTAIN to JESSE PENDERGRASS, GEORGE CARSON & JOHN HALL, all of Macon, eleven Negroes: ISHAM, NED, BOSTON, WILLSON, RANSOM, SUSAN, MARLBOROUGH, EASTHER, JANE, SARAH & CLAREY. Condition: Pendergrass, Carson & Hall have this day executed a bond to THOS. J. ROANE, Sh'ff of Macon, for $16,000. Seven of the slaves—Ned, Boston, Willson, Ransom, Easther, Sarah, Clairy—are to be sold in a Sheriff's sale on the 3rd Monday of August next, if delivered to the Sheriff by Pendergrass, Carson & Hall. No date. *B.S. Brittain.* Wit: *THOS. J. ROAN, SILAS MCDOWELL.* Proven by McDowell in Jun, 1838 court. Registered June 30, 1838.

617 WILLIAM W. PIERCY to JAMES W. GUINN, both of Macon, for $30, 28+ ac., part of Sec. 42, Dis. 11, originally granted to WILLIAM ROGERS. June 17, 1838. *Wm. W. Piercey.* Wit: *THOS. J. ROANE,* who proved in court, Jun. 1838. Registered July 4, 1838 by J.F. GRANT, clk.

618 WILLIAM W. PIERCEY to JAMES W. GUINN, both of Macon, for $67.625, 95 ac. on Sugartown R., Dis. 11, granted to Piercey in 1838. June 16, 1838. *Wm. W. Piercey.* Wit: *THOS. J. ROANE.* Registered July 4, 1838.

620 JOSEPH SHEPHERD of Yancey Co. NC to WILLIAM ROANE of Macon, for $450, 116 ac., Sec. 6, Dis. 16. June 30, 1837. *Jos. Shepherd.* Wit: *C.D. SMITH, J.W. GUINN.* Proven by J.W. Guinn, July 4, 1838. Registered July 5, 1838.

621 JOHN MCCLURE of Macon to WILLIAM ROANE of Burke Co. NC, for $600, 116 ac., Sec. 6, Dis. 16. Oct. 11, 1834. *John McClure.* Wit: *J.R. ALLMAN, LUKE BARNER.* Proven in court by J.R. Allman, Jun. 1838. Registered July 5, 1838.

623 SG 99, SETH HYATT, $10/100 ac., 150 ac. on Deep Cr., Dis. 1. Granted Feb. 26, 1838; registered Sep. 11, 1838.

624 SG 98, JASON L. HYATT, $10/100 ac., 50 ac. on Elarkey Cr., Dis. 8. Granted Feb. 26, 1838; registered Sep. 11, 1838.

625 JAMES MCCLURE to ULRICH KEENER, both of Macon, for $330, 133 ac., Sec. 29, Dis. 11, runs with LAIRD line. Jan. 25, 1838. *James McClure.* Wit: *JOHN DESYHANY, DAVID PASSMORE.* Proven in court by John Deseahenny, Jun. 1838. Registered Sep. 12, 1838.

626 JOHN MCCLURE of Macon to WILLIAM ROANE of Burke Co. NC 116 ac., Sec. 6, Dis. 16. Oct. 11, 1834. *John McClure.* Wit: *J.R. ALLMAN, LUKE BARNARD.*

627 JOHN SUTTEN to JACOB MASON, both of Macon, for $100, tract on Savannah Cr., Sec. 149, Dis. 8. May 21, 1838. *John Sutten.* Wit: *WM. R. BUCKHANNON, ISAAC MORRISON.* Registered Sep. 13, 1838.

628 JOHN HALL to THOMAS W.P. POINDEXTER, both of Macon, for $800, a certain Negro woman named PATSY & her child, MARY ANN. Apr. 27, 1838. *John Hall.* Wit: *JUDY POINDEXTER, MARY F. HALL.* Registered Sep. 13, 1838.

628 THOMAS W.P. POINDEXTER of Macon, for love & affection I have for my daughter, REBECCA C. HALL, give to JOHN HALL in trust for his wife (my daughter), Rebecca, a certain Negro girl child named MARYANN, the eldest & only child of a Negro woman named PATSY, which I have this day purchased from said John Hall. Apr. 27, 1838. *Thos. W.P. Poindexter.* Wit: JUDY POINDEXTER, MARY F. HALL. Registered Sep. 13, 1838.

End of Volume A

Macon County Deed Book B

630 SG 307, WILLIAM ROAN, $23.49, 116 ac., Sec. 29, Dis. 16. Granted Dec. 12, 1836; registered Sep. 16, 1838.

631 SG 239, JOSEPH SHEPPERD, assignee of JOHN WOODY, for $232.50, 116 ac., Sec. 6, Dis. 16. Granted Dec. 12, 1836; registered Sep. 6, 1838.

632 SG 367, AMOS BROWN, $225.50, 150 ac., Sec. 6, Dis. 10. Granted Mar. 1, 1838; registered Sep. 6, 1838.

633 REBECAH MCDANIEL to THOMAS MCDANIEL, both of Macon, for $1,500, 300 ac. on "Cartugajay" (Cartoogechaye) Cr., Sec. 12, Dis. 15. Mar. 7, 1838. *Rebecah (her X mark) McDaniel.* Wit: *A.J. PATTON, J. HOWARD.* Proved by John Howard, Apr. 1838 court. Registered Sep. 6, 1838.

634 REBECAH MCDANIEL to ANDREW MCDANIEL, both of Macon, for $1,500, Sec. 11, Dis. 16, near an Indian grave, crossing "Cartogajay" (Cartoogechaye) Cr. Mar. 7, 1838. *Rebecah (her X mark) McDaniel.* Wit: *A.J. PATTON, J. HOWARD.* Proved by John Howard, April 1838 court. Registered Sep. 6, 1838.

635 EZEKEL GRIBBLE to JAMES BUCKHANAN, both of Macon, for $75, Sec. 143, Dis. 8, on E. fork of Little Savannah. May 29, 1838. *E. Gribble.* Wit: *JAMES WILSON, W.R. BUCKHANAN.* Registered Sep. 8, 1838.

636 Power of Attorney: JOHN WELCH, a Cherokee resident in N.C., appts. JONATHAN BLYTH & JONATHAN PARKER, both of Macon, my attorneys for benefit of wife, ELIZABETH WELCH & her children: EDWARD, MARY, DAVID, JAMES, JONATHAN, JOHN COBB, NANCY, RICHARD, DENNIS, MARTHA ANN & REBECCA CATHERINE; to take charge of all property in which I have any right: 8 Negroes (ISAAC, a man abt 40; NELLY, a woman of 36 & her child, JANE; PHILLIS, a woman of 26 & her 3 children, BILL, CLARIE & HENDERSON; and FRANK, abt 6), 150 cattle, 26 sheep, 125 hogs, 15 horses, improvement where I now live, lands & growing crops. To take charge as though Welch were personally present & act according to rights to which I would be entitled were I a citizen of N.C. I sell Blyth & Parker all my property, provided they do all things that concern the welfare of my wife & children. June 20, 1838. *John (his X mark) Welch.* Wit: *R.A. HALL, JOHN EARLEY, J.P., & WM. ROANE.* Proven by John Earley, Sep. 1838 court. Reg. Sep. 17, 1838.

637 SG 371, HUGH GIBBS, $450, 300 ac., Sec. 19, Dis. 8, crossing Dick Wesser's Cr. Granted Mar. 15, 1838; registered Sep. 21, 1838.

638 SG 88, WILLIAM H. BRYSON, $5 per 100 ac., 25 ac. on Cullowhee Cr., Dis. 7, on corner of Sec. 20, on line of Sec. 16. Granted Feb. 26, 1838; registered Sep. 21, 1838.

639 SG 89, WILLIAM H. BRYSON, $5 per 100 ac., 100 ac. in Dis. 7, on corner of Sec. 7 and Sec. 38. Granted 26 Feb. 1838; registered Sep. 21, 1838.

640 SG 113, JOHN JOHNSTON, $5 per 100 ac., 50 ac. in Dis. 16, on waters of DAVID JOHNSTON's Mill Cr. Granted Mar. 1, 1838; registered Sep. 21, 1838.

641 SG 117, WILLIAM W. PEARSEY, $5 per 100 ac., 95 ac. in Dis. 12, on N. side of Sugar Town (Cullasaja) R., on corner of Sec. 43, 42 and 48. Granted Apr. 17, 1838; registered Sep. 21, 1838.

642 SG 114, JAMES BARTON, $5 per 100 ac., 50 ac. in Dis. 16, on DAVID JOHNSTON's Mill Cr., on Johnston's line, corner of Sec. 22. Granted Mar. 1, 1838; registered Sep. 21, 1838.

643 HUMPHREY POSEY of Franklin Co., GA, to WILLIAM MORRISON of Macon, for
     $3,000, 460 ac. on SW side of Tennessee R., S. bank of "Iolee" (Iotla) Cr., Sec. 63 and
     65 and part of Sec. 43 in Dis. 16, on HALL's corner, with mill & all appurtenances. Jan.
     5, 1838. *Humphrey Posey*. Wit: *N.S. JARRETT, N. HILL*. Proven by N.S. Jarrett in June
     1838 court. Registered Sep. 22, 1838.

644 SG 105, STEPHEN PACE, $10 per 100 ac., 200 ac. on S. side of mtn. div. "Iola" (Iotla)
     Cr. and Tennessee R. on W. side of R. Granted Feb. 26, 1838; registered Sep. 21, 1838.

645 Scots Cr., Haywood County NC, ROBERT LANEY to WM. H. THOMAS and A.
     FISHER. Laney owes Thomas & Fisher by bond $10, exec. Apr. 11, 1838, also book (ac-
     count?) for $18 due Aug. 1, 1838. To secure payment & in consideration of one shilling
     pd by Thomas and Fisher, Laney conveys 57 ac. adj. land of ABRAM SELLERS &
     JOSHUA HALLS, also standing crop of corn on the land, cow and calf, 9 hogs, small
     horse, bed & furniture, 2 pots and other household furniture, etc. Sep. 21, 1838. *Robert
     Laney*. Wit: *ISAAC ASH*. Registered Sep. 24, 1838.

646 SG 110, JACOB D. WELCH, $5 per 100 ac., 30.5 ac. on the Tennessee R., Dis. 10,
     corner of Sec. 6, on MORRISON's line. Granted Feb. 26, 1838; registered Sep. 22, 1838.

647 JOSEPH SHERREL to JOHN DEHART, both of Macon, for $850, a tract on Junulus-
     kees Cr., Sec. 30, Dis. 8. Apr. 17, 1838. *Joseph (his X mark) Sherrell*. Wit: *J.L.H. WIG-
     GINS, JOHN R. EDWARDS*. Proven by John Edwards in Sep. 1838 court. Registered
     Sep. 24, 1838.

648 SG 90, WILLIAM COCKERHAM, $5 per 100 ac., 50 ac. on STUART
     COCKERHAM's Branch, Dis. 8, on corner of Sec. 106. Granted Feb. 26, 1838;
     registered Sep. 26, 1838.

649 SG 122, MALECHA ROLING, $5 per 100 acre, 50 ac. on S. fork of Cowee Cr., corner
     of Sec. 105, on sd Roling's field. Granted Aug. 21, 1838; registered Sep. 26, 1838.

650 Bond: JOHN HALL, LEWIS VANDYKE, DILLARD LOVE, JOHN MCDOWEL, J.L.
     MOORE, J.R. ALLMAN, pledge $2,000 bond for John Hall, elected Clerk of Court of
     Pleas & Qtr Sessions. Sep. 26, 1838. Wit: J. HOWARD.

650 Bond: JOHN HALL, LEWIS VANDYKE, DILLARD LOVE, JOHN MCDOWEL, J.L.
     MOORE, J.R. ALLMAN, pledge $10,000 bond for John Hall, elected Clerk of Court of
     Pleas & Qtr Sessions. Sep. 26, 1838. Wit: J. HOWARD.

651 JOEL (JAEL?) SAWYERS to DAVID WEST, both of Macon, for $50, my right to a cer-
     tain tract on a creek named Sweet Water, Sec. 61, Dis. 9. Sep. 21, 1838. *Jael Sawyers*.
     Wit: *J.W. HENRY, GEORGE W. DICKEY*. Proven by George W. Dickey in Sep. 1838
     court. Registered Sep. 26, 1838.

651 CLEMMON HOOPER to JOHN HOWARD, both of Macon, 55 ac. on the Tennessee R.,
     Sec. 16, Dis. 14. Sep. 21, 1838. *C. Hooper*. Wit: *JOSEPH HICK*. Proven by Joseph Hick
     in Sep. 1838 court. Registered Oct. 4, 1838.

652 SG 388, ROBERT LOVE, Jr. & JOHN MOORE, for $1925, 275 ac., Sec. 32, Dis. 11,
     jcn Sugar Town and Tennesssee R. Granted Sep. 21, 1838; registered Oct. 4, 1838.

653 THOMAS SHEPHERD to JOHN MCCLURE, both of Macon, for $450, 116 ac., Sec. 6,
     Dis. 16. *Thomas (his X mark) Shepherd*. Wit: *ASAPH ENLOW, J. HOWARD*. Proven by
     John Howard, June 1838 court. Registered Oct. 4, 1838.

654 SG 96, MARTHA GREEN, $5 per 100 ac., 50 ac. on Middle Cr., Dis. 13. Granted Feb.
     26, 1838; registered Oct. 4, 1838.

655 SG 294, SAMUEL LOVINGGOOD Jr., $17, tract of 84 ac., Sec. 56, Dis.17, beg. on S.
     corner of SIX KILLER Reservation, on "Ioa" (Iotla) Cr. Granted Dec. 16, 1836;
     registered Oct. 4, 1838.

656 SG 295, SAMUEL LOVINGGOOD Jr., for $10.14, 50 ac., Sec. 61, Dis. 17, crossing
     Burning town Cr. Granted Dec. 12, 1836; registered Oct. 4, 1838.

657 SG 378, JOHN WIKE, $45.55, 217 ac., Sec. 1, Dis. 6, on SW side of "Tuckaseegie" R. Granted Mar. 1, 1838; registered Oct. 4, 1838.

658 SG 380, HENCY QUEEN, assignee of ALFORD BROWN, for $__pd by Brown, 53.75 ac. on Tennesee R., Sec. 29, Dis.17. Granted Mar. 1, 1838; registered Oct. 4, 1838.

659 SG 116, SAMUEL WIKEL, $5 per 100 ac., 95 ac. on Savannah Cr. Granted Apr. 5, 1838; registered Oct. 5, 1838.

660 SG 123, JAMES H. MCLEOD, $5 per 100 acre, 75 ac. on Mud Cr., near the Georgia line. Granted Sep. 21, 1838; registered Oct. 5, 1838.

661 SG 104, ZACHARIAH PEEK, $5 per 100 ac., 100 ac. on E. side of "Ellijaye" Cr., Dis. 11, corner of Sec. 58. Granted Feb. 26, 1838; registered Oct. 5, 1838.

662 WILLIAM ROANE to JAMES ROBINSON, for $4.06, 16+ ac., part of Sec. 29, Dis. 16, granted to William Roane on Dec. 12, 1836. June 30, 1837. *Wm. Roane.* Wit: *J.S. GRANT, N.H. PALMER.* Registered Oct. 5 1838.

663 Bond: SILAS MCDOWELL, JESSE R. SILER & JAMES K. GRAY pledge bond of $5,000 for Silas M. McDowell, elected Clerk of Superior Court of Macon County. Sep. 27, 1838. Registered Sep. 27, 1838.

663 Bond: SILAS MCDOWELL, JESSE R. SILER, & J.K. GRAY pledge bond of $10,000 for Silas McDowell, elected Clerk of Superior Court of Macon County. Sep. 27, 1838. Registered Sep. 27, 1838.

664 Deed of Gift: PHEBE or FEREBY BELK, being old & in infirm state of health, in consideration of services rendered to me by my daughter, REBECAH & her daughters, CYNTHEY & NANCY, give all my small estate both of household furniture, stock, & everything else with which the Lord has blest me, (retaining) only so much as shall be necessary to bury me in a decent & Christian manner & to pay my just debts. Deed to take effect immediately after my decease. Rebecah is to have the management of the property, to give each of her daughters their equal 1/3 part whenever they stand in need of same. June 11, 1830. *Pheby or Fereby (her X mark) Belk.* Wit: *HUMPHREY POSEY, LEMUEL A. ADKINS.* The handwriting of Humphrey Posey was proved by SILAS MCDOWELL, that of Lemuel A. Adkins by ELI COLLINS. McDowell and Collins testify that Posey and Adkins are not inhabitants of this state. Registered Sep. 29, 1838.

665 PETER LEDFORD to JOHN CONNELLEY, both of Macon, for $100, 54 ac., Sec. 9, Dis. 14, located on Tennessee R. Sep. 6, 1838. *Peter (his X mark) Ledford.* Wit: *J.W. GUINN.* Ack. in Sep. 1838 court. Registered Oct. 20, 1838.

666 JEREMIAH R. PACE of Macon to CHARLES HAYS of Buncombe County, NC, for $100, Sec. 45, Dis. 16, near the plains of "Iola" (Iotla Cr.). Sep. 27, 1838. *J.R. Pace.* Wit: *J. HOWARD.* Proven in Sep. 1838 session of court. Registered Oct. 20, 1838.

667 JOHN SHULAR to ABEL B. HYATT, both of Macon, for $1,000, Sec. 5, Dis. 1, on THE BEARE's line, on Deep Cr. Sep. 27, 1834. *John Shular.* Wit: *J. HOWARD.* Proven by J. Howard in Sep. 1838 court. Registered Oct. 20, 1838.

668 JOHN P. MOORE of Rabun Co. GA to ABNER MOORE of Macon, for val. rec'd, 58 ac., Sec. 52, Dis. 11, purchased Oct. 7, 1823 at land sale. June 9, 1838. *John P. Moore.* Wit: *ISAAC C. MOORE.* Proven in Sept. 1833 court by Isaac Moore. Registered Oct. 20, 1838.

669 Bond: SAUL SMITH, ELY MCKEE, JOHN HOWARD, J.W. GUINN pledge $4,000 bond for Saul Smith as Clerk & Master for the Court of Equity. Sep. 29, 1838. Registered Oct. 26, 1838.

670 Bond: SAUL SMITH, ELY MCKEE, JOHN HOWARD, J.W. GUINN pledge $10,000 bond for Saul Smith as Clerk and Master for the Court of Equity. Sep. 29, 1838. Registered Oct. 26, 1838.

671 WILLIAM P. POTEAT to WILLIAM ALLIN Junr., both of Macon, for val. rec'd, 65
ac., Sec. 109, Dis. 10, which Poteat purchased at the land sale Oct. 27, 1836 in Franklin.
Sep. 28, 1838. *Wm. P. Poteat.* Wit: *J.R. JOHNSTON, JAMES WITHOW.* Proven by
Joseph R. Johnston, Sep. 1838 court. Registered Oct. 20, 1838.

672 LEWIS FORE to DANIEL GARLAND, both of Macon, for $70, 277+ ac. on Tennessee
R., Sec. 25, Dis. 14. July 31, 1837. *Lewis (his X mark) Fore.* Wit: *JAMES H. SMITH,
SAMUEL SMITH.* Proven on oath of Samuel Smith, Sep. 1838 court. Registered Oct. 20,
1838.

673 DANIEL GARLAND to WILLIAM GARLAND, both of Macon, for $50, 277+ ac. on
Tennessee R., Sec. 25, Dis. 14, William to pay what is due the State from LEWIS FORE.
Aug. 31, 1838. *Daniel Garland.* Wit: *J. HOWARD.* Registered Oct. 20, 1838.

674 State of Tennessee, Henry Co. JAS. B. LOVE for val. rec'd, to THOMAS LOVE Senr.
of Henry Co. TN, 78 ac. in Haywood, now Macon Co., Sec. 45, Dis. 11, purchased 1820
at the land sale. Nov. 20, 1838. *Jas. B. Love.* Wit: *A.G. LOVE, ALLIN RAMSEY.* James
B. Love appeared before THOMAS K. PORTER of Henry Co. to acknowledge deed.
Town of Parris, Nov. 21, 1838. WILLIAM PORTER, Chairman of the county court of
Henry Co. certified that Thomas K. Porter was acting clerk of court at the time.
Registered Dec. 18, 1838.

675 STEPHEN S. PACE to ELIJAH M. HALL, both of Macon, for $75, a tract on the S. side
of mtn dividing "Iola" (Iotla) Cr. and Tennessee R., on W. side of the R. Apr. 13, 1838.
S.S. Pace. Wit: *S.G. SMITH, WM. CUNNINGHAM.* In an addendum, Elijah M. Hall
released Stephen Pace from all warrants in the deed except one, general warranty having
been made by mistake. E.M. Hall, Sep. 29, 1938. Wit: *WILLIAM ROANE, JOHN HALL.*
Proved by William Cunningham, Sep. 1838 court. Reg. Jan. 13, 1839.

676 Sheriff's Sale: N.G. HOWELL Esq., High Sheriff of Haywood Co., to CHARLES
HAYES of Macon, 400 ac. in 2 tracts, Sec. 45, Dis. 16, on waters of "Iola" (Iotla) Cr.,
111+ ac., and Sec. 47, Dis. 16, on "Iola" Cr., 288 ac., known by name of "Pars" tract.
Sold subsequent to judgment from Superior Court of Burke Co. against property of J.R.
PACE, BENJAMIN S. BRITTIAN, WILLIAM A. BRITTIAN and THOS. J. ROANE
for $5,649.73. Recovered by ISAAC T. AVERY, Agent of the Bank of the State at Mor-
ganton. In the sale of property, Charles Hayes had high bid of $300. Sep. 27, 1838. *N.G.
Howell, Sh'ff.* Wit: *J. HOWARD, Thos. J. Roane.* Proven by John Howard in Sep. 1838
court. Registered Jan. 13, 1839.

678 THOMAS W.P. POINDEXTER to JAMES POINDEXTER, both of Macon, for $1,000,
Negro woman named PATSEY which I lately purchased of JOHN HALL. Sep. 11, 1838.
Thomas W.P. Poindexter. Wit: *EVENS POINDEXTER.* Ack. in Sep. 1838 court.

679 SG 383, for $346.50 paid by JOHN POSEY, grant by Sheriff deed to HUMPHREY
POSEY 231 ac. on W. bank of Tennessee R., Sec. 43, Dis. 16. Granted Mar. 1, 1838;
registered Jan. 13, 1839.

680 JAMES POINDEXTER of Macon, to better secure to THOS. W.P. POINDEXTER a
debt of $1,000, have mortgaged a certain Negro woman named PATSEY. Sep. 11, 1838.
James Poindexter. Wit: *EVEN POINDEXTER, SAMUEL ROBISON. Ack. in Sep. 1838
court. Registered Jan. 14, 1839.*

680 THOMAS W.P. POINDEXTER of Macon, to my youngest daughter, HARIETT POIN-
DEXTER, for love & affection, the EQUCHNETTY tract on Tennessee R. and on bank
of Aqunetla (Ekaneetlee?) Sec. 35, Dis. 1. Jan. 11, 1838. *Thos. W.P. Poindexter.* Wit:
JUDY POINDEXTER, JOHN P. (his X mark) BREWER. Ack. in Sep. 1838 court.
Registered Jan. 14, 1839.

681 On Jun 27, 1834, an execution from the Superior Court of Macon, at suit of JOSEPH
DAVES vs. SAMUEL WOODFIN was levied on tract where PHEREBE BELK lived &
was sold at public sale. I, B.S. BRITTIAN became last & highest bidder. For $54, I sell
to Pherebe Belk all my right & title in the land. Feb. 22, 1837. *B.S. Brittian*. Wit: *S.
MCDOWELL, JAMES WITHEROW*. Ack. in Sep. 1838 court. Registered Jan. 14, 1839.

682 WESTLEY JOHNSTON of Macon to JESSE R. GREGG, for $100, 69 ac. on S. bank of
Thompson's fork of "Cartoogachey" Cr., Sec. 61, Dis. 15. May 19, 1838. *Westley (his X
mark) Johnston*. Wit: *JOHN H. BLACK, P.D. CLABURN*. Proven by Philip D. Claburn
in Sep. 1838 court. Registered Jan. 15, 1839.

683 WM. P. PIERCEY to THOS. M. ANGEL, both of Macon, for $290, 90 ac. on Sugartown
Fork of the Tennessee R., Sec. 43, Dis. 11. Mar. 16, 1838. *Wm. P. Piercey*. Wit: *S.
MCDOWELL*. Proven by Silas McDowell in Sep. 1838 court. Registered Jan. 15, 1839.

684 JOSEPH SHERRILL to JOHN DEHART, both of Macon, for $25, 100 ac. on Junelus-
kees Cr., Sec. 39, Dis. 8. Apr. 17, 1838. *Joseph (his X mark) Sherrill*. Wit: *J.L.H. WIG-
GINS, JOHN R. EDWARDS*. Proven by John R. Edwards in Sep. 1838 court. Registered
Jan. 15, 1839.

685 DANIEL GARLAND to JANE GARLAND, both of Macon, 2 horse beasts, 9 cattle, 20
sheep, 40-50 hoggs & all my plantation tools of every description, all my kitchens furniture, bedding, household furniture. Aug. 31, 1838. *Daniel Garland*. Wit: *J. HOWARD*.
Proven by John Howard, Sep. 1838 court. Registered Jan. 15, 1839.

686 WM. W. PEARSEY to THOMAS M. ANGEL, both of Macon, for $100, all my right
etc. in the dower of land of ELIZABETH ANGEL, wife of WILLIAM ANGEL, dec'd.
Mar. 16, 1838. *Wm. W. Piercey*. Wit: *S. MCDOWELL*. Proven by Silas McDowell, Sep.
1838 court. Registered Jan. 15, 1839.

687 WILLIAM ROGERS to WM. W. PIERCEY, both of Macon, for $7.75, part of Sec. 42,
Dis. 11, containing 28+ ac. Feb. 6, 1838. *Wm. F. Rogers*. Wit: *DILLARD LOVE*, who
proved in Sep. 1838 court. Registered Jan. 16, 1839.

688 Agreement between DAVID MCRAY, JOHN W. RAY, JOHN W. GARLAND, JOEL
VERNAY. They have bid off at their joint interest the following tracts, all in District 7:
No. 4, No. 5 & No. 41. They have jointly paid 1/8 of the purchase money down & given
bonds for other purchase money. The object of this agreement is that each member of
company is to pay equal share of all & every expense of purchase & every other expense
that a majority deems advisable. Each to have equal share of property arising from purchase either by mining operations or rent either of gold or other mineral, or from agricul-
tural pursuits or any other business on the land. Agreement subject to disposition of
property as majority may deem advisable. Sep. 17, 1838. *David McRay, John W. Ray,
John W. Garland, Joel Vernay*. Wit: *JOHN HALL, B.S. BRITTIAN*. Proven by Benjamin
S. Brittin in Sep. 1838 court. Registered Jan. 18, 1839.

689 WILLIAM P. POTEAT to WILLIAM ALLIN, Junr. for $100, 50 ac. of a certain tract on
Watauga Cr., on lines of No. 47 in Dis. 10 and No. 1 in Dis. 11. Jan. 3, 1838. *William P.
Poteat*. Wit: *J.R. JOHNSTON, J. COOKS*. Proven by Joseph R. Johnston. Registered Jan.
17, 1839.

690 SG 287 to RICHARD WILSON $5 per 100 ac., 100 ac. on waters of Savannah Cr., Dis.
8, of sd Wilson's entered land, W. side of a mountain. Granted Dec. 15, 1838; registered
Jan. 21, 1839.

691 SG 195 to JOHN HOWARD $5 per 100 ac., 75 ac. on the W. side of Tennessee R., both
sides of "Coweter" (Coweeta) Cr., Dis. 14. Granted Dec. 15, 1838; registered Jan. 21,
1839.

692 SG 268 to LEVI WILSON $5 per 100 ac., 90 ac. on the Tuckaseigee R., Dis. 8, above sd
Wilson's farm. Granted Dec. 15, 1838; registered Jan. 21, 1839.

693 SG 192 to NICHOLAS F. HOWARD $5 per 100 ac., 100 ac. on Clear Cr. waters of "Chattuega" (Chatooga R.), incl. improvement of JAMES WOODY. Granted Dec. 15, 1838; registered Jan. 22, 1839.

694 SG 502 to WILEY R. SHEARER, $10, 50 ac., Sec. 122, Dis. 2 on a branch of "Guskies" Cr., on side of hill in line of No. 121. Granted Jan. 7, 1839; registered Jan. 22, 1839.

695 SG 257 to JOHN SETTEN, $5 per 100 ac., 75 ac. on Savannah Cr. in Dis. 8, on line of No. 149, line of Setten's entered land. Granted Dec. 15, 1838; registered Jan. 22, 1839.

696 SG 167 to JESSE BERRY, $5 per 100 ac., 50 ac. on Deep Cr. in Dis. 1, beg. near the top of a ridge that divides sd creek from Newtons Mill Cr. near what is called the Bench. Granted Dec. 15, 1838; registered Jan. 22, 1839.

697 SG 313 to JOHN HOWARD, $5 per 100 ac., 50 ac. on W. side of the Tennessee R. and W. side of "Coweter" (Coweeta) Cr., on corner of No. 34 and No. 6, Dis. 14. Granted Dec. 24, 1838; registered Jan. 23, 1839.

698 SG 153 to JESSE BERRY, $5 per 100 ac., 100 ac. on W. side of Newtons Mill Cr. in Dis. 1, on corner of JESSE BRECK's land, corner of GILES C. HAYES' land. Granted Dec. 15, 1838; registered Jan. 23, 1839.

699 SG 267 to JOSIAH WARD, $5 per 100 ac., 50 ac. on E. side of Tennnessee R., Dis. 13, on corner of Sec. 20. Granted Dec. 15, 1838; registered Jan. 23, 1839.

700 SG 155 to WILLIAM R. BUCKANON, $5 per 100 ac., 50 ac. on Savannah Cr. in Dis. 8. Granted Dec. 15, 1838; registered Jan. 23, 1839.

701. Mortgage: BENJAMIN S. BRITTIAN & JAMES K. GRAY, both of Macon, to HENRY GRADY & JOHN HALL, property as collateral for note of $2,000, to be used to procure a further indulgence for Brittian & further suspension on the sale of his property to satisfy LT. AVERY, agent of Bank of State of NC at Morganton. Gray for $1 further consideration receives title to the following property. Lands in Dis. 10: 250+ ac., Sec. 49, on which Brittian now lives; 300 ac., Sec. 48 adj. part of plantation occ. by Brittian; 136+ ac., Sec. 50 adj. part of plantation & orchard occ. by Brittian; 60 ac., Sec. 80; 52 ac., Sec. 86 contiguous on "Ioli" (Iotla) Cr., purchased by said B.S. Brittin of the State many years since, money not yet entirely paid; also, in Dis. 16, 640 ac., Sec. 3; 640 ac., Sec. 4; 117 ac., Sec. 76; 111 ac, Sec. 259, contiguous to lands first described; also, half an moiety of 6 other tracts granted to Brittian & Hall in Dis. 8: Sections 43, 40, 42, 44, 46, 49; also, lot & house in Franklin purch. by JOSEPH WELCH, adj. public lots of JAMES ROBISON, w. growing crops, fodder, hay, oats, grain, etc. on these lands; also, Negro woman, ESTHER, abt. 35 yrs. old & her child; also, 40 cattle, 50 hogs, 25 sheep, saddle horse, 5 feather beds & furniture, pony, mule colt, pony colt, wagon, 2 yoke of oxen, set of blacksmith tools, cupboard, sideboard, set of tables, fine bed stead & all Brittin's farming tools. Hall & Grady may sell property at public sale for money to apply to note. Sep. 27, 1838. *B.S. Britten, H. Grady, John Hall, J.K. Gray.* Wit: *N.W. WOODFIN* who proved before JOHN M. DICK, judge of Sup. Ct., Sep. 17, 1838. Registered Jan. 24, 1839.

703 JOHN HALL to JAMES ROBISON, both of Macon, for $600, a certain Negro girl named EMELIN, 17 or 18 years old. Jan. 2, 1839. *John Hall.* Wit: *J.F. GRANT* who proved Jan. 1839 session of court. Registered Jan. 26, 1839.

704 JAMES POTTEAT to JESSE R. SILER, both of Macon, for $1,000, 174 ac., Sec. 27, Dis. 16. Dec. 1, 1838. *James Poteat.* Wit: *D.R. LOWRY, B.M. POTEAT.* Proven by B.M. Poteat in Jan. 1839 session. Registered Jan. 26, 1839.

705 SG 284 to ANDREW WELCH, $5/100 ac., 50 ac. on Deep Creek, Dis. 7. Granted Dec. 15, 1838; registered Jan. 26, 1839.

706 SG 164 to JAMES BUCKANON $5/100 ac., 50 ac. on Big Savannah Creek, Dis. 8. Granted Dec. 15, 1838; registered Jan. 28 1839.

707 SG 168 to JAMES BUCKANON $5/100 ac., 50 ac. on Little Savannnah Cr., Dis. 8. Granted Dec. 15, 1838; registered Jan. 28, 1839.

708 SG 157 to JAMES BUCKANON $5/100 ac., 40 ac. on Big Savannah Cr., Dis. 8, corner of Sec. 10, bd. JOSEPH BUCKANON. Granted Dec. 15, 1838; registered Jan. 28, 1839.

709 SG 312 to SETH W. HYATT, $10/100 ac., 640 ac. on Horse Pasture fork of Toxaway R., Dis. 18, on line of Sec. 14. Granted Dec. 24, 1838; registered Jan. 28, 1839.

710 SG 154 to JESSE BRACKS/BRACK, $5/100 ac., 100 ac. on Newtons Mill Cr., Dis. 7, bd. HAYES land. Granted Dec. 15, 1838; registered Jan. 28, 1839.

711 SG 414 to JOHN CONNELLY, assignee of PETER LEDFORD for $112.17 pd by Ledford, 55 ac. on Tennessee R., Sec. 9, Dis. 14. Granted Jan. 7, 1839; registered Jan. 28, 1839.

712 SG 433 to REBECAH MCDANIEL, $___, 122+ ac., Sec. 33, Dis. 15. Granted Jan. 7, 1839; registered Jan. 29, 1839.

713 SG 482 to JAMES ROBISON, $23.95, 97 ac., Sec. 21, Dis. 7. Granted Jan. 7, 1839; registered Jan. 29, 1839.

714 SG 436 to DAVID ROGERS, $___, 58 ac., Sec. 37, Dis. 7. Granted Jan. __, 1839; registered Jan. 29, 1839.

715 SG 278 to THOMAS WEST, $5/100 ac., 100 ac. on "Cowwee" (Cowee) Cr., Dis. 10, on corner of Sec. 20. Granted Dec. 15, 1838; registered Jan. 29, 1839.

716 SG 525 to DANIEL WEST, $517.65, 348 ac., Sec. 61, Dis. 9. Granted Jan. 7, 1839; registered Jan. 29, 1839.

717 SG 230 to WILLIAM PARTON, $5/100 ac., Greens Fork of Savannah Cr., Dis. 8, beginning above Parton's improvement. Granted Dec. 15, 1838; registered Jan. 30, 1839.

718 SG 425 to JEREMIAH R. PACE, $185.85, 111+ ac., Sec. 45, Dis. 16, near planes of "Iola" (Iotla Cr.). Granted Jan. 7, 1839; registered Jan. 30, 1839.

719 SG 265 to AARON THOMAS, $5/100 ac., 50 ac., Middle Cr., Dis. 13, on W. bank of N. fork, above sd Thomas's mill. Granted Dec. 15, 1838; registered Jan. 30, 1839.

720 SG 329 to ELISHA THOMAS, $5/100 ac., 100 ac. in Flats of Middle Cr., Dis. 13. Granted Jan. 1839; registered Jan. 30, 1839.

721 SG 183 to MARK FORTENBURY, $5/100 ac., 50 ac. on Tennessee R., Dis. 14. Granted Dec. 15, 1838; registered Jan. 30, 1839.

722 SG 305, SETH W. HYETT for $10/100 ac., 200 ac. in Dis. 18 on Horse Pasture of Toxaway R., corner of Sec. 13, bd. JOHN CLARK. Granted Dec. 24, 1838; registered Jan. 30, 1839.

723 SG 307, BARRACK NORTON, THOMAS MILLSAPPS, WILLIAM BRYSON, JOHN DOBSON for $___,100 ac., 50 ac. on White Water Cr., Dis. 18. Granted Dec. 24, 1838; registered Jan. 30, 1839.

724 SG 308, BARRICK NORTON, THOMAS MILLSAPPS, DAVID MILLSAPPS, WILLIAM BRYSON, JOHN DOBSON for $5/100 ac., 100 ac. on Toxaway R., Dis. 18. Granted Dec. 24, 1838; registered Jan. 30, 1839.

725 SG 197, JACKSON HAYS, $5/100 ac., 100 ac. on Deep Creek, Dis. 1. Granted Dec. 15, 1838; registered Jan. 30, 1839.

726 SG 198, GEORGE W. HAYS, $5/100 ac., 50 ac. on W. bank of Newtons Mill Cr. Granted Dec. 15, 1838; registered Jan. 30, 1839.

727 SG 311, PHILIP S.C. HOWARD, $5/100 ac., 100 ac. on Tennessee R., Dis. 13, on corners of Sections 70, 71 and 37. Granted Dec. 24, 1838; registered Jan. 30, 1839.

728 SG 199, GEORGE W. HAYS, $5/100 ac., 50 ac. on Newton's Mill Cr., Dis. 1. Granted Dec. 15, 1838; registered Jan. 31, 1839.

729 SG 201, GEORGE W. HAYES, $5/100 ac., 100 ac. on W. bank of Newtons Mill Cr., Dis. 1. Granted Dec. 15, 1838; registered Jan. 31, 1839.

730 SG 235, ZACHARIAH PEEK, $5/100 ac., 50 ac. on "Elijee" (Ellijay) Cr., Dis. 11, bd. HAGAN. Granted Dec. 15, 1838; registered Jan. 31, 1839.

731 SG 211, JOHN LOWRY, $5/100 ac., 50 ac. in Dis. 15, on "Cartoogahgee" (Cartoogechaye) Cr., bd. WALDROP. Granted Dec. 15, 1838; registered Jan. 31, 1839.

732 SG 327, ULRICK KEENER, $5/100 ac., 42 ac. in Dis. 11, on Sugartown (Cullasaja) R., on corner of Sec. 29. Granted Dec. 27, 1838; registered Jan. 31, 1839.

733 SG 440 to JOHN DEHART, assignee of JOSEPH SHERREL, for $33.71, 123+ ac., Sec. 30, Dis. 8 on Junaluskies Creek. Granted Jan. 7, 1839; registered Jan. 31, 1839.

734 SG 287, LEVI WILSON, $5/100 ac., 100 ac. on E. fork of Savannah Cr., Dis. 8. Granted Dec. 15, 1838; registered Jan. 31, 1839.

735 SG 426, JOHN HOWARD, assignee of SAMUEL BRODWAY/BRODAWAY for $85.23, 52 1/2 ac. on Commmissioners Cr., Sec. 22, Dis. 14. Granted Jan. 7, 1839; registered Jan. 31, 1839.

736 SG 191, JOHN HOWARD, $5/100 ac., 25 ac. on W. side of Tennessee R., Dis. 14. Granted Dec. 15, 1838; registered Jan. 31, 1839.

737 SG 412, WILLIAM H. BRYSON, assignee of P. MATHEWS for $___, 57 ac., Sec. 37, Dis. 7. Granted Jan. 7, 1839; registered Jan. 31, 1839.

738 SG #___, NATHAN TABER, $5/100 ac., 50 ac. on Mill Creek in Dis. 9. Granted Dec. 15, 1838; registered Feb. 1, 1839.

739 SG 255, JOSEPH SHERRELL, $5/100 ac., 100 ac. on "Tuckaseegie" R. in Dis. 8, beg. near road leading to Franklin. Granted Dec.15, 1838; registered Feb. 1, 1839.

740 SG 295, ZACHARIAH EVENS, $5/100 ac., 50 ac. on Burningtown Cr, in Dis. 17. Granted Dec. 20, 1838; registered Feb. 1, 1839.

741 SG 180, JOHN DAVIS, $5/100 ac., 70 ac. on "Eliga" (Ellijay) Cr., Dis. 11, on line of Sec. 96. Granted Dec. 15, 1838; registered Feb. 1, 1839.

742 SG 241, DAVID W. SILER, $5/100 ac., 53 ac., Cartoogechaye Cr., Dis. 15, on BRITTAIN's old line, bd. MCCLURE. Granted Dec. 15, 1838; registered Feb. 1, 1839.

743 SG 489, JACOB SILER, $27.50, 137 ac., Sec. 38, Dis. 6. Granted Jan. 7, 1839; registered Feb. 1, 1839.

744 SG 439, JACOB SILER, $180, 80 ac. on "Cartoogahgee" (Cartoogechaye) Cr., Sec. 26, Dis. 15. Granted Jan. 7, 1839; registered Feb. 1, 1839.

745 SG 509, JACOB SILER, $23.31, 63 ac., Sec. 49, Dis. 6. Granted Jan. 7, 1839; registered Feb. 1, 1839.

746 SG 510, JACOB SILER, $15.75, 63 ac., Sec. 50, Dis. 6. Granted Jan. 7, 1839; registered Feb. 1, 1839.

747 SG 222, ISAAC MORRISON, $5/100 ac., 100 ac. on Savannah Cr., Dis. 8. Granted Dec. 15, 1838; registered Feb. 1, 1839.

748 SG 224, JAMES MORRISON, $5/100 ac., 100 ac. on Savannah Cr., Dis. 8, bd. JOHN WILSON. Granted Dec. 15, 1838; registered Feb. 1, 1839.

749 SG 225, ISAAC MORRISON, $5/100 ac., 100 ac. on Savannah Cr., Dis. 8, bd. BUCKANAN. Granted Dec. 15, 1838; registered Feb. 1, 1839.

750 SG 365, JOHN STEPHENSON, $20, 205 ac. on E. side of Tennessee R., mouth of Kelly's Branch, Sec. 1, Dis. 13. Granted Mar. 1, 1838; registered Feb. 1, 1839.

751 SG 190, HENRY HAGAN, $5/100 ac., 75 ac. on "Eliga" (Ellijay) Cr., Dis. 11, bordering Sec. 56, 57, 100. Granted Dec. 15, 1838; registered Feb. 5, 1839.

752 SG 185, JULES N. GARRETT, $5/100 ac. on Tuckaseegee R., Dis. 1, on corner of Sec. 2. Granted Dec. 15, 1838; registered Feb. 5, 1839.

753 SG 422, MATHEW GARRETT for $____, 50 ac., Sec. 3, Dis. 1, on NE bank of the "Tuckaseigee" R., at mouth of Rock Creek, at location of 2 "Nattle Boxes" (Rattle Boxes) on riverbank. Granted Jan. 7, 1839; registered Feb. 15, 1839.

754 SG 296, MATHEW GARRETT, $5/100 ac., 50 ac. on E. bank of Tuckasegee R. below Garrett's house, corner of Sec. 3. Granted Dec. 20, 1838; Feb. 15, 1839.

755 SG 249, SAMUEL BRYSON, $11.14, 55 ac., Sec. 36, Dis. 10, on NE side of Tennessee R., on upper line of Sec. 35. Granted Dec. 12, 1836; registered Feb. 6, 1839.

756 SG 350, HENRY WILSON, $77.32, 83 ac., Sec. 17, Dis. 7. Granted Dec. 28, 1836; registered Feb. 6, 1839.

757 SG 454, ANDREW COLVERT, $10, 50 ac., Sec. 89, Dis.9. Granted Jan. 7, 1838; registered Feb. 6, 1839.

758 SG 239, AGNES RUDDLE, $5/100 ac., 100 ac. on Savanah Cr., Dis. 8, bd. JOHN WILSON's entered land, WILLIAM BUCKANAN's line. Granted Dec. 15, 1838; registered Feb. 6, 1839.

759 SG 434, MATHEW N. RUSSEL, assignee of JOHN TATHAM, for $49 pd by Tatham, 52 ac., Sec. 33, Dis. 11. Granted Jan. 7, 1839; registered Feb. 6, 1839.

760 SG 87, JOHN BROWN, $5/100 ac., 50 ac. on Wautauga Cr., Dis. 10. Granted Feb.25, 1838; registered Feb. 6, 1839.

761 SG 394, ABEL B. HYATT assignee of JOHN SHULAR for $731.23 paid by Hyatt, 300 ac., Sec. 5, Dis.1 (?), E. of THE BEAR's NE corner, crossing Deep Cr. Granted Dec. 24, 1838; registered Feb. 6, 1839.

762 SG 115, WILLIAM B. CRUSE, $5/100 ac., 75 ac. in Dis. 16, bordering Sec. 36, MOORE's land. Granted Mar. 31, 1838; registered Feb. 6, 1839.

763 SG 314, JOSEPH J. WELCH, $5/100 ac., 50 ac. on Tuckaseegee R., Dis. 1, corner Sec. 1. Granted Dec. 27, 1838; registered Feb. 6, 1839.

764 SG 315, JOSEPH J. WELCH, $5/100 ac., 50 ac. on branch running into the Tennessee R. on N. side, below mouth of Tuckaseegee. Granted Dec. 27, 1838; reg. Feb. 6, 1839.

765 SG 277, FRANCIS WARD, $5/100 ac., 75 ac. on Green Fork of Savannah Cr., Dis. 8. Granted Dec. 15, 1838; registered Feb. 7, 1838.

766 SG 163, SAMUEL BRYSON, $5/100 ac., 100 ac. on N, side of Tennessee R., Dis. 10, bd. DANIEL GABBY's fence. Granted Dec. 15, 1838; registered Feb. 7, 1839.

767 SG 523, HENRY WILSON, $11.60, 58 ac., Sec. 54, Dis. 2, both sides of "Tesquittee" (Tusquittee Creek). Granted Jan. 7, 1839; registered Feb. 7, 1839.

768 SG 247, AMOS SHEPHERD, $5/100 ac., 50 ac., S. side Tuckaseegee R., Shepherd's Cr., incl. Shepherd's lower improvement. Granted Dec. 15, 1838; registered Feb. 7, 1839.

769 SG 504, EMANUEL SHULAR, $10.20, 51 ac., Sec. 154, Dis. 5,on W. side of Cane Cr. Granted Jan. 7, 1839; registered Feb. 7, 1839.

770 SG 273, WILLIAM WILLIAMS, $5/100 ac., 100 ac. on "Eligeye" (Ellijay) Cr., Dis. 11, bd. V. AMMONS. Granted Dec. 11, 1838; registered Feb. 8, 1839.

771 SG 455, EZEKIEL DOWDLE, $19.50, 78 ac. on Tusquittee (Cr.), corner of Sec. 7, Sec. 9. Granted Jan. 7, 1839; registered Feb. 8, 1839.

772 SG 121, ROMULUS A. BROWN, $5/100 ac., 100 ac. on "Culowhee" Cr., incl. improvement. Granted May 24, 1838; registered Feb. 8, 1839.

773 SG 479, JAMES D. FRANKS, $15.30, 58 ac. on "Hiwasee" R., Sec. 80, Dis. 2. Granted Jan. 7, 1839; registered Feb. 8, 1839.

774 SG 220, MASON MCLEOD, $5/100 ac., 50 ac. on Middle Cr. Granted Dec. 18, 1838; registered Feb. 8, 1839.

775 SG 214, AMOS LEDFORD, $5/100 ac., 50 ac. on Standridge's Cr., above last old survey (#109) in Dis. 15. Granted Dec. 15, 1839; registered Feb. 8, 1839.

776 SG 289, SAMUEL WIKEL, $5/100 ac., 35 ac. on both sides of Savannah Cr., Dis. 8. Granted Dec. 15, 1838; registered Feb. 8, 1839.

777 SG 270, SAMUEL WIKLE, $5/100 ac., 50 ac. on Savannah Cr., Dis. 8, on line of Sec. 137. Granted Dec. 15, 1838; registered Feb. 8, 1839.

778 SG 282, WILLIAM BURTON WIGGINS, $5/100 ac., tract on "Elearky" (Alarka or Yalaka) Cr., Dis. 8, incl. an improvement. Granted Dec. 15, 1838; registered Feb. 9, 1839.

779 SG 272, JAMES WELBURN WIGGINS, $5/100 ac., 50 ac. on branch of "Eleuky" (Alarka) Cr., Dis. 8, incl. an improvement. Granted Dec. 15, 1838; reg. Feb. 9, 1839.

780 SG 216, JOHN LAMM, $5/100 ac., 50 ac. on Sugar Town R., Dis. 12?, on line of 69. Granted Dec. 15, 1838; registered Feb. 9, 1839.

781 SG 254, WILLIAM SAWYERS, $5/100 ac., 75 ac. on Tuckaseegee R., Dis. 8, on corner of Sec. 29, Sec. 64. Granted Dec. 15, 1838; registered Feb. 9, 1839.

782 SG 286, JAMES WILSON, $5/100 ac., 50 ac. on Little Savannah Cr., Dis. 7. Granted Dec. 15, 1838; registered Feb. 9, 1839.

783 SG #285, JOHN WILSON, $5/100 ac., 100 ac. on Savannah Cr., Dis. 8, corner of Sec. 8. Granted Dec. 15, 1838; registered Feb. 9, 1839.

784 SG 229, ZACHARIAH PEAK, $5/100 acre, 50 ac. on Indian Camp Branch of "Elijah" (Ellijay) Cr., Dis. 11. Granted Dec. 15, 1838; registered Feb. 9, 1839.

785 SG 215, HOSEA LAND, $5/100 ac., 100 ac. on Coon Cr., beg. on ridge above sd Land's house. Granted Dec. 15, 1838; registered Feb. 9, 1839.

786 SG #258, JOHN STRAIN, $5/100 ac., 49 ac. on Love's Mill Cr. Granted Dec. 15, 1838; registered Feb. 9, 1839.

787 SG 428, JOHN LAMB, $____, 49 ac., Sec. 69, Dis. 12, crossing the River. Granted Jan. 7, 1838; registered Feb. 11, 1839.

788 SG 295, TRAVES ELMORE, $5/100 ac., 50 ac. on Rabbit & "Wataugah" Creeks, Dis. 11, corner of sd Ellmore's entered land, on line of 66. Granted Dec. 20, 1838; registered Feb. 11, 1839.

789 SG 430, SAMUEL LOVENGOOD, $____, 154 ac., Sec. 59, Dis. 17, crossing N. fork of Burning town Creek. Granted Dec. 7, 1838; registered Feb. 13, 1839.

790 SG 300, JOHN STRAIN, $50/100 ac., 50 ac. on "Elijah (Ellijay) Cr., Dis. 11. Granted Dec. 20, 1838; registered Feb. 13, 1839.

791 SG 259, JOHN STRAIN, $10/100 ac., 200 ac. on Cat Creek, Dis. 11, line of Sec. 12. Granted Dec. 15, 1838; registered Feb. 13, 1839.

792 SG 299, JOHN STRAIN, 10/100 ac., 200 ac. on "Eligah" (Ellijay) Cr., Dis. 11, near First Gap, on corner of 119. Granted Dec. 20, 1838; registered Feb. 13, 1839.

793 SG 260, JOHN STRAIN, $10/100 ac., 200 ac. in Dis. 11, corner of Sec. 73. Granted Dec. 15, 1838; registered Feb. 14, 1839.

794 SG 298, JOHN STRAIN, $5/100 ac., 100 ac. on "Elijah" (Ellijay) Cr., Dis. 11. Granted Dec. 20, 1838; regitered Feb. 14, 1839.

795 SG 202, JAMES HONECUT, $5/100 ac., 100 ac. on Gray's Tanyard Branch, Dis. 15, corner of BATES's land. Granted Dec. 15, 1838; registered Feb. 15, 1839.

796 HORATIO FORD to THOMAS FORD, both of Macon, for $175, 8 cattle, 9 hogs, 5 sheep, waggon & harnesss, sorrell mare, 4 beds & furniture, all household furniture, farming utensils. Aug. 10, 1838. *Horatio Ford.* Wit: *U. KEENER.* Reg. Feb. 13, 1839.

796 JAMES LEDBETTER to JAMES KIRKLAND, both of Macon, for $71, 50 ac. in Dis. 8, E. fork of Cockerhams Cr. *James Ledbetter.* Wit: *NOAH BURCHFIELD, MERREL B. CRISP.* Registered Feb. 13, 1839.

797 SG 355, JOHN DOBSON, $219, 146 ac., Sec. 7, Dis. 12, on Tennessee R., lower corner Dis. 13. Granted Jan. 17, 1837; registered Feb. 26, 1839.

798 SG 93, JOHN F. DOBSON, $5/100 ac., 100 ac., E. side of Tennessee R., Dis. 12, corner of Dobson's entry. Granted Feb. 26, 1838; registered Feb. 26, 1839.

799 SG 94, JOHN DOBSON, $5/100 ac., 100 ac. on E. side Tennessee R., Dis. 12. Granted Feb. 28, 1838; registered Feb. 29, 1839.

800 SG 200, JOHN HALL, $75, 50 ac. on S. side of Tennessee R., Dis. 17, opposite BRITTAIN's and Hall's lands. Granted Dec. 15, 1838; registered Mar. 4, 1839.

801 SG 507, THOMAS SHEPHERD, $19.20, 96 ac., Sec. 1, Dis. __, in TUNAUGH HEE ALL's reservation, on corner of old survey No. 15, with line of Sec. 15 to a stake in RAMSEY'S yard. Granted Jan. 7, 1839; registered Mar. 4, 1839.

802 SG 233, FRANCES POINDEXTER, $5/100 ac., 50 ac. on SW side of Hightower Branch, below GARRETT's improvement. Granted Mar. 15, 1838; reg. Mar. 4, 1839.

803 SG 512, THOMAS SHEPHERD, $10, 50 ac., Sec. 1, Dis. __, beginning in BEVER CARRIER's Reservation, on SW corner of No. 74, on south side of Middle Fork of Cowee Creek, on line of Sec. 26. Granted Jan. 7, 1839; registered Mar. 4, 1839.

804 SG 252, THOMAS SHEPHERD, $5/100 ac., 100 ac. on Cowee Creek, Dis. 10, on line of Sec. 84. Granted Mar. 30, 1837; registered Mar. 5, 1839.

805 N.S. JARRETT to JOHN WELCH, both of Macon, for $100, 83 ac., Sec. 42, Dis. 13. Oct. 20, 1838. *N.S. Jarrett*. Wit: *J. HOWARD*. Acknowledged in court by Nimrod S. Jarrett, Jan. 1839 session. Registered Mar. 7, 1839.

806 N.S. JARRETT to JOHN WELCH, both of Macon, for $200, part of Sec. 20, Dis. 13 crossing Tessenty Creek, 51 ac. Oct. 20, 1837. *N.S. Jarrett*. Wit: *J. HOWARD*. Acknowledged by Nimrod S. Jarrett in Jan. 1839 session of court. Registered Mar. 7, 1839.

807 JONOTHAN PHILLIPS, Ch'man of Court of Pleas and Qtr Sessions of Macon Co., to MARY BRAZEAL of Macon, for $108, part of lower 100 ac. of Town of Franklin, one acre, No. 44 on the lower plat, on Main Street. Jan. 25, 1839. *J. Phillips, Ch*. Wit: *S. MCDOWELL*. Acknowledged in Jan. 1839 session. Reg. Mar. 14, 1839.

808 Mortgage: WILLIAM BROWN to HOWELL MOSS Senr., 168 ac. on Peach Tree Creek, Dis. __, Sec. 46. Sep. 6, 1838. *William (his X mark) Brown*. Condition: Moss is security for Brown for $700 in notes given to State of NC. Brown will pay & satisfy obligation. *William (his X mark) Brown*. Wit: *C.T. ROGERS, THOS. J. ROANE*. Proven by Thomas J. Roane in Jan. 1839 session of court. Registered Mar. 14, 1839.

809 THOMAS LOVE to JESSE R. SILER for $2,000, 275 ac., E. side of Tennessee R., Dis. 11, Sec. 32, purchased of the State of NC by ROBERT LOVE Jr. & JOHN MOORE in 1820 & granted Sep. 21, 1838, jcn of Sugartown & Tennessee R. Thomas Love was legal representative of Robert Love Jr., dec'd, & Moore had executed a deed relinquishing title. Oct. 22, 1838. *Thos. Love*. Wit: *G.W.I. MOORE, SAMUEL ROBISON*. Proven by George W.I. Moore in Jan. 1839 session. Registered Mar. 14, 1839.

810 JACOB R. LINSEY of Macon to JASON L. HYITT for $129.16, 62 ac. on Lick Log Creek, Dis. 2, Sec. 144, surveyed on Oct. 22, 1837 by ROBERT HENRY, D.S. and REUB DEVER(?), P.S., shown by certificate of the commissioners, J.F. PATTISON & C.L. HENTON on Sep. 6, 1838. Jan. 23, 1839. *J.R. Linsey*. Wit: *WILLIAM ROANE*. Proven in Jan. 1839 session of court. Registered Mar. 14, 1839.

811 JOHN BROWN to E.V. AMMONS, both of Macon, for $150, 50 ac. in Dis. 10, on corner of Sec. 126; entered for claim May 2, 1836. Apr. 19, 1838. *John (his X mark) Brown*. Wit: *HOWELL MOSS*. Proven by Moss in Jan. 1839 session of court. Registered Mar. 14, 1839.

812 WILLIAM TATHAM to RICHARD WILSON for $80, 73 ac., part of Entry No. 494 on Savannah Creek, line of No. 20. Dec. 17, 1838. *W.M. Tatham*. Wit: *JOHN TATHAM, SAMUEL KELLY*. Acknowledged in Jan. 1839 court. Registered Mar. 15, 1839.

813 JOSEPH MILLER to CHARLES RIDLY, both of Macon, for $800, 144 ac., Dis. 10, Sec. 45 on Tennessee R. (by) Rattlebox on river. Sep. 8, 1838. *Joseph Miller*. Wit: *M. WIKLE, HENSON QUEEN, JOHN HALL*. Proven by John Hall in Jan. 1839 session. Registered Mar. 15, 1839.

814 JOHN BROWN Senr. to E.V. AMMONS, both of Macon, for val. rec'd, 55 ac. joining Sec. 126 in Dis. 10, which I bought at 1836 sale in Franklin. Apr. 19, 1838. *John Brown*. Wit: *HOWELL MOSS*, who proved in Jan. 1839 court. Registered Mar. 15, 1839.

815 JOHN SUTTON to JACOB MASON, both of Macon, for $65, 100 ac. on Savannah Creek, Dis. 8, on corner of Sec. 149. Jan. 12, 1839. *John Sutton*. Wit: *FRANCIS (his X mark) WARD, LEVI WILSON*. Proven by Francis Ward in Jan. 1839 court. Registered Mar. 15, 1839.

816 NATHAN B. THOMPSON to JAMES PARKER (no $ amount given), Sec. 12, Dis. 8 on S. fork of Tuckaseegah River. Oct. 6, 1839. *Nathan B. Thompson*. Wit: *JESSE C. COCK- ERHAM, CHARLES SWENNS*. Ack. in Jan. 1839 court. Registered Mar. 15, 1839.

817 RICHARD WILSON to PETER LONG, both of Macon, 75 ac., Sec. 53, Dis. 4, which Wilson purchased at the land sale in Franklin, Oct. 24, 1836. Dec. 31, 1838. *Richard (his X mark) Wilson*. Wit: *B. KERSLEY or KERSHEY, ENOCH UNDERWOOD*. Proven by B. Kershy in Mar. 1839 session. Registered Mar. 18, 1839.

818 SG 209, SAMUEL KELLY, $5/100 ac., 50 ac. on N. side of Tennessee River, Dis. 15, on corner of Sec. 3. Granted Dec. 15, 1838; registered Mar. 18, 1839.

819 SG 251, JESSE SANDERS, $5/100 ac., 60 ac. on "Skenner" (Skeenah) Creek in Dis. 15 on north boundary of Sec. 27. Granted Dec. 15, 1838; registered Mar. 18, 1839.

820 SG 207, SAMUEL KELLY, $5/100 ac., 50 ac. on Mud Creek, Dis. 13, on W. side of JOHN DERRICK's improvement. Granted Dec. 15, 1838; registered Mar. 18, 1839.

821 SG 208, SAMUEL KELLY, $5/100 ac., 50 ac. on Mud Creek, Dis. 13, on lower side of MATHESON's improvement. Granted Dec. 15, 1838; registered Mar. 18, 1839.

822 SG 432, MOSES MAYFIELD, for $___, 106 ac., Sec. 92, Dis. 10. Granted Jan. 7, 1839; registered Mar. 26, 1839.

823 SG 424, JAS. BUCKHANAN, assignee of EZEKEL GRIBBLE, for $__ , 55 ac., Sec. 14, Dis. 8, right hand fork of E. part of Litttle Savannah Creek. Granted Jan. 7, 1839; registered Mar. 27, 1839.

824 SG 165, JESSE BURRELL, $5/100 ac., 50 ac. on Chattooga River, on corner of Sec. 8, Dis. 18. Granted Dec. 15, 1838; registered Mar. 28, 1839.

825 BENJAMIN S. BRITTIAN of Macon, to JONATHAN BIRD of Burke Co. NC, for $600, 142 ac. on "Iolie" (Iotla) Creek, Sec. 56, Dis. 16. Mar. 28, 1839. *B.S. Brittin*. Wit: *LEMUEL BIRD, CLEARK BIRD*. Ack. in March 1839 court, H.G. WOODFIN, Deputy Clerk. Registered Mar. 28, 1839.

826 ANDREW NORTON of Macon, JAMES NOCKS & his wife EDITH, and CORNELUS HOWELL & his wife MATILDA, all of Cherokee Co., GA to MARTIN NORTON of Macon, for $25 pd to each of above, tract on Tennessee R. that GIDEON NORTON died possessed of & fell to Andrew Norton, Edith Norton & Matilda as heirs, their lawful part of 3 tracts yet undivided in Dis. 14 & Sec. 6(?), 13, 14 & 16, also their undivided part of the widow's dowry, all rights they received by the death of their father, Gideon Norton, dec'd. Jan. 28, 1838. *Andrew (his X mark) Norton, James Nock, Edith (her X mark) Noxx, Cornelius Howel, Matilda (her X mark) Howel*. Wit: *WILLIAM DRYMAN*, who proved in Jan. 1839 court. Registered June 3, 1839.

827 SG 156 to WILLIAM BARNS, $5/100 ac., 50 ac. in Dis. 18, on head of Big Creek, on line of Sec. 3. Granted Dec. 15, 1838; registered Mar. 28, 1839.

828 SG 508, JOHN SILER, $15.20, 76 ac. on E. side of "Nuntahaly" (Nantahala) River, crossing river, Sec. 28, Dis. 13. Granted Jan. 7, 1839; registered Mar. 29, 1839.

829 SG 139, EPHRIM AMMONS, $10/100 ac., 300 ac. on Toxaway and "Cattoga" (Chatooga) Rivers in Dis. 18, W. of Chimney Top Mountain, on line of No. 82, on HYATT's line. Granted Dec. 15, 1838; registered Mar. 29, 1839.

830 SG 187, THOMAS GREBLE/GRIBLE, $5/100 ac., 50 ac. on "Tuckaseigah" (Tuck- aseigee) River, Dis. 7. Granted Dec. 15, 1838; registered Apr. 2, 1839.

831 SG 124, NATHANIEL CARRELL, $5/100 ac., 50 ac. on "Skenner" (Skeenah) Cr., Dis. 15. Granted Oct. 10, 1838; registered Mar. 30, 1839.

832 SAMUEL Y. JAMISON to JESSE R. SILAR, $84, Sec. 75, Dis. 17 on bank of Tennessee River. Mar. 25, 1839. *S.Y. Jamison.* Wit: *B.S. BRITTAN, J.H. TRUETT.* Proved by J.H. Truett in Mar. 1839 court. Registered May 18, 1839.

833 GEORGE W. HISE to JESSE R. SILAR for $750, Negro woman named VINA abt 30 yrs old & her boy-child NELSON abt 2 yrs old, the woman now delivered to him at his own house & the child to be delivered to him or his agent at my father's in Walker Co., GA. I warrant them to be healthy & sensible. Feb. 1839. *G.W. Hise.* Wit: *N.S. JARRETT, T.P. SILER.* Proven by N.S. Jarrett in court, Mar. 1839. Registered (no date).

833 JOHN A. BELL to JESSE R. SILAR for $800, a Negro man named ISAAC, 21 yrs of age, sound, healthy and sensible. Feb. 25, 1839. *J.A. Bell.* Wit: *BURTON DICKY, A. HESTER.* Proven by B.K. Dicky in court, Mar. 1839 session. Registered May 18, 1839.

834 JAMES BRYSON Senr. to MATHEW RUSSELL for $200, 87 ac. on Sugartown R., Sec. 47, Dis. 11, bought Oct. 1822 from state. Feb. 18, 1839. *James Bryson.* Wit: *J.R. SILAR, D.R. LOWRY.* Proven by J.R. Silar in Mar. 1839 court. Registered May 18, 1839.

834 GEORGE SHERRILL of Haywood Co. NC to JESSE R. SILAR of Macon, for $50, land on the "Nantihalee" (Nantahala) River, Dis. 12, No. 25, containing 119 ac. Jan. 21, 1837. *George Sherrill.* Wit: *JOHN HYDE, LEMUEL BIRD.* Proven by Lemuel Bird in May 1839 session of court. Registered May 18, 1839.

835 JOHN H. KIRKLAND of Macon, to JESSE R. SILAR for $140, 4 tracts on "Nantihalee" (Nantahala) R., Dis. 12, Sec. 17(68 ac.); Sec. 18 (68 ac.); Sec. 20 (88 ac.); Sec. 21 (61 ac.), 285 ac. in all, which Kirkland purchased in Sept. 1838, pd 1/8 of purchase money down & gave bonds for balance. Jan. 18, 1839. *John H. Kirkland.* Wit: *BURTON K. DICKY, J.M. BRYSON.* Proven by Burton K. Dicky in Mar. 1839 session. Registered May 18, 1839.

836 SAM'L Y. JAMISON to JESSE R. SILAR for $29, 79 ac., Sec. 9, Dis. 17. Mar. 25, 1839. *S.Y. Jamison.* Wit: *B. BRITTAN, J.H. TRUITT.* Proven by J.H. Truitt in Mar. 1839 court. Registered May 18, 1839.

837 SAM'L Y. JAMISON to JESSE R. SILAR for $60, 60 ac., Sec. 74, Dis. 17 on N. bank of Tennessee R., N. bank of Tellico Creek. Mar. 25, 1839. *S.Y. Jamison.* Wit: *B.S. BRITTAIN, J.H. TRUITT.* Proven by Truitt in Mar. 1839 session. Registered May 18, 1839.

837 Mortgage: BENJ. S. BRITTAIN to MICHAEL WIKLE the following tracts in the Franklin Town Land: Lot No. 11 (150 poles), Lot No. 7 (5+ ac.), Lot No. 8 (5+ ac.), Lot No. 14 (5+ ac.); also 2 tracts in the Cherokee Nation in Dis. 8, No. 90 & 91, containing 175 ac. each. Condition: Wikle endorsed note from Brittain to STEPHEN S. PACE for $73 with interest, and stayed 5 judgments in favor of Pace against Brittain as principal, Wikel as secondary for $160; if Brittain pays the several amounts of money, this instrument is void. Jan. 29, 1839. *B.S. Brittain.* Wit: *JAMES W. WAYNE, JOHN HALL.* Ack. in March 1839 court. Registered May 18, 1839.

839 SAM'L Y. JAMISON to JESSE R. SILAR for $53, 53 ac., Sec. 18, Dis. 18 on Toxaway R. Mar. 25, 1839. *S.Y. Jamison.* Wit: *B.S. BRITTAIN, J.H. TRUITT.* Proven by Truitt in Mar. 1839 court. Registered May 18, 1839.

840 WILLIAM H. THOMAS to JESSE R. SILAR for $100, land on S. side of Tennessee R., 4 poles below the fort Lindsay ford, running with old Treaty line, 640 ac. granted by the state on Dec. 24, 1838. Mar. 15, 1839. *WM. H. Thomas.* Wit: *B.K. DICKY, W.M. DEWESE.* Proven by B.K. Dicky in Mar. 1839 court. Registered May 18, 1839.

841 GEORGE W. ANGEL to JESSE R. SILER, both of Macon for $600, 120 ac., Sec. 18, Dis. 11 on Tennessee R. Nov. 10, 1838. *Geo. W. Angel.* Wit: *MARTIN MCCOY, B.K. DICKY.* Proven by Burton K. Dickey in Mar. 1839 session. Registered May 18, 1839.

842 SG #244, EPHRAIM AMMONS, $10.14, 50 ac. on Sec. 88, Dis. 17. Granted Dec. 12, 1836; registered May 25, 1839.

843 SG #143, EPHRAIM AMMONS, $10/100 ac., 150 ac. on Hickory Knoll Creek in Dis. 13. Granted Dec. 15, 1838; registered May 25, 1839.

844 SG 242, EPHRAIM AMMONS, $90, 65 ac., Sec. 37, Dis. 18. Granted Dec. 12, 1836; registered May 25, 1839.

845 SG 297, S. MCDOWELL & EPHRAIM AMMONS, $15.18, 75 ac., Sec. 67, Dis. 12. Granted Dec. 12, 1836; registered May 25, 1839.

846 SG 243, EPHRAIM AMMONS, $10.19, five ac., Sec. 86, Dis. 17, crossing Wiggins Creek. Granted Dec. 12, 1836; registered May 25, 1839.

847 SG 246, EPHRAIM AMMONS, $12.18, 62 ac., Sec. 89, Dis. 17. Granted Dec. 12, 1836; registered May 25, 1839.

848 SG 248, EPHRAIM AMMONS, $12.72, 61 ac., Sec. 85, Dis. 17. Granted Dec. 12, 1836; registered May 25, 1839.

849 SG 145, EPHRAIM AMMONS, $5/100 ac., 100 ac. on E. side of Tennessee R. Dis. 12 and 13, on DOBSON's SE corner. Granted Dec. 15, 1838; registered May 25, 1839.

850 SG 118, EPHRAIM AMMONS, $5/100 ac., 200 ac. on Horse Pasture, fork of Toxaway River, Dis. 18. Granted Dec. 15, 1838; registered May 25, 1839.

851 SG 120, ALLEN AMONS, $5/100 ac., 100 ac. on Horse Pasture, fork of Toxaway River, Dis. 18, on line of Sec. 13. Granted May 24, 1838; registered May 25, 1839.

852 SG 245, EPHRAIM AMMONS, $12.39, 61 ac., Sec. 87, Dis. 17. Granted Dec. 12, 1836; registered May 25, 1839.

853 SG 247, EPHRAIM AMMONS, $18.54, 90 ac., Sec. 84, Dis. 17, crossing Wiggins Creek. Granted Dec. 12, 1836; registered May 25, 1839.

854 SG 142, EPHRAIM AMMONS, $10/100 ac., 640 ac. on Silver Mine & White Water Creeks, beginning at fork of the creeks. Granted Dec. 15, 1838; registered May 25, 1839.

855 SG 141, EPHRAIM AMMONS, $5 pre 100 ac., 65 ac. on Haselnut Creek, Dis. 1; incl. the Poplar Grove. Granted Dec. 15, 1838; registered May 26, 1839.

856 SG 144, EPHRAIM AMMONS, $10/100 ac., 300 ac. on west bank of White Water Creek. Granted Dec. 15, 1838; registered May 27, 1839.

857 SG 119, EPHRAIM AMMONS, $5/100 ac., 200 ac. on Horse Pasture Creek of Toxaway River, above where JOHN CLARK lives, on line of Sec. 13, in Dis. 18. Granted May 24, 1838; registered May 27, 1839.

858 SG 148, EPHRIM VANSE AMMONS, $5/100 ac., 50 ac. on E. side of Noland Creek, Dis. 1. Granted Dec. 10, 1838; registered May 27, 1839.

859 SG 168, JACOB TRAMELL, assignee of LINCOLN FULRIM, 171 ac. on N. side of Cartoogachaye Creek, Sec. 2, Dis. 16. Granted Dec. 22, 1831; reg. May 27, 1839.

860 SG 335, BENJAMIN TRAMMELL, $14.56, 71 ac., Sec. 28, Dis. 18, bd. AMOS PODGIN'S improvement, crossing Flat Cr. Granted Dec. 12, 1836; reg. May 27, 1839.

861 SG 379, JOHN LEDFORD, assignee of HENRY DRYMAN for $23.60, 118 ac. on Sec. 13, Dis. 13, on the river. Granted Mar. 1, 1838; registered May 27, 1839.

862 SG 139, JACOB DEITZ, $5/100 ac., 50 ac. on W. fork of Tuckasegee River, Dis. 7, on corner of Sec. 24. Granted Dec. 12, 1838; registered May 27, 1839.

863 SG 242, WILLIAM SUTTON, $5/100 ac., 100 ac. in Dis. 8, on Savannah Creek of Tuckaseegee, corner of Sec. 147. Granted Dec. 15, 1838; registered May 28, 1839.

864 SG 179, WILLIAM COWEN, $5/100 ac., 50 ac. on Little Savannah Creek in Dis. 7, on J. FRIEZLE line. Granted Dec. 15, 1838; registered May 28, 1839.

865 SG 431, JOHN MOORE, $444.84, 87 ac., Sec. 52, Dis. 15, crossing "Cartoogayeye" (Cartoogechaye) Creek. Granted Jan. 7, 1839; registered May 28, 1839.

866 SG 242, DAVID SUTTON, $5/100 ac., 50 ac. on Tuckaseegee River, Dis. 8, on line of Sec. 147. Granted Dec. 15, 1838; registered May 28, 1839.

867 SG 174, JOSEPH CLEMENTS, $5/100 ac. W. side of Tennessee River, Dis. 17, on corner of Sec. 30. Granted Dec. 15, 1838; registered May 28, 1839.

868 SG 186, GEORGE W. GREEN, $5/100 ac., 50 ac., Green's fork of Savannah Cr. of
Tuckasegee R., Dis. 8, bd. Sec. 152. Granted Dec. 15, 1838; reg. May 28, 1839.

869 SG 123, ISAAC MORRISON, $5/100 ac., 3 ac. 96 poles on W. side of Tuckasegee River
in Dis. 8, on corner of what is called the HEX Tract, running with HALL's line, SILER's
line. Granted Dec. 15, 1838; registered May 28, 1839.

870 SG 134, BENJAMIN F. MORRISON, $5/100 ac., 100 ac. on waters of Savannah Creek
in Dis. 8, on corner of Sec. 9. Granted Dec. 15, 1838; registered May 28, 1839.

871 SG 269, JAMES WEATHEROWE, $5/100 ac., 80 ac. on Watauga Creek, Dis. 10, on
NW corner of Sec. 112. Granted Dec. 15, 1838; registered May 28, 1839.

872 SG 444, JAMES WEATHEROWE, assignee of ELIJAH JOHNSON for $_____, 105 3/4
ac., Sec. 50, Dis. 10. Granted Jan. 7, 1839; registered June 3, 1839.

873 SG 203, BENJAMIN JOHNSTON Sr., $5/100 ac., 50 ac., Dis. 15, Cartoogechaye) Cr.,
bd. JOSEPH SMITH. Granted Dec. 15, 1838; registered June 3, 1839.

874 SG 442, SAMUEL SMITH Jr., $___, 60 ac., Sec. 18, Dis. 13, crossing Tessenty Creek.
Granted Jan. 7, 1839; registered June 3, 1839.

875 SG 335, WILLIAM MCCLURE, $5/100 ac., 50 ac. on N. side of Tennessee River, Dis.
13, on corner of Sec. 4. Granted Apr. 17, 1839; registered June 3, 1839.

876 SG 334, WILLIAM MCCLURE, $5/100 ac., 50 ac. on N. side of Tennessee River, Dis.
13, on corner of Sec. 2, on corner of KELLY's land.

877 SG 503, SAMUEL SMITH for $1940.84, 53 ac., Sec. 132, Dis. 3. Granted Jan. 7, 1839;
registered June 3, 1839.

878 SG 333, JOHN MCCLURE for $5/100 ac., 100 ac. on Sugar Town Creek near the Bleue
Ridge, Dis. 12, beginning a short distance below JEFFESON BRISON's cabbin.
Granted Apr. 17, 1839; registered June 3, 1839.

879 SG 533, JOHN TATHAM for $45.26, 208 ac., Sec. 107, Dis. 6. Granted Jan. 7, 1839;
registered June 3, 1839.

880 SG 534 to JOHN TATHAM for $20, 100 ac., Sec. 1, Dis. 9, beginning on side of a mtn.
20 poles W. of tract leading from COL. JOHN TATHAM's to Cheoee on head waters of
S. fork of Cheoee (Cheoah) River. Granted Jan. 7, 1839; registered June 3, 1839.

881 THOS. GRIBBLE to THOMAS MONTEATH, both of Macon, for $250, a tract of land
beginning on Tuckaseejah River, to mouth of small branch known as the Dividing
Branch. July 5, 1837. *Thomas (his X mark) Gribble.* Wit: *J.B. LOVE, ALLEN FISHER.*
Ack. in Mar. 1839 court. Registered June 4, 1839.

881 JOHN DEHART to ALLEN FREEMAN for $35, 100 ac. in Dis. 8, beginning near road
leading to Franklin, on corner of No. 34. Mar. 18, 1839. *John Dehart.* Wit: *JAS. H. (his X
mark) WIGGINS, ABRAM (his X mark) WIGGINS.* Ack. by John D. Heart in Mar. 1839
court. Registered June 4, 1839.

882 JAMES MCDOWELL of Burke Co., NC to JOHN GIBBS Jr. of Haywood Co. NC,
Negro girl, JANE, aged 14-15, for $400. Oct. 6, 1825. *James McDowell.* Wit: *HUGH
GIBBS, GUS SHETLUN(?).* Proven by Hugh Gibbs, Mar. 1839 court. Reg. June 4, 1839.

883 J.R. JOHNSON to MILES SANDERS, both of Macon, for $40, 12+ac. on S. side
Watauga Creek. Feb. 2, 1838. *Joseph R. Johnson.* Wit: *JAMES WETHEROWE, HENRY
SANDERS.* Ack. in March 1839 court. Registered June 4, 1839.

884 JOSEPH SHERREL to JOHN DEHART for $50, 100 ac. in Dis. 8, on line of Sec. 34.
Mar. 16, 1839. *Joseph (his X mark) Sherrel.* Wit: *JOHN CHAMBERS, JAMES COL-
VERD.* Proven by James Colvard in March 1839 session. Registered June 4, 1839.

885 LEVY WILSON to WILLIAM WEST, both of Macon, for $80, 100 ac. on E. fork Savan-
nah Creek, Dis. 8, near what is called the JOHN HEGDEN improvement. Jan. 21, 1839.
Levi Wilson. Wit: *JOHN HOWARD, DANIEL WEST.* Proven by John Howard in Jan.
1839 court. Registered June 4, 1839.

886 JAMES POTEAT, WILLIAM P. POTEAT & BARNET M. POTEAT of Macon to
JOHN N. DEYTON for $100, 88 ac., Sec. 1, Dis. 11 on Tennessee R. near mouth of
Watauga Cr., near the County Rd.; tract orig. purchased from state by ENOS SHIELDS.
Dec. __, 1838. *B.M. Poteat, W.P. Poteat and James Poteat.* Wit: *SAMUEL SANDERS,
J.R. JOHNSON.* Proven by J.R. Johnson in Jan. 1839 session. Registered June 4, 1839.

887 PETER MILLER to SAMUEL BRYSON for $200, 50 1/2 ac., Sec. 4, Dis. 9, and 67 ac.,
Sec. 5, Dis. 9 on Georges Creek. Jan 25, 1839. *Peter Miller.* Wit: *J.W. GUINN.* Ack. in
March 1839 session. Registered June 4, 1839.

888 SILAS LITTLEJOHN of Macon to THOMAS GRIBBLE for $70, 50 ac. on corner of
Sec. 30, on line of Sec. 31 (no District given). Dec. 2, 1837. *Silas Littlejohn.* Wit:
SAMUEL MONTIETH, JACOB DEITZ. Proven by Monteith in March 1839 session.
Registered June 4, 1839.

888 UTE SHERREL to JOHN GIBBS, both of Macon, for $400, Negro man, BEN, age be-
tween 30 & 40 years. Mar. 14, 1832. *Ute Sherrell.* Wit: *W.H. THOMAS.* Proven by Wm.
H. Thomas in March 1839 court. Registered June 12, 1839.

889 JOSEAH WARD to JOHN HOWARD, both of Macon, for $100, 71 ac. on Tennessee
R., Sec. 70, Dis. 13, the tract where Ward now lives, bought at the land sale in Franklin
in 1836. Ward has not yet obtained grant. Jan. 7, 1839. *Joseah Ward.* Wit: *HUGH
WHITE, SAMUEL RUNNELS.* Proven by Runnels in June 1839 session. Registered June
30, 1839.

890 SG 498 to JESSE R. SILAR for $31.15, 115 ac., Sec. 23, Dis. 6, description mentions
rich hollow. Granted Jan. 7, 1839; registered June 5, 1839.

891 SG 302, WILLIAM H. THOMAS for $10/100 ac., 640 ac. on S. side Tennessee R.,
beginning on bank of river, 4 poles below the Fort Lindsey ford, running with the old
treaty line. Granted Dec. 24, 1838; registered June 5, 1839.

892 SG 304, JESSE R. SILAR for $5/100 ac., 100 ac. on NE side of Tenesee R., District 8,
on corner Sec. 57, line of Sec. 37. Granted Dec. 24, 1838; registered June 5, 1839.

893 SG 303, JESSE R. SILAR for $5/100 ac., 50 ac. on E. bank of Tennessee River, bd. tract
where JAMES SHERER lives. Granted Dec. 24, 1838; registered June 5, 1839.

894 SG 489, JESSE R. SILER for $17.60, 88 ac., Sec. 31, Dis. 12, on SE bank of Nantahalee
River on upper end of an island. Granted Jan. 7, 1839; registered June 5, 1839.

895 SG 486, J.R. SELAR for $13.20, 66 ac., Sec. 29, Dis. 12, on NW bank of Nantahalee
River, on corner of Sec. 27. Granted Jan. 7, 1839; registered June 5, 1839.

896 SG 487, JESSE R. SILER for 139 ac., Sec. 14, Dis. 12 , on W. bank of Nantahalee River,
on upper corner of Sec. 13. Granted Jan. 7, 1839; registered June 5, 1839.

897 SG 488, J.R. SILAR for $12.40, 62 ac., Sec. 26, Dis. 12, on Nantahalee River, upper
corner of Sec. 25, near a clift of rock. Granted Jan. 7, 1839; registered June 5, 1839.

898 SG 491, J.R. SILAR for $16.06, 73 ac., Sec. 28, Dis. 12, Nantahala R., opposite the
Town House on Nantahala. Granted Jan. 7, 1839; registered June 5, 1839.

899 SG 499, J.R. SELAR for $14, 70 ac., Sec. 1, Dis. 12, on S. bank of Tennessee R. op-
posite lower end of J.R. Siler's plantation, above what is called the Gap in the Tennessee
Rd. Granted Jan. 7, 1839; registered June 5, 1839.

900 SG 500, JESSE R. SILER for $15.60, 52 ac., Sec. 27, Dis. 12, on NW bank of Nan-
tahalee River. Granted Jan. 7, 1839; registered June 5, 1839.

901 SG 492, J.R. SILAR for $12.40, 62 ac., Sec. 30, Dis. 12, on NW bank of Nantahalee
River, on upper corner of Sec. 29. Granted Jan. 7, 1839; registered June 5, 1839.

902 SG 493, J.R. SELEIR for $16.40, 82 ac., Sec. 16, Dis. 12, on W. bank of Nantahalee
River, on line of Sec. 14. Granted Jan. 7, 1839; registered June 5, 1839.

903 SG 495, JESSE R. SILER for $14.20, 121 ac., Sec. 78, Dis. 12, on ridge dividing Tenn.
& Nantahalee R., on Macon Co. or treaty line. Granted Jan. 7, 1839; reg. June 6, 1839.

904 SG 496, JESSE R. SELAR for $39.90, 190 ac., Sec. 17, Dis. 6. Granted Jan. 7, 1839; registered June 6, 1839.

905 SG 497, JESSE R. SILER for $16.40, 82 ac., Sec. 22, Dis. 12, on E. bank of Nantahalee R. Granted Jan. 7, 1839; registered June 6, 1839.

906 SG 494, J.R. SILAR for $12.20, 61 ac., Sec. 19, Dis. 12, on W. bank of Nantahalee R. Granted Jan. 7, 1839; registered June 6, 1839.

907 SG 501, J.R. SILAR for $17, 85 ac., Sec. 24, Dis. 12, E. bank of Nantahalee R. opposite an Indian Town House. Granted Jan. 7, 1839; registered June 6, 1839.

908 SG 505, J.R. SILAR for $10, 50 ac., Sec. 28, Dis. 12, beginning near top of a ridge. Granted Jan. 7, 1839; registered June 6, 1839.

909 SG 538, JESSE R. SILER asssignee of ENOS SHIELDS for $13 paid by Shields, 53 ac., Sec. 44, Dis. 11. Granted Mar. 13, 1839; registered June 6, 1839.

910 SG 530, JESSE R. SILEIR, assignee of JAMES POTEAT, for $631.05 1/2 paid by Poteat, 175 ac., Sec. 27, Dis. 16. Granted Feb. 7, 1839; reg. June 6, 1839.

911 SG 529, JAMES BRYSON Sr., $16.24, 65 ac., Sec. 84, Dis. 11, beg. where an Indian Reservation line intersects line of Sec. 47. Granted Jan. 19, 1839; registered June 6, 1839.

912 GEORGE CUNNINGHAM of Haywood Co. NC to MILES SANDERS of Macon for $300, 82+ ac., Wattaga Creek, Sec. 52, Dis. 10. Mar. 26, 1839. *George (his X mark) Cunningham.* Wit: *J.K. GRAY, U. KEENER.* Ack. June 1839 court. Reg. June 12, 1839.

913 E. AMONS to ALEXANDER ZACHARY of Macon, for $5, 300 ac., Toxaway & Chattooga R., Chimney Top Mtn., Sec. 99, Dis. 18. Jan. 26, 1839. *Ephrim Ammons.* Wit: *JONATHAN ZACKARY, S. MCDOWELL.* McDowell proved in Mar.1839 court. Reg. June 13, 1839.

914 SG 438, ARON ROBISON for $___, 50 ac., Sec. 120, Dis. 10. Granted Jan. 7, 1839; registered June 13, 1839.

915 SG 437, ARON ROBISON for $___, 51 ac., Sec. 118, Dis. 10. Granted Jan. 7, 1839; registered June 12, 1839.

916 SG 238, ARON ROBISON for $5/100 ac., 95 ac. on Tennessee R., Dis. 10, on corner of Sec. 120. Granted Dec. 15, 1838; registered June 13, 1839.

917 R.V. MICHAUX rec'd of JESSE R. SILAR, JOHN HALL, JAMES ROBISON, DAVID R. LOWRY, JAMES K. GRAY, THOMAS J. ROAN, SILAS MCDOWELL, N.S. JARRETT, SAUL SMITH & JOHN HOWARD, $2,500 for 5/6 of Stallion Marblieu, purch. of the late HON. JOHN RANDOLPH of Roanoke, Charlotte Co. VA, & of the following pedigree from original ms.furnished by WYATT CARDWELL, mgr. for estate of John Randolph, dec'd. Marblieu was foaled in1832, got by old Monsurr(?) Tonson, his dam got by (Imp) Blustir, G-dam, Slaterd by Alexander, the GG-dam by (Imp) Buzzard, GGG-dam Rose by Sweet Brier, GGGG-dam Miss Morleton by Snap, GGGGG-dam Miss Windor by the Godolphin Arabian Young Belgrade Barlets Childers Devonshire Chestnut Arabian Ceorven bay Back old Shot old Woodcock. Jun.13, 1839. *R.V. Michaux.* Wit: *ROBERT HUGGINS,* who proved, June 1839. Registered June 15, 1839.

918 SG 393, SAMUEL SMITH for $___, 212 ac., Sec. 14, Dis. 13, on Tennessee River, crossing Tessenty Creek. Granted Dec. 24, 1838; registered July 17, 1839.

919 SG #391, SAMUEL SMITH for $___, 120 ac., Sec. 15, Dis. 13 on Tennessee R., on SW corner of Sec. 14. Granted Dec. 24, 1838; registered July 19, 1839.

920 JAMES WALKER to JOSEPH BRINDLE, both of Macon, for val. rec'd, 65 ac., Sec. 56, Dis. 10, purch. 1836 at Franklin. Aug. 9, 1838. *James Walker.* Wit: *WM. O. MULE, WM. HICKS.* Proven by Wm. Hicks in June 1839 session. Registered Sep. 15, 1839.

920 JONATHAN PHILIPS, Esq., Ch'man of County Court of Macon, to JAMES ROBIN-
     SON, of Macon, for $226.50, Lot 15 in Franklin, N. side of main street, adj. public
     square & Robinson's own lot, 150 poles, orig. purch. by JOSEPH WELCH for $250,
     secured by note pd with interest by James Robinson, who has purchased interest of
     Joseph Welch & B.S. BRITTAIN, and obtained certificate of sale executed May 22,
     1835 to Welch by J.R. SILAR & JOHN HALL, commissioners. June 15, 1839. *J. Philips
     Ch.* Wit: *SAUL SMITH, JOHN HOWARD.* Ack. June 1839. Reg. Sep. 15, 1839.

922 CLARK BIRD to GOLDMAN BRYSON, both of Macon, for $27.50, 55 ac. on Tellico
     Creek, Sec. 3 of the SUWAGAH's Reservation. Apr. 20, 1839. *Clark Bird.* Wit: *JAMES
     MORGAN.* Ack. in June 1839 session. Registered Sep. 13, 1839.

922 Sheriff's Sale: ELI MCKEE Esq, High Sh'ff of Macon, to JAMES ROBINSON of
     Macon, to satisfy 2 judgments of County Ct. against JOSEPH WELCH, one of $52.50,
     int. & cost, in favor of G. BLACKWELL; the other, $126.36, int. & cost, in favor of
     BAKER & SPROWLS: in Franklin, house, Lot 15, 150 poles, N. side Main St., & cross
     st. At sale Jun. 13, 1839, Robinson had high bid of $125. June 14, 1839. *Eli Mckee.* Wit:
     N.W. WOODFIN, JOHN HOWARD. Ack. in June 1839 court. Reg. Sep. 13, 1839.

924 Sheriff's Sale: THOMAS J. ROANE Esq, High Sh'ff of Macon, to DILLARD LOVE of
     Macon, to satisfy judgment of Burke Co. Sup. Ct. against JOSEPH WELCH & others for
     $417.54 & costs recovered by ISAAC T. AVERY, agent, of Welch & others: 640 ac. on
     Tuckaseige R., a reservation taken by YONA AWKWA alias BIG BEAR. At sale Nov.
     21, 1838. Love had high bid of $56. Jun. 12, 1839. *Thos. J. Roan, Shff.* Wit: (none). Ack.
     in court. Reg. Sep. 13, 1839.

926 Sheriff's Sale: ELI MCKEE Esq., High Sh'ff of Macon to JAMES ROBINSON, to satis-
     fy judgments of Supr. Ct. of ___ against BENJAMIN S. BRITTAIN (1) in favor of
     JAMES BRITTAIN for $244.85 & costs; (2) in favor of DAVID NEWLAND for
     $17.74; (3) in favor of J.B. TRAMMELL for costs, $91.40: Lot 15 in Franklin, 150 poles
     adj. James Robinson's lot & public square, N. side Main St., with houses & improve-
     ments made by JOSEPH WELCH & others. At sale, June 13, 1839, Robinson gave high
     bid of $125. June 15, 1839. *Eli Mckee, Shff.* Wit: *N.W. WOODFIN, JOHN HOWARD.*
     Ack. in June 1839 session. Registered Sep. 13, 1839.

928 Sheriff's Sale: THOMAS J. ROAN Esq., High Sh'ff of Macon, to DILLARD LOVE of
     Macon, to satisfy judgments of Co. Ct. of Macon against JOSEPH WELCH for $67.21 &
     $13.21 costs in favor of G. BLACKWELL & one of $141.10 & $9.35 costs in favor of
     SAM'L SPROWLS, J.W. BAKER & E.F. GREGORY, partners in trade under name of
     BAKER, SPROWL & CO: 54 ac., N. side Tennessee R. & confluence of Tenn. & Tuck-
     aseige R., Sec. 1, Dis. 1; also 53+ ac., Sec. 38, Dis. 8, intersection of Tenn. & Tuckaseige
     R. At sale, Sep. 28, 1838, Love had high bid of $50. June 24, 1839. *Thos. J. Roane,
     Sh'ff.* Wit: *J.W. GUINN, WM. M. PENLAND.* Ack. Mar. 1839 ct. Reg. Sep. 13, 1839.

931 CLARK BIRD to GOLDMAN BRYSON, both of Macon, for $13, 63 ac. on Tellico
     Creek, Dis. 17, Sec. 1 of SAWAGAH's Reservation. Apr. 13, 1839. *Clark Bird.* Wit:
     JAMES MORGAN. Ack. in June 1839 court. Registered Sep. 16, 1839.

932 WILLIAM MORE to THOMAS J. ROANE, both of Macon, for val. rec'd, 223 ac., Sec.
     105, Dis. 2, both sides of Shooting Creek, purchased Sep. 5, 1838, at sale in Franklin.
     Nov. 13, 1838. *Wm. More.* Wit: *J.K. GRAY, JAMES ROBINSON.* Reg. Sep. 17, 1839.

932 JOSEPH R. JOHNSON to JAMES WITHROW, both of Macon, for $350, 66+ ac, Sec.
     48, Dis. 10, crossing Watauga Cr. June 28, 1839. *J.R. Johnson.* Wit: *WM. G. WATTS,
     E.I. JOHNSON.* Proven by Wm. G. Watts in Mar. 1839 court. Registered Sep. 17, 1839.

933 JOSEPH R. JOHNSON to JAMES WITHROW, both of Macon, for $50, Sec. 54, Dis.
     10, 25 ac. on line between Johnson & COOK, near State Rd. & on cond. line between
     Johnson & SAUNDERS. June 28, 1839. *J.R. Johnson.* Wit: *WM. G. WATTS, E.
     JOHNSON.* Proven by Wm. G. Watts in Mar. 1839 court. Registered Sep. 18, 1839.

934 Mortgage: JOHN A. BELL of 1st part to JOHN H. LEDFORD, ULRIC KEENER, JAMES ROBINSON & DANIEL NICHOLDS of 2nd part and SILAS MCDOWEL of 3rd part. Bell mortgages to McDowel the following lots in Franklin: No. 33 (1 ac.), No. 34 (1 ac.), No. 35(1 ac.), No. 36 (155 poles), No. 37 (150 poles), No. 38 (150 poles), No. 39 on Main Street (150 poles), No. 40 (150 poles). Bell to pay agent of Bank of State of NC at Morganton $300 in discharge of note sec. by Ledford & Keener; $100 to Robinson on note; also balance due State for land whereon Bell lately lived; also, pay Nicholds to the use of a SILAR PETER (Peter Siler). Mar. 30, 1839. *J.A. Bell.* Wit: *JOHN HOWARD, DAVID PASSMORE.* Ack. in Mar. 1839 court. Reg. Sep. 18, 1839.

936 THOMAS J. ROANE to WILLIAM HICKS, both of Macon, for $650, tract of land, Sec. 28, Dis. 16. Oct. 27, 1835. *Thos. J. Roane.* Wit: *JONATHAN B. HUNT, J.R. SILER.* Proven by J.R. Siler in June 1839 court. Registered Sep. 18, 1839.

937 Deed of Gift: HENRY WILLSON of Macon, for further encouragement of two of JOHN MATHEWS' children, ADAM N. MATHIS & SARAH MELVINA N. MATHIS, & for $4, sell to the children 3 cattle, one brown & white cow to Adam and a heifer & calf to Sarah Melvina. Apr. 3, 1839. *Henry Willson.* Wit: *ENOCH UNDERWOOD.* Ack. in June 1839 court. Reg. Sep. 18, 1839.

938 JOS. R. JOHNSON to JAMES WITHROW, both of Macon, 89 ac., Sec. 112, Dis. 10, purchased of State at Oct. 27, 1836 land sale. June 28, 1837. *J.R. Johnson.* Wit: *WM. G. WATTS, E. JOHNSON.* Proven by Watts in Mar. 1839 court. Reg. Sep. 18, 1839.

939 SILAS MCDOWEL to WILLIAM M. LAMBERT, both of Macon, for $26.34, tract on S. side of Sugartown Fork of Tennessee R., Sec. 26, Dis. 12, originally granted to SAM'L D. FENDLY & by him conveyed to McDowel Dec. 29, 1835 by patent No. 26. Jun. 1, 1839. *S. McDowel.* Wit: *J.A. BELL, J. ROBINSON.* Proven in June 1839 session. Registered Sep. 19, 1839.

940 Deed of Gift: WILLIAM BIRD of Macon to WILLIAM B. MORGAN for nat'l love & affection for WILLIAM K. MORGAN, grandson by marriage of sd William Bird, & infant son of William B. Morgan by ANN BIRD, Wm. Bird's wife; give to William K. Morgan, the infant child, 50 ac. on Rabit Creek on which William B. Morgan now lives, Sec. 16, Dis. 11, for purpose of enabling William B. Morgan to raise William K. Morgan on sd tract. Mar. 15, 1839. *Wm. (his X mark) Bird.* Wit: *WM. ROANE,* who proved in March 1839 court. Registered Sep. 19, 1839.

941 SG 95, JOHN GALLISPEE, $5/100 ac. for 50 ac. on Cartoogachaye in Dis. 15. Granted Feb. 26, 1838; registered Sep. 19, 1839.

942 SG 372, JOHN GILLISPIE for $___, 51 ac., Sec. 144, Dis. 15. Granted Mar. 1, 1838; registered Sep. 19, 1839.

943 SG 537, JESSE R. SILAR assignee of JOHN WOODY, for $333.96 paid by Woody, 116 ac., Sec. 5, Dis. 16. Granted Mar. 15, 1838; registered Sep. 19, 1839.

944 SG 328, ABNER MOORE, $5/100 ac., 50 ac. in Dis. 11 on Sugartown River, on corner of Sec. 54. Granted Jan. 5, 1839; registered Sep. 19, 1839.

945 SG 539, JOHN STEVENSTON for $673.79, 300 ac., Sec. 4, Dis. 16, in a marshe at a spring having crossed the "Cautoogajay" (Cartoogechaye Cr.). Granted Mar. 13, 1839; registered Sep. 20, 1839.

946 SG 291, WILLIAM G. WATTS for $5/100 ac., 40 ac. in Dis. 10 on Tennessee R. Granted Dec. 15, 1838; registered Sep. 20, 1839.

947 SG 172, JOHN CLURE for $5/100 ac., 50 ac. on Lowry's fork of Cartoogachaye Creek in Dis. 15. Granted Dec. 15, 1838; registered Sep. 20, 1839.

948 SG 271, ELI WALDROOP, $5/100 ac., 50 ac. S. side Lowry's Fork of Cartoogachaye Creek, Dis. 15, near the mile road, on corner of Sec. 133. Granted Dec. 15, 1838; registered Sep. 21, 1839.

949 SG 246, THOMAS AMMONS for $11.75, 58 ac. on W. side Sugartown fork of Tennessee R., Sec. 68, Dis. 12. Granted Dec. 12, 1836; registered Sep. 21, 1839.

950 SG 542, JONATHAN BIRD assignee of BENJAMIN S. BRITTAIN for $__, 142 ac. on S. side Iolee (Iotla) Cr., Sec. 56, Dis. 16. Granted Apr. 13, 1833; registered Sep. 21, 1839.

951 SG 266, JAMES THOMAS, $5/100 ac., 50 ac. on Brush Creek, Dis. 8, on line of Sec. 48. Granted Dec. 15, 1838; registered Sep. 21, 1839.

952 SG 290, FRANCIS WARD, $5/100 ac., 50 ac. on Savannah Creek, Dis. 8, on line of Sec. 151. Granted Dec. 15, 1838; registered Sep. 23, 1839.

953 SG 184, BUCKNER GUYE, $5/100 ac., 100 ac. on Julyes Branch on S. side of Sugar Town R., Dis. 11. Granted Dec. 15, 1838; registered Sep. 23, 1839.

954 SG 151, THOMAS AMMONS, $5/100 ac., 100 ac. on Walnut Creek waters of Sugartown fork, Dis. 12. Granted Dec. 15, 1838; registered Sep. 23, 1839.

955 SG 366, THOMAS AMMONS, assignee of ROBERT PHILLIPS, for $100 paid by Phillips, 50 ac., mouth of Walnut Cr., Sec. 30, Dis. 12. Granted Mar. 1, 1838; registered Sep. 23, 1839.

956 SG 181, MATHEW DAVES, $5/100 ac., 50 ac. S. side of "Elijah" (Ellijay) Cr., Dis. 11, on S. boundary of Sec. 89. Granted Dec. 15, 1838; registered Sep. 23, 1839.

957 SG 42, JOSEPH BRENDLE, $5/100 ac., 100 ac. on Tennessee R., on line of Sec. 54 (Dis. not given). Granted Jan. 25, 1837; registered Sep. 23, 1839.

958 SG 129, ISAAC ASHE, $5/100 ac., 100 ac. in Dis. 8, bounded by Sec. 5 & Sec. 3. Granted Dec. 12, 1838; registered Sep. 23, 1839.

959 SG 125, JOHN ZACKARY, $5/100 ac., 640 ac. on "Chattoogee" (Chattooga R.), Dis. 18, bd. S.J. ZACHARY's entered line. Granted Nov. 21, 1838; registered Sep. 23, 1839.

960 SG 196, JOSEPH HICKS, $5/100 ac., 75 ac. on Croain Fork of "Coweter" (Coweeta) Creek, Dis. 14, corner of Sec. 38. Granted Dec. 15, 1838; registered Sep. 23, 1839.

961 JOHN LEDFORD to ASKU CURTIS for $500, 118 ac., Tennessee R., Sec. 13, Dis. 13, incl. farm where Ledford formerly lived. Dec. 26, 1838. *John Ledford.* Wit: *BRYANT GIBBS, JOHN MCDOWELL.* McDowell proved in Mar.1839 court. Reg. Sep. 23, 1839.

962 ENOS CRAWFORD to JOHN GILISPIE, both of Macon, for $175, 54 ac., Sec. 36, Dis. 15, on the "Warior" (Wayah) fork of Cartoogachaye Creek. Feb. 27, 1838. *Enos Crawford.* Wit: *JACOB SILAR, HARRIET E. SILAR.* Proven by Jacob Silar in June 1839 court. Registered Sep. 23, 1839.

963 REBECAH MCDANIEL to JOHN GILLISPIE, both of Macon, for $15, 61+ ac., part of Sec. 33, Dis. 15. Jan. 29, 1839. *Rebecca (her X mark) McDaniel.* Wit: *ANDREW MCDANIEL, THOMAS H. MCDANIEL.* Ack. in June 1839 court. Reg. Sep. 23, 1839.

964 A.B. DONALDSON to J.R. ALLMAN, both of Macon, for $500, 1 ac., Lot 44 on main st., Franklin, corner of Lot 30 occupied by MRS. LAMBERT. May 22, 1839. *A.B. Donaldson.* Wit: *WM. M. PENLAND, CALVIN M. MCCLOUD.* Ack. in June 1839 court. Registered Sep. 23, 1839.

965 MATHEW DAVES of Cass Co., GA to ABNER MOORE of Macon, for $1500, 3 tracts in Dis. 11: 96 ac., Sec. 54; 50 ac. adj. LEDFORD's land on the east, incl. a (cave? cove?) known as M. Daves' Still House (Cave? Cove?); and 3 ac. transferred by T.B. MOORE to Daves, on a ridge down to Mill Pond, below old Road, part of Sec. 53 on Ellijah (Ellijay Creek). Feb. 7, 1839. *Mat Daves.* Wit: *L. BRADLEY, H. HAGIN.* Proven by Hagin in June 1839 court. Registered Sep. 23, 1839.

966 LEVI WILLSON to RICHARD WILLSON for $10, 90 ac. on Savannah Cr. of Tuckaseigee, Dis. 8, above sd Willson's farm. Feb. 15, 1839. *Levi Willson.* Wit: *W.M. TATHAM, WALTER SOMES?* Proven by Tatham in Mar.1838 court. Reg. Sep. 23, 1839.

967 SG 123, BENJAMIN HIDE, $5/100 ac., 100 ac. on Tuckaseige R. Dis. 8, on corner of Sec. 69. Granted Dec. 15, 1838; registered Sep. 24, 1839.

968 SG 323, BERRICK NORTON, $5/100 ac., 200 ac. in Dis. 18, on Thompson's fork of Toxaway R. Granted Dec. 27, 1838; registered Sep. 25, 1839.

969 SG 126, JOSEPH KEENER & J.B. ALLISON, $10/100 ac., 200 ac., near top of mountain, near an E. course from SAM'L HICKS' house on Savannah Creek, Dis. 8, corner of Sec. 161. Granted Nov. 22, 1838; registered Sep. 25, 1839.

970 SG 318, HUGH BROWN, $5/100 ac., 50 ac. in Dis. 5, on W. side of S. fork of Tuckaseige R. Granted Dec. 27, 1838; registered Sep. 1839.

971 SG 376? (blotted), HUGH BROWN, $5/100 ac., 50 ac. in Dis. 5, S. fork of Tuckaseige R., incl. improvement in Poplar Cove. Granted Dec. 27, 1838; reg. Sep. 25, 1839.

972 SG 177, WILLIAM COCKERHAM, $5/100 ac., 50 ac. on Tuckaseige R. Dis. 8, about 30 poles from sd Cockerham's old still house. Granted Dec. 15, 1838; reg. Sep. 25, 1839.

973 SG 127, NATHAN B. THOMPSON, $5/100 ac., 50 ac., Tuckaseige R., Dis. 8, near head of WM. COCKERHAM's Mill Branch. Grant Nov. 22, 1838; reg. Sep. 25, 1839.

974 I, JAMES ROBINSON have rec'd of PETER, a mulatto slave abt 37, $500 for balance of time he is bound to service & release all control I have over him, authorizing him to act as a free man as far as the laws of any of the states may justify him in doing so, etc., justifying him in passing out of NC, conforming to laws of states through which he may go until he takes up his abode in Ohio or elsewhere. Peter (now called PETER SILAR) was born property of JOHN MCLAINE of Rutherford Co. NC, sold to JAMES MURRAY of Buncombe Co. NC & raised by him, by him sold to JESSE R. SILAR & by him to myself. He is abt 5 ft., 9 in. high, mulatto, spare made, rather stoop-shouldered, scar on right cheek running from corner of his mouth, one tooth out & scar on forefinger of left hand, very complaisant when he talks. Sep. 25, 1839. *James Robinson.* Wit: *H.G. WOODFIN, N.S. JARRITT.* In Sep. 1839 court, SILAS MCDOWELL swore he was acquainted with all signators. Reg. Sep. 25, 1839. RICHMOND M. PEARSON, judge of Superior Ct., certified that McDowell is clerk of court. Reg. Sep. 25, 1839.

975 BENJAMIN S. BRITTAIN of Macon, to CHARLES HAYS of Buncombe Co., NC, for $100, land on Iolee (Iotla) Cr., Sec. 47, Dis. 16. Sep. 27, 1838. *B.S. Brittain.* Wit: *JOHN HOWARD.* Proven in Sep. 1839 session of court. Registered Sep. 26, 1839.

976 Mortgage: ULRICK KEENER to JOS. KEENER for performance of debts he owes the following: ALEXANDER ROBISON, $72 & interest, JAMES ROBINSON, J.R. ALLMON & J.A. BELL, security; ditto, $75 & interest, WILY JONES, security; James Robinson, note of $25 & his book acc't, not known; J.R. SILAR a book acc't of more than $125; JACOB SILAR by note & book acc't, $40; heirs of DAVID FULTON, dec'd, $145.75; SAM'L Y. JAMISON, $45; MATTHEW RUSSELL, $100 due 25 Dec. next; ABIA JONES, $15 & interest; Wily Jones, $18; GUDGER & SMITH, $50 & interest; JAMES M. SMITH, $127& interest; JNO. REYNOLDS, $16; T.K. CATLET, bal. of note $30; JAMES M. ALEXANDER, $70; State of NC, $100; WILLIAM CUNNINGHAM, $14; N.S. JARRETT, $31; J.R. Allmon, $21; J. & W.W. DOBSON $52, judgment stayed for JAMES MCLURE to ROB'T HUGGINS, $5. To secure payment of debts, (Ulrick) Keener has appt'd Joseph Keener trustee & conveyed following property: 40 ac. in Dis. 11, bounded by the lands of THOS. ROGERS, J.R. SILAR & WM. DEAL; 50 ac. in Cherokee Co. on headwaters of TUNEE's (Tuni) Cr., Dis. 2, No. 38, $15 incumbrance. Also, 3 mares, 2 Brimer(?) colts horses, 6 cows, 6 young cattle, 35 hogs; small wagon & harness; brass brushed clock; silver watch; 5 beds & furniture; all my household & kitchen furniture; cupboard & ware; my book case & library; chest; trunk; loom; man's saddle; side saddle; 3 bridles; several tubs or barrels; 10 stacks of oats; all my crop of corn including my rent of LOUDERMILK & what I am to get of DEAL & WATTS; crop of potatoes, Irish, sweet & yams; 4 hay stacks; 4 bee stands; all my farming utensils. Sep. 24, 1839. *U. Keener.* Wit: *C.T. ROGERS, WM. B. MOSS.* Ack. in Sep. 1839 court. Registered Sep. 26, 1839.

978 SG 228, WILLIAM NEWTON, $5/100 ac., 50 ac. on Deep Creek, Dis. 1. Entered May 2, 1836; granted Dec. 15, 1838; registered Sep. 26, 1839.

979 SG 471, GIDEON F. MORRIS, $31.80, 150 ac., Sec. 90, Dis. 6. Granted Jan. 7, 1839; registered Sep. 27, 1839.

980 JOHN MASON to JOSEPH CLEMMONS for $254, 79+ ac. on W. side Tennessee R., Sec. 30, Dis. 17. Sep. 24, 1829. *John Mason*. Wit: *J. PHILLIPS*. Proven in Sep. 1839 court. Registered Sep. 27, 1839.

981 SG 218, JAMES LEDFORD, $5/100 ac., 50 ac. W. side of Tuckaseigee R. Entered May 2, 1836; granted Dec. 15, 1838; registered Oct. 18, 1839.

982 SG 288, THOMSON WILSON, $5/100 ac., 100 ac. on Tuckaseigee R., Dis. 6, on line of Sec. 36. Entered May 2, 1836; granted Dec. 15, 1838; registered Nov. 25, 1839.

983 SG 213, JAMES LEDFORD, $5/100 ac., 50 ac. on Tuckaseigee R. & Knob Creek, Dis. 6. Entered May 2, 1836; granted Dec. 15, 1838; registered Oct. 18, 1839.

984 SG 275, ALFORD WILSON, $5/100 ac., 100 ac. on East Fork of Tuckaseigee R. Dis. 6, corner of Sec. 25. Entered Sep. 20, 1836; granted Dec. 15, 1838; reg. Nov. 25, 1839.

985 SG 132, WILLIAM R. BUCKANAN, $5/100 ac., 50 ac., S. bank of Tuckaseigee R. Dis. 8. Entered May 2, 1836; granted Dec. 12, 1838; registered Nov. 18, 1839.

986 SG 317, BENJAMIN S. JOHNSTON, $5/100 ac., 15+ ac., David Johnston's Mill Cr., Dis. 16, on his line. Entry Sep. 26, 1837; grant Dec. 27, 1838; registered Nov. 18, 1839.

987 SG 236, ARCHIBALD ROADS, $5/100 ac., 75 ac. on Burningtown Creek, Dis. 17, corner of Sec. 54. Entered Mar. 29, 1837; granted Dec. 15, 1838; reg. Nov. 19, 1839.

988 SG 547, MATTHEW RUSSELL, assignee of JAMES BRYSON, Junr., $71.31, Sec. 47, Dis. 11, Sugar town River. Granted July 9, 1839; registered Nov. 19, 1839.

989 SG 279, ALEXANDER WILSON, $5/100 ac., 100 ac. on Tuckaseigee R. Dis. 6, on corner of Sec. 36. Entered Oct. 3, 1836; granted Dec. 15, 1838; registered Nov. 26, 1839.

990 SG 170, JOHN CONLEY, $5/100 ac., , 50 ac. on "Wessor's Creek," (Wesser) Dis. 8. Entered Aug. 22, 1836; granted Dec. 15, 1838; registered Nov. 26, 1839.

991 SG 276, ALEXANDER WILSON, $5/100 ac., 50 ac. on E. fork Tuckaseigee R. Dis. 6, corner of Sec. 29. Entry May 2, 1839; grant Dec. 15, 1838; registered Nov. 26, 1839.

992 SG 175, JAMES CONLEY, $5/100 ac., 10 ac., on "Weseur's Creek" (Wesser), Dis. 8, on line of Sec. 22. Entry Mar. 17, 1838; grant Dec. 15, 1839; registered Nov. 26, 1839.

993 SG 274, ALEXANDER WILSON, $10/100 ac., 200 ac. on Tuckaseigee R. Dis. 6, beginning about 40 poles south of the hickory knob. Entered Oct. 3, 1836; granted Dec. 15, 1838; registered Nov. 26, 1839.

994 SG 420, JASON FRIZZLE, $12.50, 50 ac., Sec. 142, Dis. 8, on E. fork of Little Savannah. Granted Jan. 7, 1839; registered Dec. 15, 1839.

995 SG 527, SAMUEL SMITH Junr., $___, 90 ac., Sec. 65, Dis. 13, on bank of the river, on corner of Sec. 69, Dis. 15. Granted Jan. 10, 1838; registered Dec. 5, 1839.

996 SG 541, WILLIAM SILER, $12.50, 50 ac., Sec. 138, Dis. 15. Granted Apr. 8, 1839; registered Dec. 5, 1839.

997 SG 368, JESSE R. SILER, assignee of JOHN BRODWAY, for $175, 128 ac., Sec. 21, Dis. 14, on Tennessee R. crossing Commissioners Creek. Granted Mar. 1, 1838; registered Dec. 5, 1839.

998 SG 178, WILLIAM CONLEY, $5/100 ac., 50 ac., E. Side of Creek, Dis. 8, on said Conley's line. Entered Mar. 17, 1838; granted Dec. 15, 1838; registered Dec. 5, 1839.

999 SG 234, WILLIAM PEEK, $5/100 ac., 100 ac. on Sugar town fork of Tennessee R. Dis. 12. Entered May 2, 1836; granted Dec. 15, 1838; registered Dec. 5, 1839.

1000 SG 325, BENJAMIN S. JOHNSTON, $5/100 ac., 50 ac. on DAVID JOHNSTON's Mill Creek, Dis. 16. Entry Jun. 16, 1837; grant Dec. 27, 1838; registered Dec. 5, 1839.

1001 SG 475, FRANCIS POINDEXTURE, $11.80, 59 ac., Sec. 12, Dis. 12, on SW bank of Tennessee R. Granted Jan. 7, 1839; registered Dec. 5, 1839.

1002 SG 227, RODERICK NORTON, $5/100 ac., 50 ac. on top of Elicott Mountain in Dis. 18. Entered May 2, 1836; granted Dec. 15, 1838; registered Dec. 5, 1839.

1003 SG 474, FRANCIS POINDEXTURE, $10.40, 53 ac., Sec. 2, Dis.__, in PARCH CORNFLOWER's Reservation, on W. boundary line.Granted Jan. 7, 1839; registered Dec. 5, 1839.

1004 SG 232, FRANCIS POINDEXTURE, $5/100 ac., 50 ac. on N. side Tennessee R., Dis. 8, corner of Sec. 55. Entry May 2, 1836; grant Dec. 15, 1838; reg. Dec. 5, 1839.

1005 SG 128, LARKIN C. HOOPER, $5/100 ac., 50 ac. on "Culleehee" (Cullowhee) Creek, Dis. 7, corner of Sec. 17. Entered Jan. 31, 1838; granted Dec. 12, 1838; registered Dec. 5, 1839.

1006 SG 188, JAMES HALLAN, $5/100 ac., 50 ac. on "Ellijah" (Ellijay) Creek, Dis. 11, on line of Sec. 71. Entered July 4, 1837; granted Dec. 15, 1838; registered Dec. 5, 1839.

1007 SG 337, WILLIAM MOSS, Junr., $5/100 ac., 100 ac. on Tuckaseigee River, Dis. 6, corner of Sec. 14. Entered Mar. 29, 1837; granted Aug. 28, 1839; registered Dec. 5, 1839.

1008 SG 1008, JOHN H. WATSON, $5/100 ac., 100 ac. on "Culluwhee" Creek, Dis. 7, bd. HENRY WILSON's land. Entry Feb. 5, 1838; grant Dec. 12, 1838; reg. Dec. 5, 1839.

1009 SG 467, MICHAEL LONG, $8.50, 17 ac., Sec. 1, Dis. __, in TEG-IN-TOSEE's Reservation, corner of Survey No. 45 & 11 in Dis. 7. Granted Jan. 7, 1839; reg. Dec. 6, 1839.

1010 SG 212, MICKLE LONG, $5/100 ac., 100 ac. on "Cullewhee" Creek, Dis. 7, bd. DAVID ROGER. Entry Mar. 8, 1838; grant Dec. 15, 1838; registered Dec. 6, 1839.

1011 SG 42, HIRAM DODGIAN, $5/100 ac., 100 ac., Dis. 7, on "Cullewhee" Creek. Entered Oct. 21, 1837; granted SEp. 4, 1839; registered Dec. 6, 1839.

1012 SG 332, RICHARD WILSON, $5/100 ac., 35 ac. on "Cullewhee" Creek, Dis. 7, on line of Sec. 18. Entered May 2, 1837; granted Apr. 13, 1839; registered Dec. 6, 1839.

1013 SG 223, WILLIAM E. MULL, $5/100 ac., 50 ac. on Sugar town Fork of Tennessee R., Dis. 11, corner of Sec. 8. Entry May 2, 1836; grant Dec. 15, 1838; reg. Dec. 6, 1839.

1014 SG 158, JOHN BROWN, $5/100 ac., 50 ac. on "Cullewhee" Creek, both sides of Hamburg Road. Entered May 2, 1836; granted Dec. 15, 1838; registered Dec. 6, 1839.

1015 SG 392, SAMUEL SMITH, $___, 75 ac., Sec. 36, Dis. 13. Granted Dec. 24, 1838; registered Dec. 6, 1839.

1016 SG 338, DAVID GUYER, $5/100 ac., 100 ac. in Dis. 10, on Brown's Creek, on sd Guyer's corner. Entered June 16, 1839; granted Aug. 28, 1839; registered Dec. 6, 1839.

1017 SG 249, SAUL SMITH, $5/100 ac., 30 ac. on Middle Creek, Dis. 13. Entered May 2, 1836; granted Dec. 15, 1838; registered Dec. 6, 1839.

1018 SG 246, SAUL SMITH, $5/100 ac., 30 ac. on Middle Creek, Dis. 13. Entered May 2, 1836; granted Dec. 15, 1838; registered Dec. 6, 1839.

1019 SG 253, SAUL SMITH, $5/100 ac., 40 ac. on Middle Creek, Dis. 13. Entered May 2, 1836; granted Dec. 15, 1838; registered Dec. 6, 1839.

1020 SG 226, RODERICK NORTON, $5/100 ac., 50 ac. on "Chattoogah" River, Dis. 18, corner of Sec. 76 & 79. Entry May 2, 1836; grant Dec. 15, 1838; registered Dec. 6, 1839.

1021 SG 322, BERRICK NORTON, $10/100 ac., 200 ac. on "Chattoogah" River, Dis. 18, line of Sec. 76. Entered July 10, 1836; granted Dec. 27, 1838; registered Dec. 6, 1839.

1022 SG 324, ELIAS NORTON $5/100 ac., 100 ac. on Chattooga River, Dis. 18. Entered May 2, 1836; granted Dec. 27, 1838; registered Dec. 6, 1839.

1023 SG 411, B.W. BELL, $___, 63 ac., Sec. 79, Dis. 18, on Norton Fork of "Chattuega" River. Granted Jan. 7, 1839; registered Dec. 6, 1839.

1024 SG 319, ELIZABETH NORTON, $5/100 ac., 100 ac. on Chattooga R., E. side of Big
      Creek, incl. a small improvement. Entered July 10, 1836; granted Dec. 27, 1838;
      registered Dec. 7, 1839.

1025 SG 320, MIRA NORTON, $5/100 ac., 100 ac. on Chattooga River, Dis. 18. Entered July
      10, 1836; granted Dec. 27, 1839; registered Dec. 7, 1839.

1026 SG 321, WILLIAM NORTON, $5/100 ac., 50 ac. on headwaters of Chattooga River,
      Dis. 18. Entered July 10, 1836; granted Dec. 27, 1838; registered Dec. 7, 1839.

1027 SG 560, JOHN HOWARD, assignee of CLEMENT HOWARD for $55, 550 ac., Sec. 18,
      Dis. 14, on Tennessee River. Granted Dec. 6, 1839; registered Dec. 15, 1839.

1028 SG 349, DELA FAYETTE HOWARD, $5/100 ac., 50 ac. on Tennessee R. Dis. 14, on
      line of Sec. 26. Entered Jan. 1, 1839; granted Dec. 6, 1839; registered Dec. 15, 1839.

1029 SG 347, JOHN HOWARD, $5/100 ac., ___ ac., W. side Tennessee R. Dis. 14, on corner
      of Sec. 26. Entered May 2, 1836; granted Dec. 6, 1839; registered Dec. 15, 1839.

1030 SG 350, NICHOLAS F. HOWARD, $5/100 ac., 100 ac. on Middle Creek, Dis. 13.
      Entered Jan. 1, 1839; granted Dec. 6, 1839; registered Dec. 15, 1839.

1031 SG 348, JOHN HOWARD, $5/100 ac., 25 ac. on "Coweter" (Coweeta) Creek, Dis. 14,
      on sd Howard's line, corner of Sec. 5. Entered Mar. 28, 1838; granted Dec. 6, 1839;
      registered Dec. 15, 1839.

1032 JAMES BRYSON Senr. to MATHEW RUSSELL for $250, Sec. 49, Dis. 11, on the
      river. Feb. 18, 1839. *James Bryson*. Wit: *J.R. SELER, D.R. LOWERY*. Proven by
      Lowery in Sep. 1839 court. Registered Dec. 15, 1839.

1033 JAMES BRYSON Sr. to MATHEW RUSSELL Sr. for $200, Sec. 84, Dis. 11, N. side
      Sugartown R. where Indian Res. line intersects Sec. 47. Feb. 18, 1839. *James Bryson*.
      Wit: *J.R. SILER, D.R. LOWERY*. Lowery proved, Sep. 1839 court. Reg. Dec. 15, 1839.

1034 Deed of Trust: LEVI NIGHT of Macon to ARCHABALD RUSSELL for $12.92, 60 ac.,
      Sec. 76, Dis. 11, which JESSE MCCLURE purchased Oct. 27, 1836. Condition: Night is
      to pay Russell $12.92 plus interest by Oct. 2, 1839. *Levi S. Night*. Wit: *E. DOWDLE,
      J___ RUSSELL*. Proven by Dowdle in Sep. 1839 court; registered Dec. 15, 1839.

1035 Sheriff's Sale: THOS. J. ROANE Esq., High Sheriff of Macon County, to WILLIAM
      ALLIN Junr. of Haywood Co. NC, to satisfy judgment of the Macon Co. Court against
      ENOS SHIELDS, JOHN ARNELL, WILLIAM ROGERS, WILLIAM P. POTEAT for
      $146.75 recovered by the State: Sec. 48 in Dis. 10, on "Watagua" Creek. Allin had high
      bid of $161.71 at public sale. Sep. 26, 1838. *Thos. J. Roane*. Wit: *J. HOWARD, N.G.
      HARWELL*. Proven by Howard in Jan. 1839 session. Registered Dec. 15, 1839.

1037 Agreement between WM. ROANE of 1st part & SALLY BELK, widow of DARLING
      BELK, dec'd, DARLING BELK, son & heir of D. Belk dec'd; HENRY SANDERS &
      wife NESA, formerly NESA BELK, dau. of Darling Belk dec'd, parties of 2nd part, all
      of Macon. The parties of 2nd part, for $400 due Roane, sell him a tract on both sides of
      Tuckaseegee R., known as BIG BEAR's Reservation, as run out by surveyor & commis-
      sioners of State in 1820 & called the Tuckeleechee old Town. Land is in possession of
      JOSEPH WELCH Esq., guardian of the Belk heirs. Roane had a demand of $322 against
      the bargainers for services performed for Welch as guardian in defending the heirs. When
      sum is paid with interest, Roane to convey back land. Jan. 14, 1839. *Sally (her X mark)
      Belk, Darling Belk, Henry W. Sanders, Nesy (her X mark) Sanders*. Wit: *SAMUEL
      SANDERS, JOSEPH KELFRABUIK, JONATHAN BLYTH*. Proven by Samuel Sanders
      before RICHARD M. PEARSON, judge of superior court. Registered Dec. 15, 1839.

1038 Power of Attorney: For purpose of allowing WILLIAM ROANE to protect our interest & to secure to him the sum of $332 due by JOSEPH WELCH to Roane for services rendered in prosecuting suit of widow & heirs of DARLING BELK, dec'd, for tract of land called BIG BEAR's Reservation, both sides of Tuckaseegee R., including the Tuckaleechee old Town, we, SALLY BELK, widow, DARLING BELK, son, HENRY SANDERS, married to NESA, the daughter of Darling Belk, dec'd, appoint Roane our attorney at law to represent our interest in our tract of land. Jan. 14, 1839. *Sally (her X mark) Belk, Darling Belk, Henry W. Sanders, Nesa (her X mark) Sanders.* Wit: *SAMUEL SANDERS, JOSEPH KELFRABUIK, JONATHAN BLYTH.* Proven by Samuel Sanders before RICHARD M. PEARSON, judge of superior ct, Reg. Dec. 15, 1839.

1040 ELIZABETH DRYMAN to JOHN HOWARD, both of Macon, for $75, 171 ac. on Tennessee R., Sec. 67 in Dis. 13, a tract that sd Elizabeth bought of the State Oct. 24, 1836, in Franklin. Jan. 19, 1837. *Elizabeth (her X mark) Dryman.* Wit: *L. LONG, MARTIN NORTON.* Proven by Laban Long in Mar. 1839 session. Registered Dec. 15, 1839.

1041 SG 248, ABRAM SELLERS, $5/100 ac., 100 ac. in Dis. 8, on bank of a branch being waters of Barker Creek.Entered May 2, 1836; granted Dec. 15, 1838; reg. Dec. 14, 1839.

1042 SG 256, JOHN STILLWELL, $5/100 ac., 50 ac., Dis. 8, Mill Branch of Seekalaw's Cr., near Hughs flat. Entry May 2, 1836; grant Dec. 15, 1838; reg. Dec. 14, 1839.

1043 SG 261, NATHAN B. THOMPSON, $5/100 ac., 50 ac. in Dis. 8, S. of Thompson's Entry 1138, on Mill Branch of Sackatowe's Creek. Entered May 2, 1836; granted Dec. 15, 1838; registered Dec. 14, 1839.

1044 SG 262, NATHAN B. THOMPSON, $5/100 ac., 50 ac., Dis. 8, Messer's Cr., above where JS. CONLEY lives. Entry Mar. 29, 1837; grant Dec. 15, 1838; reg. Dec. 14, 1839.

1045 SG 263, NATHAN B. THOMPSON, $5/100 ac., 50 ac. in Dis. 8, on Barker's Creek, bd. SELLER's Entry #660. Entry May 2, 1836; grant Dec. 15, 1838; reg.ec. 14, 1839.

1046 SG 245, JOHN STILLWELL, $5/100 ac., 50 ac. in Dis. 8 on Seekalowe's Creek. Entered May 2, 1836; granted Dec. 15, 1838; registered Dec. 14, 1839.

1047 BINUM W. BELL of Cass County, GA, to RODRICK NORTON of Macon, for $30, 63 ac., Sec. 79, Dis. 18. Sep. 25, 1839. *B.W. Bell.* Wit: *J. HOWARD, D.R. LOWRY.* Proven by John Howard in Sep. 1839 court. Registered Dec. 14, 1839.

1048 WILLIAM SETTIN, Senr. to WILLIAM SETTIN, Junr., both of Macon, for $100, land on Savannah Creek of Tuckaseigee R. in Dis. 8, on corner of 147, entered May 27, 1836. Sep. 28, 1839. *William Settin, Senr.* Wit: *SAUL SMITH.*

1049 ELI COLLINS to THOMAS J. ROAN, both of Macon County, for $10, 50 ac. on Burningtown Creek in Dis. 17. Sep. 27, 1839. *Eli Collins.* Wit: J.K. GRAY, S. MCDOWELL. Ack. in Sep. 1839 court. Registered Dec. 14, 1839.

1050 ELI COLLINS to THOMAS J. ROANE, both of Macon, for $50, 50 ac., Dis. 17, Sec. 46. Sep. 25, 1839. *Eli Collins.* Wit: *J.K. GRAY, S. MCDOWELL.* Ack. by Eli Collins in Sep. 1839 court. Registered Dec. 14, 1839.

1051 JOSEPH WELCH to JAMES MAGAHA, both of Macon, for $50, 150 ac.on Cowee Cr., Sec. 15, Dis. 10, purch. at Franklin sale, JOHN PATTON, commissioner. Sep. 26, 1838. *Joseph Welch.* Wit: *J. HOWARD,* who proved in Sep. 1839 court. Reg. Dec. 14, 1839.

1051 ELI COLLINS to THOS. J. ROANE, both of Macon, for $50, 142 ac., Sec. 9, Dis. 4, on Collins Creek, surveyed May 6, 1837. Sep. 25, 1839. *Eli Collins.* Wit: *J.K. GRAY, S. MCDOWELL.* Ack. in Sep. 1839 court. Registered Dec. 14, 1839.

1053 SG 149, JOUSHUA AMMONS, $5/100 ac., 88 ac. on Cat Creek, Dis. 11, on corner of Sec. 9. Entered May 2, 1836; granted Dec. 15, 1838; registered Dec. 14, 1839.

1054 SG 171, ELI COLLINS, $5/100 ac., 40 ac. on Burningtown Creek, Dis. 17. Entered Apr. 15, 1837; granted Dec. 15, 1838; registered Dec. 14, 1839.

1055 SG 552, JERSHUA AMMONS, $____, 105 ac., Sec. 9, Dis. 11, crossing creek. Granted Aug. 25, 1839; registered Dec. 14, 1839.

1056 EPHRIM ASH of Haywood Co., NC, to AMOS ASH of Macon, 50 ac., W. side Tuckaseegee R. near tract on which AMOS ASH has an improvement. Aug. 28, 1837. *Ephrim
Ash.* Wit: *LUCAS (LISNODS?), JOS. KEENER.* Proven by Joseph Keener in Sep. 1839
court. Registered Dec. 14, 1839.

1057 MARTIN ANGEL to SILAS MCDOWELL, both of Macon. for $900, 230 ac., Sec. 38,
Dis. 16 on W. bank Tennessee R. Sep. 10, 1838. *Martin Angel.* Wit: *JOHN HALL, JOHN
SELEIR.* Proven by Hall in Sep. 1839 session. Registered Dec. 14, 1839.

1059 SG 102, RUDS MORGAIN, $5/100 ac., 50 ac. on Burningtown Creek, Dis. 17. Entered
May 2, 1836; granted Feb. 26, 1838; registered Dec. 14, 1839.

1060 SG 221, JOHN D. MORELAND, $5/100 ac., 95 ac. on Watauga Creek, Dis. 10, on
corner of Sec. 114. Entered May 2, 1836; granted Dec. 15, 1838; registered Jan. 18, 1840.

1061 SG 341, MILTON MOSS, $5/100 ac., 100 ac. on Walnut Creek, Dis. 12. Entered Apr.
28, 1838; granted Aug. 28, 1839; registered Jan. 18, 1840.

1062 SG 340, JOHN H. LEDFORD, $5/100 ac., 7 ac., on "Ellijah" (Ellijay) Cr. & Sugartown
R., Dis. 11, corner of Sec. 90. Entry Apr. 26, 1838; grant Aug. 28, 1839; registered Jan.
18, 1840.

1063 THOMAS W. BIRD to JACOB DIETS, both of Macon, for $60, 50 ac., Tuckaseegee R.,
bd. tract where AMOS ASH formerly lived. June 9, 1838. *Thos. W. Bird.* Wit: *FIULDEN
UNDERWOOD, J. KEENER.* Keener proved, Sep. 1839 court. Reg. Jan. 18, 1840.

1064 DAVID LEDFORD to JOHN BRYSON Jr. for $175, 50 ac. on "Kulleehee" (Cullowhee)
Cr., Sec. 20, Dis. 7. Jan. 15, 1833. *David (his X mark) Ledford.* Wit: *THOS. ROGERS,
JESSE SANDERS.* Ack. Sep. 1839 court. Reg. Jan. 18, 1840.

1065 THOMAS MCCLURE & SARAH MCCLURE of Union Co., GA, to REBECAH
MCDANIEL of Macon, for $400, 127 ac., Sec. 32, Dis. 15, Cartoogechaye Cr. Aug. 23,
1839. *Thos. McClure, Sarah (her X mark) McClure.* Wit: *J.K. GRAY, J.S. ROBISON.*
Proven by James Robison in Sep. 1839 session. Registered Jan. 18, 1840.

1066 AMOS ASH to THOMAS W. BIRD, both of Macon, for $50, 50 ac. on W. side of Tuck-
aseegee R., near tract on which Amos Ash has an improvement. June 24, 1839. *Amos
Ash.* Wit: *WM. A. BRYSON, J.B. LEWIS.* Ack. in Sep. 1839 court. Reg. Jan. 18, 1840.

1067 JESSE F. PADGETT to THOMAS WEST, both of Macon, for $60, land, Cowee Cr.
Aug. 21, 1839. *Jesse F. Pagett.* Wit: *DAVID GUYER.* Reg. Jan. 18, 1840.

1068 SAMUEL REYNOLDS to JOHN WILLIAMSON, both of Macon, for $75, 75 ac. on
Vandyke's Creek, Dis. 14, on W. line of Sec. 37. Dec. 21, 1838. *Samuel Reynolds.* Wit:
J. HOWARD, who proved in Sep. 1839 court. Registered Jan. 18, 1840.

1069 RODRICK NORTON to GARRETT HEDDING/HEDING, both of Macon, for $30, 50
ac. Dec. 17, 1839. *Rodrick (his X mark) Norton.* Wit: *J. HOWARD, MARTIN SHEETS.*
Proven by John Howard in Jan. 1840 court. Registered Jan. 30, 1840.

1070 JAMES LEDFORD to ELIAS PACK, both of Macon, for $40, 50 ac. on Tuckaseigee R.
Oct. 18, 1839. *James (his X mark) Ledford.* Wit: *J. HOWARD,* who proved in Jan. 1840
court. Registered Jan. 30, 1840.

1071 SG 344, ABEL B. HYATT, $5/100 ac., land on Tuckasegee R., bd. BIG BEAR's &
TEGANITEE's reservations. Entry Sep. 28, 1838; grant Nov. 11, 1839; reg. Jan. 21, 1840.

1072 Power of Att'y: JAMES MCHAN of Macon, duly appt'd guardian of MARION, ANN SARAH (SARAH ANN), MALINDA, BURKET & WEAKLY MCHAN, minor heirs of MILLY MCHAN, alias MILLY HIX, whereas TOLIVER HIX of Cobb Co., GA is shortly going to Cherokee Co., Miss., appoints Toliver/Tolerford Hix/Hicks lawful attn'y to take possession of all Miss. land & personal est. of any kind belonging to the minor heirs, to convey property, etc. in rights of their mother, Milly, who was the heir & child of THOMAS HIX, who lately died in Cherokee Co., Miss.: for HILDY(?) HIX, minor child of Milly before marrieage with myself, & our children, Marion, Sarah Ann, Malinda, Burcket & Weakly McHan. Jan. 23, 1840. *James McHan.* Wit: *J.W. GUINN,* who proved, Jan. 1840 ct. Reg. Jan. 23, 1840.

1074 JAMES WITHEROW to CURTIS SANDERS, both of Macon, for $50, 20 ac., Sec. 54, Dis. 10 on conditional marked line between JOHNSTON & COOK, near State Rode, on conditional line between Johnston & MILAS SANDERS; entry by JOSEPH R. JOHNSON and conveyed to Witherow. No date. *James Witherow.* Wit: *MATHEW MASHBURN, Miles Sanders.* Ack. in Jan. 1840 court. Registered Jan. 30, 1840.

1076 JAMES WITHEROW to CURTIS SANDERS of Macon, for $350, 66+ ac., Sec. 48, Dis. 10, crossing Watagua Creek. No date. *James Witherow.* Wit: *MATHEW MASHBURN, MILES SANDERS.* Ack. in Jan. 1840 court. Registered Jan. 30, 1840.

1077 SG 389, JOHN AMMONS, assignee of LEWIS TILLY, for $122.48, 59+ ac., Sec. 31, Dis. 12, on SW side of Sugar town fork of Tennessee R. Granted Dec. 4, 1838; registered Jan. 25, 1840.

1078 SG 339, JOHN H. LEDFORD, $5/100 ac., 50 ac. on Sugar town River in Dis. 11. Entered Apr. 26, ___; granted Aug. 28, 1839; registered Jan. 26, 1840.

1079 SG 551, GEORGE T. LEDFORD, assignee of TAVNER B. MORE, for $___, 64 ac., Sec. 51, Dis. 11 on bank of Sugartown R. below a whirl. Granted Aug. 28, 1839; registered Jan. 26, 1840.

1080 MAT DAVES to JOHN H. LEDFORD for $12.25, 60 1/2 ac. on Ellijah Creek, Dis. 11, part of Sec. 89, on conditional line between Daves & Ledford. Mar. 9, 1838. *Mat Daves.* Wit: *GEORGE (his X mark) T. LEDFORD, PHILIP KIRBY.* Proven by George T. Ledford in Jan. 1840 court. Registered Mar. 5, 1840.

1081 JESSE R. SILER of Macon to JACOB PLEMMONS for $600, 128 ac. on W. side of Tennessee R., Sec. 21, Dis. 14, to a post on boundary between GA & NC, crossing Commissioners Creek. Sep. 7, 1838. *Jesse R. Siler.* Wit: *BURTON P. DICKEY, THAD P. SILER.* Ack. in Jan. 1840 court. Registered Mar. 5, 1840.

1082 JESSE R. SILER to N.S. JARRETT for $35, 70 ac. on Nantehala R., Sec. 7, Dis. 13, containing 70 ac. Jan. 23, 1840. *Jesse R. Siler.* Wit: *J.H. TRUITT, T.P. SILER.* Ack. in Jan. 1840 court. Registered Mar. 5, 1840.

1082 Sheriff's Sale: ELI MCKEE, Esq., High Sheriff of Macon, to J.C. (C.J.) COOK of Augusta, GA, to satisfy judgment of County Court of Macon against J.A. BELL for $409.88 debt & 40 cents cost recovered by Cook of said John A. Bell: 8 lots in Franklin purchased by RUDDS MORGAN at land sale in May 1835, Nos. 33, 34 & 35, all on Main Street, containing one acre each; Nos. 36, 37 & 38, containing 150 poles each; No. 39, as per deed of JONATHAN PHILLIPS, bearing date ____, beginning on the Main Street, containing 150 poles; No. 40, containing 150 poles. S. & E. of Main Street, 135 yards from the court house - all lots joining each other & lying on the Main street, and making nearly a square. At the public sale Dec. 23, 1839, C.J. Cook was high bidder by agent with a bid of $440. Jan. 25, 1840. *Eli McKee.* Wit. *H.G. WOODFIN.* Ack. in Jan. 1840 court. Registered Mar. 6, 1840.

1085 Sheriff's Sale: ELI MCKEE, Esq., High Sheriff of Macon County, to ABRAM ENLOE
assignee of JAMES W. GUINN of Haywood Co., NC, on execution of judgment from
County Court of Macon against ROBERT H. ENLOE, SARAH ANN ENLOE, WM. B.
ENLOE, A.H. ENLOE, ASH T. ENLOE, ALFORD P. ENLOE, dec'd., & CHRIS-
TOPHER C. ENLOE, minor heirs of ASAPH ENLOE, dec'd, for $1101.89 recovered by
the State of NC, exposed to public sale 300 ac. on W. bank of Tuckaseegee R. on lower
corner of Sec. 15, known as Stecoa old fields. At the sale, held on the second Mon.
before last Mon. in Aug. 1839, Abram Enloe had high bid of $1. Jan. 23, 1840. *Eli
McKee, Shff.* Wit: *J. KEENER, J.H. WIGGINS.* Ack. in Jan. 1840 court. Registered Mar.
6, 1840.

1087 WILLIAM HECK of Macon to JAMES ROBISON for $86.50, 10+ ac, part of Sec. 29,
Dis. 16, on edge of State Rd, on line of Sec. 28. June 3, 1839. *Wm. Heck.* Wit: *S.
MCDOWELL, J.T. GRANT.* Proven by S. McDowell in Jan. 1840 court. Registered Mar.
6, 1840.

1088 WILLIAM DODGEN to DAVID B. LEDFORD, both of Macon, for val. rec'd, 56 ac.,
Sec. 22, Dis. 6. Feb. 22, 1839. *William (his X mark) Dodgin.* Wit: *H. CONLEY(?), JEF-
FERSON MOSS.* Proven by Moss in Jan. 1840 court. Registered Mar. 9, 1840.

1088 HENCEY MOSS of Macon, to JOHN CORBIN for val. rec'd, tract of land, Sec. 69, Dis.
11, sold by commissioners Oct. 27, 1836, at land sale in Franklin. Jan. 23, 1839. *Henry
Moss.* Wit: *H.G. WOODFIN, C.T. ROGERS.* Proven by C.T. Rogers in Jan. 1840 court.
Registered Mar. 9, 1840.

1089 ISBEL JAMES to RUDDS MORGAN of Cherokee County, NC, for $100, 65+ ac., Sec.
120, Dis. 10. Nov. 9, 1838. *Isbell James.* Wit: *W.B. MORGAN, J.W. SANDERS.* Proven
by Wm. B. Morgan in Jan. 1840 session. Registered Mar. 9, 1840.

1090 WILLIAM PATTON to HENRY ADDINGTON for $200, 70 ac. Oct. 9, 1839. *William
(his X mark) Patton.* Wit: *J.M. GRIFFITH, WM. JAMES.* Proven by Wm. James in Jan.
1840 session. Registered Mar. 9, 1840.

1091 GEORGE T. LEDFORD to JOHN H. LEDFORD, Jr., both of Macon, for $1,000, 48 ac.
on Shugartown fork River, (Cullasaja) crossing mill poon (pond?), running with conditional line between MOORE & DAVES, passing mouth of "Ellijah" (Ellijay) Cr. Mar.
12, 1839. *George (his X mark) T. Ledford.* Wit: *J.W. GUINN.* Proven by J.W. Guinn in
Jan. 1839 session of court. Registered Mar. 10, 1840.

1092 JAMES ANGEL to NIMROD S. JARRETT, both of Macon, for $300, 179 ac. on Ten-
nessee R., Sec. 2, Dis. 11, crossing Mill Creek. May 31, 1837. *James Angel.* Wit: *G.W.J.
MOORE.* Proven by G.W.J. Moore in Jan. 1840 session. Reg. Mar. 11, 1840.

1093 ANN BROWN to PETER DAVES & SALLY DAVES his wife, all of Macon, for love &
good will I have for sd Peter & Sally, and for care & troble the sd Peter & Sally have and
is to bestow on me, so long as I may live, 38 ac. in Dis. 10, Sec. __, and an Entry for 50
ac. made by NATHAN PILKY & SAUL TRUITT on Brown's Creek, and the place
where Ann Brown now lives. Also, one mare named Polly, a sorrel about 11 years, three
cows one (bullock?) & a steer, the stock hogs, gentle & wild, number not known. No
date. *Ann (her X mark) Brown.* Wit: *BENJ. DUVAL, AARON MILLER, L.C. DUVAL.*
Proven by Duval in Jan. 1840court. Reg. Mar. 11, 1840.

1094 HUGH WHITE of Macon, to ELIZABETH DRYMAN for $150, 152+ ac. on "Cowetier"
(Coweta) Creek, Sec. 34, Dis. 14, purchased Oct. 24, 1836 at land sale. Jan. 19, 1837.
Hugh White. Wit: *JAMES HUNNICUTT, J. HOWARD.* Proven by John Howard in Jan.
1840 court. Registered Mar. 11, 1840.

1095 WILLIAM PATTON to HENRY ADDINGTON for $100, 50 ac. on "Cartugage" (Car-
toogechaye) Creek, Dis. 15, on NW corner of Sec. 67. Oct. 1, 1839. *William (his X mark)
Patton.* Wit: *J.M. GRIFFITH, WILLIAM JAMES.* Proven by William James in Jan. 1840
court. Registered Mar. 11, 1840.

1096 Deed of Trust: WEST TRUITT to DANIEL GARLAND, both of Macon, for $35, 100
ac. on Middle Creek, Dis. 13, Sec. 50, which was sold at the land sale of 1836. Jan. 24,
1840. *West (his X mark) Truitt*. Wit: *J.W. GUINN*. Registered Mar. 12, 1840.

1096 GEORGE W. GREEN to FRANCIS WARD, both of Macon, for $75, 50 ac. on Greens
fork of Savannah Creek, Dis. 8, on N. line of Sec. 152, entered May 2, 1836. Mar. 1,
1839. *George W. (his X mark) Green*. Wit: *WM. R. BUCKANNON, JAMES BUCKAN-
NON*. Proven by James Buckannon in Jan. 1840 session. Registered Mar. 12, 1840.

1097 JONATHAN PHILLIPS, Ch'man of Court of Macon County, for $72 pd by H.G.
WOODFIN to J.K. GRAY, treasury, Town Lot in Franklin, No. 46 on Main Street, one
ac., also Lot No. 38 on the Big Road, 2+ ac. Jan. 24, 1840. *J. Phillips*. Wit: *J.K. GRAY*.
Proven by J.K. Gray in Jan. 1840 court. Registered Mar. 13, 1840.

1098 J.R. SILER to H.G. WOODFIN, both of Macon, for $10, part of the 400-acre tract of the
town of Franklin, on SE corner of town land No. 38, containing 140 poles. Oct. 12, 1839.
J.R. Siler. Wit: *BURTON K. DICKEY*. Ack. in Jan. 1840 court. Registered Mar. 13, 1840.

1100 H.G. WOODFIN to J.R. SILER, both of Macon, for $10, part of town commons land on
State Road, containing 1+ ac. Oct. 12, 1839. *H.G. Woodfin*. Wit: *BURTON K. DICKEY*.
Ack. in Jan. 1840 court. Registered Mar. 13, 1840.

1101 FRANCIS POINDEXTUER of Cherokee Co., NC, to JESSE R. SILER for $100, 59 ac.
on SW side of Tennessee R., Sec. 12, Dis. 12. Date? *F. Poindexter*. Wit: *L. LONG, T.P.
SILER*. Proven by L. Long in Jan. 1840 court. Registered Mar. 13, 1840.

1102 ISAAC ASH to DAVID W. ASH, both of Macon, for $50, 100 ac. on Savannah Cr.,
corner of Sec. 5 in Dis. 8, entered May 2, 1836. Oct. 5, 1839. *Isaac Ash*. Wit: *WILLIAM
STILES, ELEANAH ASH*. Ack. in Jan. 1840 court. Registered Mar. 10, 1840.

1103 F. POINDEXTER of Cherokee Co. NC to JESSE R. SILER of Macon, for $75, 50 ac. on
N. side of Tennessee R., Dis. 8, corner of Sec. 55. Jan. 23, 1840. *Francis Poindexter*.
Wit: *L. LONG, T.P. SILER*. Proven by L. Long in Jan. 1840 court. Reg. Mar. 16, 1840.

1104 ISAAC ASH to DAVID W. ASH, both of Macon, for $450, 71+ ac. on Big Savannah
Creek on north line of Sec. 3. Oct. 5, 1839. *Isaac Ash*. Wit: *WILLIAM STILES, ELLER-
NAH ASH*. Ack. in Jan. 1840 court. Registered Mar. 16, 1840.

1105 SG 423, HUGH GIBBS for $___, 70 ac., Sec. 90, Dis. 8, W. bank of Wessers Creek.
Granted Jan. 7, 1839; registered Mar. 17, 1840.

1106 SG 555, MILES SANDERS, assignee of GEORGE CUNNINGHAM, for $61.72 paid by
Cunningham, 82+ ac., Sec. 52, Dis. 10, crossing "Wattauga" Creek. Granted Aug. 28,
1839; registered Mar. 17, 1840.

1107 SG 189, GARRETT HEDDY, $5/100 ac., 100 ac. on "Chattuga" R., both sides of road
leading to Pickens (SC). Entry May 2, 1836; grant Dec. 15, 1838; reg.Mar. 17, 1840.

1108 SG 152, WILLIAM BRYSON, $5/100 ac., 50 ac. on Sugartown fork of Tennessee R.
Dis. 12, at head of JOHN BRYSON's Branch. Entered May 2, 1836; granted Dec. 15,
1838; registered Mar. 18, 1840.

1109 SG 194, DAVID HIGDON, $5/100 ac., 100 ac. on E. fork of Savannah Creek, Dis. 8, on
corner of Sec. 57. Entry May 2, 1836; grant Dec. 15, 1838; registered Mar. 16, 1840.

1110 ISAAC ASH is bound to DAVID W. ASH, both of Macon, for $1,000; Isaac Ash is to
make sufficient deed of two tracts he sold to David W. Ash. Sep. 22, 1838. *Isaac Ash*.
Wit: *JAMES W. KEENER*. Ack. in Jan. 1840 session. Registered Mar. 18, 1840.

1111 SG 240, MOSES REDMAN, $5/100 ac., 100 ac. in Dis. 7, on forks of Bettes Branch be-
tween SAUL REDMAN's improvement (and?). Entered May 2, 1836; granted Dec. 15,
1838; registered Mar. 18, 1840.

End of Volume B

Macon County Deed Book C

1112 SG 361, WILLIAM GARLAND, $5/100 ac., 100 ac. on Middle Creek, Dis. 13. Entered Jan. 1, 1839; granted Apr. 28, 1840; registered June 1, 1840.

1113 SG 360, JOHN HOWARD, $5/100 ac., 100 ac. on Coweeta Creek,, Dis. 14, on NE corner of Sec. 48. Entered Jan. 1, 1839; granted Apr. 28, 1840; registered June 1, 1840.

1114 SG 558, ELIJAH STANDRIDGE, $___, 67 ac., Sec. 122, Dis. 15. Granted Aug. 28, 1839; registered June 1, 1840.

1115 SG 554, GEORGE DICKY, $80.20, 150 ac., Sec. 12, Dis. 10, crossing Mill fork of Cane Creek. Granted Aug. 28, 1839; registered June 1, 1840.

1116 SG 359, JOHN HOWARD, $5/100 ac., 100 ac. on Mulberry Creek, Dis. 14, on corner of Sec. 48. Entered Aug. 23, 1837; granted Apr. 1840; registered June 1, 1840.

1117 SG 362, JOHN H. HOWARD, $5/100 ac., 50 ac. on Mulberry Creek, Dis. 14. Entered Feb. 12, 1839; granted Apr. 28, 1840; registered June 1, 1840.

1118 SG 343, WILLIAM HANEY, $10/100 ac., 150 ac. on Bushy fork of Savannah Creek. Entered Aug. 26, 1836; granted Nov. 4, 1839; registered June 2, 1840.

1119 SG 277, JAMES FOUTS, $10.14, 50 ac., Sec. 44, Dis. 17. Granted Dec. 12, 1836; registered June 2, 1840.

1120 SG 278, JAMES FOUTS, $31, 153 ac., Sec. 59, Dis. 16, crossing a large branch. Granted Dec. 12, 1836; registered June 2, 1840.

1121 SG 204, JOHN JUSTICE, $5/100 ac., 50 ac. on Tessenty Creek, Dis. 13, on SE corner of Sec. 48. Entered May 2, 1836; granted Dec. 15, 1838; registered June 2, 1840.

1122 SG 205, JOHN JUSTICE, $5/100 ac., 50 ac. on Tesenty Creek, Dis. 13, on corner of Sec. 47. Entered May 2, 1836; granted Dec. 15, 1838; registered June 2, 1840.

1123 SG 556, ELI MCKEE, $44.73 for 149 1/2 ac., Sec. 65, Dis. 15, crossing Cartoogachaye. Granted Aug. 28, 1839; registered June 2, 1840.

1124 SG 557, ELI MCKEE for $___, 55 ac., Sec. 120, Dis. 15. Granted Aug. 28, 1839; registered June 2, 1840.

1125 SG 97, JACKSON HUGHS, 75 ac. on Wattauga Creek, NW corner of Sec. 122 in Dis. 10. Entered May 2, 1836; granted Feb. 26, 1838; registered June 2, 1840.

1126 SG 280, THOMAS J.(I?) WILLIAMS, $5/100 ac., 50 ac. S. fork of "Ellijah" (Ellijay) Cr., Dis. 12 . Entry Mar. 29, 1837; grant Dec. 15, 1838; registered June 2, 1840.

1127 SG 330, LEWIS HUGINS, $5/100 ac., 50 ac. on "Skeener" (Skeenah) Creek, on line of Sec. 106, Dis. 16. Entered Sep. 26, 1838; granted Apr. 1, 1839; registered June 3, 1840.

1128 SG 331, LEWIS HUGINS, $5/100 ac., 50 ac. on line of Sec. 108, on Skeener Creek. Entered Sep. 26, 1838; granted Apr. 1, 1839; registered June 3, 1840.

1129 SG 176, PHILAMON CRAIN, $10/100 ac., 200 ac. on waters of Chattooga called Nickleson's(?) lick log Creek, incl. improvement where DAVID MORGAN lives. Entered May 2, 1836; granted Dec. 15, 1838; registered June 3, 1840.

1130 SG 159, MOSES BUTLER, $10/100 ac., 200 ac. on Gum Bottom Cr. of Thompsons R., incl. improvement. Entry May 2, 1836; grant Dec. 15, 1840; registered June 3, 1840.

1131 To the County Ct. of Macon, the Bd. of Supertendance of Common Schools, (assigned to lay off the County into School Districts) in Complyance with the act of the Gen'l Assembly of NC: Respectfully ask leave to Report That the Board met & Made preliminary arrangements Among (the Board) the best feelings of friendship & Compromise have Prevaled & Neither Sectional values nor Sectional Interest have (interfered) with the Grand & primary object of this Board, That of Making the Common School System a boon of Great value to all Classes & Conditions of our Community.

The first & Highest object of the Board (is) to Erect a Common School in reach of every Individual & Make them accessable to the poorest & most obscure Citizen of Macon County. This we designed to do with as little Expense to the Citizens by taxation as poseable - We had only to Direct our attention to the population & territory of our County to Discover obsticles of no Small Magnitude that the Differant neighbourhood(s) were so Situated that lines drawn parallel to Each other & others Crossing them at Right angles & Imbrasing in the Square of Such lines the requisite amount of territory would have Divided Settlements Conveniently Situated to each other on the one had & Imbrased those on the other hand which are Separated by Insuffferable Natural barriers.

The Board therefore.. (visited) the Different Sections of the County in person. The result was, 1st that a More Deep & lively Interest was felt and a greater anxiety manifested by the community in General than we had anticipated, and 2ndly, in order to Meet the Wants of the Community a Much Greater Number of School Districts Would be required than we had (contemplated?) - We have Indevered to Give to Each District Such Boundarie as to Include none but Such as may be in Reach of the Center of Such District Without having a formidable Mountain or River to Cross. The Tennessee R. & the various mountains & Dividing ridges are therefore made our Principal boundaries - In view of this together with the fact that many of our neighbourhoods lie in long and narrow valleys on Creek(s) and Branches, Some of our District are Made to Contain a much Greater number of children than could be concluded in others - the whol(e) number of Common Schools District(s) for the County of Macon is twenty-six, and are as follows.

District No. 1 - Beginning at top of Ridge between MRS. R. MCDANIEL's & D. JOHNSTON's Mill Creek, Runs S. with Ridge to Cartoogachaye Cr., Crossing Same at JOHN SILER ford, continuing S. to top of ridge S.W. of JOHN DOWDLE Senr., then E. with Dividing Ridge between Cartoogachaye & Tennessee River to S. end of ISAAC MAUNEY's lane then to Mouth of Cartoogacheye Creek thence N. with Tennessee R. to point of a Ridge below SILAS MCDOWELL's farm known as the MARTIN ANGEL place, then W. with the Ridge Crossing the Ten. R. Road at top of Ridge between DAVID ALLEN's & DAVID DAUSEY's old plase continuing with Ridge so as to Imbrase all the Inhabitants on its south side to the beginning.

District 2nd - Beginning on top of Ridge between Johnson's Mill Creek & Mrs. McDaniel's at N.W. Corner of District 1, Runs S. with W. line of said District to the S.W. corner of No. 1, thence W. & S. with Ridge between the Skeener Creek & Tennessee R. & those of Cartoogachaye so as to Imbrase all the Inhabitants on the N. and W. side of said Ridge to H. ADDINGTON's Saw Mill then W. & N. so as to Imbrase all Inhabitants on E. side of Mountain which Divides the Waters of Nantahaly & Cartoogacheye to the State Road above DANIEL JARRETT's then E. to point of beginning.

District 3rd - Commences on the Ten. R. at the Mouth of Cartoogachaye, SE Corner of No. 1 Runs thence Southwardly with the River and Crosses the River opposite the point of a Ridge Which Runs between Z. CABE's and JOHN DOBSON's thence with sd Ridge E. to the base of the Mountain thence S. to JAMES M. SMITH's Farm, thence Westwardly Crossing the River & running With the line which Divid(es) the land District of Macon Co. No. 14 & No. 15 to Ridge Divid(ing) the Waters of Tennessee & Cartoogachaye thence N. with said ridge so as to Include all the Inhabitants on its E. Side to the S. End of Isaac Mauney's lane thence to the beginning.

District 4th - Beginning at GA line on E. side of Tennessee R. on Ridge that divides the Waters of Tennessee R. from those of Middle Creek, Running to the Head of Balard's Branch thence down said Branch to the River, down said River to the point Where the S. line of District No. 3, thence with said line W. Crossing the River to Include all the Waters of "Coweteer" (Coweeta Creek) & Settlements on Mulberry, Commissioners & Bettey's Creek on W. Side of Tennessee R. thence S. to GA line and With the line to the beginning.

District 5th - Beginning on Tennessee R. at line of No. 3, Running up Tennessee R. to line of No. 4, thence E. to the GA line thence E. With Sd line to Include all Waters of Middle Creek & Tessenty and Down Tennessee R. on E. Side to JAMES M. SMITH's farm to the Beginning.

District 6th - Beginning on Tennessee R., N.E. corner of District No. 1 and Runs With S. line of Sd District W. to top of Mountain opposite upper settlement on "Iola" (Iotla) Creek thence Northwardly to top of ridge that Divid(e)s the Waters of Iola & Burningtown then N. in a Strate line to Tennessee R. at the Mouth of Roses Creek thence up the River to the Beginning.

District 7th - Beginning at point of Mountain opposite the Widow PEGGY BRYSON's thence S. & E. to point of Mountain that Divides the Waters of Sugartown & "Ellijah" (Ellijay) thence to Head of Crow's Branch thence to the head of Walnut Creek thence to the Sugartown falls thence Westwardly to the "Neck-o-Jack" (Nickajack) thence N. along Mountain to the beginning to Include all the Settlements on Sugartown R. from Beginning to the Sugartown Falls.

District 8th - Beginning on E. Side of Tennessee R. Where line of No. 3 Crosses River, thence with said line E. including all inhabitants on Sugartown R. to W. line of No. 7, thence N. with that line Crossing Sugartown R. with a Ridge to Gap of Mountain near WILLIAM HOLBROOK's thence with the Ridge between Cat's Creek & Sugartown to the fork of State Rd thence W. to the River N.E. corner of No. 1, thence with the River to the beginning.

District 9th - Running with Mountain that Divides the Waters of Cat's Creek & "Ellijah" (Ellijay) to the head of Ellijah Waters thence S. to mountain Dividing waters of Ellijah & Sugartown, thence with sd Mountain W. to a point opposite the lower Settlement on "Allijah" (Ellijay), thence N. to the beginning so as to Include every Inhabitants on the Waters of Allijah Creek.

District 10th - Beginning on Ridge between WM B. MORGAN's & WM. BURD'S, Runs E. with Ridge Dividing Waters of Love's Mill Creek & those of Wataga to the Cowe Mountain, thence S. with Cowee Mountain to Mountain which Divides the Waters of Cat's Creek & "Allijah" (Ellijay) thence W. with said Dividing Ridge to line of District No. 8, thence N. to Inbrace all the Inhabitants of Cat's Creek & Rabbit's Creek E. of line of No. 8 District to the beginning.

District 11th - Beginning at Bridge between WM. B. MORGAN's & WM. BURD's N.W. and beginning corner of No. 10, thence with line of Sd. District to Base of Cowee Mountain thence N. & S. with base of Sd. Mountain to W. Bank of Tennessee R. at "Iola" (Iotla) ford, thence S. with River to N.W. Corner of No. 8, thence E., Crossing the Mountain to the beginning incl. all inhabitants of Wataga & the MCCAY's settlement.

District 12th - Beginning at E. bank of Tennessee R. at "Iola" (Iotla) ford running E. to Base of Mountain, thence N. with Base of Mountain surrounding all the Cowee Settlements to a point opposite Truit's Bridge, then W. with River to the beginning.

District 13th - Commencing at Truitt's Bridge on Tennessee R., running N. with River to N.E. corner of District No. 6, then Crossing the River W. to Mountain, then N., Imbrasing all Settlements on Tellico thence E. Crossing the River below JULIOUS DEAN's thence S. with Mountain to the NE Corner of No. 12 thence W. to the beginning.

District 14th - Includes every Inhabitant on Waters of Burning town Creek bounded by Tennessee R. by the Mountains on Either side of the Burningtown Creek & by the Ridge Which Divides the Waters of Burningtown & Iola.

District 15th - Beginning at the upper End of WM. COCKERHAM's farm on South Side of Tuckaseegee R., Running Down sd River opposite end of Ridge on N. Side of River below MARKE COLEMAN's farm, thence Crossing & up the River so as to include all Inhabitants to the Haywood line & thence to the Beginning.

District 16th - Beginning on N. Side of Tuckaseegee R. on lower line of District 15th, Running Down both Sides of River so as to include all inhabitants on both Sides as low down as MATHEW GARRETT & JOHN DEHART.

District 17th - Beginning at Mouth of Tuckaseegee R. and Running down S. Side of Mountain so as to Include all Inhabitants on N. side of River & all Inhabitants of Hazelnut Creek as low down as JAMES HEBBEART's.

District 18th - Begining at Gap of mountain on Tennessee R. where JESSE CORNWELL now lives & Runs up both Sides of River and Bounded by Mountains on Either Side as high up as to Include fort Linsey & all its Inhabitants.

District 19th - Beginning at WM. ELDERS on N. Side of Tennessee R. and Runs up both Sides of River bounded by Mountains on Either Side, Includes all the Inhabitants on both Side(s) as far up as JAMES MCHANN's.

District 20th - Bounded Northward by the Shut-in on Nantehala River below G.F. CALER's, E. & W. by Mountains on Either Side of Said River & S. by Mouth of Alan Creek so as to Include all Inhabitants on Waters of Nantehala above sd Shut-in.

District 21st - Beginning on S. Side of Tuckaseegee R. at lower end of WM. H. BRYSON's farm running S. to top of Ridge between Wm. H. Bryson's & AMOS ASHE's, then with Dividing ridge between Waters of Cullewhee & Savanah Round to main Mountain thence with Mtn to point opposite DAVID ROGERS, then w. Main Ridge between Rogers & JOHN WIKE's incl. BEARDING then Down Ridge to Tuckaseegee, thence with River to beginning.

District 22nd - Beginning at Tuckaseegah R., SE Corner of district 21st, Running S. With Ridge between Bearding & John Wike so as to include H. BROWN & M. WATSON, thence to Haywood line then Down the River to the beginning.

District 23rd - Beginning at point of Ridge Dividing Culluehee & Savannah waters thence down Tuckaseegah R., low Enough to Imbrase the MESSERS Settlement thence W, to the top of ridge between SETTON's & "Lowral" (Laurel) Branch, then S. with said Ridge Crossing the Savannah above SAMUEL WIKLE's to ridge between big & little Savannah thence w. sd ridge to Main Collecohee Ridge, then down sd ridge E. to Beg.

District 24th - Beginning at S.E. Corner of District No. 23, Running with line to N.W. Corner of sd District so as to Include DAVID SETTON's then W., Including all the inhabitants of the Waters of Savannnah to the top of Cowee Mountain thence S. with sd Mountain to main ridge Dividing Waters of Culluohee & Savannah, then Eastwardly to the Beginning.

District 25th - Beg. on ridge a little N. of old JOHN CLARK's then W. so as to Include JAMES MCKEMSEY, A. ZACHARY's, the NORTONS, DAVID MORGAN, GARRET HEDDY & WM. QUEEN, then to Mouth of Silver run, thence to head Waters then to beginning.

District 26th - beginning at falls of Tuckaseege R., running W. to take in JOHN START(?) then S. to Include E. PEAKE, thence E. to Haywood line, then N. to Peak Mountain, then to falls of River at the Beginning.

All of which is respectfully submitted. (No signatures -possibly prepared by school superintendent H.G. WOODFIN.) Received in open court, March 1840 Session, and ordered to be registered. Registered June 8, 1840.

1137 JACOB SILER to JOHN SELER, both of Macon, for $600, 176 ac. on DAVID JOHNSTON's fork of "Cartoogehege" (Cartoogechaye) Cr., part of Sec. 19, all of Sec. 21, bd. John Siler, running w. Hughes Summit, incl. a grist mill. Nov. 29, 1839. *Jacob Siler*. Wit: *J.K. GRAY*. Ack. in Mar. 1840 session. Registered June 9, 1840.

1138 JOHN SILER to JACOB SILER, both of Macon, for $1400, 235 ac. on Cartoogechaye Cr., Dis. 15, part of Sec. 3, 22, 19 & 20, all of Sec. 23 to top of a ridge, div. line between John Siler & MOSES ADDINGTON. Mar. 23, 1840. *John Siler*. Wit: *J.K. GRAY, DARLING BELKS*. Proven by J.K. Gray in Mar. 1840 session. Registered June 9, 1840.

1139 JAMES POINDEXTER & THOS. W.P. POINDEXTER to JESSE R. SILER, for $900, a
Negro woman, PATSEY abt 20 yrs old & her child ALBERT abt one yr., warrant to be
sound, healthy & sensible. Mar. 25, 1840. *James Poindexter, Thos. W.P. Poindexter.*
Wit: *J.H. QUIET.* Proven by Quiet in Mar. 1840 court. Registered June 9, 1840.

1140 Sheriff's Sale: ELI MCKEE, Esq., High Sh'iff of Macon, to SAMUEL REED of Burke
Co. NC, property to satisfy judgment of County Ct. against JOHN N. DEYTON & others
for $4.2 principal, 8 1/2 cents int., 40 cents cost and $67 subject to (illeg.) of $50 on Sep.
26, 1838, recovered by N.S. JARRETT, B.M. POTEAT & others. Sold at public auction:
80 ac. in Sec. 1, Dis. 11 on Tennessee R. to branch div. lands of JOHN POTEAT &
Deyton; 8 ac. on Tennessee R. near mouth of Watauga Cr., also 30 ac. tract. Reed had
high bid of $230. Aug. 12, 1839. *Eli McKee, Shff.* Wit: *J.W. GUINN.* Ack. in Mar. 1840
session. Registered June 10, 1840.

1142 JONATHAN H. WHITESIDES of Cass County, GA, to JOHN SILER of Macon, for
$300, 115 ac., Sec. 16, Dis. 16 on Cartoogecheye at mouth of a branch. Dec. 12, 1839.
J.H. Whitesides. Wit: *J.W. GUINN.* Proven in Mar. 1840 court. Reg. June 10, 1840.

1143 SAMUEL H. WATERS to JAMES FOUTS, both of Macon, for $200, 72 ac. on Burning
town Cr., Sec. 25, Dis. 17. Nov. 12, 1836. *S.H. Waters.* Wit: *ELI COLLINS, WILLIAM
(his X mark) FOUTS.* Proven by Eli Collins in Mar. 1840 ct. Registered June 10, 1840.

1144 WILLIAM HICK to JONATHAN H. WHITESIDES for $300, 115 ac. where G.W. CAR-
SON now lives, lying between ANDREW MCDANIELS & J.H. Whitesides, Sec. 16,
Dis. 16, on Cartoogecheye at mouth of a branch, purchased from state by J. HARRISON
and transferred Nov. 1822, to Wm. Hicks. Dec. 29, 1835. *William Hick.* Wit: *J.K. GRAY,
J.R. SILER.* Proven by J.R. Siler in Mar. 1840 court. Registered June 11, 1840.

1145 MICHEL WATERS to JACOB FOUTS for $500, land on "Iolee" (Iotla) Creek, Sec. 60,
Dis. 16, 140 ac. Mar. 7, 1836. *Michael (his X mark) Waters.* Wit: *JAMES FOUTS,
GEORGE ROLAND.* Proven in Mar. 1840 court. Registered June 11, 1840.

1146 WILLIAM SAWYERS to ELIZABETH SHERRELL, both of Macon, for $75, 75 ac. in
Dis. 8, on Tuckaseegee R. corner of Sec. 29 & 64. Dec. 27, 1839. *William (his X mark)
Sawyers.* Wit: *JAMES SELLARS, JAEL (or JOEL) SAWYERS.* Proven by Jael Sawyers in
Mar. 1840 court. Registered June 11, 1840.

1147 WILLIAM SAWYERS to ELIZABETH SHERRELL, both of Macon, for $100, 50 ac.,
Sec. 29, Dis. 8. Mar. 17, 1840. *Wm. (his X mark) Sawyers.* Wit: *NATHAN THOMPSON
Sr., JOEL SAWYERS.* Proven by Sawyers in Mar. 1840 ct. Registered June 11, 1840.

1147 SAUL SMITH, Clk & Master—Ct. of Equity, Macon Co., by virtue of a decree at Apr.
1836 term, returned Oct. 1836, did on Feb. 21, 1837 expose to public sale property of
JORSHUA LEDFORD, dec'd. ZACHARIAH CABE had high bid of $100 for 56 ac.,
Sec. 34, Dis. 13, near a mill shoal on Middle Cr. Mar. 27, 1840. *Saul Smith, M.C.M.E.*
Wit: *J. PHILLIPS, JOHN KIMSEY.* Ack. Mar. 1840 session. Reg. June 11, 1840.

1149 WILLIAM SAWYERS to ELIZABETH SHERRELL, both of Macon, for $125, 78 ac.,
Sec. 66, Dis. 8. Mar. 17, 1840. *William (his X mark) Sawyers.* Wit: *NATHAN
THOMPSON Senr., JOEL SAWYERS.* Proven by Sawyers in Mar. 1840 session.
Registered June 11, 1840.

1149 Mortgage: agreement between JOHN HALL of Macon, JACOB SILER of Macon, &
DAVID L. SWAIN of Orange Co., NC. John Hall drew bill of exchange in favor of
MILLER REPLY & CO., merchants of Charleston for $1110 due next Sept. & payable at
Bank of State of N.C. at Raleigh. To secure note, Hall grants Jacob Siler, for $1 further
consideration, 2 tracts, the first where John Hall resides, 218 ac., Sec. 41, Dist. 16, conveyed to Hall by MOSES WHITESIDES; second, 253+ ac., Sec. 64, Dis. 16, a tract purchased by Hall from JOHN WHITESIDES Oct. 9, 1827. If bill of exchange is not pd to
David L. Swain before Oct. 1, land to be sold to satisfy note, otherwise void. June 17,
1840. *John Hall, Jacob Siler, David L. Swain.* Wit: *J.K. GRAY,* who proved in June 1840
court. Registered June 25, 1840.

1152 SG 364, STEPHEN GRAVES, $5/100 ac., 100 ac. on Branch running by GRAY's Tanyard, Dis. 14, beginning on THOMAS line, crossing at the high falls, incl. cabbin made by JOSEPH BLACK. Entry May 12, 1836; grant July 6, 1840; reg. Sep. 21, 1840.

1153 SG 363, CLARK GUY, $5/100 ac., 100 ac. on Sugartown R. Dis. 12, corner of WIDOW BRYSON's land, runs with HIRAM GIPSON's land. Entered Jan. 22, 1839; granted June 29, 1840; registered Sep. 21, 1840.

1154 SG 358, DUCY OLIVER, $5/100 ac., 50 ac. on "Skenner" (Skeenah) Creek, Dis. 15, incl. an improvement. Entry Sep. 23, 1839; grant Apr. 28, 1840; registered Sep. 21, 1840.

1155 WILLIAM M. ASH to JACOB DETZ (could be DEBY or DOTY), both of Macon, for $53, 56 ac. on Tuckaseegee R. Feb. 28, 1838. *William M. Ash.* Wit: *AMOS ASH, J. KEENER.* Ack. in Mar. 1840 court. Registered Sep. 21, 1840.

1156 JAMES COCKERHAM to ANDREW B. GARRETT for $52, 58 ac., Sec. 76, Dis. 8. Feb. 7, 1840. *James Cockram.* Wit: *NOAH BURCHFIELD, M. GARRETT.* Proven by Noah Burchfield in Mar. 1840 court. Registered Sep. 21, 1840.

1157 WILLIAM LAMBERT of Macon to J.R. ALLMAN for $300, 59+ ac., Sec. 26, Dis. 12, crossing the river, originally granted to SAMUEL D. FINLY Dec. 29, 1835 by Patent No. 32. July 1, 1839. *William Lambert.* Wit: *S. DAVRELL?, J.R. LAMBERT.* Ack. in June 1840 court. Registered Sep. 21, 1840.

1158 JOHN W. DOWDLE of Macon to EZEKIEL DOWDLE, for val. rec'd, 3 tracts in Dist. 15: Sec. 134, 108 ac.; Sec. 155, 71 ac.; Sec. 156, 71 ac., all purchased by John W. Dowdle Oct. 28, 1836 in Franklin. Nov. 12, 1839. *John W. Dowdle.* Wit: *D.R. LOWERY.* Ack. in March 1840 court. Registered Sep. 21, 1840.

1159 JESSE BERRY of Macon to JOHN SHERREL of Burke Co., NC for $300, 49 ac., N.E. bank of Tuckaseigee R. & Newtons Mill Creek, Sec. 11, Dis. 1. June 7, 1839. *Jesse Berry.* Wit: *DAVID ELDER, SAMUEL SHERREL.* Proven by Samuel Sherrel in June 1840 court. Registered Sep. 21, 1840.

1161 JESSE R. SILER to JAMES ROBISON for $400, 99+ ac., part of Sec. 27, Dis. 16, at edge of State Rd leading from Franklin to "Murphrey" (Murphy). Mar. 24, 1840. *Jesse R. Siler.* Wit: *JOEL SAWYER, S.Y. JAMASON.* Ack. in Mar. 1840 court. Reg. Sep. 22, 1840.

1162 AVELINE CARPENTER to LABEN LONG, both of Macon, for $50, all my interest in legasees of my father's estate & all the interest in rents of all lands my father had to rent or lease, which my father owned & willed to me; my part of WILKINS plase if it should fall back to estate of my father... except what is or was in hands of my guardian, Z.J. THOMAS. Jan. 31, 1840. *Avalena (her X mark) Carpenter.* Wit: *SAUL SMITH, J.D. DRYMAN.* Proven by Smith in Mar. 1840 court. Registered Sep. 22, 1840.

1163 ELI MCKEE to Z.J. THOMAS, both of Macon, for $___, 2 tracts, one of 100 ac. on W. side Tennessee R., Sec. 74, Dis. 15, mouth of "Coweter" (Coweeta) Cr., the other adjoining, being one-half of a tract granted to RUSH & CARPENTER. June 18, 1833. *Eli McKee.* Wit: *M. KILLIAN.* Ack. in June 1840 court. Registered Sep. 22, 1840.

1164 NATHANIEL CARRELL to NANCY CARRELL, both of Macon, for val. consideration, 50 ac., Sec. 107, Dis. 15. Apr. 20, 1840. *Nathaniel (his X mark) Carrel.* Wit: *ELI MCKEE,* who proved in June 1840 session. Registered Sep. 22, 1840.

1165 BENJAMIN STILES of Macon to DAVID CARPENTER for $15, 59 ac. on "Coweter" (Coweeta) Creek, Sec. 52, Dis. 14. Apr. 23, 1839. *Benjamin Stiles.* Wit: *J.B. STILES, H.P. STILES.* Ack. in June 1840 court. Registered Sep. 24, 1840.

1166 BENJAMIN STILES to ZEBULON J. THOMAS for $10, 50-acre tract on "Turkle" (Turtle) Pond Cr.of Sugartown R., Dis. 12. Mar. 11, 1839. *Benjamin Stiles.* Wit: *SAUL SMITH, SAMUEL KELLY.* Ack. in June 1840 session. Registered Sep. 24, 1840.

1166 JAMES TRUITT to NATHAN TABER one tract of land as set forth in this certificate and quitclaim my right. Feb. 5, 1839. *J.P. Truitt.* Wit: *E.M. KILPATRICK, E.M. HALL.* Proven by E.M. Hall in Mar. 1840 session. Registered Sep. 29, 1840.

1167 CHARLES GRANT to HENRY BURNETT for $50, 81+ ac., Sec. 9, Dis. 9. May 22, 1840. *Charles Grant.* Wit: *THOS. B. GRANT.* Ack. in June 1840 session. Registered Sep. 29, 1840.

1168 SG 161, ANDREW BRYSON, $5/100 ac., 25 ac. on Cullewhee Creek, Dis. 7, beginning below the FRADY improvement, near an old line of said Bryson's land. Entered May 2, 1836; granted Dec. 15, 1838; registered Sep. 29, 1840.

1169 SG 162, HENDERSON BRYSON, $5/100 ac., 50 ac. on Cullewhe Cr., Dis. 7, on north corner of Sec. 36. Entered May 2, 1836; granted Dec. 15, 1838; registered Sep. 29, 1840.

1170 ROBERT JOHNSTON to THOMAS J. ROANE, both of Macon, for $200, 73 ac. on Cartoogechaye Cr., Dis. 15, Sec. 130. Mar. 4, 1840. *Robert Johnson.* Wit: *U. KEENER, DANEL PAYNE.* Proven by U. Keener in March 1840 court. Registered Sep. 29, 1840.

1171 DAVID CARPENTER to ZEBULON J. THOMAS, both of Macon, for $40, 59 ac. on "Coweter" (Coweeta) Creek, Dis. 14, Sec. 52. Jan. 15, 1840. *David Carpenter.* Wit: *JACOB CARPENTER.* Ack. in June 1840 court. Registered Sep. 29, 1840.

1172 J.R. ALLMAN to N.S. JARRETT for $20, 160 ac. on "Nantihaly" R., Sec. 8, Dis. 13. Apr. 10, 1840. *J.R. Allman.* Wit: *J.L. MOORE, WM. M. PENLAND.* Proven by Wm. M. Penland in June 1840 court. Registered Oct. 5, 1840.

1173 ADAM CORN to WILLIAM H. BRYSON, both of Macon, for $40, land on Cullowhee Cr., Sec. 40, Dis. 7 . Oct. 29, 1839. *Adam Corn.* Wit: *JOS. KEENER, JOHN C. BRYSON.* Proven by Jos. Keener before J.L. BAILEY in Haywood Co. NC, Oct. 6, 1840. Registered Oct. 29, 1840.

1174 ADAM CORN to WILLIAM H. BRYSON, both of Macon, for value received, land on Collowhee Cr. adj. lands of JOHN BRYSON Senr., Sec. 8, Dis. 7, containing 168 ac., originally purchased from the state by Adam Corn and JACOB TRAMEL. Corn's part supposed to be 84 ac., known by conditional line between the parties. Oct. 29, 1839. *Adam Corn.* Wit: JOS. KEENER, JOHN C. BRYSON. Proven in Haywood Co. NC by Joseph Keener before J.L. BAILEY. Registered Oct. 29, 1840.

1175 JESSE GUY to WALTER JEFFERS (JEFFREYS), both of Macon for $20, 58 ac. in Dis. 12, on corner of Sec. 20 and 36. Jun. 17, 1840. *Jesse (his X mark) Guy.* Wit: *M. RUSSEL, A.N. RUSSEL.* Proven by A.N. Russel in Sep. 1840 court. Reg. Oct. 29, 1840.

1176 THOMAS T. (or J.) POSTELL of Cherokee County, N.C. for value received to WILLIAM EVETT, a tract purchased at the land sale in Franklin in Oct. 1836, 50 ac., Sec. 60, Dis. 12. Jan. 21, 1840. *T.T. Postell.* Wit: *JOHN MCDOWELL, SILAS MCDOWELL.* Proven by Silas McDowell in Sep. 1840 court. Reg. Oct. 29, 1840.

1176 JOHN REDMAN to ABNER MOORE, both of Macon, for $32.50, 130 ac., Sec. 77, Dis. 11, purchased at the sale in Franklin, Oct. 28, 1836. Mar. 9, 1840. *John Redman.* Wit: *H.G. WOODFIN.* Proven by H.G. Woodfin in Sep. 1840 court. Reg. Oct. 29, 1840.

1176 WALTER N. BURRELL to WILLIAM BARNS, both of Macon, for $100, 123 ac. on Big Creek, crossing a fork of Big Creek, Sec. 3, Dis. 18, bought at 1836 sale in Franklin. ___ 1838. *Walter Burrel.* Wit: *DAVID MORGAN, JESSE BURRELL.* Proven by Jesse Burrell in Sep. 1840 court. Registered Nov. 2, 1840.

1178 JEREMIAH HARRISON to WM. HICKS for $300, 115 ac., the land where on I now live, lying between LUKE BARNARD's and JONATHAN H. WHITESIDE's, Sec. 16, Dis. 16, on "Cartugage" (Cartoogechaye Cr), purchased from the State in Nov. 1822. Oct. 11, 1833. *Jeremiah Harrison.* Wit: *H. ADDINGTON, J.A.R. HANKS.* Proven by Addington in Sep. 1840 court. Registered Nov. 2, 1840.

1179 JOSEPH MILLER to NOAH MILLER, both of Macon, for $150, 75 ac. (no location). Apr. 13, 1839. *Joseph Miller.* Wit: *WILLIAM HARRISON.* Proven by Harrison in Sep. 1840 court. Registered Nov. 2, 1840.

1180 MATHIAS WIKE to GEORGE FOX for $12, 50 ac. on SW side of Tuckasegee R., Dis.
6, beginning near WILBURN's improvement to above Fox's improvement. Sep. 25,
1839. *Mathias Wike. Wit: A.D. CATHEY, ROBERT FOX*. Proven by Fox in Sep. 1840
court. Registered Nov. 2, 1840.

1181 JOHN W. CRISP to HUGH GIBBS, both of Macon for $15, Sec. 91, Dis.8, purchased at
sale in Franklin, Oct. 26, 1836. July 28, 1840. *John W. Crisp*. Wit: *WM. WELCH, ISAAC
CARINGER*. Proven by Welch in Sep. 1840 session. Registered Nov. 3, 1840.

1182 WILLIAM KINSLAND to DANIEL GABBY for $500, Sec. 55, Dis. 10 containing 50
ac. and Sec. 3, Dis. 10 containing 13 ac., granted to Kinsland; 95 ac. on "Wattaga"
(Watauga) Creek, on both sides of the State Road, running though same place where
Kinsland now lives. Gabby to pay the State of N.C. $116.69 1/2 due on tract No. 55,
$5.82 1/2 due on No. 3. Apr. 8, 1840. *William Kinsland*. Wit: *WM. ROANE, SAMUEL
(his X mark) BRYSON*. Proven by Bryson in Sep. 1840 session of court. Registered Nov.
3, 1840.

1183 JOHN DOBSON to EPHRAIM AMMONS, both of Macon, for $78.25, part of Sec. 7,
Dis. 12, from corner of Dobson's fence near JOHN LEDFORD's, near the Road, near the
top of a ridge between Dobson's & Ammon's, containing 48+ ac. Apr. 25, 1837. *John
Dobson*. Wit: *MARY L. DOBSON, JOSEPH DOBSON*. Ack. in Sep. 1840 court.
Registered Nov. 3, 1840.

1184 WILLIAM KINSLAND to DANIEL GABBY for $500, Sec. 55, Dis. 10, containing 50
ac., and Sec. 3, Dis. 10, per BARNE's lot, granted to Kinsland, containing 95 ac. on
"Wattogee" (Watauga) Cr., on both sides of State Rd. (see 1182) Apr. 8, 1840. *William
Kinsland*. Wit: *WILLIAM ROANE, SAMUEL (his X mark) BRYSON*. Proven by Bryson
in Sep. 1840 session.

1185 JOHN LEDFORD to GEORGE PENLAND, both of Macon, for $1500, land on E. side
of Tennessee R. granted to JOHN STEPHENSON and conveyed to the said Ledford,
above the mouth of Kelly's Branch. Feb. 1, 1840. *John Ledford*. Wit: *J. HOWARD,
CHARLES DRYMAN*. Proven by Howard in Sep. 1840 session. Registered Jan. 10, 1841.

1186 CLARK BIRD of Macon to JONATHAN BIRD of Burke County, NC, for $30, 110.5 ac.
on W. bank of Tennessee R., Sec. 3, Dis. 17. May 13, 1840. *Clark Bird*. Wit: *LEMUEL
BIRD*. Ack. in Sep. 1840 session. Registered Jan. 10, 1841.

1187 JOHN HALL to MARY D. MOORE, both of Macon, for $30, 30 ac. in Dis. 16, on begin-
ning corner of Sec. 60. Jul. 24, 1840. *John Hall*. Wit: *JOHN F. PENDERGRASS, TIL-
MAN MOORE*. Ack. in Sep. 1840 session of court. Registered Jan. 12, 1841.

1188 WILLIAM WELCH to THOMAS WELCH of Sevier Co. TN,all my right, title & interest
in the plat annexed, No. 18, Sec. 8, containing 300 ac., given under my hand for value
received. Oct. 27, 1820. *Wm. Welch*. Wit: *MARK COLMAN, ANDREW WELCH*. Thomas
Welch to ASAPH ENLOE, JOSEPH WELCH and ABRAM ENLOE of Haywood Co.
NC, all my right, etc. to within tract of land, No. 18, Sec. 8, containing 300 ac., given
under my hand and seal. Jul. 5, 1827. *Thomas Welch*. Wit: *Wm. Welch, THOS. WELCH
Jr*. Proven by Wm. Welch in June session. Registered Jan. 12, 1841.

1189 I, ISAAC MORRISON of Macon, being parrent and guardian for BENJAMIN F. MOR-
RISON, a minor heir of said Isaac Morrison, for $10 sell all his right etc. in land on Big
Savanah Creek in Dis. 8, containing 16+ ac., to WILLIAM R. BUCKANON of Macon.
B.F. Morrison to make his own title when he comes of age. Apr. 17, 1837. *Isaac Mor-
rison*. Wit: *JOHN WILSON, JOSEPH BUCKANAN*. Proven by John Wilson in Sep. 1840
court. Registered Jan. 13, 1841.

1190 JOHN REDMAN to ABNER MOORE for $100, 2 tracts, 59 ac., Sec. 28, Dis. 11 and 50 ac., Sec. 30, Dis. 11, purchased at land sale in Franklin, Oct. 31, 1822; also an entry made by Redman in entry taker's office of Macon on May 2, 1836, Dis. 11, on corner of SETSER's land, corner of STRAIN's entered land; one other entry made on same day in Dis. 11, on bank of creek, containing 200 ac. Redman reserves to himself 20 ac. Mar. 9, 1840. *John Redmond.* Wit: *H.G. WOODFIN.* Proven by H.G. Woodfin in Sep. 1840 court. Registered Jan. 13, 1841.

1192 ROBERT JOHNSTON to THOMAS J. ROANE, both of Macon, for $300, land in Dis. 15, on Cartoogechaye Cr., part of tract No. 54, containing 28 ac., 12 poles. Mar. 5, 1840. *Robert Johnston.* Wit: *ULRICK KEENER, DANIEL PAYNE.* Proven by U. Keener in Mar. 1840 court. Registered Jan. 13, 1841.

1193 JOHN CORN to WILLIAM H. BRYSON, both of Macon, for $300, 55 ac. on "Colewhee" (Cullowhee) Creek, Sec. 12, Dis. 7. Oct. 11, 1838. *John Corn.* Wit: *J.B. AL-LISON, ROBT. A. ALLISON.* Proven by John B. Allison in Sep. 1840 court. Registered Jan. 13, 1841.

1194 JAMES WILSON of Macon to JAMES BUCHANAN Junr. for $5, 14 ac., 95 poles on line of Sec. 143 (no District given). Jun. 4, 1839. *James Willson.* Wit: *WM. R. BUCHANON, SAMUEL BUCKANON.* Proven by Wm. R. Buchanon in Sep. 1840 court. Registered Jan. 13, 1841.

1195 Sheriff's Sale: ELI MCKEE, Esq., High Sheriff of Macon, to JESSE R. SILER and DAVID R. LOWRY of Macon, for $4,000, 2,323 ac. on "Iole" (Iotla) Creek, beginning at the NE corner of Sec. 48 Dis. 16, on N. side of creek. Land was sold at public auction on order of Superior Court of Burke Co. NC in a judgment against JAMES TRUITT, JOSEPH WELCH, ROBERT HALL, J.M. BRYSON & B.S. BRITTON for $1,634.49 recovered by ISAAC T. AVERY, agent of the Bank of the State of North Carolina. The sale was Apr. 22, 1839; JAMES W. GUINN, bidding for Jesse R. Siler & David R. Lowry gave the high bid. Aug. 10, 1840. *Eli McKee, Sheriff.* Wit: *JAMES ROBISON, H.G. WOODFIN.* Proven by H.G. Woodfin in Sep. 1840 session. Reg. Jan. 13, 1841.

1198 Mortgage: BENJAMIN S. BRITTEN to JESSE R. SILER & DAVID R. LOWERY: whereas on Jul. 1, 1839, by covenant of the parties, Siler & Lowery agreed to return the tracts of land named therein which had been conditionally transferred to J.W. GUINN (see 1195). Britten transferred the property to Siler & J.R. Lowery with the promise that on repayment of several sums by Mar. 1, 1840, Siler & Lowery were to reconvey the tracts to Britten, otherwise Britten was to release his interest in the land to Siler & Lowery. Britten has failed to repay the sums, therefore, for further consideration of $1, he now sells to Siler & Lowery all his interest in the 9 tracts, including the plantation on which he lives, containing 2,290 ac. Aug. 18, 1840. *B.S. Brittian.* Wit: *JOHN SILER, JOHN CLURE.* Proven by John Clure in Sep. 1840 session. Registered Jan. 14, 1841.

1199 JONATHAN PHILLIPS, Ch'man of Court of Pleas & Qtr Sessions of Macon County to C.J. COOK of Augusta, GA, for $150, several lots in the town of Franklin: Lot 33 (1 ac.); Lot 34 (1 ac.) - 25 poles in front, on the Main St., abreast of last lot; Lot 35 (1 ac.) - five poles in front on Main St.; Lot 36 (155 poles); Lot 37 (150 poles); Lot 38 (150 poles); Lot 39 (150 poles) beginning on Main Street corner of Lot 38; Lot 40 (150 poles). All 8 lots being abreast & adj. on the Main St. Apr. 4, 1840. *J. Phillips.* Wit: *W. ROAN, W. MCCONNELL.* Ack. in Sep. 1840 session. Registered Jan. 14, 1841.

1200 JUDAH POINDEXTER to THOS. W.P. POINDEXTER, for valuable consideration, 135
ac., Sec. 35, Dis. 1 on Tennessee R., on bank of Aquella. Sep. 1, 1837. *Juday Poindexter.*
Wit: *JOHN P. BREWER, HARRELL (his // mark) POINDEXTER.* Proven by John P.
Brewer in Sep. 1840 session. Registered Jan. 14, 1841.

1202 NOAH HALL of Georgia to GEORGE CALER of Macon, for $200, 96 ac., Sec. 61, Dis.
16. Feb. 3, 1840. *N. Hall.* Wit: *B.S. BRITTEN.* Proven by B.S. Britten in Sep. 1840 session. Registered Jan. 14, 1841.

1202 Bond: JOHN HALL, CLARK BIRD, DAVID LOWERY, MICHEL WIKEL bound for
$10,000 for John Hall, duly elected clerk of court of pleas and quarter sessions. Sep. 29,
1840. Registered Jan. 14, 1841.

1203 ISAAC MORRISON to ABRAHAM SELLERS, both of Macon, land near the State ford
of Tuckaseegee R., at beginning corner of what is called the HISE tract, on Sellar's line.
Land was entered May 2, 1836; containined 3+ ac. Dec. 4, 1839. *Isaac Morrison.* Wit:
ELBERT HALL. Acknowledged in Sep. 1840 session. Reg. Jan. 14, 1841.

1203 JOHN SETTIN of Cherokee County, NC to JACOB MASON of Macon County for $75,
land on Savannah Creek, Dis. 8, on West boundary of No. 149, running with line of
Suttin's entered land. Entered Apr. 27, 1837; containing 75 acres. Oct. 2, 1839. *John
Settin.* Wit: *W.R. BUCKANAN, ISAAC MORRISON.* Proved by W.R. Buckanan in Sep.
1840 session. Registered Jan. 14, 1841.

1204 GEORGE BLACK of Macon County to JOHN H. BLACK for $500, 71 acres, Dis. 15,
Sec. 63.Sep. 13, 1834. *George Black.* Wit: DANIEL NICHOLAS, RUTH (my X mark)
BLACK. Acknowledged in Sep. 1840 session. Registered Jan. 14, 1841.

1205 JOHN R. ALLMAN of Macon County to ZEBULON J. THOMAS for $2,000, 290 ac.
on W. bank of Tuckasegee R., Oct. 1, 1831. *J.R. Allman.* Wit: *J.R. WILLIAMSON.* Acknowledged in June 1840 session. Registered Jan. 15, 1841.

1206 MATHEW MASHBURN to TELENIUS MOORE, both of Macon, for $600, two tracts
adjoining each other, lying on the west side of the Tennessee R., Dis. 16, Sec. 44, containing 76 acres; Sec. 39, 122 acres, 198 acres in all. July 23, 1840. *Mathew Mashburn.* Wit:
J.R. SILER, B.K. DICKEY, JOHN HALL. Proved by John Hall in Sep. 1840 session.
Registered Jan. 15, 1841.

1208 SG 345, to JOHN WILD, $5/100 ac., 50 acres on Burningtown Creek, Dis. 17, to a hick-
ory on the Reservation line, on line of Sec. 48. Entered Apr. 15, 1837; granted Nov. 11,
1839; registered Jan. 15, 1841.

1209 SG 413, AMOS CABE, $75. 50 acres, Sec. 6, Dis. 8 on Big Savannah Creek.Granted
Jan. 7, 1839; registered Jan. 15, 1841.

1210 SG 346, MARTIN HOGENS, $5/100 ac., 50 acres on Skeener Creek, Dis. 15, oon corner
of Sec. 106.Entered Jan. 19, 1839; granted Nov. 19, 1839; registered Jan. 15, 1841.

1211 JOHN MOORE to THOMAS J. ROANE, both of Macon, for $1,000, 87 acres on line of
Sec. 41, crossing Cartoogachaye Creek, 15 poles above a good shoal for a mill. Oct. 1,
1840. *John Moore.* Wit: *G.W. CRAFORD, JOHN H. BLACK.* Proven by John H. Black
in Sep. 1840 court. Registered Jan. 16, 1841.

1212 MOSES A. REDMON to MICHAL CLURE, both of Macon, for $75, 100 acres in Dis.
1, on fork of Bets Branch, below Redmon's improvement. Nov. 9, 1839. *Moses A. Redmon.* Wit: *ANDREW WELCH, MARK COLEMAN.* Proven by Mark Coleman in Jan.
1840 session. Registered Jan. 16, 1841.

1213 JAMES MORRISON to ISAAC MORRISON, both of Macon, for $100, 100 acres in
Dis. 8, on Big Savannah Creek, to JOHN WILLSON's beginning corner. Apr. 19, 1839.
James Morrison. Wit: *J.C.B. TRAMMEL, W.C. TATHAM.* Proven by J.B. Trammel in
June 1840 session. Registered Jan. 16, 1841.

1214 Bond: SILAS MCDOWELL, JESSE R. SILER, JAMES K. GRAY bound for $10,000
for McDowell, elected Clerk of Superior Court. Oct. 3, 1840. Registered Jan. 16, 1841.

1214 JONATHAN PHILLIPS, Ch'man of the County Ct. of Macon, to H.G. WOODFIN of
Macon, for $140.48, part of the 400 acres called the town commons, lots 7 & 8, adj. the
field recently owned by B.W. BELL, containing 10+ ac., being the 2 lots of land bought
by B.S. BRITTEN at the sale of lands in Franklin, May 21, 1835. Sep. 30, 1840. *J. Phillips.* Wit: *JOHN HALL.* Acknowledged in Sep. 1840 session. Registered Jan. 16, 1841.

1216 Bond: SILAS MCDOWELL, JESSE R. SILER, JAMES K. GRAY bound for $5,000 for
Silas McDowell, Clerk of Superior Court.   Oct. 3, 1840. Acknowledged Oct. 3, 1840.
Registered Jan. 16, 1841.

1217 SG 352, MICHAEL J. WIKLE, $5/100 ac., 50 acres on Shoal Creek, Dis. 13. Entered
Jan. 12, 1839. Granted Dec. 6, 1839. Registered Jan. 16, 1841.

1218 SG 351, MICHAEL J. WIKLE, $5/100 ac., 50 acres in Dis. 14, on Middle Cr., including
improvement on which NATHANIEL STUART now lives. Entered Jan. 12, 1839;
granted Dec. 6, 1839; registered Jan. 16, 1841.

1219 SG 355, WILLIAM DEWEESE, $5/100 ac., 50 acres on Burningtown Creek, Dis. 17,
on corner of Sec. 64. Entered Apr. 15, 1837; granted Feb. 24, 1840; registered Jan. 16,
1841.

1220 SG 160, JOHN H. BLACK, $5/100 ac., 50 acres in Dis. 15, on corner of Sec. 63, on Car-
toogechaye Creek, Thomson's fork. Entered Sep. 19, 1836; granted Dec. 15, 1838;
registered Jan. 16, 1841.

1221 Sheriff's sale: ELI MCKEE, Esq., High Sheriff of Macon, to THOMAS M. ANGEL, assignee of WILLIAM LAMBERT of Macon, several pieces of property to satisfy a judgement against HENRY HIGGINS in favor of JOHN ROBERTS for $92.67 and one in
favor of JAEL B. JAMES for $8.31, plus $10.55 cost from Superior Court and judgment
from the County Court for $221.24 plus interest; also, cost of $10.80 in favor of JESSE
R. SILER. To satisfy execution, the following property was sold at public auction on
Mar. 24, 1840: In District 11, 1st, Sec. 55 on "Elijah" (Ellijay) Creek, down the creek to
a ditch that MOORE cut, to a stoney point on SE side of creek at a cross fence to a white
oak on side of the mill pond, containing 70 acres; 2nd, Sec. 56, crossing "Elijah" (Ellijay) Cr. except 4 or 5 acres where A. VAUGHNES lives, 114 acres; 3rd, Sec. 92, 50
acres; 4th, Sec. 93, 65 acres; 5th, Sec. 95, on corner of a sand beach, 70 acres; 6th, Sec.
112, 70 acres; 7th, Sec. 101, 50 acres. Wm. Lambert bid $411. Mar. 24, 1840. *Eli
McKee, Sheriff.* Wit: *JS. ZACKARY, DILLARD LOVE.* Ack. in Jan. 1841 session.
Registered Feb. 15, 1841. I assign to Thomas M. Angel my bid for the Hagen (sic) lands
purchased by me, etc. *Wm. Lambert.* Wit: *S.B. LAMBERT.* Ack. Jan. 1841 session.
Registered Feb. 15, 1841.

1224 ISAAC MAUNEY & ZEBULON J. THOMAS, as administrators of GEORGE RISH,
dec'd, of Macon, to ELI MCKEE of Macon, 100 ac., Sec. 74, Dis. 15, on W. side of Tennessee R. at mouth of "Coweter" (Coweeta) Creek and another tract adjoining this, being
one-half of a tract granted to Rush & CARPENTER, Dis. 15, Sec. 90. ____ 1833. *Isaac
Mauny, J. Thomas.* Wit: *M. KILLIAN.* Ack. by I. Mauny & Z.J. Thomas in Jan. 1841 session. Registered Feb. 15, 1841.

1226 JAMES HUNNICUTT of Rabun Co., GA, to WILLIAM BATES of Macon for $30, 100
acres bordering Sec. 117 and 92 (no district given), bd. CARPENTER & Bates. Oct. 8,
1840. *James Hunnicutt.* Wit: *J. HOWARD, JOHN HALL.* Proven by J. Howard in Jan.
1841 session. Registered Feb. 16, 1841.

1227 JOHN STEVENSON of Union County, GA, to JOHN LEDFORD of Macon for $1,200,
205 acres, Sec. 1, Dis. 13, on E. side of Tennessee R. above Kelly's Branch.Aug. 11,
1838. *John Stevenson.* Wit: *THOS. JN. CURTIS, WM. LEDFORD.* JOHN HOWARD &
J.L. MOORE swore to prove the handwriting of John Stephenson in Jan. 1841 session.
Registered Feb. 16, 1841.

1228 ZEBULON J. THOMAS & ISAAC MAUNY, administrators of GEORGE RUSH, deceased, to JOHN R. ALLMAN for $2,000, land on the W. side of little Tennessee R. Oct. 1, 1831. *Zebulon J. Thomas, Isaac Mauny.* Wit: *JOHN WILLIAMSON.* Ack. by makers, Jan. 1841 session. Registered Feb. 16, 1841.

1229 JOHN JUSTICE to ANDREW JUSTICE, both of Macon, for $100, 50 ac. in Dis. 13, on Tennessee R., bordering Sec. 47 & 48. Mar. 17, 1840. *John Justice.* Wit: *JOHN HOWARD.* Ack. in Jan. 1841 session. Registered Feb. 17, 1841.

1230 JOHN SETTEN to JACOB MASON, both of Macon, for $75, 100 ac. tract on Savannah Cr., corner of Sec. 149, entered May 2, 1836. May 21, 1838. *John Sutten.* Wit: *W.R. BUCKANAN, ISAAC MORRISON.* Ack. Jan. 1841. Registered Feb. 17, 1841.

1231 JAMES L. JOHNSTON to JAMES ROBISON, my right in Dis. 16, Sec. 94, 97+ ac. as per certificate dated Oct. 19, 1836. Robison is to pay the State the purchase money. Dec. 24, 1840. *James L. Johnston.* Wit: *H.R. KIMZEY, I.F. GRANT.* Proven by I.R. Grant in Jan. 1841 session. Registered Feb. 17, 1841.

1232 CHARLES MCDOWELL of Burke Co., NC by his agent and attorney in fact, N.W. WOODFIN, for $300, to JOHN HOWARD of Macon, 3 undivided on-fourths of one share, or 1/6 part interest in the stud horse Marbleieu now at Franklin, which share I purchased of R.L. MICHAUX, and the other 1/4 part to HENRY G. WOODFIN for value rec'd, total 1/6 share in horse for future but not to pass any right to any claim for former shares. Jan. 20, 1841. *Charles McDowell per N.W. Woodfin.* Wit: *N.S. JARRETT.* Ack. by N.W. Woodfin, Jan. 1841 session. Registered Feb. 17, 1841.

1233 SG 63, GEORGE BLACK, $131, 71+ ac., Sec. 62, Dis. 15, crossing Thompson's? Fork of Cartoogajaye Cr. Granted Feb. 9, 1829; registered Feb. 17, 1841.

1234 SG 356, SAMUEL WATERS, $5/100 ac., 55 ac. on Burningtown Cr., Dis. 17, on corner of No. 3, crossing creek. Entered Dec. 26, 1838; granted Feb. 24, 1840; registered Feb. 17, 1841.

1235 DAVID HIGDON to JOSEPH BUCKANON for $100, Sec. 157, Dis. 8, 66 ac. on Savannah Cr. Jan. 15, 1841. *David Hegdon.* Wit: *W.C. TATHAM, ISAAC ASH.* Proven by Ash in Jan. 1841 session. Registered Feb. 18, 1841.

1236 JOHN HOWARD to LEWIS VANDYKE, both of Macon, for $10, 25 ac. beginning on Howard's line. Jan. 31, 1840. *J. Howard.* Wit: *C.M. Stiles.* Ack. in Sep. 1840 session. Registered Feb. 18, 1841.

1237 JOHN J. ROSE to RILEY MARTIN, both of Macon, for $500, 78 ac., Sec. 30, Dis. 17. Mar. 4, 1840. *John J. Rose.* Wit: *ALFORD HALL, ZACKARIAH DOWNS.* Proven by Hall, Jan. 1841 session. Registered Feb. 18, 1841.

1238 DAVID ROGERS to ANDREW BRYSON, both of Macon, for $300, 50 ac. on Cullowhee Cr., part of Sec. 11, Dis. 7, beginning at A. CORN's line. Sep. 19, 1839. *David Rogers.* Wit: *WM. NORTON, B. KERBEY.* Proven by Baily Kerbey in Jan. 1841 session. Registered Feb. 18, 1841.

1239 HENDERSON BRYSON to ANDREW BRYSON, both of Macon, for $1, 50 ac. on Cullowhee Cr., Dis. 7, on corner of Sec. 13. Mar. 10, 1840. *Henderson (his X mark) Bryson.* Wit: *B. KERBY, SAMUEL BRYSON.* Proven by B. Kerby in Jan. 1841 session. Registered Feb. 18, 1841.

1240 ELIJAH COX to JACOB SIMS, both of Macon, for $25, 100 ac. on big Savannah Cr., entered Mar. 29, 1836. Jun. 6, 1840. *Elijah Cox.* Wit: *W.R. BUCKANON, JACOB MASON.* Proven by W.R. Buckanon, Jan. 1841 session. Registered Feb. 18, 1841.

1241 ELIJAH COX of Macon to JACOB SIMS, for $25, 60 acres on W. side of Big Savannah Cr., part of entry made by JAMES MORRISON, in Dis. 8, on line of No. 8, to top of ridge that points down near to JOHN WILSON's stable, to Wilson line, entered May 2, 1836. Jun. 6, 1840. *Elijah (his X mark) Cox.* Wit: *W.R. BUCKANON, JACOB MASON.* Proven by W.R. Buckanon, Jan. 1841 session. Registered Feb. 18, 1841.

1242 ELIJAH COX to JACOB SIMS, both of Macon, land on E. side of Savannah Creek, Dis. 8, 100 ac. bd. BUCKANON, entered May 2, 1836. June 6, 1840. *Elijah (his X mark) Cox.* Wit: *W.R. BUCKANON, JACOB MASON.* Proven by W.R. Buckanon in Jan. 1841 session. Registered Feb. 18, 1841.

1243 SG 357 GEORGE W. CRAFORD, $5/100 ac., 100 ac. on "Warier" fork of Cartoogachaye Creek (Wayah Creek), Dis. 15, corner of No. 34, running with WILLIAM SILER's line. Entered _____; granted Apr. 6, 1840; registered Feb. 22, 1841.

1244 Mortgage: WILLIAM KINSLAND to WILLIAM BIRD of Macon, one iron grey horse, one red and white cow with her yearling calf, one white pided heifer and her calf. The obligation is that Bird has bound himself with Kinsland, plaintiff in case in which TRAVES ELMORE was defendant. If Kinsland fail to prosecute case with effect, he & myself should pay $100. No date. *William Kinsland.* Wit: *W.B. MORGAN.* This bill of sale is to stand good against William Kinsland until he shall pay to JAMES ROBISON the sum of about $14 or $15. Ack. by William Kinsland in June, 1840 court. Registered Feb. 24, 1841.

1245 LARKIN C. HOOPER to HENRY WILSON for $25, 19 ac. of land on Cullowhee Cr., SE corner of JOHN WATSON's land, on boundary line of Hooper's tract. Mar. 8, 1839. *L.C. Hooper.* Wit: W.W.(? smeared) BRYSON, JOHN (his X mark) WILLSON. Proven by John Willson in Jan. 1841 court. Registered Feb. 25, 1841.

1246 ISAAC MORRISON of Macon to ELIJAH COX of Haywood County, NC, for $50, 100 ac. on Big Savannah, entered Mar. 27, 1837. Jan. 6, 1840. *Isaac Morrison.* Wit: *W.R. BUCKANON, JAMES BUCKANON.* Proven by Wm. R. Buckanon in Jan. 1841 court. Registered Feb. 25, 1841.

1246 CHARLES GRANT of Macon to JAMES GRANT, son of said Charles Grant, for natural love & affection and for better maintenance & livelihood of him the sd. Charles Grant, a certain colt, two head of sheep, two sows with five pigs with their increase. Jan. 20, 1841. *Charles (his X mark) Grant.* Wit: *E.M. KILPATRICK, PETER DAVES.* Proven by E.M. Kilpatrick in Jan. 1841 court. Registered Feb. 25, 1841.

1248 JONATHAN PHILLIPS, Ch'man of County Court of Macon, to JOHN R. ALLMAN of Macon, for $125, lots in town of Franklin, No. 9 (1 ac.); also No. 21 (1 ac.) for $25, on S. side of Main Street; No. 22 (1 ac.), for $50; No. 23 (1 ac.) for $60; in Town Commons, No. 26(8+ ac.) for $70; No. 27 (5 ac.) for $52; No. 28, (5+ ac.) for $55; No. 29 (5+ ac.), $81; No. 30 (5 ac.) for $25. Dec. 1, 1840. *Jonathan Phillips.* Wit: *W.M. TATHAM, MOSES HALL.* Ack. in Jan. 1841 court. Registered Mar. 3, 1841.

1249 MOSES HALL to THOMAS SHEPPERD, both of Macon, for $256, right & title to Sec. 8, Dis. 9, containing 120 acres.Oct. 30, 1840. *Moses Hall.* Wit: *ELIJAH SHEPPARD.* Proven by Elijah Sheppard in Jan. 1841 court. Registered Mar. 3, 1841.

1250 MOSES HALL to THOMAS SHEPPERD, both of Macon, for $106, Sec. 11, Dis. 9, 53 acres. Oct. 30, 1840. *Moses Hall.* Wit: *ELIJAH SHEPHERD.* Proven by Elijah Shepherd in Jan. 1841 court. Registered Mar. 3, 1841.

1251 SG 380, JAMES A. DRYMAN, $5/100 ac., to 50 ac. on "Coweteer"(Coweeta) Creek, Dis. 14. Entered Feb. 12, 1839; granted Nov. 24, 1840; registered Mar. 3, 1841.

1252. SG 379, CHARLES DRYMAN, $5/100 ac., 50 ac., both sides of Coweter Creek, Dis. 14. Entered Feb. 12, 1839; granted Dec. 24, 1840; registered Mar. 4, 1841.

1253. SG 589, HANNAH FORTENBURY, for $24.50, 98 ac., Sec. 28, Dis. 14. Granted Dec. 17, 1840; registered Mar. 4, 1841.

1254. SG 373, ASA BRADLEY, $5/100 ac., 50 ac. on Cowee Cr., Dis. 10, on corner of Sec. 81 & 82. Entry Jan. 21, 1839; grant Nov. 24, 1840; reg. Mar. 4, 1841.

1255 SG 433, BENJAMIN STILES, $5/100 ac., 100 ac. on Hickory Knoll Creek, Dis. 13, corner of No. 11. Entered Jan. 28, 1839; granted Feb. 10, 1841; registered Mar. 5, 1841.

1256 SG 409, GEORGE WIKLE, $5/100 ac., 100 ac. on Tesenty Creek, Dis. 13, including
      LOYD's corner and NEWELL ROBISON's improvement. Entered Jan. 12, 1839;
      granted Nov. 24, 1840; registered Mar. 5, 1841.

1257 SG 608, for $122.22 to JOHN HOWARD, assignee of ARON PINSON, 85 ac., Sec. 37,
      Dis. 13, on bank of Tennessee River opposite to a rock in the river. Granted Dec. 28,
      1840; registered Mar. 6, 1841.

1258 SG 421, JOHN HOWARD, $5/100 ac., 25 ac. on waters of "Coweteer"(Coweeta) Creek,
      Dis. 14, on corner of Sec. 33. Entered Sep. 25, 1839; granted Dec. 28, 1840; registered
      Mar. 6, 1841.

1259 SG 609, JOHN HOWARD assignee of AUSTIN BANISTER, for $63.03, 89 ac., Sec. 2,
      Dis. 14 on bank of Tennessee River, crossing Commissioners Creek. Granted Dec. 28,
      1840; registered Mar. 6, 1841.

1260 SG 571, GEORGE WIKLE, $15.845, 74 ac., Sec. 63, Dis. 13. Granted Nov. 25, 1840;
      registered Mar. 6, 1841.

1261 SG 570, GEORGE WIKLE, $15/845, 70 ac., Sec. 53, Dis. 14, on bank of Tennessee
      River. Granted Nov. 26, 1840; registered Mar. 6, 1841.

1262 JOSEPH BUCKANON to JAMES WILLSON, both of Macon, for $550, all my interest
      in tract No. 4, Dis. 8, crossing little Savannah, containing 116 ac.. Dec. 7, 1835. *Joseph
      Buckanon*. Wit: *JOHN WILSON, JAMES BUCKANON*. Proven by John Wilson, Jan.
      1838 court. Registered Mar. 11, 1841.

1263 MOSES HALL to THOMAS SHEPPARD Senr., both of Macon, for $180, Sec. 20, Dis.
      9(?), containing 54 ac.. Oct. 20, 1840. *Moses Hall*. Wit: *ELIJAH SHEPHERD*. Proven in
      Jan. 1841 court by Elijah Shepherd. Registered Mar. 12, 1841.

1263 MOSES HALL to THOMAS SHEPPARD Senr. of Macon, for $300, 50 ac., Sec. 10,
      Dis. 9 on NE bank of Tennessee River. Oct. 20, 1840. *Moses Hall*. Wit: *ELIJAH
      SHEPHERD*. Proven by Elijah Shepherd in Jan. 1841 court. Registered Mar. 12, 1841.

1264 MOSES HALL to THOMAS SHEPPARD Senr., both of Macon, for $300, 64 ac., Sec. 3,
      Dis. 9, on east bank of Tennessee River. Oct. 20, 1840. *Moses Hall*. Wit: *ELIJAH
      SHEPHERD*. Proven by Elijah Shepherd in Jan. 1841 court. Registered Mar. 12, 1841.

1265 MOSES HALL to THOMAS SHEPPARD Senr., both of Macon, 152 ac., Sec. 2, Dis. 9,
      crossing Georges Creek, to a post on the river bank. Oct. 20, 1840. *Moses Hall*. Wit:
      ELIJAH SHEPHERD. Proven by Elijah Shepherd in Jan. 1841 court. Registered Mar. 12,
      1841.

1266 ISAAC MORRISON of Macon to ELIJAH COX of Haywood Co., NC, for $150, 100
      ac., entered May 2, 1836, on Savannah Creek, Dis. 8. Jan. 6, 1840. *Isaac Morrison*. Wit:
      W.R. BUCKANON, JAMES BUCKANON. Proven by W.R. Buckanon in Jan. 1841 court.
      Registered Mar. 12, 1841.

1266 HENRY HUGIN of Macon to JOHN DAVES for $20, 35 ac., part of a tract in Dis. 11 on
      "Ellijah" (Ellijay) Creek, on E. side of Battle Branch, on top of ridge to Z. PEAK's line,
      surveyed Jan. 5, 1838. Jan. 16, 1841. *Henry Hugin*. Wit: *THOS. LONG, WM (his X
      mark) BIRD*. Acknowledged by H. Hagen in Jan. 1841 court. Registered Mar. 12, 1841.

1268 ISAAC MORRISON to ELIJAH COX, both of Macon, for $50, 60 ac. on west side of
      Big Savannah Creek, part of an entry made by I. Morrison cornering on west boundary
      line of No. 8, Dis. 8, running with line of No. 8 to the top of a ridge that points down
      near to JOHN WILSON's stable... to Wilson's line. Feb. 24, 1840. *Isaac Morrison*. Wit:
      W.R. BUCKANON, JACOB MASON. Proven by Wm. R. Buckanon in Jan. 1841 court.
      Registered Mar. 12, 1841.

1269 Sheriff's sale: ELI MCKEE, Esq., High Sheriff of Macon to T.J. ROANE of Macon, to satisfy an execution of the County Court of Macon against JOHN H. BLACK for $66.20 principal plus $6.375 interest and cost recovered by MARTIN BAKER of Black, sold at public sale a tract owned by Black: part of Sec. 61, Dis. 15, on south bank of Thompson's fork of "Cartoogahee" (Cartoogachaye) Creek, containing 10.5 ac.. At the sale held Mar. 24, 1840, T.J. Roane had high bid of 57 cents. Mar. 24, 1840. *Eli Mckee, Shff.* Acknowledged in Jan. 1841 court. Registered Mar. 12, 1841.

1271 Sheriff's sale: ELI MCKEE, Esq., High Sheriff of Macon to SAMUEL WATERS of Macon, to satisfy an execution of the County Court of Macon against JOHN HANNAH for $29.50 principal plus 40 cents cost recovered by JOAB L. MOORE of Hannah, sold at public sale a tract of 50 ac. owned by Hannah on W. bank of Brown's Creek, Sec. 63, Dis. 17. At the sale held Aug. 24, 1840, Samuel H. Waters had high bid of $7.50. Aug. 24, 1840. *Eli Mckee, Shff.* Wit: THOS. J. ROAN, LEMUEL BIRD. Proven by T.J. Roan in Jan. 1841 court. Registered Mar. 15, 1841.

1273 Sheriff's sale: ELI MCKEE, Esq., High Sheriff of Macon to SAMUEL WATERS of Macon, to satisfy an execution of the County Court of Macon against JOHN HANNAH for $29.50 principal plus 40 cents cost recovered by JOAB L. MOORE of Hannah, sold at public sale a tract owned by Hannah, Sec. 62, Dis. 17. At sale held Aug. 24, 1840, Waters had high bid of $7.50. Nov. 12,, 1840. *Eli Mckee, Shff.* Wit: THOS. J. RONE, LEM'L BIRD. Proven by T.J. Roane in Jan. 1841 court. Registered Mar. 17, 1841.

1275 Sheriff's sale: ELI MCKEE, Esq., High Sheriff of Macon to T.J. ROANE of Macon, to satisfy an execution of the County Court of Macon against JOHN H. BLACK for $66.20 principal plus $6.37 interest and cost recovered by MARTIN BAKER of Black, sold at public sale a tract owned by Black: Sec. 63, Dis. 15, containing 71.5 ac. At sale held Mar. 24, 1840, Roane had high bid of $49. Mar. 24, 1840. *Eli Mckee, Shff.* Ack. in Jan. 1841 court. Registered Mar. 19, 1841..

1277 Sheriff's sale: ELI MCKEE, Esq., High Sheriff of Macon to T.J. ROANE of Macon, to satisfy an execution of the County Court of Macon against JOHN H. BLACK for $66.20 principal plus $6.37 interest and cost recovered by MARTIN BAKER of John H. Black, sold at public sale a tract owned by Black: 50 ac. on Thompsons fork of "Cartoogahee" (Cartoogachaye) Creek, on east corner of Sec. 63, Dis. 15. At sale held Mar. 24, 1840, Roane had high bid of $3.125. Mar. 24, 1840. *Eli Mckee, Shff.* Acknowledged by maker in Jan. 1841 court. Registered Mar. 19, 1841.

1279 JONATHAN H. WHITESIDES, executor of estate of CALEB A. HOOD of Cass County, GA, to MOSES ADDINGTON of Macon for $58, 56+ ac. on "Cautagah" (Cartoogechaye) Creek, crossing Wolf (Wayah) Cr., Sec. 38, Dis. 15, sold in land sale in 1820. Dec. 12, 1839. *J.H. Whitesides.* Wit: J.W. GUINN, D.R. LOWRY. Proven by Guinn in Mar. 1841 court. Registered June 1841.

1280 ENOS SHEALS to LEVI BUCKNER, both of Macon, 157 ac. on Sec. 3, Dis. 16, purchased at land sale in Franklin, Sep. 24, 1838; Buckner to pay amount due State. Mar. 20, 1841. *Enos Shealds.* Wit: HENRY DEWESE, JOHN WILDE. Proven by John Wilds in Mar. 1841 court. Registered June 7, 1841.

1281 Mortgage: JOHN HALL of Macon to DILLARD LOVE, for $5 and other consideration, to secure Love against hazard, (Love having put up bond as security of John Hall as guardian of his children by sd Hall's first wife), mortgages to Love 4 Negro slaves, DANNY, ELIAS, MERIAN, & BECK, and two tracts in Macon, Sec. 64, Dis. 16, conveyed by JOHN WHITESIDES to Hall by deed registered in Haywood Co. NC, Book B, page 469 on July 10, 1828, containing 252+ ac., the other adjoining the tract said Hall now lives on, Sec. 41, Dis ?, containing 213 ac. The property is to remain in the possession of Hall; mortgage to be void when the bond is discharged. _____ 1841. *John Hall, Dillard Love.* Wit: H.G. WOODFIN, T.M. ANGEL. Acknowledged by makers in Mar. 1841 court. Registered June 7, 1841.

1282 JOHN STILES of Macon to ISAAC ASH, land purchased Oct. 28, 1820, Sec. 5, Dis. 8.
       Oct. 23, 1831. *John Stiles*. Wit: *JESSE ASH*. Proven by Jesse Ash in Mar. 1841 court.
       Registered June 7, 1841.

1283 ABNER MOORE to WILLIAM ARNOLD, both of Macon, for $90.70, Sec. 52, Dis. 11,
       containing 58 ac. on Sugartown fork of Tennessee River. Nov. 25, 1839. *Abner Moore*.
       Wit: *SAMUEL BRYSON, ENOCH UNDERWOOD*. Ack. in Mar. 1841 court. Registered
       June 9, 1841.

1284 SG 602, THOMAS WEST, assignee of JESSE F. PAGET, for $12.50, 50 ac., Sec. 25,
       Dis. 10, on Middle Fork of Cowee Creek. Granted Dec. 12, 18__(1831); registered June
       9, 1841.

1285 SG 435, THOMAS WEST, $5/100 ac., 50 ac. on N. fork of Cowee Creek, Dis. 10, on
       corner of Sec. 64. Entered Sep. 24, 1839; granted Feb. 18, 1841; registered June 10, 1841.

1286 SG 374, JOSEPH BUCKHANAN, $5/100 ac., 100 ac. on Savannah Creek, Dis. 8, on
       corner of W.R. BUCKANAN's land. Entered June 9, 1838; granted Nov. 24, 1840;
       registered June 10, 1841.

1287 SG 601, THOMAS WEST, assignee of J.F. PAGET, for $12.50, 50 ac., Sec. 64, Dis. 10.
       Granted Dec. 17, 1840; registered June 10, 1841.

1288 SG 403, RICHARD WILSON, $5/100 ac., 100 ac. on Savannah Cr., Dis. 8. Entered Oct.
       2, 1838; granted Nov. 24, 1840; registered June 10, 1841.

1289 SG 593, to PETER LONG, assignee of RICHARD WILSON, for $18, 75 ac., Sec. 53,
       Dis. 7, crossing Cullowhee. Granted Dec. 17, 1840; registered June 10, 1841.

1290 SG 410, RICHARD WILSON, $5/100 ac., 30 ac. on Savannah Creek. Entered Feb. 15,
       1839; granted Nov. 24, 1840; registered June 10, 1841.

1291 SG 619, HUGH ROGERS, $22, 88 ac., Sec. 44, Dis. 7. Granted Jan. 12, 1841; registered
       June 10, 1841.

1292 SG 540, MOSES ADDINGTON, $25, 100 ac., Sec. 11, Dis. 15. Granted Apr. 4, 1839;
       registered June 10, 1841.

1293 SG 310, WALES W. DOBSON, $5/100 ac., 100 ac. on JOHN HALL's Mill Creek, Dis.
       16, on NW corner of JAMES ROBISON's line, on CRUSE's line. Entered May 2, 1836;
       granted Dec. 24, 1838; registered June 10, 1841.

1294 SG 401, RICHARD WILSON, $5/100 ac., 70 ac. on Savanah Creek, Dis. 8. Entered June
       3, 1837; granted Nov. 24, 1840; registered June 10, 1841.

1295 SG 578, SAMUEL H. WATERS & JOHN DAVIS, for $43.80, 219 ac., Sec. 3, Dis. __,
       on boundary of SIX KILLER's Reservation, NE corner of No. 1. Granted Nov. 28, 1840;
       registered June 10, 1841.

1296 SG 406, JAMES WILSON, $5/100 ac.. 50 ac. on east side of "Cullewhee" (Cullowhee)
       Creek, Dis. 7, on corner of No. 62. Entered Feb. 28, 1838; granted Dec. 24, 1840;
       registered June 10, 1841.

1297 SG 595, THOMAS P. MOORE, $32, 98 ac., Sec. 52, Dis. 16. Granted Dec. 17, 1840;
       registered June 10, 1841.

1298 SG 612, to TRAVIS ELMORE, for $___, 63 ac., Sec. 13, Dis. 11. Granted Dec. 30,
       1840; registered June 10, 1841.

1299 SG 597, MICHAEL WIKLE, $14, 56 ac., Sec. 76, Dis. 17, on W. bank of Tennessee
       River. Granted Dec. 17, 1840; registered June 10, 1841.

1300 SG 371, to JAMES BUCKANON, JOHN WILSON, JACOB MASON, trustees, for
       $5/100 ac., 37 ac. on Savannah Cr., including a meeting house and for that purpose
       entered Jan. 7, 1839; granted Nov. 24, 1840; registered June 10, 1841.

1301 SG 591, JOHN KIMSEY, $15.60, 62+ ac., Sec. 89, Dis. 15. Granted Dec. 17, 1840;
       registered June 11, 1841.

1302 SG 405, WILLIAM WILSON, Junr., $5/100 ac., 50 ac., E. side of Cullewhee Cr., Dis. 7, on line of No. 25. Entered Feb. 28, 1838; granted Nov. 24, 1840; registered June 11, 1841.

1303 SG 600, JOHN WILSON, for $16, 56 ac., Sec. 160, Dis. 8, beginning at a stony point near Betts Branch. Granted Dec. 17, 1840; registered June 11, 1841.

1304 ENOS SCROGGS of Macon to SAMUEL W. DOWDLE, for $400, 133 ac. tract on E. side of Tennessee R., on N. corner of WILLIAM CABE's survey. Dec. 3, 1839. *Enos Scrogg.* Wit: *JETH BRYSON, JOHN SCROGGS.* Proven by Jeth Bryson in Mar. 1841 court. Registered June 12, 1841.

1305 SG 615, JAMES CONNELLY, for $38.40, 125 ac., Sec. 23, Dis. 8, crossing Wessers Creek. Granted Dec. 31, 1840; registered June 28, 1841.

1306 SG 616, JAMES CONNELLY, for $13, 52 ac., Sec. 22, Dis. 8, crossing W. fork of Wesser's Creek. Granted Jan. 2, 1841; registered Jun. 28, 1841.

1307 SG 614, JAMES CONNELLY, for $26.62, 63+ ac., Sec. 24, Dis. 8, crossing Wesser's Creek. Granted Dec. 31, 1840; registered June 8, 1841.

1308 SG 623, JESSE BERRY, for $319.785, 161+ ac., Sec. 26, Dis. 8, on bank of "Tuckasejah" (Tuckaseegee) River. Granted Apr. 26, 1840; registered June 28, 1841.

1309 SG 622, MOSES WHITESIDES, for $385.32, 218 ac., Sec. 41, Dis. 16. Granted Apr. 24, 1841; registered June 28, 1841.

1310 SG 396, DANIEL ROGERS, $5/100 ac., 100 ac. on "Culliwhee" (Cullowhee) Cr., Dis. 7, on SE corner of said Roger's line. Granted Nov. 24, 1840; registered June 28, 1841.

1311 SG 617, JAMES CONNELLY, $13.75, 55 ac., Sec. 98, Dis. 8. Granted Jan. 2, 1840; registered June 28, 1841.

1312 SG 382, BUCKNER GUY, $5/100 ac., 50 ac. on Silas or Silers Branch, joining GUY's land. Entered Sep. 25, 1838; granted Nov. 24, 1840; registered June 28, 1841.

1313 SG 579, JOHN BRYSON Senr. & WILLIAM A. BRYSON, assignees of JACOB B. TRAMMELL & ADAM CORN, for $___, 168 ac., Sec. 8, Dis. 7, crossing Cullowhee Creek. Granted Nov. 28, 1840; registered June 28, 1841.

1314 SG 38, WILLIS GUY, $5/100 ac., 50 ac. on "Sileyes" Branch, Dis. 12, on boundary line of said Guy's land. Entered Aug. 10, 1838; granted June 28, 1841; registered Nov. 27, 1840.

1315 SG 625, MOSES ADDINGTON, assignee of DRURY LOGAN, $13.75, 65 ac., Sec. 153, Dis. 15. Granted Apr. 27, 1841; registered June 28, 1841.

1316 SG 430, ALFORD WILSON, $5/100 ac., 100 ac. on Tuckaseegee R., Dis. 6, to top of a ridge between Beetree Cr. and head of Wilson's Mill Branch. Entered May 2, 1836; granted Jan. 12, 1841; registered June 28, 1841.

1317 SG 626, MOSES ADDINGTON, for $30, 121+ ac., Sec. 15, Dis. 15. Granted Apr. 28, 1841; registered June 28, 1841.

1318 SG 375, JOHN CLURE, $5/100 ac., 50 ac. on Lowery fork of "Cartugahay" (Cartoogechaye) Cr., Dis. 15, on corner of said Clure's entered land No. 909. Entered Jan. 21, 1839; granted Nov. 24, 1840; registered June 28, 1841.

1319 SG 629, LEVI WILLSON, $27, 50 ac., Sec. 131, Dis. 8. Granted Apr. 27, 1841; registered June 28, 1841.

1320 SG 376, JOHN COCKRAN, $5/100 ac., 100 ac., Dis. 10, on N. fork of Cowee Cr., corner of No. 67. Entered Jan. 22, 1839; granted Nov. 24, 1840; registered June 29, 1841.

1321 SG 599, SAMUEL WIKLE, $12, 50 ac., Sec. 145, Dis. 8, on W. bank of big Savannah Creek. Granted Dec. 17, 1840; registered June 29, 1841.

1322 SG 397, JOHN B. STILES, $5/100 ac., 100 ac. on Bets fork of Savannah Cr., Dis. 8. Entered Mar. 30, 1841; granted Nov. 24, 1841; registered June 29, 1841.

1323 SG 596, NATHAN TABER, assignee of JAMES TRUITT, for $12.56, 50 ac., Sec. 33, Dis. 9, on left-hand fork of Mill Cr., crossing Mill Creek. Granted Dec. 17, 1840; registered June 29, 1841.

1324 SG 412, ALEXANDER ZACHARY, $5/100 ac., 50 ac. on Chattooga R., Dis. 18, on line of No. 74. Entered Sep. 6, 1838; granted Dec. 24, 1840; registered June 29, 1841.

1325 SG 598, SAMUEL WIKLE, $14.75, 59 ac., Sec. 137, Dis. 8. Granted Dec. 17, 1840; registered June 29, 1841.

1326 SG 426, LEVI BUTLER, $5/100 ac., 100 ac. on Gum Bottom Cr., Dis. 18, on corner of MOSES BUTLER's survey. Entered Dec. 8, 1838; granted Dec. 30, 1840; registered June 29, 1841.

1327 SG 427, MOSES BUTLER, $5/100 ac., 50(?) ac. on Bear Camp Cr., Dis. 18. Entered Dec. 8, 1838; granted Dec. 30, 1840; registered June 27, 1841.

1328 SG 425, ARON BUTLER, $5/100 ac., 100 ac. on Laurel Creek, Dis. 18. Entered Dec. 8, 1838; granted Dec. 30, 1840; regsitered June 29, 1841.

1329 SG 394, SILAS MCDOWELL, $5/100 ac., 50 ac. on Sugartown River. Entered Oct. 10, 1838; granted Nov. 4, 1840; registered June 29, 1841.

1330 SG 424, PETER BUTLER, $5/100 ac., 60 ac. on Bear Camp Cr., Dis. 18, near a mill shoal, including AMOS DAGGINS improvement. Entered Dec. 8, 1838; granted Dec. 30, 1840; registered June 29, 1841.

1331 SG 293, WALLICE W. DOBSON, $5/100 ac., 50 ac. beginning on a ridge dividing "Iola" (Iotla) and "Cartoogyaye" (Cartoogechaye) waters, Dis. 16, on line of Sec. 54 & 55. Entered May 2, 1836; granted Nov. 20, 1838; registered June 29, 1841.

1332 SG 372, LOGAN BERRY, $5/100 ac., 50 ac. on Elijah and Cats Cr. in Dis. 11. Entered June 11, 1836; granted Nov. 24, 1840; registered June 29, 1841.

1333 SG 393, SILAS MCDOWELL, $5/100 ac., 50 ac. on Sugartown R. above the falls, beginning where a trace crosses a branch. Entered Oct. 10, 1838; granted Nov. 24, 1840; registered June 29, 1841.

1334 ARCHABALD MORRISON of Haywood Co. NC to ANDREW PREASLEY of Macon, for $100, two tracts, Sec. 58, Dis. 7, containing 63 ac. and Sec. 59, Dis. 7, containing 57 ac. Oct. 6, 1840. *Archabald Morrison.* Wit: *J. KEENER, J.B. ALLISON.* Proven by John B. Allison before JOHN L. BAYLEY, one of the judges of the Superior Court of Law and Equity, Oct. 7, 1840. Registered June 29, 1841.

1334 SAMUEL SMITH to BRYANT CONNELLY for $3,000, land in Dis. 13, Sections 14, 15 and 17, beginning at a post on the E. bank of the Tennessee R., crossing Tessenty (Tessentee) Cr., containing 463+ ac. Mar. 27, 1839. *Sam'l Smith.* Wit: *JOHN MCDOWELL, ANDREW J. CONNELLY.* Ack. in June 1841 court. Registered June 29, 1841.

1336 Mortgage: JEREMIAH NATIONS of Macon to WILLIAM H. THOMAS of Haywood Co. NC, for one shilling, one horse 4 years old, one blend gray mare, two cows & calves, all my stock hogs, 25 head, all my geese, chickens, ducks, seven head of sheep, 25 bushels of corn, 100 pounds of bacon, all my household and kitchins furniture and my standing crop of corn & oats. The condition being that whereas Nations is indebted to Thomas to the amount of one note of hand dated Jan 1, 1841, for sum of $99.84, if he repay loan, this mortgage is void. May 24, 1841. *Jeremiah (his X mark) Nations.* Ack. at courthouse in Franklin, May 26, 1841, at an extra court. Registered July 15, 1841.

1338 SG 370, WILLIAM S. ANDERSON, $5/100 ac., 100 ac. on the Smoky Mountain, beginning at a sugartreee in the State line. Entered Nov. 20, 1839; granted Nov. 24, 1840; registered Sep. 7, 1841.

1339 SG 292, JOHN MOORE, $292.50, 97+ ac., Sec. 34, Dis. 15, crossing "Woolf" (Wayah) Creek. Granted Apr. 23, 1840; registered Sep. 7, 1841.

1340 SG 368, MARY ANDERSON, $5/100 ac., 100 ac. on the Smoky Mountain, beginning at
a sugartreeeon the bank of a branch, including the head of Eagle Creek. Entered Nov. 20,
1839; granted Nov. 24, 1840; registered Sep. 7, 1841.

1341 SG #___, ROBERT MCCAMPBELL, $5/100 ac., 100 ac. on the Smoky Mountain in
Dis. 1, beginning on south side of "Egle" (Eagle) Creek. Entered Nov. 20, 1839; granted
Nov. 24, 1840; registered Sep. 7, 1841.

1342 SG 369, SAMUEL E.H.B. ANDERSON, $5/100 ac., 100 ac. on the Smoky Mountain,
beginning at a sugartree in the State line. Entered Nov. 20, 1839; granted Nov. 24, 1840;
registered Sep. 7, 1841.

1343 SG 388, ROBERT MCCAMPBELL, $5/100 ac., 100 ac. on the Smoky Mountain, begin-
ning at a beech in the State line. Entered?; granted Nov. 24, 1840; registered Sep. 7, 1841.

1344 SG 390, WILLIAM MCCAMPBELL, $5/100 ac., 100 ac. on the Smoky Mountain, Dis.
1, beginning at a beech in the State line. Entered Nov. 20, 1839; granted Nov. 24, 1840;
registered Sep. 8, 1841.

1345 SG 400, AARON THOMAS, $5/100 ac., 50 ac. on Middle Cr., on SW corner of his mill
tract. Entered Sep. 21, 1837; granted Nov. 24, 1840; registered Sep. 8, 1841.

1346 SG 389, JANE MCCAMPBELL, $5/100 ac., 100 ac. on the Smoky Mtn, beginning at a
sugartree in the State line, to beginning which is 40 poles east of the four mile tree.
Entered Nov. 20, 1839; granted Nov. 24, 1840; registered Sep. 8, 1841.

1347 SG 402, LEONARD WOOD, $5/100 ac., 100 ac. on the Smoky Mtn, beginning at a
beech, on s. side of "Egle" (Eagle) Cr., including a cabin. Entered Nov. 20, 1839; granted
Nov. 24, 1840; registered Sep. 8, 1841.

1348 NATHAN B. THOMPSON of Macon to WILLIAM H. THOMAS of Haywood Co. NC,
for $300, land on Wessers Cr., Sec. 20, Dis. 8, containing 67+ ac. June 15, 1841. *Nathan
B. Thompson.* Wit: *J.L. MOORE, M. WIKLE.* Ack. in June 1841 court. Registered Sep. 9,
1841.

1349 DAVID MCCONNELL, JOHN SCROGGS & his wife POLLY, SARAH MCCON-
NELL, JONATHAN DENTON & his wife AGNES, DAVID CARPENTER guardian of
the heirs of WILLIAM CARPENTER, dec'd, PEGGY CARPENTER widow of William
Carpenter dec'd, CHARLES STILES & his wife KIZZY, WILLIAM MCCONNELL,
WILLIAM CABE & his wife ELIZABETH, ENOS SCROGGS & his wife JANE,
MILAS MCCONNELL, JOHN D. DRYMAN & his wife RACHEL, SANFORD CAR-
PENTER & his wife PATIENCE, heirs at law of William McConnell, dec'd, to JOHN
MCCONNELL, for $500, a tract granted to William McConnell, dec'd, on a conditional
line made by William McConnell, dec'd and THOMAS KIMSEY ... to the river, to a con-
ditional line between David McConnell & William McConnell, dec'd, containing 150
ac., except the widow's thirds during her lifetime. Feb. 14, 1840. *David (his X mark) Mc-
Connell, Sarah (her X mark) McConnell, Jonathan (his X mark) Denton, Agnes (her X
mark) Denton, Milas (his X mark) McConnell, Enos Scroggs, Jane Scroggs, William Mc-
Connell, Sanford Carpenter, Patience (her X mark) Carpenter, Charles (his X mark)
Stiles, Kizzy (her X mark) Stiles, William Cabe, Elizabeth (her X mark) Cabe, John D.
Dryman, Rachel (her X mark) Dryman, John Scruggs, Mary (her X mark) Scruggs,
Peggy (her X mark) Carpenter. David Carpenter* signed as guardian of Wm Carpenter's
heirs. Wit: *ELISHA L. KIMSEY, J. HOWARD.* Proven by Elijah Kimsey in June 1841
court. Registered Sep. 10, 1841.

1351 JOHN B. LOVE of Haywood Co., NC, to JOHN SHULAR Senr. of Macon, for $2,500, 640 ac. on Tuckasegee R., near mouth of Deep Creek, known by the name of BIG BEAR's Reservation in consequence of its having been granted by the United States to a Cherokee Indian by the name of YONA, alias Big Bear, under a treaty of 1819, beginning on a ridge on the north side of the river, crossing the river, to the side of a ridge in the head of a hollow. May 26, 1841. *John B. Love*. Wit: *ALLEN FISHER, WM. H. THOMAS*. Proven by William H. Thomas in June 1841 court. Registered Sep. 11, 1841.

1352 JOHN DOBSON of Macon to JAMES W. GUINN, my Negro boy JOHN, abt 9 years of age, for $450 as well as 8 month's work by sd boy, commencing on today; I warrant him to be sound & sensible and to be a slave for life, and free of all other claims. Mar. 3, 1841. *John Dobson*. Wit: *J.K. GRAY*. Proven by J.K. Gray in June 1841 court. Registered Sep. 11, 1841.

1353 WILLIAM H. THOMAS to UTE HYATT, both of Haywood Co. NC, for $2,000, 173 ac. on bank of Tuckasegee River, Sec. 27, Dis. 8. Dec. 25, 1838. *Wm. H. Thomas*. Wit: *GEORGE SHERRILL, JOHN C. SHERRILL*. Acknowledged in Jun. 1841 court. Registered Sep. 11, 1841.

1354 RICHARD WILSON to WILLIAM TATHAM for $300, 85 ac. in Dis. 8 on Savannah Cr., an moiety of tract 11, to the still house branch, with meanders of branch to the creek, to the State Road, westward with the lane to the first ridge. Dec. 9, 1840. *Richard Wilson*. Wit: *JOHN MCDOWELL, LEVI WILSON*. Ack. in June 1841 court. Registered Sep. 11, 1841.

1355 JOHN MOORE of Cherokee County, NC to GEORGE W. CRAWFORD of Macon, for $400, Sec. 34, Dis. 15, containing 97+ ac., crossing "Woolf" (Wayah) Creek. June 18, 1841. *John Moore*. Wit: *G.W.I. MOORE*. Proven by G.W.I. Moore in June 1841 court. Registered Sep. 11, 1841.

1356 WILLIAM LAMBERT to H.G. WOODFIN, both of Macon, for $120, land in Franklin, Lots #48, 50, 51, 52 and 53. Feb. 17, 1841. *Wm. Lambert*. Wit: *J.R. ALLMAN, JAMES ROBISON*. Ack. in June 1841 court. Registered Sep. 11, 1841.

1357 Deed of Gift: DAVID SHULAR of Macon to NANCY L. JULETTY HYDE, minor daughter of CATHERINE HYDE, one pale red cow and calf with a crop in the left and split in the right ears, with all their increase, for benefit of Nancy L. Julettey, yet cow and calf with increase remains virtually mine. June 10, 1841. *David Shular*. Wit: *N. BURCHFIELD, WILLIAM HYDE*. Proven by N. Burchfield in June 1841 court. Registered Sep. 11, 1841.

1358 Deed of Gift: JOHN B. LOVE of Haywood County, for natural love and affection for ELIZABETH ANN WELCH, daughter of WM. WELCH of Macon formerly, but now of Cherokee County, NC, three beds and furniture, two ovens and lids, three pots, one spider or baker, two sets of fire dogs, four ? and cards, one table and six plates, a set of knives and forks, a set of tea cups and sausers, four "bales," six chairs, two tin trunks, one trunk, one chest, a chair base, six hogheads and other barrels and sundry other small articles, "two tedeous to mention" including whole of property that I bought at Sheriff sale by agency of JOHN GIBBS and sold as property of the aforesaid Wm. Welch some years past and left by me in his possession, etc. Mar. 23, 1841. *John B. Love*. Wit: *John Gibbs, HUGH GIBBS*. Acknowledged in my office Mar. 23, 1841, JOHN HALL, Clerk. Registered Sep. 11, 1841.

1358 JACOB SIMS to JOHN WILSON & WILLIAM TATHAM, for $100, three tracts, one of 100 ac. on Big Savannah, on corner of JACOB MASON's land, running with line of No. 8, occupied by ELIZA (ELIJAH?) COX, including a mill; the second, 100 ac. on east side of Savannah, running to a stake on WM. BUCKANON's line; the third 6 ac. on west boundary of No. 8, running to atop of a ridge pointing down near John Wilson's stable, running with Wilson's old tract. Feb. 27, 1841. *Jacob Sims*. Wit: *W.R. BUCKANON, JAEL SIMS*. proven by Wm. R. Buckanon in June 1841 court. Registered Sep. 11, 1841.

1360 ANDREW WELCH to WILLIAM COCKERHAM, my right and interest in annexed certificate, Sec. 105, Dis. 8. Apr. 17, 1837. *Andrew Welch.* Wit: *JESSE C.C. COCKER-
HAM.* Proven by J.C. Cockerham. Registered Sep. 12, 1841.

1360 WILLIAM GARLAND to SAUL SMITH, both of Macon, for $27.85, 100 ac. on Middle
Creek, Dis. 13. Oct. 12, 1840. *William Garland.* Wit: *H.G. WOODFIN, ELIJAH
THOMAS.* Proven by Woodfin in June 1841 court. Registered Sep. 12, 1841.

1362 SG 367, DAVID GUYER, $5/100 ac., 50 ac. on Burningtown Cr., Dis. 17, on SW corner
of JOHN WELCH's entered land No. 1676, near line of Sec. 59. Entered Feb. 6, 1840;
granted Nov. 17, 1840; registered Sep. 13, 1841.

1363 SG 572, to PHILLIP GUYER, assignee of BENJAMIN S. BRITTAIN, for $5/100 ac.,
117+ ac., Sec. 57, Dis. 16, crossing the Creek "Iolee" (Iotla). Granted Nov. 23, 1840;
registered Sep. 13, 1841.

1364 SG 439, DAVID GUYER, $5/100 ac., land on Iola (Iotla) Creek, Dis. 16, beginning at a
hickory on the south side of LEACHE's Reservation corner No. 87.Entered Sep. 28,
1838; granted Aug. 23, 1841; registered Sep. 13, 1841.

1365 SG 419, JOHN SUTTON, $5/100 ac., 50 ac. on Savannah Creek, Dis. 8, running with
boundary line of CARPENTER's entered land. Entered Oct. 4, 1837; granted Dec. 28,
1840; registered Sep. 13, 1841.

1366 JESSE R. SILER of Macon to DAVID L. SWAIN of Orange Co., NC, for $2,500, land
on "Iolee" (Iotla) Creek, corner of No. 48, Dis. 16 on N. side of "Iola" & N. of Methodist
Provident Meeting House, west to line of Sec. 96, crossing both forks of Iola, to a stake
at THOMAS MOOR's fence, to bank of a ditch, containing 2,323 ac., embracing Sec. 48,
part of 47, part of 51, 49, 50, 96, 86, 80, Entry No. 982 & Entry No. 984. Aug. 1, 1841.
J.R. Siler. Wit: *WM. H. THOMAS, N.S. JARRETT.* Siler acknowledged within before
MATTHIAS E. MANLY, one of the judges of Superior Court, Sep. 16, 1841. Registered
Sep. 20, 1841.

1368 SG 416, JESSE HALL, $5/100 ac., 43 ac. on Savannah Cr., on corner of JORSHUA
HALL's land. Entered Sep. 21, 1838; granted Dec. 22, 1840; registered Sep. 30, 1841.

1369 SG 365, WILLIAM WILLIAMS, $5/100 ac., 50 ac. on "Elejaye" (Ellijay) Creek, Dis.
11, to a stake on Williams' line. Entered May 2, 1836; granted Nov. 2, 1840; registered
Oct. 30, 1841.

1370 SG 395, ASHBEL ROADS, $5/100 ac., 100 ac. on Burningtown Cr., Dis. 17, on corner
of Sec. 55. Entered Nov. 27, 1838; granted Nov. 24, 1840; registered Oct. 30, 1841.

1371 SG 385, RICHARD JONES, $5/100 ac., 100 ac. on Big Savannah Creek, Dis. 8. Entered
Mar. 29, 1837; granted Nov. 24, 1840; registered Oct. 30, 1841.

1372 SG 383, THOMAS GRANT, $5/100 ac., 50 ac., Dis. 9, on corner of Sec. 17. Entered
May 2, 1836; granted Nov. 24, 1840; registered Oct. 30, 1841.

1373 SG 387, JOHN LOWDERMILK, $5/100 ac., 50 ac. on "Elijah" (Ellijay) Creek, Dis. 11,
beginning at a beech in the bank of a branch. Entered Oct. 27, 1838; granted Nov. 24,
1840; registered Oct. 30, 1841.

1374 SG 309, JAMES W. GUINN, $5/100 ac., 50 ac. on Sugartown (Cullasaja) River, Dis. 12,
crossing the river, including STILES's old camp. Entered May 2, 1836; granted Dec. 24,
1838; registered Oct. 30, 1841.

1375 WILLIAM WILLIAMS to JEREMIAH BURTON, both of Macon, for $75, 100 ac. on
"Elijah" (Ellijay) Creek, on corner of V. AMMONS' land. Oct. 3, 1840. *Wm. Williams.*
Wit: *JOSEPH (his X mark) BALLARD, HENRY HAGIN.* Proven by Hagin in Sep. 1841
court. Registered Oct. 30, 1841.

1376 JONATHAN PHILLIPS, Chairman of the County Court of Macon, to WILLIAM LAM-
BERT for $110, two lots joining the town of Franklin in NE part of town: No. 22, 4+ ac.;
No. 23, 4+ ac. Dec. 25, 1840. *J. Phillips, Chmn.* Wit: *S.R. LAMBERT, THOS. M.
ANGEL.* Proven by Angel in June 1841 court. Registered Nov. 1, 1841.

1377 Performance bond: SILAS MCDOWELL, JESSE R. SILER, JAMES K. GRAY, $10,000 bond for Silas McDowell, duly elected Clerk of Superior Court of Law of Macon. Sep. 1841. Acknowledged before me, M.E. MANLY, judge of Superior Court of Law and Equity. Registered Nov. 1, 1841.

1377 JONATHAN PHILLIPS, Chairman of the County Court of Macon, to WILLIAM LAMBERT for $30, lot in the town of Franklin, containing one acre, 10 poles, on corner of lot 47. Dec. 25, 1840. *J. Phillips*. Wit: *S.R. LAMBERT, T.M. ANGEL*. Proven by Angel in June 1841 court. Registered Nov. 1, 1841.

1379 WEST TRUIT to BENJAMIN W. KILPATRICK, both of Macon, for value received, 70 ac., Sec. 2, Dis. 18, crossing the fork of Silver Run. June 2, 1841. *West (his X mark) Truitt*. Wit: *J. HOWARD*. Proven by Howard in June 1841 court. Registered Nov. 1, 1841.

1380 MARTHA OSBURN & ROLAND OSBURN, executor and executrix of JONATHAN OSBURN of Haywood County NC, to JOSEPH HICKS of Macon, for $1200, Sec. 4, Dis. 14, crossing "Coweter" (Coweeta) Creek. Apr. 3, 1841. *Martha (her X mark) Osburn, Roland (his X mark) Osburn*. Wit: *P.J. (or S.) NATIONS, J.J. RITTERS? BETTERS?* Proven by Nations in June 1841 court. Registered Nov. 1, 1841.

1381 Performance bond: SILAS MCDOWELL, JESSE R. SILER, JAMES K. GRAY, post $5,000 bond for Silas McDowell, duly elected Clerk of Court. Sep. 1841. Acknowledged in fall term, 1841. Registered Nov. 1, 1841.

1382 Performance bond: SILAS MCDOWELL, JESSE R. SILER, JAMES K. GRAY, post $2,000 bond for J.K. Gray, Clerk of the Court of Pleas and Quarter Courts. Sep. 13, 1841. Registered Nov. 1, 1841.

1382 Performance bond: SILAS MCDOWELL, JESSE R. SILER, JAMES K. GRAY, post $10,000 bond for J.K. Gray. Sep. 13, 1841. Registered nov. 1, 1841.

1383 Mortgage: N.S. THOMPSON of Macon to JAMES PARKER of Cass County, GA, 244 ac., Sections 17, 109, 110 and 113 in Dis. 8. Parker may have the land by paying $125 more; otherwise, Thompson may redeem certificates by paying $50 and interest. May 17, 1841. *N.S. Thompson*. Wit: *WARREN CLATAN*. Ack. in Nov. 1841 court. Registered Nov. 10, 1841.

1384 Deed of Gift: POWELL STOVAL for natural love and affection to MARY ELIZABETH CUNNINGHAM, daughter of JAMES and LUCINDA CUNNINGHAM of Macon, a certain mare pony two years old, a bay with two particular white spots. Mary Elizabeth is a minor five years old in March 1841. Stoval also appoints ALFERD HESTER of Macon to be guardian of Mary Elizabeth Cunningham to see that her right in said pony is not in any way invaded. Nov. 8, 1841. *Powell Stoval*. Wit: *E. DOWDLE, J.M. BRYSON*. Ack. in Nov. 1841 court. Registered Nov. 10, 1841.

1384 Power of Attorney: CHIULAH, or DEAD WORKS, a Cherokee, only heir and representative of OCENEWASTAH, a Cherokee reservee under treaties N.304, appoint D. LOVE of Macon my "trew and lawfull" attorney to demand from the Commissioners of the United States under the late treaty a certain certificate of debts due me amounting to whatever sum of money they may adjudge me to receive for above reservation. Sep. 13, 1837. *Chiulah (his X mark) or Dead Work*. Wit: *JOHN MOORE Senr., JOHN C. MOORE*. Proven by John C. Moore. Registered Nov. 10, 1841.

1385 Power of Attorney: We, the heirs and widow of WILL or WILLIAM JONES, an Indian of the Cherokee Nation of People, PEGGY JONES, WILLITOO JONES, SAM'L JONES, WILLIAM JONES, sons and legal heirs of Will Jones, dec'd, who took a reservation in the year 1817, appoint D. LOVE of Macon our attorney to recover whatever is due them from the Commissioners of the United States under the treaty. July 21, 1837. *Peggy Jones (her X mark), Sam'l (his X mark) Jones, Willitoo (his X mark) Jones, Wm. (his X mark) Jones*. Wit: *JOHN MOORE, J.P.* Proven by John Moore. Registered Nov. 10, 1841.

1386   Deed of Gift: DILLARD LOVE to MOURNING and MARGARET REDDICK, daughters of WM. REDDICK of Macon, for natural love and affection, two certain muly heiffers which Dillard Love bought at private sale from Wm. Reddick. *Dillard Love.* Wit: *WILLIAM HICKS, H.B. DUNEDSON.* Acknowledged by maker. Registered Nov. 10, 1841.

1387   MILES CARROLL of Macon to LOGAN BERRY, for $50, Section 43 (73?), Dis. 11, 200 acres, on Rabbit Creek. Oct. 9, 1840. *Miles Carrol.* Wit: *M.B. STRAIN, JOHN SETSER.* Ack. in Sep. 1840 court. Registered Nov. 10, 1841.

1388   JONATHAN PHILLIPS, Chairman of the Macon Court, to JAMES JAMES for $130, town lots No. 26 and 30, one acre each; No. 30 is on the Main Street. Oct. 3, 1840. *J. Phillips.* Wit: *JOHN HALL, E. DOWDLE.* Ack. in Sep. 1841 court. Registered Nov. 11, 1841.

1389   JASON LEDFORD of Union Co., GA, to ANDREW BRADLEY for $50, 53 acres, on S. side of Tennessee R., Dis. 14, beginning on CONLEY's line, on line of No. 7. Mar. 21, 1838. *Jason Ledford.* Wit: *HARVY M. PENLAND, GEORGE (his X mark) PENLAND.* Proven by H.N. Penland in Sep. 1841 court. Registered Nov. 11, 1841.

1390   W.W. DOBSON of Macon to JAMES JAMES of Haywood Co., NC, for $15, a parcel in Franklin, part of Lot No. 26. The lot begins on south bank of branch on J.R. SILER's line and contains one acre, 50 poles; the part sold was west of a fence between JAMES W. GUINN and W.W. Dobson, that ran from the corner of Lot No. 21 to the long ditch dividing the lands of Dobson, ALLMAN and Guinn.   June 23, 1841. *W.W. Dobson.* Wit: *J.R. Siler.* Ack, in Sep. 1841 court. Registered Nov. 11, 1841.

1391   JAMES W. GUINN to W.W. DOBSON for $5, part of town lots, No. 25, being one-third of lot 25. Mar. 26, 1841. *J.W. Guinn.* Wit: *J. Phillips.* Proven by Phillips in Sep. 1841 court. Registered Nov. 11, 1841.

1391   JOHN R. ALLMAN to W.W. DOBSON & JAMES W. GUINN for $25, part of lot No. 26 on J.R. SILER's line opposite the Maple corner. Mar. 10, 1841. *J.R. Allman.* Wit: *MOSES ADDINGTON.*

1392   Agreement between W.W. DOBSON to J.W. GUINN, for $10 paid to each other, to make a division line between us. They agreed to make the fence between them, from the SE end of lot No. 25 to a long ditch dividing the lands of Dobson, ALLMAN & Guinn. Mar. 10, 1841. *J.W. Guinn, W.W. Dobson.* Acknowledged by makers in Sep. 1841 court. Registered Nov. 11, 1841.

1393   SG 621, to JAMES WILSON associate of JOSEPH BUCHANAN, $240, 116 ac., Sec. 4, Dis. 8, crossing the little Savannah Creek. Granted Apr. 23, 1841; registered Nov. 12, 1841.

1394   SG 440, JAMES CONLEY, $5/100 ac., 100 ac. on "Wesers" (Wessers) Creek in Dis. 8. Entered ? (no date); granted Oct. 2, 1841; registered Nov. 12, 1841.

1395   SG 428, THOMPSON WILSON, $5/100 ac., 100 ac. on Tuckasegee River, Dis. 6, on line of Sec. 26, including an improvement. Entered Apr. 30, 1838; granted Jan. 2, 1841; registered Nov. 12, 1841.

1396   SG 420, LOGAN BERRY, $5/100 ac., 50 ac. near the head of "Elijah" (Ellijay) Creek, near the branch. Entered Oct. 24, 1839; granted Dec. 28, 1840; registered Nov. 12, 1841.

1397   SG 584, LOGAN BERRY, $14, 56 ac., Sec. 70, Dis. 11. Granted Dec. 17, 1840; registered Nov. 13, 1841.

1398   SG 407, ELI WALDROOP, $5/100 ac., 50 ac. on Lowry fork of Cartoogechaye Creek, Dis. 15, on corner of No. 133. Entered Jan. 22, 1839; granted Nov. 24, 1840; registered Nov. 13, 1841.

1399   SG 408, ELI WALDROOP, $5/100 ac., for 50 ac. on Lowry fork of Cartoogechaye Creek, Dis. 15, on corner of No. 137 and 133. Entered Jan. 22, 1839; granted Nov. 24, 1840; registered Nov. 13, 1841.

1400 SG 457, JOHN H. HOWARD, $5/100 ac., 100 ac. "on the Blew Ridge," beginning near
      the top of a ridge, including an improvement. Entered Nov. 27, 1789 (1839?); granted
      Oct. 28, 1841; registered Jan. 1, 1841 (1842).

1401 Sheriff's sale: ELI MCKEE, Esq., High Sheriff of Macon, to SAMUEL SMITH of
      Macon, property sold to satisfy a judgment against S.G. SMITH for $8.75 debt & 50
      cents interest. The sum was recovered by JAMES ROBISON, together with sum of
      $8.30. Sold were lands & tenements of sd. Samuel G. Smith, Sec. 65, Dis. 13, 90 ac., at a
      public sale on Aug. 9, 1841. Samuel Smith had high bid of $18.72. Sep. 13, 1841. *Eli
      McKee, Shff.* Wit: *JOHN HALL*. Proven by John Hall in Sep. 1841 court. Registered Jan.
      3, 1842.

1402 Sheriff's sale: ELI MCKEE, Esq., High Sheriff of Macon, to SAMUEL SMITH of
      Macon, property sold to satisfy a judgement in the County Court of Macon against
      SAMUEL G. SMITH for $8.75 & another for $27.10, with total cost of $110.88,
      recovered by JAMES ROBISON & JAMES K. GRAY. Sold at public sale, Aug. 9, 1841,
      was land, crossing Tessenty Cr. above a Mill Shoal, Sec. 18, Dis. 13. Samuel Smith, Sr.
      had high bid of $16. Sep. 15, 1841. *Eli McKee, Shff.* Wit: *JOHN HALL*. Proven by John
      Hall in Sep. 1841 court. Registered Jan. 3, 1842.

1404 Sheriff's sale: ELI MCKEE, Esq., High Sheriff of Macon, to EZEKIEL DOWDLE of
      Macon, property sold to satisfy a judgement against JAMES NICHOLS for $41.79 1/2,
      less sum recovered by SAMUEL KELLY. Sold was 50 ac., Sec. 49, Dis. 13, at public
      sale, Aug. 24, 1840. Ezekiel Dowdle had high bid of 37 1/2 cents. Aug. 14, 1840. *Eli
      McKee, Shff.* Wit: *J.L. MOORE*. Proven by J.L. Moore in Sep. 1841 court. Registered
      Jan. 4, 1842.

1406 SG 455, BENJAMIN STILES, $5/100 ac., 50 ac. in Dis. 13, on corner of Sec. 9. Entered
      Jan. 28, 1839; granted Oct. 25, 1841; registered Jan. 4, 1842.

1407 SG 470, WILLIS JONES, $5/100 ac., 75 ac. on Skeener (Skeenah) Cr., Dis. 15, includ-
      ing a poplar cove. Entered Sep. 26, 1839; granted Nov. 30, 1841; registered Jan. 6, 1842.

1408 SG 451, LEWIS VANDYKE, $5/100 ac., 50 ac. on Coweeter (Coweeta) Cr., Dis. 14,
      near Vandyke's lick log. Entered Jan. 22, 1838; granted Oct. 25, 1841; registered Jan. 7,
      1842.

1409 SG 454, CALEB NORTON, $5/100 ac., 50 ac. on Mulberry Cr., Dis. 14, on line of Sec.
      16. Entered Jan. 1, 1839; granted Oct. 25, 1841; registered Jan. 7, 1842.

1410 SG 469, JOHN HOWARD, $5/100 ac., 100 ac. on Middle Cr., to a stake in ELISHA
      THOMAS'S line. Entered Sep. 9, 1839; granted Nov. 30, 1841; registered Jan. 7, 1842.

1411 SG 471, M.L. WIKLE, $5/100 ac., 70 ac. on Middle Cr., Dis. 13, on SW corner of sd.
      Wikle's survey, runs with HOWARD's line. Entered Nov. 27, 1839; granted Nov. 30,
      1841; registered Jan. 7, 1842.

1412 SG 456, GEORGE WIKLE, $5/100 ac., 50 ac. on Tennessee R., Dis. 14, on corner of
      Sec. 33. Entered Mar. 27, 1839; granted Oct. 25, 1841; registered Jan. 17, 1842.

1413 SG 452, TELITHA NORTON, $5/100 ac., 50 ac. in Dis. 14, on corner of JOHN
      HOWARD's survey, on line of Sec. 17. Entered Jan. 1, 1839; granted Oct. 25, 1841;
      registered Jan. 7, 1842.

1414 SG 468, L.C. WIKLE, $5/100 ac., 50 ac. on Middle Cr., Dis. 13, on E. side of Goulards
      (?) Branch. Entered Jan. 12, 1839; granted Nov. 30, 1840; registered Jan. 7, 1842.

1415 SG 453, TELITHA NORTON, $5/100 ac., 50 ac. on Mulberry Cr., Dis. 14, on NW
      corner of No. 17. Entered Mar. 7, 1839; granted Oct. 25, 1841; registered Jan. 7, 1842.

1416 ELI MCKEE, Esq., High Sheriff of Macon, to JOHN HOWARD of Macon, property to satisfy a judgment of the County Court against JOHN D. DRYMAN, WM. DRYMAN, ELIZA DRYMAN, MARTAIN NORTON & his wife ELVIRA, MARTAIN T. LONG & his wife DORCAS, CHARLES S. DRYMAN, JAMES DRYMAN, JANE DRYMAN, VIRGIL DRYMAN, ELIZABETH DRYMAN, heirs at law of HENRY DRYMAN, dec'd, for $184.41, with interest from Sep. 24, 1839 and costs of $7.75; the sum recovered by SAUL SMITH of sd. J.D. Dryman, William & Eliza Dryman, M. Norton & wife, M.T. Long & wife, Charles, James, Jane, Virgil & Elizabeth Dryman. Sold at public sale, a certain parcel of land on the W. side of the Tennessee R., including the mouth of Mulberry Cr., three tracts in Dis. 14, two of which were bought by GIDEON NORTON, dec'd, at Waynesville, Haywood County, in 1820, another, Sec. 15, all three tracts joining. Out of this land, the widow of Gideon Norton took her dowry. "Now I have sold one-seventh of sd. three tracts which Henry (Dryman) in his life time bought from two of Gideon Norton's sons-in-laws to wit MOSS & BRADLEY, who had married two of sd. Norton's daughters & by marriage became legal heirs of one seventh part. By the death of Dryman became the right of his heirs. At public sale, Jan. 20, 1841, John Howard had high bid of $200. Sep. 20, 1841. *Eli McKee, Shff.* Wit: *ISAAC ASH, J.K. GRAY.* Ack. in open court. Registered Jan. 8, 1842.

1418 SG 481, EBENEZER MCLEOD, $5/100 ac., 50 ac. on Middle Cr., on NW corner of his old survey. Entered Dec. 28, 1838; granted Dec. 20, 1841; registered Jan. 31, 1842.

1419 SG 631, to JOHN HOWARD, assignee of SAMUEL BRODWAY, for $34.65, 50 ac., Sec. 19, Dis. 14, on Tennessee R.. Granted Jan. 3, 1842. Registered Jan. 31, 1842.

1420 SG 487, JOHN HOWARD, $5/100 ac., 100 ac. on Middle Cr., on N. boundary line of land occupied by WM. WHITE. Entered Dec. 20, 1839; granted Dec. 20, 1841; registered Jan. 31, 1842.

1421 SG 478, ELISHA J.(I?) LONG, $5/100 ac., 61 ac. on "Coweeter" (Coweeta) Cr., Dis. 14, on line of Sec. 4. Entered May 2, 1836; granted Dec. 20, 1841; registered Jan. 31, 1842.

1422 SG 482, HENRY ADDINGTON, $5/100 ac., 50 ac. on "Cartoogaye" (Cartoogechaye) Cr., Dis. 15, on NE corner of Sec. 67. Entered Jan. 12, 1839; granted Dec. 20, 1841; registered Jan. 31, 1842.

1423 SG 483, JOSEPH HICKS, $5/100 ac., 100 ac., Dis. 14, between "Coweter" (Coweeta) Cr. & the Tennessee R., on SE corner of Sec. 35. Entered Jan. 7, 1839; granted Dec. 20, 1841; registered Jan. 31, 1842.

1424 ALFORD HALL to JOSEPH BRENDLE, both of Macon, for $15, 59 ac., Sec. 114, Dis. 10. Jan. 28, 1842. *Alford Hall.* Wit: *JAS. ROBISON, N.H. PALMER.* Proven by N.H. Palmer in Jan. 1842 court. Registered Jan. 31, 1842.

1425 JAMES BRADLEY, MARY BRADLEY, HANNAH FORTENBURY of Macon to RICHARD WILSON of Hall County, GA, for $20, land in Cleaveland County, NC, on Williams Cr. of French Broad R., it being the place where ISAAC FORTENBURY & ELIZABETH FORTENBURY lived & died and near or joining LEWES? (LUVES?) & COVINGTONs & others, 100 ac., it being two shares of six in sd. tract. Jan. 28, 1842. *James (his X mark) Bradly, Mary (her X mark) Bradly, Hannah (her X mark) Fortenbury.* Wit: *ANDREW BRADLY, SAMUEL P. BRADLEY.* Proven by Samuel P. Bradley in Jan. 1842 court. Registered Feb. 1, 1842.

1426 SG 491, MARTIN NORTON, $5/100 ac., 25 ac. on Tennessee R., Dis. 14. Entered Sep. 25, 1839; granted Jan. 7, 1842; registered Feb. 2, 1842.

1427 SG __, ANDREW HOGGINS, $5/100 ac., 50 ac. on headwaters of "Skeener" (Skeenah) Cr., on line of Sec. 118, passing ELI MCKEE's line. Entered Jan. 19, 1839; granted Dec. 20, 1841; registered Feb. 2, 1842.

1428 SG 444, ALEXANDER WILSON, $5/100 ac., 50 ac. on Tuckasegee R., Dis. 6. Entered Feb. 5, 1839; granted Oct. 15, 1841; registered Feb. 8, 1842.

1429 SG 437, WILLIAM MOSS, $5/100 ac., 50 ac. on Tuckasegee R., Dis. 6, on line of Sec.
      16, including his mill. Entered Mar. 29, 1837; granted Apr. 23, 1841; registered Feb. 3,
      1842.

1430 SG 432, CHARLES WOODRING, $5/100 ac., 50 ac. on Tuckasegee R., including a
      peach orchard & a mill shoal. Entered Apr. 28, 1838; granted Jan. 12, 1841; registered
      Feb. 3, 1842.

1431 SG 422, GEORGE LOWDERMILK, $5/100 ac., 42 ac. in Dis. 11, on corner of Sec. 62.
      Entered Sep. 26, 1838; granted Dec. 28, 1840; registered Feb. 4, 1842.

1432 SG 381, WILLIAM EVET, $5/100 ac., to 50 ac. on Walnut Cr.. Entered Feb. 23, 1838;
      granted Nov. 24, 1840; registered Feb. 4, 1842.

1433 SG 445, ALEXANDER WILSON, $5/100 ac., 100 ac. on Chatooga R., Dis. 18, to a
      stake in TRAMMEL's line. Entered Sep. 5, 1840; granted Oct. 15, 1841; registered Feb.
      7, 1842.

1434 SG 130, WILLIAM R. KERBY, $5/100 ac., 50 ac. on Cullehee Cr., Dis. 7. Entered Oct.
      27, 1838; granted Dec. 12, 1838; registered Feb. 7, 1842.

1435 SG 489, LABURN LONG, $5/100 ac., 100 ac. on "Coweteer" (Coweeta) Cr., Dis. 14.
      Entered Jan. 17, 1839; granted Dec. 20, 1841; registered Feb. 7, 1842.

1436 SG 479, LABRON LONG, $5/100 ac., 28 ac. on "Coweteer" (Coweeta) Cr., Dis. 14,
      beginning, in the gap of a ridge near a Trail, on line of Sec. 117. Entered Dec. 20, 1839;
      granted Dec. 20, 1841; registered Feb. 7, 1842.

1437 SG 297, WOODY GRIGGS, Senr., $5/100 ac., 50 ac. in Dis. 15, on Cartoogechaye Cr.,
      on SW corner of Sec. 124. Entered May 14, 1836; granted Dec. 20, 1838; registered Feb.
      9, 1842.

1438 SG 611, to WILLIAM EVITT assignee of THOMAS POSTELL, for $11.76 3/4, 50 ac.,
      Sec. 6, Dis. 12. Granted Dec. 29, 1840; registered Feb. 9, 1842.

1439 SG 605, GEORGE F. CALER, for $30, 74 ac., Sec. 94, Dis. 10. Granted Dec. 23, 1840;
      registered Feb. 9, 1842.

1440 SG 607, NOAH HALL, for $25, 96 ac., Sec. 61, Dis. 16. Granted Dec. 23, 1840;
      registered Feb. 10, 1842.

1441 SG 604, GEORGE F. CALER, for $12.50, 50 ac., Sec. 71, Dis. 10. Granted Dec. 23,
      1840; registered Feb. 11, 1842.

1442 SG 606, GEORGE F. CALER, for $13, 52 ac., Sec. 105, Dis. 10. Granted Dec. 23, 1840;
      registered Feb. 11, 1842.

1443 SG 493, D. LAFAYETTE HOWARD, $5/100 ac., 100 ac. on Middle Cr., Dis. 13, on the
      Georgia line. Entered Nov. 27, 1839; granted Jan. 7, 1842; registered Feb. 23, 1842.

1444 SG 492, NICHOLAS F. HOWARD, $5/100 ac., 100 ac. on Middle Cr., Dis. 13, begin-
      ning on the NW corner of sd. Howard's survey. Entered Nov. 27, 1839; granted Jan. 7,
      1842; registered Feb. 23, 1842.

1445 SG 562, JONATHAN OSBURN, for $_.99, to 290 ac., Sec. 4, Dis. 14, croosing
      "Coweter" (Coweeta) Cr., on S. boundary of Sec. 2. Granted June 19, 1840; registered
      Feb. 24, 1842.

1446 SG 490, EBENEZER MCCLOUD/MCLEOD $5/100 ac., 50 ac. on Middle Cr.. Entered
      Mar. 27, 1839; granted Jan. 7, 1842; registered Feb. 24, 1842.

1447 SG 336, JAMES WALKER, $5/100 ac., 100 ac. on little Birch Cr., Dis. 12, beginning
      below improvement where sd. Walker formerly lived, on N. side of creek. Entered May
      2, 1836; granted Aug. 28, 1839; registered Feb. 25, 1842.

1448 BALEY KERBY to ROBERT BRYSON, both of Macon, for $300, land on "Cullewhee"
      waters of Tuckaseegee R., tract on which sd. Kerby now lives, Sec. 50, Dis. 7, containing
      80 ac.. Jan. 10, 1842. *B. Kirby.* Wit: *J. KEENER, WM. STALLCUP.* Ack. in Jan. 1842
      court. Registered Mar. 14, 1842.

1449 MARY D. MOORE to THOMAS P. MOORE, both of Macon, for $100, 30 ac. in Dis. 16, on corner of Sec. 47. Jan. 23, 1842. *Mary D. Moore*. Wit: *J.K. GRAY, N.H. PALMER*. Proven by J.K. Gray in Jan. 1842 court. Registered Mar. 14, 1852 (1842).

1450 JAMES WALKER to ABNER MOORE, both of Macon, for $54, land on Little Birch Cr., Dis. 12,beginning below improvement where sd. Walker lives on the N. side of creek, containing 100 ac., entered May 2, 1836. Jan. 21, 1840. *James Walker*. Wit: *ELIZABETH (her X mark) TAYLOR, ABRAHAM MOORE*. Proven by Abraham Moore in Jan. 1842 court. Registered Mar. 14, 1842.

1451 BENJAMIN STILES of Macon to JAMES K. GRAY for $1480, land on E. side of Tennessee R., Dis. 13, below mouth of Hickory "Nole" (Knoll) Cr., containing 184 ac.. Jan. 25, 1842. *Benjamin Stiles*. Wit: *N.S. JARRETT, WM. ANGEL*. Proven by N.S. Jarrett in Jan. 1842 session. Registered Apr. 29, 1842.

1452 BENJAMIN STILES of Macon to JAMES G. GRAY for $10, 100 ac. on Hickory "Nole" (Knoll) Cr., Dis. 13, on SW corner of Sec. 11, Jan. 25 (1842). *Benjamin Stiles*. Wit: *N.S. JARRETT, WM. ANGEL*. Proven by N.S. Jarrett in Jan. 1842 session of court. Registered Apr. 29, 1842.

1452 A. PICKLESIMER to WILSON PICKLESIMOR, both of Macon, my right in 73 ac., Sec. 12, Dis. 5, Willson Picklesimor to pay amount due state.Jan. 24, 1842. *A. Picklesimer*. Wit: *JOHNSON (his X mark) MCCALL, SAMUEL MCCALL*. Proven by Johnson McCall in Jan. 1842 session. Registered June 6, 1842.

1453 ABRAM PICKLESIMAR to WILLISON PICKLESIMON, both of Macon, 78 ac., Sec. 9, Dis. 6, Willison Picklesimon to pay amount due state.Jan. 24, 1842. *A. Picklesimar*. Wit: *JOHNSON (his X mark) MCCALL, SAMUEL MCCALL*. Proven by Johnson McCall in Jan. 1842 session. Registered June 6, 1842.

1454 JOHN HOWARD to JACOB PLEMMONS for $250, Sec. 22, Dis. 14, on Commissioners Cr., crossing the creek. Oct. 20, 1841. *J. Howard*. Acknowledged in Jan. 1842 session. Registered June 6, 1842.

1455 MARTIN TEAGUE of Union Co., GA, to ANDREW WIKE of Macon, 217 ac., Sec. 1, Dis. 6, on SW side of Tuckasegee R.. Teague makes title to only 27+ ac., "it being my undivided part of said tract." Jan. 21, 1842. *Martin (his X mark) Teague*. Wit: *C. McD. PAXTEN, JOHN WIKE*. Proven by Wike in Jan. 1842 court. Registered June 6, 1842.

1456 SG 112 $5/100 ac., to ABRAM WIGGINS, 50 ac. on Junaluskee Cr., Dis. 13, below where JAMES PELKERTON lives, to a hickory on the bank of the creek near an old Hominy Mill. Entered May 2, 1836; granted Feb. 26, 1838; registered June 6, 1842.

1457 SG 111 $5/100 ac., to ABRAM WIGGINS, 50 ac. on "Elarkey's" (Alarka) Cr., Dis. 8, on corner of Sec. 32. Entered May 2, 1836; granted Feb. 26, 1838; registered June 6, 1842.

1458 SG 182 $5/100 ac., to JOHN DEHART, 50 ac. in Dis. 8, on N. side of Tennessee R., near EDWARD's (?) corner. Entry May 2, 1836; grant Dec. 15, 1838; registered June 6, 1842.

1459 SG 302, for $12.61, to NATHAN PILKINGTON, 63 1/2 ac., Sec. 33, Dis. 8, on E. bank of "Chunaluskee's" (Junaluska) Cr., on upper line of Sec. 32. Granted Dec. 12, 1836; registered June 6, 1842.

1460 SG 137 $5/100 ac., to JAMES HOOPER, 50 ac. on W. side of Tuckasegee R., Dis. 6, including a small improvement. Entered May 2, 1836; granted Dec. 12, 1838; registered June 6, 1842.

1461 SG 418 $5/100 ac., to MARTIN NORTON, 50 ac. on Tennessee R., Dis. 14, on corner of Sec. 25. Entered Sep. 19, 1838; granted Dec. 22, 1840; registered June 6, 1842.

1462 STEPHEN GRAVES of Cherokee Co., NC, to WILLIAM C. GRAY of Macon, for $55, 100 ac. on THOMAS's line, crossing the Branch at the High Falls, incl. the cabin made by JOSEPH BLACK. Mar. 20, 1841. *Stephen (his X mark) Graves*. Wit: *J.W. DOWDLE, SAMUEL SELLARS*. Proven by Samuel Sellars in March 1842 session. Registered June 7, 1842.

1463 WILLIS JONES to ELIZABETH GRAY, both of Macon, for $20, 75 ac. on "Skeener"
      (Skeenah) Cr., Dis. 15, beginning on S. corner of NATHAN CARRELL's survey, to top
      of a mountain. Mar. 11, 1842. *Willis (his X mark) Jones.* Wit: *WM. BATES, W.C. GRAY.*
      Proven by W.C. Gray in Mar. 1842 session. Registered June 7, 1842.

1464 Mortgage: JOHN HALL to DILLARD LOVE, both of Macon, Negro woman named
      REBECA, about 17 years old, as collateral to protect Love, who had become security for
      Hall in his guardianship of the orphan children of his former wife, CAROLINE HALL.
      June 16, 1841. *John Hall.* Wit: *JAS. ROBINSON, H.L. HUNDER.* Registered June 7,
      1842.

1464 Mortgage: SAMUEL BRYSON to JOHN PHILLIPS, both of Macon, for valuable con-
      sideration, 50 ac. on S. side of Sugar Fork, bounded on NW by widow MARGARET
      BRYSON's land and on SE by land of WM. BRYSON, dec'd; also, all my right to a
      child's part of the lands of ANDW. BRYSON, dec'd, of which estate I am heir at law, on
      which said land Margaret Bryson now lives on S. side of Sugartown fork of Tennessee
      R.; also, a one-year-old fily, 32 head of hogs. This mortgage to be void on condition that
      Samuel Bryson pay or cause to be paid to N.S. JARRETT of Macon a certain judgement
      by him this day recovered against Samuel Bryson for $66.23. Sep. 16, 1840. *Samuel
      Bryson.* Wit: *E. DOWDLE.* Proven by E. Dowdle. Registered June 7, 1842.

1466 ABRAM SELLARS to WM. STALCUP, both of Macon, for $300, 63+ ac. on the bank
      of Tuckasegee R., Dis. 8. Oct. 1, 1839. *Abram Sellars.* Wit: *FRANKLIN KILLIAN, M__
      STALLCUP.* Ack. in June 1841 session. Registered June 7, 1842.

1466 Deed of Gift: JASON SHERRELL of Haywood Co., NC, to JANE SIMS, daughter of
      JACOB SIMS, a 3-year-old filly, in consideration of the trouble the family of Jacob Sims
      has had with the filly—the property got crippled taking it to range & I could get it no fur-
      ther. Aug. 18, 1841. *Jason Sherrell.* Wit: *JOHN CARRELL, JAMES CARRELL.*
      Registered June 7, 1842.

1467 GEORGE SHULAR of Macon to U.C.B. TIDUS and MALINDA G__ BATTLE,
      minors, one bed & furniture, a woman's saddle, one pot, one oven, one skillet, one set of
      knives and forks, some dresser ware, to have and hold against all suits or claims against
      their parents or guardians. Oct. 28, 1841. *George (his X mark) Shular.* Wit: *N.
      BURCHFIELD, URIAH C. BURNS.* Proven by N. Burchfield in Jan. 1842 session.
      Registered June 7, 1842.

1468 WM. F. MCKEE to JACOB TRAMMELL & B.W. BELL, all of Macon, for $250, 76 ac.
      on a branch of the Sugartown fork of the Tennessee R., Dis. 11, Sec. 40, McKee to have
      possession of building & improvement made on lands until Dec. 25, 1831. Nov. 18,
      1830. *Wm. F. McKee.* Wit: *JOHN SCROGGS, JAS. MCCLURE.* Ack. in Mar. 1842 ses-
      sion. Registered June 7, 1842.

1469 JOSEPH SMITH of Cherokee Co., NC to WILLIAM SILER of Macon, for $150, 96 ac.
      on "Cartoogachage" (Cartoogachaye) Cr., Sec. 132, Dis. 15, which Smith purchased Oct.
      1836 at Franklin. Jan. 10, 1842. *Joseph Smith.* Wit: *H.G. WOODFIN.* Proven by H.G.
      Woodfin in Mar. 1842 session. Registered June 11, 1842.

1470 MARGARETT BRYSON to ALLISON CLARK GUY, both of Macon, to said Guy or
      his heirs, etc., Sec. 42, Dis. 12, which I purchased Oct. 28, 1836 in Franklin. Aug. 24,
      1839. *Margret (her X mark) Bryson.* Wit: *M. RUSSEL, JAMES H. BRYSON.* Proven by
      M. Russell in June 1842 session. Registered June 7, 1842.

1470 JOHN SHULAR to GEO. SHULAR, both of Macon, for $1200, 280 ac. on Deep Cr.,
      Sec. 6, Dis. 1. Oct. 20, 1835. *John Shular.* Wit: *JOHN DOBSON, W.H. THOMAS.*
      Proven by W.H. Thomas in Mar. 1842 session. Registered June 7, 1842.

1471 HUGH BROWN, Junr. to CHARLES WOODRING for $50, 50 ac., including an im-
      provement in the poplar cove. Mar. 2, 1841. *Hugh Brown Jr.* Wit: *HUGH BROWN Sr.,
      ABSOLAM WOODRING.* Ack. in June 1841 session. Registered Jun 7, 1842.

1471 MARTHA KERBY to LEWIS TILLY, both of Macon, for $22.50, 50 ac., Sec. 61, Dis. 7. Feb. 26, 1842. *Martha (her X mark) Kerby*. Wit: *WM. CARSON, ELIAS CARSON*. Ack. in Mar. 1842 session. Registered June 7, 1842.

1472 HUGH BROWN Junr. to CHARLES WOODRING, for $50, 50 ac.. Mar. 2, 1842. *Hugh Brown Jr.* Wit: *HUGH BROWN Senr., ABSOLOM WOODRING*. Ack. in June 1841 session. Registered June 7, 1842.

1473 ABRAM WIGGINS to JOHN WEST Senr., both of Macon, for $50, 52 ac. on N. side of "Elarkey" (Alarka) Cr., Dis. 8, entered May 2, 1836. Mar. 1, 1842. *Abram (his X mark) Wiggins*. Wit: *J.Y. GRANT*. Proven by J.Y. Grant in Mar. 1842 session. Registered June 8, 1842.

1474 ABRAM WIGGINS Jr. to DANIEL WEST, both of Macon, 50 ac. on "Olarkee" (Alarka) Cr., Dis. 8. Mar. 1, 1842. *Abram (his X mark) Wiggins*. Wit: *J.Y. GRANT*. Proven by J.Y. Grant in Mar. 1842 session. Registered June 8, 1842.

1475 ABRAM WIGGINS, Jr. to JOHN WEST, Sr., both of Macon, for $100, 50 ac. on "Elenoy" Cr., including an improvement; entered May 2, 1836 and deeded to W.B. WIGGINS. Mar. 1, 1842. *Abram (his X mark) Wiggins*. Wit: *J.Y. GRANT*. Proven by J.Y. Grant in Mar. 1842 session. Registered June 8, 1842.

1476 ABRAM WIGGINS Jr. to JOHN WEST Senr., both of Macon, for $200, land on E. bank of Junelusky Cr., crossing "Chunaluskee," containing 68 ac. on corner of No. 31. Mar. 1, 1842. *Abram (his X mark) Wiggins*. Wit: *J.Y. GRANT*. Proven by J.Y. Grant in Mar. 1842 session. Registered June 8, 1842.

1477 ABRAM WIGGINS Junr. to JOHN WEST Senr., both of Macon, for $150, 63 ac. on "Chunaluskea" (Junasluskee) Cr., on line of No. 32. Mar. 1, 1842. *Abram (his X mark) Wiggins*. Wit: *J.Y. GRANT*. Proven by J.Y. Grant in Mar. 1842 session. Registered June 8, 1842.

1478 SG 443 $5/100 ac., to BRYANT CONLEY, 100 ac. on Middle Cr.. Entered Nov. 27, 1839; granted Oct. 11, 1841; registered June 24, 1842.

1479 Mortgge: JOEL BINGHAM to JOHN HOWARD, both of Macon, one sorrel mare and mule, two cows, one a white speckle cow the other a brindle with bell on also the bell, for $55.75 and interest on said sum from 25th Dec. last. The condition is that Bingham bought a beast of a certain WILSON P. ROBISON some time last year and give his note to the said Robison and John Howard was security for $55.25 due Dec. 25, 1841. In April the note came against Bingham & Howard for collection and they confessed judgment and stayed same by giving for security L. VANDYKE, which stay will be out the last of October. This deed of trust is to keep Howard harmless in transaction. June 24, 1842. *Joel Bingham*. Wit: *N.F. HOWARD*. Proven by N.F. Howard June 24, 1842. Registered June 25, 1842.

1480 Mortgage: JOHN WILLIAMSON to JOHN HOWARD, all my interest in the crops now growing in that place where I now live, having rented the same from said Howard, one-third being his and two-thirds mine. Howard to let me have 40 bu. of corn on Mar. 7 at 20 3/4 cents per bushel, also Howard has lifted a judgment for $31.25, with 40 cents cost on or about April 15, held on me by ANDREW BRADLEY. If Williamson pay John Howard the above sums with interest from the time that Howard let him have the corn and from the time when he lifted the judgment from Bradley, the understanding is that the said Williamson gets only half the crop of oats in the rent and sells the other half. June 20, 1842. *John Williamson*. Wit: *L. VANDYKE, N.F. HOWARD*. Proven June 24, 1842; registered June 25, 1842.

1481 WILLIAM GUFFIE to T.J. ROANE, DANIEL NICHOLS & JOHN PENDERGRASS, a white cow about four years old with calf that Guffie bought of T.J. Roane, one lot of hogs that he bought at JOHN LOWRY's sale, 14 head in number, to wit, one black sow and pigs, one red sow and pigs and 7 shoats, together with his growing crop of corn and oats, for $15. *William Guffie*. The condition of the above is that T.J. Roane, Daniel Nichols and John Pendergrass have gone security for $5 fine imposed by Superior Court of Macon, spring 1842 term, in a state prosecution. If Guffie satisfy judgment, this deed to be void. April 5, 1842. *William Guffie*. Wit: *JAMES ROBISON*. Proven by James Robison in June 1842 session. Registered June 25, 1842.

1482 SG 472, DAVID BALLEW (BALEW), $5/100 ac., 50 ac. on Tesenty (Tessentee) Cr., Dis. 13, on corner of No. 25, on JUSTICE's line. Entered Oct. 7, 1839; granted Dec. 13, 1841; registered June 25, 1842.

1483 JOSEPH HICK to JOHN HOWARD, both of Macon, for $1600, Sec. (1? 4? 7?) in Dis. 14, containing 290 ac., bordering No. 3, crossing Coweter (Coweeta) Cr.. Mar. 7, 1842. *Joseph Hicks*. Wit: *JONATHAN HICKS, JACOB HICKS*. Proven by Jacob Hicks in June 1842 session. Registered July 1, 1842.

1484 JOSEPH HICKS to JOHN HOWARD, both of Macon, for valuable consideration, Sec. 35, Dis. 14; Howard to pay amount due state. Oct. 28, 1841. *J. Hick*. Wit: *THOS. M. ANGEL, E.T. LONG*. Proven by E.T. Long in June 1842 session. Registered July 4, 1842.

1484 Deed of Gift: BENJAMIN HYDE Senr. to ELIZABETH ELRINDA BATTLE, one cow, black-and-white spotted, marked with a crop and slit in each ear; also to POLLY ELIZA BATTLE, one cow, white-and-red spotted, marked same as other. Dec. 30, 1841. *Benjamin (his X mark) Hyde*. Wit: *N. BURCHFIELD, N. PILKINTON*. Proven by N. Burchfield in June 1842 session. Registered July 5, 1842.

1485 JOSEPH HICK to JOHN HOWARD, both of Macon, for $10, 100 ac.. Feb. 18, 1842. *Joseph Hick*. Wit: *JACOB HICK, MARTIN NORTON*. Proven by Jacob Hick in June 1842 session. Registered July 5, 1842.

1486 SG 494, THOMAS WEST, $5/100 ac., 100 ac. on S. side of "E. larky" (Alarka) Cr., Dis. 8, crossing creek. Entered Jan. 19, 1841; granted June 3, 1842; registered July 14, 1842.

1487 JAMES H. MCLEOD to EBENEZER MCLEOD, for $50, tract near the Georgia line, 75 ac. May 16, 1840. *James H. McLeod*. Wit: *WM. MCLEOD, SAUL SMITH*. Proven by Saul Smith in June 1842 session. Registered July 14, 1842.

1488 SG 473 $5/100 ac., to SAUL SMITH, 50 ac. on Middle Cr., on corner of Sec. 58. Entered Jan. 21, 1840; granted Dec. 13, 1841; registered July 14, 1842.

1489 GEORGE WIKLE to THOMAS CABE, both of Macon, for $100, land on Middle Cr., 75 ac., Sec. 63, Dis. 13. Dec. 13, 1841. *George Wikle*. Wit: *N.F. HOWARD, JOHN HOWARD*. Proven by John Howard in June 1842 session. Registered July 14, 1842

1490 SG 217 $5/100 ac., to JAMES LEDBETTER, 50 ac. on Middle Fork of Ledbetter's Mill Cr., Dis. 8, including his improvement. Entered May 2, 1836; granted Dec. 15, 1838; registered July 14, 1842.

1491 JOHN HOWARD to SAMUEL P. BRADLY, both of Macon, for $100, a tract in Dis. 14, part of Sec. 10 on bank of Tennessee R., crossing the river, containing 25 ac.. Feb. 18, 1842. *John Howard*. Wit: *JOSEPH HICKS, JACOB HICKS*. Proven by Jacob Hicks in June 1842 session. Registered July 14, 1842.

1492 SG 386 $5/100 ac., to TIMOTHY LINDSEY, 50 ac., Dis. 9, on Milleny? Cr., on corner of No. 5. Entered May 14, 1836; granted Nov. 24, 1840; registered July 14, 1842.

1493 Mortgage: RILEY MARTIN to ZACHARIAH DOWNS for one Spanish Mill Dollar, 78
ac., Sec. 30, Dis. 17. The considerations are that, whereas Martin purchased tract from
JOHN J. ROSE for $400, for which he gave his note with Zachariah Downs for security,
Martin is to pay off notes as they fall due. *Riley Martin.* Wit: *SILAS MCDOWELL, R.C.
ROGERS.* And further, in consideration of the security Downs gave, Martin conveys my
interest in a tract of land purchased by ALFERD HALL joining the aforesaid tract on the
E. side, of which one-half is my own by contract, 47 ac., also one bay horse, saddle &
bridle, also 7 head of cow beast cattle, 4 head of hogs, 2 head of sheep and my crop of
corn now on hand. The condition is that Martin is to pay off the $400 in bonds due John
J. Rose. Oct. 30, 1841. *Riley Martin.* Wit: *Silas McDowell, R.C. Rogers.* Proven by Silas
McDowell in July 22, 1842 court. Registered Aug. 1, 1842.

1494 Mortgage: JOHN PENDERGRASS to T.J. ROANE, one sorrel mare four years old, 2
cows & calves, 2 yearlings, 3 head of hogs, crop of growing corn and fodder, for $65. *J.
Pendergrass.* The condition of the above is that John Pendergrass is to satisfy the debt he
owes to T.J. Roan in the amount of $65. June 16, 1842. *John Pendergrass.* Wit: *WIL-
LIAM H. ROANE.* Proven by Roane in June 1842 court. Registered Aug. 1, 1842.

1495 JOHN BROWN to JOHN WILSON, both of Macon, for $150, 50 ac. on Cullowhee Cr.,
on both sides of Hamburgh Road. Aug. 19, 1839. *John Brown.* Wit: *ENOCH UNDER-
WOOD, MICHAEL (his X mark) LONG.* Proven by Michael Long in June 1842 session.
Registered Aug. 2, 1842.

1496 JOHN N. DEATON of Macon to SAMUEL REED of Burke County, NC, for $300, 88
ac. on the Tennessee R., Sec. 9, Dis. 11, beginning near the mouth of "Watargu"
(Watauga) Cr., crossing Mill Creek. Dec. 8, 1840. *John N. Deaton.* Wit: *E. DOWDLE,
J.W. GUINN.* Proven by E. Dowdle in June 1842 court. Registered Aug. 2, 1842.

1497 RICHARD WILSON to HENRY WILSON, both of Macon, for $199, Sec. 54 and 63 in
Dis. 7; Sec. 54 is on Cullowhee Cr., 62 ac.; Sec. 63 contains 64 ac. June 11, 1842.
Richard Wilson. Wit: *B. CORBY (KERBY?), MICHAEL (his X mark) LONG.* Proven by
Michael Long in June 1842 court. Registered Aug. 2, 1842.

1498 RICHARD WILSON to HENRY WILSON, both of Macon, for $99, Sec. 18, Dis. 7, on
E. fork of K Creek, 51 ac.. June 8, 1842. *Richard Wilson.* Wit: *B. KARBY (KERBY?),
MICHAEL (his X mark) LONG.* Proven by Michael Long in June 1842 court. Registered
Aug. 2, 1842.

1499 SG 475 $5/100 ac., to JAMES ZACHARY, 100 ac. on Silver Run Cr., Dis. 18. Entered
Sep. 24, 1836; granted Dec. 13, 1841; registered Aug. 2, 1842.

1500 SG 475 $5/100 ac., to JOHN ZACHARY, 100 ac. on Gum Bottom Cr., Dis. 18. Entered
Jan. 1, 1839; granted Dec. 13, 1841; registered Aug. 23, 1842.

1501 SG 477, ALFERD ZACHARY, $5/100 ac., 100 ac. on "Chatooga" R., Dis. 18, beginning
on JOHN ZACHARY's line, incl. an improvement known by name of "SAUL
MILLSAP plase." Entered Sep. 24, 1838; granted Dec. 13, 1841; registered Aug. 3, 1842.

1502 SG 474, JOHN ZACHARY, $5/100 ac., to 100 ac. on Gum Bottom Creek, Dis. 18, begin-
ning on N. side of creek. Entered Dec. 8, 1838; granted Dec. 13, 1841; registered Aug. 3,
1842.

1503 JAMES JAMES, late of Macon, had contracted with NIMROD S. JARRETT of Macon
for the sale of 80 ac. and executed to Jarrett a bond of $450, dated Oct. 31, 1838; James
James has since died and JOHN N. DETON has been legally appointed his administrator.
Jarrett having complied with the terms of the contract, I now for $225 paid by Jarrett con-
vey the land, Sec. 4, Dis. 11. Aug. 9, 1839. *John N. Deaton.* Wit: *JAS. ROBISON.* Proven
by James Robison in June 1842 session. Registered Aug. 3, 1842.

1504 C.R. HARDEN of Macon to JONAS JENKINS, for $100, 50 ac., Dis. 8, on Middle Fork
of Ledbetter's Mill Cr., incl. improvement where I now live. July 27, 1841. *C.R. (his X
mark) Hardin.* Wit: *N. BURCHFIELD, SARAH L. (her X mark) BURNS.* Proven by N.
Burchfield in June 1842 session. Registered Aug. 3, 1842.

1505 JAMES LEDBETTER of Macon to C.R. HARDIN for $100, 50 ac. on Middle Fork of
Ledbetter's Mill Cr., Dis. 8, beginning on Ledbetter's line, incl. his improvement. Dec.
12, 1840. *James Ledbetter*. Wit: *N. BURCHFIELD, JEREMIAH (his X mark) GEORGE*.
Proven by N. Burchfield in June 1842 session. Registered Aug. 3, 1842.

1505 JONAS JENKINS Senr. of Macon to ABEL B. HYETTS for $16, 50 ac. in Dis. 8, on
Middle Fork of Ledbetter's Mill Cr., beginning on LEDBETTER's line, incl. improve-
ment where C.R. HARDIN now lives. Apr. 13, 1842. *Jonas (his X mark) Jenkins*. Wit: *N.
BURCHFIELD, NATHAN JENKINS*. Proven by N. Burchfield in June 1842. Registered
Aug. 3, 1842.

1506 JOSEPH ALLIN of Haywood Co., NC, to ABRAM/ABRAHAM SELLARS of Macon,
for $400, 63+ ac. on the Tuckasegee R., Dis. 8, Oct. 1, 1839. *Joseph Allen*. Wit: *JESSE
C. COCKERHAM, NATHAN B. THOMPSON*. Proven by Nathan B. Thompson in June
1842 session. Registered Aug. 3, 1842.

1507 SAUL SMITH to WM. M. PENLAND, both of Macon, for $4.50, 50 ac. on NE side of
Middle Cr., joining Penland's land, June 14, 1842. *Saul Smith*. Wit: *L. BIRD, W.M. PAT-
TON*. Ack. in June 1842 session. Registered Aug. 3, 1842.

1508 BENJAMIN STILES of Macon to GEORGE PENLAND for $150, 12 ac. near the Ten-
nessee R., on Penland's line, Dis. 13, part of a 25-ac. tract entered by Stiles. Feb. 10,
1838. *Benjamin Stiles*. Wit: *HENRY M. PENLAND, JOHN B. STILES*. Proven by Henry
M. Penland in June 1842 session. Registered Aug. 3, 1842.

1509 SAMUEL SMITH to GEORGE PENLAND for $500, land on Tessenty waters, Dis. 13,
Sec. 18, crossing Tessenty 20 poles above a mill seat. Sep. 16, 1841. *Samuel Smith*. Wit:
D.R. LOWERY, JOHN HOWARD. Proven by John Howard in June 1842 session.
Registered Aug. 3, 1842.

1510 JASON LEDFORD to HARVY M. PENLAND, both of Macon, for $350, land on Ten-
nessee R., 97 ac., Dis. 14, Sec. 7. Nov. 4, 1836. *John Ledford*. Wit: *JOHN HOWARD,
S.P. HOWARD*. Proven by John Howard in June 1842 session. Registered Aug. 3, 1842.

1511 SG 464, WILLIAM C. CAMBELL (WILLIAM MCCAMBELL?) Junr., $5/100 ac., 100
ac. on the Smoky Mountain, on (Tennessee) state line, to beginning, which is 40 poles
east of the 42nd mile tree. Entered Nov. 20, 1839; granted Nov. 22, 1841; registered Sep.
26, 1842.

1512 SG 441, ISAAC A. MCCAMBELL, $5/100 ac., 100 ac. on the Smoky Mountain, begin-
ning at a "beach" in (Tennessee) state line, near the New Road, near Eagle Creek.
Entered Nov. 20, 1839; granted Oct. 2, 1841; registered Sep. 26, 1842.

1513 SG 462, to JOHN MCCAMPBELL & JOSEPH EASTERBROOK, for $5/100 ac., to 100
ac. on the Smoky Mountain, beginning at a "beach" in (Tennessee) state line on road
near JAMES SPINIER'S (?) improvement, incl. an improvement. Entered Oct. 9, 1839;
granted Nov. 22, 1841; registered Sep. 26, 1842.

1514 SG 442, JOHN MCCLURE, $5/100 ac., 25 ac. on the Tennessee R. Entered Mar. 26,
1839; granted Oct. 2, 1841; registered Oct. 1, 1842.

1515 SG 480, MOSES BUTLER, $5/100 ac., 50 ac. on Bear Camp Cr., Dis. 18, incl. an im-
provement. Entered Dec. 8, 1838; granted Dec. 20, 1841; registered Oct. 9, 1842.

1516 BENJAMIN STILES to ZACHARIAH PEAK, both of Macon, for $100, 55 ac. on "Ally
Jay" (Ellijay) Creek, Dis. 11, Sec. 58, incl. the tract where Zachariah Peak now lives.
June 14, 1842. *Benjamin Stiles*. Wit: *Z. CABE, JAS. RUSSEL*. Ack. in June 1842 session.
Registered Oct. 11, 1842.

1516 Mortgage: JOHN SLAGLE to H.G. WOODFIN, my standing crop of corn, supposed to
be likely to yeald 150 bu. when ripe, also 7 stacks of hay, about 200 dozen of oats, being
all the corn, hay and oats that I possess. The condition is that H.G. Woodfin has gone
security in a stay of two judgements on the property of JOHN DOBSON in sum of $109
principle, Slagle to pay Dobson. Sep. 15, 1842. *John Slagle*. Wit: *B.S. BRITTIAN*. Proven
by B.S. Brittian in Sep. 1842 session. Registered Oct. 11, 1842.

1517 S. MCDOWELL of Macon & EPHRAIM AMMONS to JAMES ROBINSON of Macon for $300, Sec. 67, Dis. 12. Sep. 14, 1842. *S. McDowell, E. Ammons.* Wit: *THOS. J. ROAN, N.H. PALMER.* Ack. in Sep. 1842 session. Registered Oct. 12, 1842.

1518 JAMES WILSON to JOHN WILSON, both of Macon, for $450, Negro girl LILLY, age abt. 19 years, a slave for life. July 25, 1842. *James Wilson.* Wit: *W.H. THOMAS, ALLEN FISHER.* Ack, in Sep. 1842 session. Registered Oct. 13, 1842.

1519 JORSHUA HALL Senr. to JOSEPH BRINDLE, Negro child VILET, nearly five years of age, for $250. Apr. 11, 1842. *Jorshua Hall.* Wit: *A. HALL.* Proven by A. Hall in Sep. 1842 session. Registered Oct. 13, 1842.

1519 DAVID BELLEW of Macon to HORATIO N. CONLEY, for $700, 206+ ac., Sections 21, 22, 23 in Dis. 13, on Tessenty Cr., also 50 ac., No. 25, Sec. 13, on Tessenty Creek. July __, 1842. *David Bellew.* Wit: *JOHN HOWARD, BRYANT CONNELLY.* Proven by John Howard in Sep. 1842 session. Registered Oct. 13, 1842.

1521 THOS. W.P. POINDEXTER of Haywood Co., NC, to JOSEPH WELCH for $100, 53+ ac. where I reside at intersection of the Tennessee & Tuckaseegee R., Dis. 8, Sec. 38. Oct. 14, 1828. *Thos. W.P. Poindexter.* Wit: *JOHN HALL, J.R. SILER.* Proven in Sep. 1842 session, registered Oct. 13, 1842.

1522 WILLIAM GARLAND to JOHN HOWARD, both of Macon, for $100, Sec. 25, Dis. 14, 77+ ac., a tract bought by LEWIS FORE at the sale in Franklin and transferred from Fore to DANIEL GARLAND and from Daniel to William Garland. Howard is to pay the notes due the state. Oct. 25, 1839. *Wm. Garland.* Wit: *JOEL BINGHAM, Daniel Garland.* Proven by Daniel Garland, 1842. Registered Oct. 14, 1842.

1523 SG 450, ELIAS NORTON, $5/100 ac., 50 ac. on White Water R. near the Terepin Mountain in Dis. 18. Entered July 23, 1839; granted Oct. 25, 1841; registered Oct. 17, 1842.

1524 SG 449, ELIAS NORTON, $5/100 ac., 50 ac. on White Water R., Dis. 18, near the Terepin Mountain. Entered July 23, 1839; granted Oct. 2, 1841; registered Oct. 17, 1842.

1525 SG 448, THOMPSON WILSON, $5/100 ac., 50 ac., Dis. 6, on the Tuckaseegee R., including both sides of the road. Entered Jan. 23, 1839; granted Oct. 25, 1841; registered Oct. 17, 1842.

1526 SG 447, THOMPSON WILSON, $5/100 ac., 26 ac. on the Tuckaseegee R., Dis. 6, on corner of No. 26, including a swamp. Entered Jan. 23, 1839; granted Oct. 25, 1841; registered Oct. 17, 1842.

1527 SG 496, WILLIAM BARNS, $5/100 ac., 50 ac. on the Chattooga R., Dis. 18, W. side of Big Cr. Entered Jan. 6, 1842; granted Sep. 29, 1842; registered Oct. 17, 1842.

1528 SG 495, JAMES M. TATHAM, $5/100 ac., 100 ac. on the Chattooga R., Dis. 18, on both sides of the track leading from the Horse Cove to Georgia, on corner of No. 8. Entered Dec. 16, 1842; granted Sep. 29, 1841 (sic); registered Oct. 17, 1842.

1529 SG 423, DAVID B. LEDFORD, $5/100 ac., 50 ac. on the Tuckasegee R., Dis. 6, on line of Sec. 23, incl. an improvement. Entered Mar. 25, 1839; granted Dec. 29, 1840; registered Oct. 17, 1842.

1530 SG 567, SAUL SMITH, $5/100 ac., land on the Chattooga R., crossing a branch. Entered Mar. 27, 1840; granted Oct. 5, 1842; registered Oct. 19, 1842.

1531 JAMES N. BRYSON of Haywood Co., NC, to ZACHARIAH PEAK of Macon, 55 ac., Sec. 58, Dis. 11, which I purchased at the land sale in Waynesville, 1822. Peak to pay state what is due. Mar. 29, 1842. *James N. Bryson.* Wit: *ABRAHAM MOORE, JACOB (his X mark) STUART.* Proven by Abraham Moore in Sep. 1842 session. Registered ct. 31, 1842.

1531 Mortgage: THOS. LONG to JOHN HOWARD & LEWIS VANDYKE, for $50, 2 horses beast, a mare & a bay; a horse colt, two years old next spring; 25 head of stock hogs; 8 head of sheep; 5 plows, 1 harrow, 3 axes, 2 mattocks, 3 hoes; a cupboard, beaurow, bench, chest, 2 bed steds with beds and furniture, 8 chairs, 2 tables with all the shelf & cooking utensils belonging to the kitchen; stack of oats & 3 stacks of hay, all the standing corn on the place & fodder; 2 cutting boxxes & knives; 2 scythes & cradles, 1 moing syth and ___ hook; 2 c___s? with 2 pair of gears; a log chain; a saddle and bridle. Condition: Vandyke & Howard have gone security for a note Long owed JAMES G. GREY for $77 with interest from Oct. 23, 1841, on which there is a judgement & execution. Long is to pay note. Oct. 14, 1842. *Thos. Long.* Wit: *N.F. HOWARD.* Ack. Oct. 15, 1842. Registered Oct. 31, 1842.

1533 SG 499, SAUL SMITH, $5/100 ac., 50 ac. on Middle Cr., Dis. 13, on corner of Sec. 36. Entered Aug. 20, 1841; granted Oct. 5, 1842; registered Nov. 3, 1842.

1534 SG 498, SAUL SMITH, $5/100 ac., 50 ac. on Chattooga R., Dis. 18, beginning on WIL-LIAM BARNES' line, crossing a small creek. Entered Mar. 27, 1840; granted Oct. 5, 1842; registered Nov. 3, 1842.

1535 JOHN HOWARD to WEST TRUITT, both of Macon, for $200, 8 tracts in Dis. 13: Sec. 28 (58 ac.); Sec. 29 (75 ac.); Sec. 51 (56 ac.); Sec. 52 (90 ac.); Sec. 53 (75 ac.); Sec. 54 (56 ac.); Sec. 56 (65 ac.); Sec. 27 (84 ac.) - all lying in the flats of Middle Creek. Sep. 26, 1841. *West (his X mark) Truitt.* Wit: *JACOB SILER.* Proven by Jacob Siler in Sep. 1842 session. Registered Nov. 3, 1842.

1535 Mortgage: JAMES ROBISON & DAVID LOWRY of 1st part to NICHOLAS W. WOODFIN, trustee, of 2nd part and JAMES C.P. REPLY, MILLER (crossed out), GEORGE N. MILLER, HENRY C. RUSSELL, EPHRIM MILLER & CHARLES W. CHAMBERLIN, merchants trading under the name of MILLER REPLY & CO. of 3rd part. James Robison, for $2,442.49 which he owes to parties of the third part, beside the further consideration of $1 paid by Nicholas W. Woodfin, trustee, mortgages to Woodfin two lots in Franklin township, No. 14 & No. 15, part of No. 19; No. 14 & part of No. 19 were conveyed to J. Robison by JESSE R. SILER by deed Dec. 12, 1837, including house & improvement where Robison now lives; No. 15 was conveyed to Robison by JONATHAN PHILLIPS, chairman of the county court, by deed June 13, 1839, also a tract of land & plantation on which GEORGE CARSON now lives, about one mile W. of Franklin, on both sides of the creek that runs by town and on publick road leading to Cherokee (County) from Franklin on N. side of road, originally in two tracts, one of 174 ac. conveyed to Robison by JAMES POTEAT, Sep. 23, 1833, the other, 99 ac., conveyed by Jesse R. Siler, Mar. 24, 1840. The purpose of this deed is to secure just debt to Miller Reply & Co. for $773.54 by note dated Aug. 18, 1841 in Charleston, SC, & two notes by the firm of ROBINSON & LOWRY, of which Robinson is a member, one due six months from Feb. 8, 1840 for $437.70, the other from Mar. 7, 1839 for $906.58, payable in Charleston. Sep. 13, 1842. *Jas. Robinson, N.W. Woodfin, Miller Reply & Co., per F. HARRELL, agt.* Wit: *B.K. DICKEY.* Proven by Dickey in Sep. 1842 session. Registered Nov. 4, 1842.

1538 JESSE R. SILER to HENRY G. WOODFIN, both of Macon, for $200, 55 ac. on "Car-tugaa gacheyi" (Cartoogechaye) Cr., Dis. 15, Sec. 60, crossing Thompson's fork, also Sec. 61, Dis. 15, containing 69 ac.; also one other tract, on corner of Sec. 123, Dis. 15, containing 50 ac. Dec. 10, 1841. *J.R. Siler.* Wit: *S. MCDOWELL.* Proven by S. Mc-Dowell in Sep. 1842 session. Registered Nov. 4, 1842.

1539 Performance bond: SILAS MCDOWELL, J.R. SILER, J.K. GRAY, $5,000 bond for Silas McDowell, duly elected clerk of superior court. Sep. 16, 1842. Ack. in Sep. 1842 session. Registered Nov. 4, 1842.

1540 Sheriff's sale: ELI MCKEE, Esq., High Sheriff of Macon, to B. STILES of Cherokee Co., NC, land sold at public auction to satisfy judgment against JAMES N. BRYSON for $47.60. The property was a tract of 55 ac. on "Ellijah" (Ellijay) Creek. Stiles had high bid of $50 at public sale, Sep. 29, 1840. Sep. 29, 1840. *Eli McKee.* Ack. in June 1842 session. Registered Nov. 4, 1842.

1541 J.R. SILER to H.G. WOODFIN, both of Macon, for $300, 122 ac. on "Cartoogachaye" Cr., Sec. 51, Dis. 15, purchased by B.W. BELL at sale in 1836 for $91.50, one-eighth of which was paid; Woodfin to pay the state the balance due; also, Sec. 62, Dis. 15, containing 60 ac., purchased by DANIEL NICHOLDS at same sale and conveyed to Siler; also Sec. 59, Dis. 16, 61 ac., purchased by WESLY JOHNSTON at same sale in 1836. Dec. 10, 1841. *J.R. Siler.* Wit: *SILAS MCDOWELL.* Proven by Silas McDowell. Registered Nov. 4, 1842.

1542 Performance bond: SILAS MCDOWELL, J.R. SILER, JAMES K. GRAY, $10,000 bond for Silas McDowell, duly elected clerk of Superior Court. Sep. 16, 1842. Ack. in Sep. 1842 session. Registered Nov. 4, 1842.

1543 Performance bond: J.K. GRAY, J.R. SILER, SILAS MCDOWELL, $10,000 bond for J.K. Gray, duly elected clerk of Court of Pleas & Qtr. sessions. Sep. 14, 1842. Registered Nov. 4, 1842.

1544 JOHN JUSTICE to ANDREW JUSTICE, both of Macon, for $50, 83 ac. on the Tennessee R., Sec. 47, Dis.13, crossing Tessenty Creek. Mar. 17, 1840. *John Justice.* Wit: *JOHN HOWARD.* Proven by Howard in Sep. 1842 session. Registered Nov. 4, 1842.

1545 DAVID BALEW to HORATIO N. CONLEY/CONNELLY, both of Macon, for $30, land on Tessenty Cr., a tract sold by JACOB PALMER to David Balew, Dis. 13, Sec. 48 & 46, containing 66 & 68 acres respectively. Oct. 5, 1841. *David Ballew.* Wit: *JOHN HOWARD, AARVIN H. CONNELLY.* Proven by Howard in Sep. 1842 session. Registered Nov. 4, 1842.

1546 SG 500, ZEBULON J. THOMAS, $5/100 ac., 40 ac. on Tennessee R., Dis. 15, on corner of Sec. 13 & 14. Entered Mar. 25, 1840; granted Oct. 24, 1842; registered Nov. 4, 1842.

1547 SG 501, JOSEAH A. CURTIS, $5/100 ac., 50 ac. on S. bank of Tessentee Cr. Entered June 16, 1840; granted Oct. 24, 1842; registered Nov. 11, 1842.

1548 JACOB PALMER to DAVID BELEW, both of Macon, for $28, two tracts, Dis. 13, Sec. 48 & 46, containing 66 & 68 acres. Balew to pay amount due state. Oct. 11, 1838. *Jacob Palmer.* Wit: *JOHN HOWARD.* Proven by Howard in Sep. 1842 session. Registered Nov. 11, 1842.

1549 Performance bond: J.K. GRAY, J.R. SILER, SILAS MCDOWELL, $2,000 bond for J.K. Gray, duly elected clerk of Court of Pleas & Qtr. Sessions. Registered Nov. 11, 1842.

1549 SG 463, JOHN MCCAMPBELL, $5/100 ac., 100 ac. on the Smoky Mountain, beginning at a mountain ash in (Tennessee) state line at the 49-mile tree. Entered Nov. 20, 1839; granted Nov. 22, 1841; registered Jan. 2, 1843.

1550 SG 460, ELIZABETH SANDERS, $5/100 ac., 50 ac. on "Watagee" (Watauga) Cr., Dis. 10, on corner of Sec. 122. Entered Jan. 21, 1839; granted Nov. 19, 1841; registered Jan. 2, 1843.

1551 SG 459, JOHN N. MATHIS, $5/100 ac., 50 ac. on "Cullewhee" (Cullowhee) Cr., Dis. 7, on line of Sec. 50. Entered Feb. 5, 1839; granted Nov. 12, 1841; registered Jan. 2, 1843.

End of Volume C

Macon County Deed Book D

1555 Mortgage: DAVID R. LOWRY, of 1st part, JACOB SILER of 2nd part & DAVID L. SWAIN of 3rd part. Swain holds $604.30 note on Lowry dated Jun. 15, 1839, JESSE R. SILER security. Swain to pay state $750 for Lowery. Swain this day advanced $250, for which Lowery has exec. his note payable one day from date. In consideration of which & for $1 paid by Jacob Siler, Lowery has sold to Siler an undiv. 1/2 of farm on which Lowry lives & 9 adj. tracts on "Iola" (Iotla) Creek, the same conveyed by ELI MCKEE, Sheriff of Macon Co. to David R. Lowery & Jesse R. Siler Aug. 18, 1840; 1/2 of which was conveyed by Jesse R. Siler to David L. Swain in trust. This void if Lowry pay Swain the amounts due by June 1. Mar. 15, 1843. *D.R. Lowery, Jacob Siler, D.L. Swain per N.W. WOODFIN, agent.* Wit: *JAS. ROBISON.* Proven by Jas. Robison in March 1843 court. Registered June 5, 1843.

1556 JESSE GRIGG to JESSE R. SILER, both of Macon, for $20, 69 ac. Sec. 61, Dis. 15, on Cartoogechaye Cr., S. side Thompson's Fork. Aug. 14, 1840. *Jesse Grigg.* Wit: *SAUL SMITH, WM. RONE.* Proven by Saul Smith in Jan. 1843 court. Registered June 5, 1843.

1557 BERRICK NORTON to JESSE R. SILER, both of Macon, for $70, 1/6 part of 100-ac. tract undiv., also 2/5 of 100-acre tract undiv.; the 1st on Toxaway R., Dis. 18, granted Berrick Norton, THOS. MILLSAPS, DAVID MILLSAPS, WM. BRYSON & JOHN DOBSON in 1838, beginning in the hickory gap of a ridge joining Sec. 82, on which Millsaps & HYATT has dug gold. 2nd on White Water Cr., Dis. 18, known as the Soap Stone Quarry tract, granted Berrick Norton, Thos. Millsaps, Wm. Bryson & John Dobson, 1838. Nov. 12, 1842. *Berrick Norton.* Wit: *B.K. DICKY, ALFERD HALL.* Proven by B.K. Dicky in Jan 1843 court. Registered June 5, 1843.

1558 CHARLES HAYES to JESSE R. SILER, both of Macon, for $2500, 300 ac. on "Ioly" (Iotla) Cr., Sec. 47, Dis. 16, purch. of State by B.S. BRITTEN in Oct. 1820 and transferred to said Hayes by him in Sep. 1838. May 2, 1841. *Charles Hayes.* Wit: *B.K. DICKY.* Proven by Dicky in Jan. 1843 court. Registered June 5, 1843.

1559 CHARLES HAYS to JESSE R. SILER, both of Macon, for $500, 111+ ac., Sec. 45, Dis. 16, as rep. in a grant to Charles Hayes, assignee of J.R. PACE, paid Jan? 7, 1839. May 29, 1841. *Charles Hayes.* Wit: *B.K. DICKY.* Proven in Jan. 1843 court by Dicky. Registered June 5, 1843.

1560 H.G. WOODFIN to J.R. SILER, both of Macon, for $1200, part of 400 ac. of Town of Franklin, 4 ac. on the Big Road, part of lots No. 38, 42 and 43, also lots 7 & 8, being 10 ac. on corner of B.W. BELL's field, 2 lots bid by B.S. BRITTEN at sale in Franklin, 1835; also in Franklin on N. side of Main St., 5 lots, total 5 ac.: No. 46, 48, 50, 51, 52, & 53. Dec. 21, 1840. *H.G. Woodfin.* Wit: *S. MCDOWELL.* Proven by McDowell in Jan. 1843 court. Registered June 5, 1843.

1562 WILLIAM HICK to JESSE R. SILER, both of Macon, for $30, 4 ac. about 1 mi. SW of Franklin, part of No. 28, Dis. 16. Apr. 28, 1840. *Wm. Hicks.* Wit: *BURTON K. DICKY.* Proven in Jan. 1843 court. Registered June 5, 1843.

1562 JOHN DEHART to JESSE R. SILER, both of Macon, for $10, 50 ac., Dis. 8, N. side Tennessee R., granted me Dec. 15, 1838. Mar. 28, 1842. *John (his X mark) Dehart.* Wit: *B.K. DICKY, CHAS. HAYES.* Proven by Dicky in Jan. 1843 court. Registered June 5, 1843.

1563 JESSE GRIGG to JESSE R. SILER, both of Macon, for $50, 50 ac. on "Cartu-u-gu-hi-gay" (Cartoogechaye), Dis. 15. Apr. 14, 1840. *Jesse Grigg.* Wit: *SAUL SMITH, WM. ROAN.* Proven by Saul Smith, Jan 1843 court. Registered June 5, 1843.

1564 J.R. ALLMAN to J.R. SILER for $60, 64 2/3 poles in town of Franklin, lot 9 on south side of the main street. May 12, 1841. *J.R. Allman.* Wit: *B.K. DICKY, E.G. MORROW(?).* Proven by Dicky, Jan. 1843 court. Registered June 5, 1843.

1565 ELIJAH M. HALL to JESSE R. SILER, both of Macon, for $100, land on Tennessee R.,
S. of ridge dividing "Ioly" (Iotla) Cr., bd. GEORGE F. CALER, MARTIN HUSK;
entered by STEPHEN PACE and conveyed to E.M. Hall in 1838. Dec. 17, 1842. *E.M.
Hall.* Wit: *E. DOWDLE, JOHN PALMER.* Proven by Dowdle, Jan. 1843 court.
Registered June 5, 1843.

1566 WM. HICK, Esq., Ch'man of Court of Pleas and Qtr Sessions for Macon, to JESSE R.
SILER, assoc. of JOHN HALL for the purchase, town lots 47 and 49, approx. 1 ac. ea.,
on N. side Main st., purchased by Hall in May 1835, pd. in full. Jan. 26, 1843. *Wm.
Heckes.* Wit: *J. HOWARD.* Ack. in Jan. 1843 court. Registered June 5, 1843.

1567 WM. MORRISON to JESSE R. SILER, both of Macon, for $300, 50-60 ac. on "Ioly"
(Iotla) including mill near mouth of creek, on W. bank Tennessee R., a few Rod below
the Ioly ford, to highest water mark of a millpond. As purchase is for express purpose of
building a good mill, Morrison agrees that should head of water necessary to make a
good mill dam up further than land conveyed, he will take from Siler or his rep. the
damage three good men may assess. Dec. 27, 1840. *William Morrison.* Wit: *GEORGE F.
CALER, MARTIN HURST.* Proven by Caler, Jan. 1843 court. Registered June 6, 1843.

1568 SAMUEL BRYSON to ISAAC MOORE, both of Macon, for $200, 75 ac. purchased
from the state by ANDREW BRYSON, dec'd, lying on Sugar Town fork of little Tennessee R. Jan. 18, 1843. *Samuel Bryson.* Wit: *NOAH C. LEDFORD.* Ack. in Jan. 1843
session. Registered June 6, 1843.

1568 JOHN HUGGINS to WM. G. WATTS, both of Macon, for $150, 78 ac., Dis. 15, Sec.
64, sold by the state to GEORGE BLACK. Feb. 23, 1842. *John Huggin.* Wit: *MILES (his
X mark) PENDERGRASS, FRACE (his X mark) NICKLE.* Proven by Pendergrass, Jan.
1843 court. Registered June 6, 1843.

1569 NIMROD S. JARRETT to SAMUEL REED, both of Macon, for $500, 80 ac., Sec. 4,
Dis. 11. Jan. 26, 1843. *N.S. Jarrett.* Wit: *JAS. ROBINSON.* Ack. in Jan. 1843 court.
Registered June 6, 1843.

1570 N.S. JARRETT to SAMUEL REED, both of Macon, for $500, Sec. 2, Dis. 11, crossing
Mill Cr., on Tennessee R. Jan. 25, 1843. *N.S. Jarrett.* Wit: *JAS. ROBINSON.* Ack. Jan.
1843 court. Registered June 6, 1843.

1570 Mortgage: WILLIAM GUYER to CHARLES HAYS & JOHN PHILLIPS, 3 horses, 5
cattle, 10 hogs as security, Hays & Phillips having secured a stay for an execution against
Guyer in favor of JORSHUA HAWSHAW for $32 & int. Oct. 1, 1842. *William Guyer.*
Wit: *B.K. DICKY.* Proven by Dicky, Jan. 1843 court. Registered June 6, 1843.

1571 JOHN HALL, who had mortgaged 4 negroes to DILLARD LOVE, sold one of the 4,
REBECCA & her male child to WILLIAM ALLMAN with consent of Love, who
released them from mortgage; Hall now surrenders to Love 3 other negroes, GEORGE,
ELIZA & CHARLOTA, same conditions. Jan. 26, 1843. *John Hall.* Wit: *FELAX AXLY,
William Allman.* Ack. in Jan. 1843 court. Registered June 6, 1843.

1571 WILLIAM HICKS, Esq., Ch'man, to J.K. GRAY, town lots 6 & 7, paid in full; both on
S. side Main St., No. 6 near Jail at SW corner Public Square & Cross St., 150 poles; No.
7 on SW corner of Public Square, one acre. Jan. 27, 1843. *Wm. Hicks.* Wit: *E. DOWDLE.*
Ack. in Jan. 1843 court. Registered June 6, 1843.

1573 JOHN LOWDERMILK to JAMES ROBINSON & DILLARD LOVE, all of Macon, for
$100, land on Elijay Cr., Dis. 11; entered Oct. 27, 1838, deeded to Lowdermilk. Feb. 28,
1842. *John Lowdermilk.* Wit: *J.Y. GRANT.* Proved in Jan. 1843 court by Jas. Y. Grant.
Registered June 6, 1843.

1573 JOHN LOWDERMILK to J.L. ROBINSON & D. LOVE, all of Macon, for $100, land
on Elijay Cr., Dis. 11. Feb. 28, 1842. *John Lowdermilk.* Wit: *J.Y. GRANT,* who proved in
Jan. 1843 court. Registered June 6, 1843.

1574 SAMUEL W. DOWDLE to EZEKIEL DOWDLE, both of Macon, for $250, 123 ac. on Tennessee R. above WILLIAM CABE survey. Nov. 8, 1842. *S.W. Dowdle*. Wit. *A. HESTER*, who proved in Jan. 1843 court. Registered June 6, 1843.

1575 JOHN HALL to WILLIAM ALLMAN, both of Macon, Negro woman BECK with her child aged 5 wks. Jan. 26, 1842. *John Hall*. Wit: *FELAX AXLY, D. LOVE*. Dillard Love quitclaims title to above Negro woman and child, Jan. 26, 1842. *Dillard Love*. Wit: *Felax Axly*. Ack. in Jan. 1843 court. Registered June 6, 1843.

1576 SAM'L W. DOWDLE to EZEKIEL DOWDLE, both of Macon, 131 ac. Sec. 14, Dis. 12, which ENOS (S)CROGG purchased at Franklin in Cherokee sales, 1836. Nov. 8, 1842. *S.W. Dowdle*. Wit: *A. HESTER*, who proved in court Jan. 1843. Registered June 6, 1843.

1576 JAMES WEATHEROW, of Macon, entered 80 ac. Mar. 28, 1837 & has a grant with WEST TRUETT; for consideration of 5 (?) to me paid, sell to West Truitt, my right to a parcel on top of a ridge, bd. W.G. WALL's old line. Jan. 29, 1843. *J. Witherow*. Wit: *SILAS MCDOWELL*, who proved in Jan. 1843 court. Registered June 6, 1843.

1577 H.M. PENLAND to ANDREW BRADLEY, both of Macon, for $400, 97 ac. on Tennessee R., Dis. 14, Sec. 7. Apr. 8, 1842. *H.M. Penland*. Wit: *C.M. PENLAND, G.N. PENLAND*. Proven by C.M. Penland in Jan. 1843 court. Registered June 6, 1843.

1578 SG 465, MARTHA KERBY, $5/100 ac., land on Culhowhee (Cullowhee) Creek, Dis. 7, corner No. 60. Entry Oct. 29, 1839; grant Nov. 30, 1842; registered June 7, 1843.

1578 SG 501, JOHN DILL, $5/100 ac., land on Tuckasegee R., Dis. 8, corner No. 30. Entry Dec. 25, 1840; grant Dec. 2, 1842; registered June 7, 1843.

1579 SG 427, JAMES JAMES, $___, 80 ac., Sec. 4, Dis. 11. Grant Jan. 7, 1839; registered June 7, 1843.

1580 SG 577, NIMROD S. JARRETT, assignee of JAMES ANGEL, assignee of MARTIN ANGEL, for $199.22, 179 ac., Sec. 2, Dis. 11, on Mill Creek. Grant Nov. 28, 1840; registered June 7, 1843.

1581 SG 510, WILLIAM SHULER, $5/100 ac., 50 ac. on Deep Cr., bd. BRAWDSHAW's line. Entry May 14, 1841; grant Dec. 2, 1842; registered June 7, 1843.

1582 SG 636, JOHN SHULAR, $1120, 280 ac. on Deep Cr., Sec. 6, Dis. 1. Grant Jan. 26, 1843; registered June 7, 1843.

1583 SG 506, ELVANDER W. ZACHARY, $5/100 ac., 100 ac. on Chatooga R., Dis. 18, near the White Side Mtn. Entry June 15, 1841; grant Dec. 2, 1842; registered June 7, 1843.

1583 SG 514, JOSEPH BUCHANON, $5/100 ac., 100 ac. on Savannah Cr. Entry Nov. 5, 1840; grant Dec. 2, 1842; registered June 7, 1843.

1584 SG 522, $5/100 ac., MARSHALL J. MULL & RISDAN COOPER, 100 ac. on "Cotteru geceahege" (Cartoogechaye) Cr. in Dis. 15, incl. some improvements. Entry Dec. 9, 1840; grant Dec. 30, 1842; registered June 7, 1843.

1585 SG 521, SAUL SMITH, $5/100 ac., 40 ac. "Cartoogie" (Chattooga) R., Dis. 18, on GA line, Buzzard Rock Mtn., bd. DANIEL L. MCDOWELL. Entry Mar. 27, 1840; grant Dec. 30, 1842; registered June 7, 1843.

1586 GEORGE W. HAYS to JOHN SHULAR, Junr., for $150, 100 ac. on Newton's Mill Cr., Dis. 1, bd. Hayes land; entered May 2, 1836. Mar. 8, 1843. *G.W. Hayes*. Wit: *SAMUEL SHERRILL, DAVID P. ADAMS*. Proven by Samuel Sherrill in Mar. 1843 court. Registered June 7, 1843.

1586 GEORGE W. HAYES to JOHN SHULAR for $25, 50 ac. on Newton's Mill Creek. Mar. 8, 1843. *G.W. Hayes*. Wit: *SAMUEL SHERRELL, DAVID P. ADAMS*. Proven by Samuel Sherrell, Mar. 1843 court. Registered June 7, 1843.

1587 ELI MCKEE, Esq., High Sheriff of Macon, to JAMES PARKER of Macon, land sold at
      public sale to satisfy judgement of county ct. against NATHAN B. THOMPSON for
      $41.95, recovered by M.S. SHERRELL: lots 107 (80 ac.), 17 (61 ac.) & 110 (50 ac.).
      High bid was $1.745, entered by WM. H. THOMAS for James Parker. Sep. 16, 1842. *Eli
      McKee, Shff.* Wit: *P. REIMS(?).* Ack. Mar. 1843 court. Registered June 8, 1843.

1588 ELI MCKEE, Esq. High Sheriff of Macon, to LAGRAN S. ROBINSON of Macon, 42
      acres to satisfy judgment of county ct. in favor of J.L. MOORE against GEORGE LOW-
      DERMILK for $37.26, recovered by Moore. Robinson had high bid of $51.06 1/4. Sep.
      15, 1842. *Eli McKee.* Wit: *J.P.M. ANGEL, J.K. GRAY.* Proven by Gray in Mar. 1843
      court. Registered June 8, 1843.

1590 ELI MCKEE, Esq. High Sh'ff of Macon to LAGRAN S. ROBINSON, 85 ac. to satisfy
      judgment against GEORGE LOWDERMILK for $4.15, recovered by J.L. MOORE.
      Robinson had high bid of $51.06. Sep. 15, 1842. *Eli McKee, Shff.* Wit: *S. MCDOWELL,
      THOS. M. ANGEL.* Proven by McDowell, Mar. 1843 court. Reg. June 8, 1843.

1592 GEORGE LOWDERMILK to LAGRAN S. ROBINSON, both of Macon, for val. rec'd,
      85 ac., Sec. 62, Dis. 11, which I purchased of JOSEPH WATTS in 1839. Mar. 17, 1843.
      George (his X mark) Lowdermilk. Wit: *W.F. ROBINSON, G.W. LOWDERMILK.* Proven
      by W.F. Robinson in Mar. 1843 court. Registered June 8, 1843.

1592 Mortgage: LABAN LONG to E.T. LONG & ANDREW NORTON for $1, 3 bedsteads &
      furniture, pot, 2 ovens & lids, pan, pot hooks, bake pan, frying pan, 4 hoes, 4 plows, 2
      scythes & cradles, 2 pr. of geares with bridle collars & hip straps, saddle, iron wedge, 2
      axes, all my shelf ware & water vessels, 3 sheaves in the mill that I am now attending;
      land agreeable to the will of WM. CARPENTER, dec'd; 62 acres that I bought & on
      which I owe state $40 or 50; two other tracts that I entered. Condition: E.T. Long is
      security to S. SMITH & WM. GRAY for 280 bu. of corn due next Nov. & Norton has
      stayed a judgment for me for $12.75 debt to J.H. HUNTER & LOVE. Mar. 29, 1843. *L.
      Long.* Wit: *JOHN HOWARD.* Proven by Howard, Apr. 3, 1843. Registered June 8, 1843.

1593 Mortgage: WILLIAM PATTON to WILLIAM ANGEL for $80.35, 3-horse wagon &
      harness, gray mare, roan mare, sorrel filly, 3 colts, 20 sheep, 11 cattle & my household &
      kitchen furniture & all my corn, say 300 bu., 40 hogs. Condition: Angel has paid Patton
      $88.35, Patton to repay with interest before Jan. 1 next. Feb. 11, 1843. *Wm. M. Patton.*
      Wit: *H.G. WOODFIN.* Proved by H.G. Woodfin in Mar. 1843 court. Reg. June 8, 1843.

1594 ABRAHAM SELLARS to WILLIAM STALLCUP, both of Macon, for $10, land near
      state ford of Tuckasegee R. & District corner of what is called the "Heet" tract; bd.
      HALL, Sellars; entered May 2, 1836. Mar. 14, 1843. *Abram Sellars.* Wit: *N.G. ALLMAN,
      M. COCKERHAND.*

1595 RICHARD WILSON of Macon to JOHN WILSON of Macon & LEVI WILSON of Gil-
      mer Co. GA, during natural life of RACHEL WILSON, wife of said Richard, Negro boy
      ALFORD, between 12 & 13 yrs.; after death of Rachel, he is to be sold & money equally
      div. among all children of Rachel, or their heirs. John & Levi to maintain Rachel during
      her natural life & keep Richard or his estate from any claim on account of her main-
      tenance. Sep. 14, 1842. *Richard (his X mark) Wilson, John Wilson, Levi Wilson.* Wit:
      JORSHUA ROBERTS. Proven by Joshua Robert, Mar. 1843 court. Reg. June 8, 1843.

1595 Gift: ISAAC ASH to MANDY C. JONES, 2 sows, 13 pigs, cow & calf, bed & furniture,
      household furniture. Mar. 10, 1843. *Isaac Ash.* Wit: *W.M. TATHAM.* Ack. in Mar. 1843
      court. Registered June 8, 1843.

1596 JOHN HALL to ROBERT HALL Jr., both of Macon, for $630, Negro man named
      ELIAS, whereas Hall was appt. guardian for heirs at law of CAROLINE HALL, dec'd,
      namely Robert Hall, MARY F. HALL, REBECAH J. HALL & ELIZABETH C.S.
      HALL, dec'd; all minor heirs of Caroline, dec'd wife of John Hall, to receive money
      from estate of GEORGE SWAIN, dec'd, father of said Caroline, amounting to $1,000.

Elizabeth C.S. Hall having died as a minor, 1/2 of her dowry reverted to John Hall, her father & guardian; there remains to Robert Hall, Mary F. Hall & JANE HESTER (i.e. Rebecah Jane Hall Hester) the sum of $630 each. Jan. 3, 1842. *John Hall, guardian.* Wit: *THOS. MASHBURN, WM. B. MORGAN.* Ack. in Mar. 1843 court. Registered June 9, 1843.

1597 JOHN HALL to MARY F. HALL, both of Macon Co., for $630, Negro woman ELIZA & her youngest child, MARGRET; her further increase, should there be any, shall be at my disposal or that of my estate. John Hall was appt'd guardian of heirs at law of CAROLINE HALL, dec'd wife of John Hall: ROBERT HALL, REBECAH JANE HALL, Mary F. Hall, ELIZABETH C.S. HALL. They to receive from estate of GEORGE SWAIN, dec'd, $1,000. Elizabeth having died, 1/2 of her share reverts to John Hall, rest to surviving heirs - Robert Hall, Jane Hester & Mary Hall - a total of $1,830, in consequence of which above bill of sale was made. Jan. 3, 1842. *John Hall, guardian.* Wit: *THOS. MASHBURN, W.B. MORGAN.* Ack. in Mar. 1843 court. Registered June 9, 1843.

1598 JOHN HALL to JANE HESTER, both of Macon, for $630, Negro girl HARRIETT, about 14 years old. John Hall was guardian of heirs of CAROLINE HALL, dec'd, namely ROBERT HALL, Rebecah Jane Hall (Hester), MARY F. HALL, ELIZABETH C.S. HALL, who are due money from estate of GEORGE SWAIN, dec'd. Rest of language same as previous deed. Jan. 3, 1842. *John Hall.* Wit: *THOS. MASHBURN, WM. B. MORGAN.* Ack. in Mar 1843 court. Registered June 9, 1843.

1599 JAMES SELLARS to JASON H. HUNTER, both of Macon, for $20, 80 ac. where Sellers now lives in Dis. 1, Sec. 65. June 6, 1842. *Jas. Sellers.* Wit: *G.W.F. MOORE, D.R. LOWRY.* Proven by Lowry in Mar. 1843 court. Registered June 9, 1843.

1599 BENJAMIN HYDE, Junr. to JASON H. HUNTER, both of Macon, for $110 paid Hyde & $40 due state, 50 acres, Dis. 8, Sec. 68, also adj. tract, 116 ac., Dis. 8, Sec. 69. Apr. 28, 1842. *B. Hyde.* Wit: *WM. H. THOMAS,* who proved in court Mar. 1843. Registered June 9, 1843.

1600 MICHAEL WIKLE to J.H. HUNTER, both of Macon, for $104, 166 ac. on W. bank Tennessee R., Sec. 34, Dis. 16. Feb. 12, 1843. *M. Wikle.* Wit: *J.F. GRAT (GRANT?), D.R. LOWRY.* Proven by Lowry in Mar. 1843 court. Registered June 9, 1843.

1600 JAMES SELLARS to JASON H. HUNTER, both of Macon, for $110, 178 ac., Sec. 64, Dis. 1. May 5, 1842. *Jas. Sellars.* Wit: *WM. H. THOMAS, G.W.F. MOORE.* Proven by Thomas in Mar. 1843 court. Registered June 9, 1843.

1601 Mortgage: CLARK BIRD of Macon to JONATHAN BIRD, by his agent BENJAMIN BIRD of Burk(e) Co., NC, whereas Clark Bird by 3 bonds is bound to Jonathan Burd for $650 with int., he mortgages several parcels to secure notes: 640 ac. known as the SKIKIN Reservation; 52 ac., Sec. 10, Dis. 17; 58 ac., Sec. 73, Dis. 17 on Tellico Cr., with buildings, improvements, etc., all my stock - 30 sheep, 30 hogs, 20 cattle, 3 horses. Dec. 3, 1842. *Clark Bird.* Wit: *LEM'L BIRD.* Proven by Lemuel Bird in Jan. 1843 court. Registered June 16, 1843.

1602 Agreement: HENRY G. WOODFIN of Macon, for $2,345.79 owing NICHOLAS W. WOODFIN of Buncombe Co. NC, & futher consideration of $1 paid by JAMES ROBINSON, of Macon, mortgages land in Buncombe whereon JOHN A. FOGG now lives on E. side French Broad R., 2 mi. N. of Warm Springs, known as the Haworth Stand, adj. lands of PHILIP H. NELSON & others, orig. 2 or more tracts conveyed to the late DR. BENJAMIN HAWORTH Sr., which descended to the heirs at law of said Haworth, an undiv. share of said real estate for life in right of ELIZA ANN, daughter & heir of Benj. Haworth dec'd, & wife of Henry G. Woodfin. Also, all interest which Henry G. Woodfin has in a stallion in Macon Co. called Marblieu, the 1/4 of a share or one 24th part, there being 6 shares, also standing crops: 20-25 ac. of corn, 20 ac. of oats, 1 ac. of potatoes, hay on 20 ac. of meadow & all the fruit on the orchard where H.G. Woodfin now lives, to James Robinson, he to hold property for purpose of repaying to N.W. Woodfin the bal. of $2,345.79 out of sales of the property on Mar. 14 & 18, 1843, under deed of trust exec. to James Robinson; also one note to D.L. SLOAN for $500; one to E.B. STODDARD, assignee, $412; one to HYETH MCBERRY & Co., assignee, $326.53; also to JACOB SILER, a judgment of about $90; also a debt of money to JOHN W. WOODFIN of about $30. All H.G. Woodfin's debts to be paid except 5 notes of $300 ea. to JOHN MOORE in purch. of farm on which H.G. Woodfin now lives, the titles of which are retained as security. Robinson to sell as much property as necessary to pay debts, selling real estate at courthouse door in Asheville, Buncombe Co., & personal prop. at such places as he deems proper; he is to pay H.G. Woodfin any surplus. May 30, 1843. *H.G. Woodfin, Jas. Robinson, N.W. Woodfin.* Wit: *D.R. LOWRY, J.M. CLARK, P. HOWARD.* Proven by P. Howard June 10, 1843. Registered June 16, 1843.

1605 Mortgage: MARSHAL J. MULL to CHARLES HAYES & ENOS MCCLURE, 2 horse wagons & harness, 2 head of horses, cow & calf, 9 head stock hogs, one clock, growing crop of corn & oats on farm where I now live, 1/3 of 3 growing crops of corn & oats on farm where WILLIS JONES now lives, 2 beds & furniture, 2 sleds, to Charles Hayes. Condition: Hayes & McClure on May 1, 1843 became security for Mull by staying an execution in favor of THOMAS J. ROAN against Mull for $34.61. June 16, 1843. *Marshal J. (his X mark) Mull.* Wit: *E. DOWDLE.* Proven by Dowdle in June 1843 court. Registered Aug. 11, 1843.

1605 Mortgage: THOMAS LONG to LEWIS VANDYKE, both of Macon, for $1, standing crop of corn & oats that I have where I now live. Long has been security for a debt of $12 to SAUL SMITH, the note now in E. DOWDLE's hand. July 22, 1843. *Thos. Long.* Wit: *J. HOWARD.* Proven by J. Howard in Aug. 5, 1843. Registered Aug. 11, 1843.

1606 JACOB PALMER of Obin Co. TN to HORATIO N. CONLEY of Macon, for $30, 2 tracts on Tessenty Cr., 50 & 100 acres; both enetered Sep. 19, 1837 & granted Nov. 30, 1841. May 3, 1843. *Jacob Palmer.* JAMES PALMER & ALEXANDER PALMER, agreeable to a commission from Ct. of Pleas & Qtr. Sessions of Macon, have taken the probate & ack. of J. Palmer to a deed for 150 ac., signed *A. Palmer, James L. Palmer.* Ack. by J.L. Palmer in June 1843 court. Registered Aug. 30, 1843.

1607 SG ___, JACOB PALMER, $5/100 ac., 100 ac. on Tessenty Cr., Dis. 13, line of Sec. 23. Entry Sep. 19, 1837; grant Nov. 30, 1841; registered Aug. 30, 1843.

1608 SG __, JACOB PALMER, $10/100 ac., 50 ac. Tessenty Cr., Dis. 13. Entry Sep. 19, 1837; grant Nov. 30, 1841; registered Aug. 30, 1843.

1609 Sheriff's sale: THOS. M. ANGEL, Esq., High Sheriff of Macon, to N.S. JARRETT of Macon, two tracts, sold to satisfy judgment against JOHN WELCH in favor of Z.J. THOMAS & LEWIS VANDYKE for $34.15. At sale on Dec. 19, 1841, the property— No. 283, 83 ac. and No. 140, crossing Tessenty, 51 ac.—went to Jarrett for high bid of $93. Dec. 19, 1841. *Thos. M. Angel.* Ack. June 1843 court. Registered Sep. 6, 1843.

1610 JOHN M. ANGEL to THOMAS M. ANGEL, both of Macon, for $90, my right in dower of land of ELIZABETH ANGEL, wife of WM. ANGEL, dec'd. June 15, 1843. *J.M. Angel.* Wit: *J.R. LAMBERT, M. WIKLE.* Ack. June 1843 court. Registered Sep. 6, 1843.

1611 Sheriff's sale: THOS. M. ANGEL, Esq., High Sheriff of Macon, to N.S. JARRETT, property sold to satisfy judgment of county court against JOHN HALL in favor of HASE & others, & in favor of J.R. ALLMAN, HYATT MCBURNEY & CO., assignee. At public sale of property—a Negro boy, GEORGE, about 12 yrs & a Negro girl, CHARLOTT, about 6 yrs—Jarrett had high bid of $525. Mar. 17, 1843. *Thos. M. Angel.* Ack. in June 1843 court. Registered Sep. 6, 1843.

1612 SG 354, JOHN MOORE, for $__, 50 ac. on "Cartoogachagee" (Cartoogechaye) Cr., Dis. 15. Entry July 14, 1836; grant Jan. 2, 1840; registered Sep. 6, 1843.

1612 NATHAN TABER of Macon to SALOMAN TRUITT for $6.25, 25 ac., part of Sec. 33, Dis. 9, on Mill Creek. Dec. 4, 1841. *Nathan Taber*. Wit: *JAMES D. TABER, WM. E. MULL*. Proven by James D. Taber in June 1843 court. Registered Sep. 6, 1843.

1613 SG ___, JOHN DOBSON, THOMAS MILLSAPS, SETH W. HYATT, for $10/100 ac., 200 ac. on Toxaway R., Dis. 18, on Blue Ridge, incl. Millsap's gold mine & camp. Entry Apr. 27, 1838; grant July 5, 1843; registered Aug. 21, 1843.

1613 SG 543, BENJAMIN S. BRITTEN, for $___, 300 ac., Sec. 48, Dis. 16, crossing "I.O. Lee" (Iotla). Granted Apr. 18, 1839; registered Sep. 6, 1843.

1614 SG 545, BENJAMIN S. BRITTEN, for $___, 136+ ac., Sec. 50, Dis. 16. Granted Apr. 18, 1839; registered Sep. 6, 1843.

1615 SG 544, BENJAMIN S. BRITTEN, for $___, 253+ ac., Sec. 49, Dis. 16, crossing "I.O. Lee" (Iotla). Granted Apr. 18, 1839; registered Sep. 6, 1843.

1616 SG 637, PHILIP GUYER, $332.12, 145 ac., Sec. 58, Dis. 18. Granted May 29, 1843; registered Sep. 7, 1843.

1617 SG 571, HUGH GIBBS, $5/100 ac., 100 ac., Dis. 8, on Tuckasegee R. Entry Sep. 5, 1840; grant Dec. 2, 1843 (sic); registered Sep. 7, 1843.

1617 SG 529, LEWIS TILLY, $5/100 ac., 50 ac., Dis. 7, Cullowhee Cr. Entry June 26, 1841; grant Apr. 7, 1843; registered Sep. 7, 1843.

1618 SG 354, ROBERT CALER, $10.55, 61 ac., Sec. 26, Dis. 9, on Tennesse R. Granted Jan. 13, 1837; registered Sep. 7, 1843.

1619 SG 528, $32.25, ROBERT CALER, 130 ac., Sec. 27, Dis. 9, NW bank Tennessee R. Granted Jan. 12, 1839; registered Sep. 7, 1843.

1620 Trustee's sale: JACOB SILER of Macon to DAVID L. SWAIN. JOHN HALL of Macon, June 17, 1840, by indenture conveyed to Jacob Siler two tracts on Watauga Cr.—a 218-ac. tract where Hall resides, Sec. 41, Dis. 16, conveyed to Hall by MOSES WHITESIDES, and a 243-ac. tract, Sec. 64, Dis. 16. Hall made a deed to Siler in trust that if a bill of exchange drawn by Hall in favor of MILLER REPLY & CO., merchants of Charlestown, for $1102, should not be paid to David L. Swain by Oct. 1, 1840, Siler, after advertising same at courthouse in Franklin, was to sell lands at public sale. The bill was not paid; Siler advertised & sold the two tracts to David L. Swain for $1,000. June 14, 1843. *Jacob Siler*. Wit: *GEORGE SWAIN*. Ack. in June 1843 court. Registered Sep. 7, 1843

1621 WILLIAM EVIT to JONATHAN EVIT, both of Macon, for $200, 2 tracts—150 ac. on Walnut Creek and 50 ac., Sec. 6, Dis. 12. May 3, 1843. *William (his X mark) Evit*. Wit: *N.H. PALMER, J.K. GREY*. Proven by J.K. Grey, June 1843 ct. Registered Sep. 8, 1843.

1623 SG 532, MAGDELINE BRYSON, $5/100 ac., 100 ac. on Georges Creek of Toxaway R. Entry Aug. 27, 1842; grant May 22, 1843; registered Sep. 9, 1843.

1624 DANIEL NICHOLAS to H.G. WOODFIN, both of Macon, for $200, 220 ac. on "Cartoogagee" (Cartoogechaye) Creek, Dis. 15, tracts bd. BELL, JOHNSTON, J.H. BLACK. Dec. 10, 1841. *Daniel Nicholas*. Wit: *J.F. GRANT*. Proven by J.F. Grant in June 1843 court. Registered Sep. 9, 1843.

1625 SG 417, JAMES L. MOFFITT, $5/100 ac., 50 ac. on "Skeener" (Skeenah) Cr., Dis. 15. Entry Oct. 9, 1838; grant Dec. 22, 1840; registered Sep. 9, 1843.

1626 Sheriff's sale: ELI MCKEE, Esq., High Sheriff of Macon, to JORSHUA AMMONS of Macon, land sold at public auction to satisfy judgment of Supreme Court of Macon Co. against JOHN DAVES & others for $19.97: 35 ac. in Dis. 11, between Battle Branch & "Ellijah" (Ellijay) Creek, bd. PEEK. May 23, 1842. *Eli McKee, Shff*. Wit: *E. DOWDLE*. Ack. June 1843 court. Registered Sep. 9, 1843.

1627 SG 438, DANIEL NICCLES, $5/100 ac., 100 ac. on "Cartoogahgee" (Cartoogechaye) Cr., Dis. 15., bd. H. BLACK's entered land. Entry Sep. 18, 1838; grant Apr. 23, 1841; registered Sep. 9, 1843.

1628 SG 436, DANIEL NICKLAS, $10/100 ac., 125 ac., Dis. 15, on Thompson's fork of "Car-
      teeogahgee" (Cartoogechaye) Cr., bd. BELL, JOHNSTON; 2 entries. Entered Apr. 2,
      1836 & Mar. 29, 1837; granted Apr. 23, 1841; registered Sep. 9, 1843.

1629 SG 517, JAMES M. TATHAM, $5/100 ac., 100 ac. on "Cattooga" (Chatooga) R., near
      White Sides Mtn. Entry Dec. 16, 1840; grant Dec. 19, 1842; registered Sep. 9, 1843.

1630 Mortgage: JON R. ALLMAN of 1st part to SILAS MCDOWELL of 2nd part, HENRY
      ADDINGTON, Z.J. THOMAS & WILLIAM ANGEL of 3rd part, for $5 pd. by Mc-
      Dowell & further consideration, Allman conveys nine lots in town of Franklin, No. 9, 21,
      22, 23, 26, 27, 28, 29 & 30, all originally conveyed to Allman by JONATHAN PHILIPS,
      ch'man of county court; also a lot purch. of A.B. DONASAL (DONALDSON?) on Main
      st., corner of lot 20 belonging to SAMUEL LAMBERT; also 59+ ac., Sec. 26 in Dis. 12
      on NW side of Sugartown R. conveyed to Allman by WM. LAMBERT. Also: Negro
      man, LEWIS, about 40 yrs, Negro woman, JENNY, about 50, Negro woman, SYVA,
      age 18, a child, a babe. Also: 37 horses, 60 cattle, 6 wagons & carts, all Allman's black-
      smith tools, tannery & tools and 100 hogs. Property secured parties of 3rd part for loans
      of $500 each which they made to Allman & executed to cashier of Branch Bank of Cape
      Fear at Asheville, NC, their several notes for $500 each. Sep. 11, 1843. *J.R. Allman.* Wit:
      J.G. BERGMAN(?), JOHN HOWARD. Ack. in Sep. 1843 court. Registered Sep. 25, 1843.

1631 Mortgage: DAVID R. LOWERY of Macon to JAMES LOWERY of Buncombe Co. NC,
      for $150, a brown bay mare which I purchased of GUYER, a black Marblieu (filly), 2(?)
      years old last spring, for security of David R. Lowry to D.L. SWAIN for $150. Sep. 16,
      1843. *D.R. Lowry.* Wit: *N.W. WOODFIN.* Ack. in Sep. 1843 court. Reg. Sep. 25, 1843.

1632 Mortgage: JOSIAH JUSTICE to MRS. LUCINDAY ROBINSON, relict of SAMUEL
      ROBINSON, my standing crop of growing corn, oats, 1/3 on tract of land I now live on,
      belonging to LAGRAN ROBINSON, as security for stay of $293 debt to WM. BEL-
      LINGER, also a note due Robinson. Aug. 5, 1843. *Josiah (his X mark) Justice.* Wit: *B.W.
      BELL, ELI ROBERTS.* Proven by Roberts, Sep. 1843 court. Reg. Sep. 25, 1842.

1633 Mortgage: ELIZABETH SHERRILL of 1st part to JOHN DEHART & ABEL B.
      HYATT of 2nd part, NOAH BURCHFIELD of 3rd part, all of Macon, whereas Elizabeth
      Sherrill is justly indebted to John Dehart & Abel B. Hyatt for $21.73, as appears from
      receipt given by THOMAS ANGEL, Shff., and honestly desires to secure payment, she
      deeds them 179 ac. on Tuckaseegee R.; if debt not paid by Dec. 25, 1843, Noah
      Burchfield to sell property at courthouse in Franklin to satisfy debt. Sep. 13, 1843.
      Elizabeth (her X mark) Sherrell, John (his X mark) Dehart, A.B. Hyatt, N. Burchfield.
      Wit: *J. MCDOWELL.* Ack. by Noah Burchfield in Sep. 1843 court. Reg.Sep. 25, 1843.

1634 Mortgage: JOHN HOWARD of 1st part to EZEKIEL DOWDLE of 2nd part, JAMES K.
      GREY, SILAS MCDOWELL & J.L. MOORE of 3rd part, for $1,200 drawn on Branch
      of Cape Fear Bank of Asheville, NC by Howard for payment of which parties of 3rd part
      are security, & for further consideration of $1 to Howard pd. by Ezekiel Dowdle,
      Howard sells Dowdle six tracts: Sec. 37, 85 ac. in Dis. 13, and in Dis. 142, Sections 20
      (85 ac.), 19 (55 1/2 ac), 4 (5 ac.), 6 (233 1/2 ac) & 33 (277 ac.). Dowdle to use land to
      secure payment of $1,200 to bank, borrowed Aug. 1843, to be repaid in 90 days. Sep. 14,
      1843. *J. Howard, E. Dowell, J.K. Gray, Silas McDowell, J.L. Moore.* Ack. in Sep. 1843
      court. Registered Sep. 25, 1843.

1636 Mortgage: DAVID R. LOWRY of Macon, of 1st part, to JESSE R. SILER & J.K. GRAY
      of 2nd part & ALFORD HESTER of Macon & HYATT MACBURNEY & CO. of Char-
      leston & other creditors, of 3rd part. Lowry is indebted to PHILIP GUYER in sum of
      $100, due by 2 judgments took before a justice of the peace & stayed by Alford Hester;
      Lowry owes Hyatt MacBurny & Co. $120, given to A. HENRY & N.W. WOODFIN,
      other debts to Hyatt MacBurney & Co., MILLER REPLY & CO., others due by late firm
      of ROBINSON & LOWRY. To secure debts & for further consideration of $1 pd. by

Siler, Lowry mortgages 9 horses, being all the horses he owns except a brown bay mare purchased of Guyer and a Marblieu filly; about 40 cattle, 50 hogs, his growing crop of corn on plantation on "Iola" (Iotla) where he lives, except portion which belongs to D.L. SWAIN, his crop of oats & other provender, all farming tools, one wagon & harness, farming implements, all household & kitchen furniture, one clock. Trustees to sell at public sale if necessary to pay debt to Guyer. Sep. 16, 1843. *D.R. Lowry, J.R. Siler, J.K. Grey, A. Hester.* Wit: *N.W. WOODFIN.* Ack. in Sep. 1843 court. Registered Sep. 25, 1843.

1637 Mortgage: JOS. DAVIS to WILLIAM & SAMUEL R. LAMBERT, all of Macon, for $52.86, four tracts in Dis. 17: Nos. 1, 2, 3 & 21(?). Condition: Jos. Davis indebted to Lamberts for $52.86. Aug. 15, 1843. *Joseph Davis.* Wit: *JON G. BYNIM, M. FRANCIS.* Ack. Sep. 1843 court. Registered Sep 26, 1843.

1638 Bedford Co., TN, LIDIA ROAN, widow of late WILLIAM ROAN, executrix & guardian to his children, nominate & appoint (my brother) CALEB P. HOUSTON my attorney to sell a lot in & adjoining the Town of Morganton, Burke Co. NC that belonged to dec'd, also to appoint local or resident agents to rent lands, collect rents, pay taxes & make bills as directed by will. Caleb B. Houston authorized to grant powers of atty to residents of state, etc. Sep. 4, 1843. *Lidia Roan.* Ack. Sep. 1843 court. Bedford Co. TN: Sep. 43, Lydia Roan, widow of late William Roan ack. this in court—ROBERT HUART clerk of county ct; THOMAS DAVIS, ch'man of county court of Bedford Co, 7 Sep. 1843. Registered Macon Co. Oct. 26, 1843.

1639 MICHAEL J. WATTERS to SAMUEL H. WATTERS, both of Macon, for $100, 57 3/4 ac., Sec. 26, Dis. 19. Jun. 1, 1843. *M.J. Waters.* Wit: *RICHARD CLAMPET, E. COLLINS.* Proven by Eli Collins, Sep. 1843 court. Registered Dec. 6, 1843.

1640 GEORGE WIKLE to ANDREW BRADLEY, both of Macon, for $25, 23 ac. on Tennessee R. Jul. 18, 1843. *George Wikle.* Wit: *C. HENSON, JOHN HOWARD.* Proven by Howard, Sep. 1843. Registered Dec. 6, 1843.

1641 W.W. DOBSON to SARAH ENLOW, both of Macon, for $300, 60 ac. Sec. 70, Dis. 15, W. bank Tennessee R. at the old Still House. I only convey interest in remainder of the heirs at law of ASAPH ENLOW, dec'd., which I purchased as Sheriff's sale. Aug. 13, 1839. *W.W. Dobson.* Wit: *J.W. GUINN, WM. M. ENLOW.* Proven by Wm. M. Enlow in Sep. 1843 court. Registered Dec. 6, 1843.

1642 JOHN DAVIS to SAMUEL H. WATERS, both of Macon, for $30, 110 ac. in Dis. 17, on S. bank of Burningtown Cr, to NW corner of SIX KILLER's Reservation. Mar. 15, 1841. *John Davis.* Wit: *W.M. DEWEESE, HENRY DEWEESE.* Proven by Henry Deweese in Sep. 1843 court. Registered Dec. 6, 1843.

1643 ABRAM WIGGINS, Senr., of Macon, for love & affection & 50 cts, to son JAMES H. WIGGINS, tract of land where I now live, 59+ ac., and 50 ac. adj. on E. side, also part of tract adj. first mentioned, separated from land now owned by ANDREW WELCH & MARK COLEMAN by a ridge known as the condition line. Reserve to self & wife NANCY the use of lands with buildings, etc. during our natural lives & whereas my son James H. Wiggins has had the misfortune to be afflicted with a white swelling which has caused him to be a cripple & in consequence less able to provide for self & family than the rest of my children, above lands are given to place him as an equal with rest of family, after which, I desire him to have an equal share of the property which may be left at death of myself & wife, same as if he had not rec'd the above. Apr. 30, 1843. *Abram (his X mark) Wiggins.* Wit: *WM. H. THOMAS.* Proved by Wm. H. Thomas in Sep. 1843 court. Registered Dec. 6, 1843.

1644 JOHN WILD to SAMUEL H. WATERS, both of Macon, for $20, 50 ac., Sec. 345 Dis. 17, on reservation line. July 13, 1840. *John Wild.* Wit: *Z. EVINS, DAVID BULLARD.* Proven by Z. Evins, Sep. 1843 court. Registered Dec. 6, 1843.

1644 Performance bond: SILAS MCDOWELL, JAMES K. GRAY, JESSE R. SILER, $10,000 bond for Silas McDowell, duly elected clerk of Superior Ct. of Macon Co. Sep. 15, 1843. Registered Dec. 6, 1843.

1645 Performance bond: SILAS MCDOWELL, JAMES K. GRAY, JESSE R. SILER, $4,000 bond for Silas McDowell, duly elected clerk of Superior Ct. of Macon Co. Sep. 15, 1843. Registered Dec. 6, 1843.

1646 Sheriff's sale: ELI MCKEE, Esq., High Sheriff of Macon Co., to GABRIEL BOLICK of Macon, property sold to satisfy judgment against JOHN DAVES and others for $19.97, recovered by State of N.C., 96 ac., Sec. 96, Dis. 11. Bolick had high bid of $4. May 23, 1842. *Eli McKee, Shff.* Wit: *E. DOWDLE.* Ack. June 1843 court. Registered Dec. 7, 1843.

1647 Performance bond: J.K. GRAY, J.R. SILER, SILAS MCDOWELL, $5,000 bond for J.K. Gray, duly elected Clerk of Court of Pleas & Qtr. Sessions. Sep. 12, 1843. Registered Dec. 7, 1843.

1648 ISAAC MILLSAPS to WILLIAM H. BRYSON, both of Macon, for $30, 100 ac. Dis. 18, on Chattooga R., entry #2223, bd. ALEXANDER WILLSON. Mar. 17, 1843. *Isaac Millsaps.* Wit: *JAMES H. BRYSON, J.C. BRYSON.* Proven by Jas. H. Bryson in Sep. 1843 court. Registered Dec. 7, 1843.

1649 CHARLES RIDLY of Macon Co., to THOS. MASHBURN, now of Macon, for $100, 29 ac., Dis. 10, to conditional corner on bank of river made by Charles Ridly & ELIJAH CLURE. Mar. 2, 1840. *Charles (his X mark) Ridly.* Wit: *MILAS SANDERS, J.C. PRICHARD.* Ack. in Sep. 1843 court. Registered Dec. 7, 1843.

1649 Performance bond: J.K. GRAY, J.R. SILER, SILAS MCDOWELL, $10,000 bond for J.K. Gray, duly elected Clerk of Court of Pleas and Qtr. Sessions. Sep. 12, 1843. Registered Dec. 7, 1843.

1650 CHARLES RIDLY of Macon Co. to THOMAS MASHBURN, now of Macon, for $700, 144 ac. on Tennessee R., to a Rattle Box on bank of river, Sec. 45, Dis. 10. May 2, 1843. *Charles (his X mark) Ridly.* Wit: *MILES SANDERS, J.C. PRICHARD.* Ack. in Sep. 1843 court. Registered Dec. 7, 1843.

1651 JOHN BRYSON, Senr. to WILLIAM H. BRYSON, whereas John & William have heretofore obtained a grant for No. 8, Dis. 7, John now in fee simple conveys same to William H. Bryson, all that part belonging to him in said grant, all payment being made by him. Land is on E. side of road leading to Pickens, incl. farm I conveyed to ADAM CORN, containing 92 ac. Oct. 15, 1841. *John Bryson Senr.* Wit: *THOS. M. ANGEL, A.B. ALLISON.* Proven by Thos. M. Angel in Sep. 1843 court. Registered Dec. 7, 1843.

1651 Sheriff's sale: ELI MCKEE, Esq., High Sheriff of Macon Co., to SARAH ENLOE of Macon, to satisfy judgment of county court of Macon against ROBERT H. ENLOE, SARAH ANN ENLOW, WM. B. ENLOW, ABRAM H. ENLOW, ASAPH T. ENLOW, ALFERD P. ENLOW, CHRISTOPHER C. ENLOW, minors heirs at law of ASAPH ENLOW, dec'd, for $1,002.89 & cost recovered by state of N.C.—145 ac. Sec. 71, Dis. 15, W. side of Tennessee R., including a mill seat on Standridges Creek. Sold at public sale Aug. 12, 1839; SARAH ENLOW had high bid of $400. *Eli McKee, Shff.* Wit: *E. DOWDLE.* Ack. in June 1843 court. Registered Dec. 7, 1843.

1654 Agreement between WILLIAM B. QUEEN of Haywood Co. NC, & JOHN MAXWELL of Pickens Dist. SC. Queen has leased to Maxwell all mining interest of tract on Chattooga R., Dis. 18, incl. samples & improvements for 12 mo. from present, liberty to use wood & water to carry on mining operations. Maxwell to pay 1/5 of all the gold that may be collected from the mine. Queen pledges his interest in land as security for $15 adv. from Maxwell. Apr. 17, 1843. *Wm. B. Queen, John Maxwell.* Wit: *ALLISON D. MCKEN-NY, JAMES MCKENNY.* Proven by A.D. McKenny, Sep. 1843 court. Reg. Dec. 7, 1843.

1654 SG 445, JOHN HOOPER, assignee of ABRAM PICKLESLIMER, for $18.69, 83+ ac. on Tuckasegee R., Sec. 5, Dis. 6. Granted Jan. 7, 1839; registered Dec. 8, 1843.

1655 SG 526, JOHN HOOPER, 99 ac, Sec. 1, Dis. 5, at jcn. E. fork of Tuckasegee R. Granted Jan. 5, 1839; registered Dec. 8, 1843.

1656 SG 524, ISAAC MILLSAPS for $5/100 acres, 100 ac, Dis. 18, Chattooga R., bd. on north by ELI WILSON's land. Entered Ja. 16, 1842; granted Dec. 31, 1842; registered Dec. 8, 1843.

1657 SG 135, JOHN HOOPER for $5/100 ac., 50 ac. on S. fork of Tuckasegee R., Dis. 5. Entered May 2, 1836; granted Nov. 12, 1838; reg. Dec. 8, 1843.

1657 SG 514, RODERICK NORTON for $5/100 ac., 100 ac. on Scotchman's Branch. Entered Jan. 20, 1844; granted Dec. 22, 1842; registered Dec. 8, 1843.

1658 SG 431, JOHN HOOPER for $5/100 ac., 100 ac. on W. bank Tuckasegee R., Dis. 5. Entered May 2, 1836; granted Jan. 12, 1841; registered Dec. 8, 1843.

1659 SG 509, JOHN DAVES for $5/100 ac., 50 ac. on Burningtown Cr., Dis. 17, N. end of SIX KILLER's reserve. Entry Jan. 1, 1840; grant Dec. 2, 1842; registered Dec. 9, 1843.

1660 SG 641, DANIEL MCCOY for $18.50, 130 ac., Sec. 110, Dis. 10. Granted Aug. 18, 1843; registered Dec. 9, 1943.

1660 SG 85, SAMUEL WATERS for $10/100 ac., 100 ac., Dis. 17, on "Telaco" (Tellico) Cr., W. side Tennessee R. Entry May 2, 1836; grant Feb. 28, 1838; registered Dec. 9, 1843.

1661 SG 512, GEORGE SHULAR, $5/100 ac., 100 ac. on Tuckasegee R., corner AMMONS & CRISP land, incl. BENNETT CRISP's improvement. Entered Jun. 15, 1841; granted Dec. 1, 1842; registered Dec. 9, 1843.

1662 SG 502, DANIEL L. MCDOWELL, for $5/100 ac., 100 ac., Dis. 18, on small branch of Chattooga R., to GA line, incl. an improvement. Entered May 12, 1841; granted Oct. 24, 1842; reg. Dec. 9, 1843.

1663 SG 538, MAGDALINA BRYSON, for $10/ac., 200 ac. on George's Creek of Toxaway R., top of the "Bleu Ridge," in Haywood line, bd. POLLY ANN BRYSON. Entered Aug. 27, 1842; granted July 10, 1843; registered Dec. 9, 1843.

1663 SG 515, ANDREW BRYSON, for $5/100 ac., 100 ac. on "Cullewhee" Cr. Entered Nov. 30, 1840; granted Dec. 2, 1842; registered Dec. 9, 1843.

1664 SG 536, POLLY ANN BRYSON, for $10/100 ac, 200 ac. on George's Creek of Toxaway R., including CLARK BARNES(?) fence(?). Entered Aug. 27, 1842; granted July 10, 1843; registered. Dec. 9, 1843.

1665 SG 537, ELIZABETH JANE BRYSON, for $10/100 ac., 200 ac. on George's Cr. of Toxaway, bd. POLLY ANN BRYSON's survey. Entered Aug. 27, 1843; granted July 10, 1843; registered Dec. 9, 1843.

1666 MARTHA OSBURN & ROLAND OSBURN of Haywood Co. NC, executrix & executor of JONATHAN OSBURN, to JOSEPH HICKS of Macon for $1200, Sec. 4, Dis. 14, on Coweta Cr. Apr. 3, 1841. *Martha (her X mark) Osburn, R. Osburn*. Wit: *J.W. PATTON, J.J.(?) PATTON*. Proven by J.W. Patton, June 1841 court. Registered Dec. 9, 1843.

1667 WEST TRUETT of Macon to JOHN W. WOODFIN of Buncombe Co. NC, for $50, 70 ac. in Dis. 2, crossing fork of Silver Run, a lot bought in 1836 in Franklin. Dec. 10, 1843. *West (his X mark) Truitt*. Wit: *J.H.L. MOORE*. Ack. in Dec. 1843 court. Registered Feb. 10, 1844.

1668 ARCHIBALD(?) STEEL for great love & affection to my grandson JAMES AR-CHIBALD(?) DALE, minor son of WILLIAM DALE, a sorrel horse abt. 12 years old named Sam, bed & furniture consisting of coverlet, 3 quilts, 2 counterpanes, blanket, sheat with pillow & bolster; also for my affections for my granddaughter, ANN YONG DALE, minor dau. of Wm Dale, 2 beds & furniture consisting of coverlet, 2 counterpanes, bolster; also for my love for MARY JANE DALE, minor dau. of Wm. Dale, bed & furniture consisting of sheat, counterpane, 2 quilts, 3 thin underbeds, also

a clock, side saddle, 6 corner chairs, 2 trunks, one covered w. seal skin and the other
with cow hide, one table w. 2 folding ____ walnut. "My grandchildren, the children of
my daughter MATILDY DALE." No date. *A. Steel*.Wit: *S. MCDOWELL, W.C.
MCDOWELL.* Proven by S. McDowell at a call court, Jan. 20, 1844. Registered Feb. 1,
1844.

1669 WILLIAM MORRISON to GEORGE F. CALER, both of Macon, for $1, 15 ac., part of
Sec. 46, Dis. 16, bd. GEORGE HUGHS tract, on "Iola" (Iotla) Cr. Feb. 21, 1841. *W.
Morrison.* Wit: *E.M. KILPATRICK,*who proved deed in court, Dec. 1843. Registered
Feb. 2, 1844.

1670 JAMES ROBISON & EZEKIEL DOWDLE to GEORGE W. ANGEL, all of Macon, for
$600, 3 tracts, one of 161 ac., Sec. 15, Dis. 11, on Tennessee R.; one of 247 ac., Sec. 14,
Dis. 11, on Tennessee River; one of 148 ac., Sec. 123, Dis. 10. Oct. 6, 1837. *Jas. Robinson, E. Dowdle.* Wit: *J.K. GRAY* as to Robinson, *B.S. JOHNSTON.* Proven by J.K. Gray
& ack. by E. Dowdle in Dec. 1843 court. Registered Feb. 2, 1844.

1671 ABNER MOORE to HOWELL MOSS, both of Macon, for $1,000, two tracts, in Dis.
11: Sec. 28, 59 ac., Sec. 30, 50 ac., which 2 tracts Moore purchased of JOHN REDMAN,
also, one entry made by Redman in entry-takers office of Macon, May 2, 1836, Dis. 11,
bd. SETSER & STRAIN, also another entry in Dis. 11 total, 200 ac. Jan. 10, 1842. *Abner
Moore.* Wit: *HIRAM LEDFORD, NOAH C. LEDFORD.* Proven by Hiram Ledford in
Dec. 1843 court. Registered Feb. 3, 1844.

1672 NOAH HILL of Georgia to GEORGE CAYLER of Macon Co., 96 ac., Sec. 61, Dis. 16.
Jan. 11, 1842. *N. Hill.* Wit: *D.R. LOWRY, B.S. BRITTEN.* Proven by D.R. Lowry in Dec.
1843 court. Registered Feb. 3, 1844.

1673 ANDREW B. GARRETT to LETTY N. GARRETT, both of Macon, for $52, 52 ac., Sec.
76, Dis. 8. Nov. 7, 1843. *Andrew B. (his X mark) Garrett.* Wit: *MATHEW GARRETT,
BENJAMIN VARNADAM(?).* Proven by Mathew Garrett in Dec. 1843 court. Registered
Feb. 3, 1844.

1673 ASHBEL ROADS to WILLIAM DEWESE, both of Macon, for $75, 100 ac. on Bur-
ningtown Cr., Dis. 17. Dec. 9, 1843. *Ashbel Rhods.* Wit: *A. HESTER* who proved in
court, Dec. 1843. Registered Feb. 7, 1843.

1674 ASHBALL ROADS to WILLIAM DEWESE, both of Macon, for $20, 74 ac on Bur-
ningtown Cr., Dis. 17. Dec. 9, 1843. *Ashbal Rhodes.* Wit: *A. HESTER* who proved in
court, Dec. 1843. Registered Feb. 7, 1844.

1675 Mortage: D.R. LOWERY to JOHN HOWARD, both of Macon, for $71.10, two oxen
and ox cart. Condition: Howard, on Nov. 28, 1843, became security of Lowery in loan to
J.R. SILER & J.K. GRAY, administrators of estate of JAMES ROBINSON, dec'd, for
$71.70, due in 11 mos. Jan. 15, 1844. *D.R. Lowry.* Wit: *N.H. PALMER* who proved Jan.
11, 1844 before J.K. Gray. Registered Feb. 7, 1844.

1676 MICHAL LONG of Macon to JAMES M. & EDWARD HOOPER for $50, 17 ac., No.
1, Dis. 7, in TININTOSS(?) (illeg.) Reservation. Dec. 9, 1843. *Michael (his X mark)
Long.* Wit: *ELIAS CHASTAIN?, ROBERT ROGERS.* Ack. in Sep. 1843 court. Registered
Feb. 7, 1843.

1677 SG 640, ENOS SHIELDS, for $31.04, 88 ac., Sec. 1, Dis. 11 on Tennessee R., near
mouth of Watauga Cr. near the County Road, crossing Mill Creek. Granted Aug. 18,
1843; registered Feb. 7, 1844.

1677 SG 461, WILLIAM NORTON, for $5/100 ac, 100 ac. on Chattooga R., Dis. 18, crossing
Scotchman's Branch, incl. an improvement. Granted Nov. 19, 1841; reg.Feb. 7, 1844.

1678 SG 502, HEBRY SCOTT, for $5/100 ac., 95 ac. in Dis. 8, on Turkey Cr. Entered Jan. 19,
1841; granted Dec. 2, 1842; registered Feb. 7, 1844.

1679 JESSE BURRELL of Union Co., GA, to MARK BURRELL, for $50, 50 ac. on both
sides of Big Creek of Chattooga R., orig. granted me Dec. 15, 1838. No date. *Jesse (his X
mark) Burrell.* Wit: *SAUL SMITH, WM. C. CONNELLY.* Proven by Saul Smith in Dec.
session. Registered Mar. 1844.

1680 MICHAEL LONG of Macon to JAMES M. & EDWARD HOOPER, for $200, 103 ac.,
Sec. 14, Dis. 7. Dec. 9, 1843. *Michael (his X mark) Long.* Wit: *ELIAS SHETTIN (CHAS-
TAIN?), ROBERT ROGERS.* Ack. in court. Registered Mar. 8, 1844.

1681 MIKLE WIKLE to THOMAS P. MOORE, both of Macon, for $30, 93 ac. on Tennessee
R., part of Sec. 36, Dis. 16. Dec. 12, 1843. *M. Wikle.* Wit: *JOHN HALL, H.W. HUG-
GINS.* Ack. in Dec. 1843 court. Registered Mar. 9, 1844.

1681 SG 543, ALEXANDER WILSON, for $5/100 ac., 100 ac. on Chattooga R., Dis. 18, bd.
W. KENNY. Entered Nov. 6, 184_; granted Sep. 26, 1843; registered Mar. 9, 1844.

1682 SG 535, ISAAC CRAIN, for $5/100 ac., 100 ac. on Chattooga R., Scotchman's Branch.
Entry May 2, 1836; granted July 10, 1843; registered Mar. 9, 1844.

1683 SG 533, THOMSON WILSON, for $5/100 ac., 50 ac. on Chattooga R., Dis. 18, bd.
ELIAS NORTON. Entry July 27, 1842; granted June 23, 1843; registered Mar. 9, 1844.

1684 JAMES M. TATHAM of Cherokee Co. to MARKE BURRELL for $9, 100 ac. on Chat-
tooga R., Dis. 18, both sides of trail leading from the Horse Cove to Georgia. Dec. 6,
1843. *James M. Tatham.* Wit: *JOHN FLEMING, RODERICK NORTON.* Proven by John
Fleming in Dec. 1843 court. Registered Mar. 9, 1844.

1685 MICHAL WIKLE to JOHN R. ALLMAN, both of Macon, for $200, 91 ac., Sec. 36, Dis.
16. Dec. 11, 1843. *M. Wikle.* Wit: *WM. BRYSON,* who proved in court, Dec. 1843.
Registered Mar. 9, 1844.

1686 JESSE BURRELL of Union Co. GA to MARK BURRELL, for $250, Sec. 8, Dis. 18, on
Big Creek, land granted me Dec. 1836. Oct. 19, 1842. *Jesse (his X mark) Burrell.* Wit:
SAUL SMITH, WM. C. CONNELLY. Proven by Saul Smith, Dec. 1843 court. Registered
Mar. 9, 1843.

1687 MICHAEL WIKLE to PHEBEE PRICHARD, both of Macon, for $250, Sec. 8, Dis. 8,
on Big Savannah Cr. *M. Wikle.* Wit: *E. DOWDLE* who proved in court, Dec. 1843.
Registered Mar. 9, 1844.

1688 MICHAEL WIKLE TO PHEBEE PRICHARD, both of Macon, for $50, 93+ ac., part of
Sec. 36, Dis. 16. Dec. 9, 1843. *M. Wikle.* Wit: *E. Dowdle* who proved in court, Dec.
1843. Registered Mar. 9, 1844.

1689 MICHAEL WIKLE TO PHEBEE PRICHARD, both of Macon, for $300, 150 poles,
town lot 16 in Franklin, NE corner of Public Square & Cross St. Dec. 9, 1843. *M. Wikle.*
Wit: *E. DOWDLE* who proved in court, Dec. 1843. Registered Mar. 9, 1844.

1690 Mortgage: TYRE/TYRA H. DAVIS to JAMES POINDEXTER, both of Macon, 2 Negro
girls, SALLY, abt. 16 yrs., ELIZA, abt. 14 yrs; also, 217+ ac., No. 36, Dis. 8, PAR-
CHED CORN place; also a bay mare & 19 cattle. Condition: property to secure several
notes of hand for $1100, $1200 & $200. No date. *Tyre H. (his X mark) Davis.* Wit:
JOHN HALL, who proved in court, Mar. 1844. Registered June 4, 1844.

1691 ZACHARIAH CABE to WILLIAM CABE, JAMES RUSSELL, SAMUEL DOWDLE,
ARCHABLE RUSSEL & JOHN MCDOWELL, trustees, all of Macon, & their succes-
sors, in trust for M.E. Church, for good will he hath for the said M.E. Church, 2+ ac. on
W. side of Public Road in Sec. 5, incl. the grave yard, to use of church, a plase of Public
worship of Almighty God. Mar. 1, 1844. *Z. Cabe.* Wit: *B.W. WILLS.* Ack. in court,
Mar. 1844. Registered June 4, 1844.

1692 ELIAS M. KILPATRICK to LEWIS C. DUVALL, both of Macon, for $300, three tracts
in Dis, 17, on Tennessee River: Sec. 4, 64+ ac., Sec. 5, 87+ ac. above an island, Sec. 27,
66 ac. Mar. 14, 1844. *E.M. Kilpatrick.* Wit: *W.M. MORRISON, JOHN Y. HICKS*
Proven by W.M. Morrison, Mar. 1844 court. Registered June 5, 1844.

1692 THOMAS SHEPHERD to JOHN INGRAM, both of Macon, for $65, town lot #18 on Main St, one acre. Mar. 14, 1843. *Thomas Shepherd.* Wit: *WM. ANGEL,* who proved in court, Mar. 1844. Registered June 5, 1844.

1693 JAMES KIRKLAND of Macon, to my beloved friend & "hier," SARAH ANN STILLWELL, one bay mare & year-old colt, one dun-colored cow & calf to her & her proper use. Mar. 13, 1844. *James (his X mark) Kirkland.* Wit: *WM. F. MCKEE.* Ack. in court Mar. 1844. Registered Apr. 20, 1844.

1694 ELIAS KILPATRICK of Macon to JULIUS DEAN, for $275, tracts on Tennessee R., Dis. 9: Sec. 13, on N. bank, 93 ac.; Sec. 21, NE bank, 82+ ac.; 195 ac. on side of reservation; Sec. 2, on boundary of reservation, N. bank of river, 51 ac. Jan. 22, 1844. *E.M. Kilpatrick.* Wit: *HENRY BURNETT, E. COLLINS.* Proven by E. Collins in Mar. 1844 court. Registered June 5, 1844.

1695 JOHN WEST to DANIEL WEST, both of Macon, for $300, a certain Negro girl slave named RACHEL, abt. 3 yrs. old. Jan. 8, 1844. *John (his X mark) West.* Wit: *J.K. GRAY* who proved in court, mar. 1844. Registered June 5, 1844.

1696 RILEY MARTAIN/MARTIN of Macon to JOHN J. ROSE of Cherokee Co. NC,, for $235, 78 ac., Sec. 9, Dis. 17. Jan. 20, 1844. *Rily Martin.* Wit: *ZACHARIAH DEWS (DOWN?), JOHN N.F.(his X mark) ROGERS.* Proven by Zachariah Dews (Down?) in Mar. 1844 court. Registered June 5, 1844.

1697 JAMES WITHEROW to CURTIS SANDERS, both of Macon, for val. rec'd, Sec. 112, Dis. 10, which I purchased of JOSEPH R. JOHNSON, the original purchaser. Jan. 9, 1844. *James Witherow.* Wit: *S. READ, MADISON SANDERS. Proven by Samuel Read, Mar. 1844 court. Registered Jun. 5, 1844.*

1697 PETER DAVES TO WILLIAM MORRISON, both of Macon, for $20, 50 ac. near William Morrison's improvement, being NE corner of Sec. 61, Dis. 10. Sep. 1, 1843. *Peter Davis.* Wit: *JAMES M. THOMPSON, JAMES M. GRANT.* Proven by James M. Grant in Mar. 1844 court. Registered June 5, 1844.

1698 WM. G. WATS to JOHN B. CLURE, both of Macon, for $150, 78 ac, Sec. 64, Dis. 15, sold by state to GEORGE BLACK. Oct. 9, 1843. *Wm. G. Watts.* Wit: *FRANCIS F. NICKLE, JOHN A. CLURE.* Ack. in Mar. 1844 court. Registered June 5, 1844.

1699 JOHN HALL to DREWRY MASHBURN, both of Macon, for $10, 164 ac., Sec. 37, Dis. 16, which Hall purchased from state in Oct. 1836. Mashburn to pay amt. due state. Jan. 10, 1844. *John Hall.* Wit: *JOHN INGRAM, LEWIS (his X mark) MASHBURN.* Ack. in court, Mar. 1844. Registered June 5, 1844.

1699 JOHN WEST to DANIEL WEST, both of Macon, for $400, a certain Negro woman slave named DORIS(?), abt. 17 yrs old. Jan. 8, 1844. *John (his X mark) West.* Wit: *J.K. GRAY* who proved in court, Mar. 1844. Registered June 5, 1844.

1700 SARAH WILSON of Macon, for great love & affection for my beloved niece, NELLY ELENER WILSON, one cow & yearling, 3 sheep. No date. *Sarah (her X mark) Wilson.* Wit: *LARKIN LINDSEY, WM. F. MCKEE.* Ack. in court, Mar. 1844. Registered June 5, 1844.

1701 ROBERT HUGGINS of Macon, to JESSE R. SILER for $600, Sec. 35, Dis. 16, 160 ac., 20 ac. of which was conveyed by the State for the use of a campground. Siler to pay state amount due. Jan. 30, 1840. *Robt. Huggins.* Wit: *M. RUSSELL* who proved in court Mar. 1844. Registered June 5, 1844.

1701 JAMES M. TATHAM of Cherokee Co. NC to EZEKIEL H. PHIPPS of Macon, for $1, three pieces which Tatham & Phipps made in entries together in connection in all the mtn. region of Chattooga & Toxaway creeks or riverlets, same conveyed by Phipps to N.W. WOODFIN of Buncombe Co. NC and by Woodfin in the name of E.H. Phipps & JAMES W. WOODFIN. Mar. 13, 1844. *J.M. Tatham.* Wit: *J.R. STALLCUP* who proved in court, Mar. 1844. Registered June 5, 1844.

1702 JAS. H. WIGGINS to JESSE R. SILER, for $225, 3 tracts on W. side Tennessee R., whereon I formerly lived, known as POUSHER's Reservation, which I bought of state Sep. 1838, rep. as Pousher's Reservation tract No. 1, 70 ac; also No. 2, same reservation, 156 ac., also No. 3, same reservation, 90 ac. Mar. 22, 1841. *Jas. H. Wiggins.* Wit: *B.K. DICKEY, J(AMES?) RUSSELL.* Proven by B.K. Dickey in Mar. 1844 court. Registered June 6, 1844.

1703 JASON H. HUNTER TO JESSE R. SILER, both of Macon, for $400, an undiv. half of 640 ac. in Dis. 18, Chattooga R., bd. WILLIAM BARNES, originally granted DAVID & JAMES SHELTON. July 1, 1843. *J.H. Hunter.* Wit: *JOHN CANSLER, ENOCH PASSMORE.* Ack. in Mar. 1844 court. Registered June 6, 1844.

1704 WM. LAMBERT to J.R. SILER, both of Macon, for $275, lots in town of Franklin, No. 21, 3 ac.; part of No. 22; No. 23, 4+ ac. Dec. 21, 1841. *Wm. Lambert.* Wit: *S.R. LAMBERT* who proved in court, Mar. 1844. Registered June 6, 1844.

1706 SG #553, WILLIAM COWEN, for $5/100 ac., 12 ac. on little Savannah Creek, Dis. 8. Entry Jan. 9, 1841; granted Jan. 27, 1844; registered June 6, 1844.

1706 SG #518, EDWARD NORTON, for $5/100 ac., 100 ac. on Chattooga R. & Scotchman's Branch, Dis. 18. Entry Jan. 15, 1840; granted Dec. 22, 1842; registered Jun. 6, 1844.

1707 SG #552, WILLIAM COWEN, for $5/100 ac., 65 ac., little Savannah Cr., Dis. 8, bd. JORSHUA HALL. Entry Jan. 9, 1841; granted Jan. 27, 1844; registered June 6, 1844.

1708 WESLEY JOHNSTON of Cherokee Co. NC to JESSE R. SILER for $150, 55 ac., Sec. 60, Dis. 15, on Thompson's fork of Cartoogachaye Cr. Jan. 20, 1840. *Wesly (his X mark) Johnston.* Wit: *JOHN INGRAM, T.P. SILER.* Proven by T.P. Siler in Mar. 1844 court. Registered Jun. 7, 1844.

1708 PATIENCE ERVIN to JESSE R. SILER, for $450, place where Patience Ervin formerly lived on State Rd., abt. 1 mi. from Franklin, part of Sec. 26, Dis. 16, 50+ ac. Nov. 14, 1840. *Patience Ervin.* Wit: *SILAS MCDOWELL, J.K. GRAY.* Proven by J.K. Gray in Mar. 1844 court. Registered Jun. 7, 1844.

1709 EZEKIEL H. PHIPPS of Macon to NICHOLAS W. WOODFIN of Buncombe Co. NC, for $100, 640 ac. on Horse Pasture fork of Toxaway R., Dis. 18, SW corner of DOBSON's & MILLSAP's survey, bd. HYATT's line, ALLISSON's survey, WALTER H. BRYSON's survey, ALEXANDER WILSON's line. Mar. 15, 1844. *E.H. Phipps.* Wit: *J.W. WOODFIN. Ack. in Mar. 1844 court. Registered June 7, 1844.*

1710 EZEKIEL H. PHIPPS of Macon to NICHOLAS W. WOODFIN of Buncombe Co. NC, for $100, 640 ac. on White Water R. in Dis. 18, bd. R. NORTONS & CO., crossing Gold Run Creek, incl. both sides of Public Road, entered Sep. 2, 1842. Mar. 15, 1844. *E.H. Phipps.* Wit: *J.W. WOODFIN.* Ack. in court Mar. 1844. Registered June 7, 1844.

1712 EZEKIEL H. PHIPPS of Macon to NICHOLAS W. WOODFIN of Buncombe Co., NC, for $1, 640 ac. on Samson's River, Dis. 18, beginning on mtn. dividing said river & Bear Camp Creek... to S. side of Rocky Knobs, entered Sep. 2, 1842. Mar. 15, 1844. *E.H. Phipps.* Wit: *J.W. WOODFIN.* Ack. in Mar. 1844 court. Registered June 7, 1844.

1713 EZEKIEL H. PHIPPS of Macon to NICHOLAS W. WOODFIN of Buncombe Co. NC, for $1, 100 ac. on White Water R. & Democrats Creek, Dis. 18. Mar. 15, 1844. *E.H. Phipps.* Wit: *J.W. WOODFIN.* Ack. in Mar. 1844 court. Registered June 7, 1844.

1714 EZEKIEL H. PHIPPS of Macon to NICHOLAS W. WOODFIN of Buncombe Co. NC, for $1, 640 ac. on Samson's R., Dis. 18, beginning on ridge adj. the river & Bear Camp Branch, entered Sep. 2, 1842. Mar. 15, 1844. *E.H. Phipps.* Wit: *J.W. WOODFIN.* Ack. in Mar. 1844 court. Registered June 7, 1844.

1715 EZEKIEL H. PHIPPS of Macon to NICHOLAS W. WOODFIN of Buncombe Co. NC, for $1, 100 ac. on Chattooga R., Dis. 18, bd. MURPHY, SHELTON, entered Sep. 21, 1844. Mar. 15, 1844. *E.H. Phipps.* Wit: *J.W. WOODFIN.* Ack. in Mar. 1844 court. Registered June 7, 1844.

1716 EZEKIEL H. PHIPPS of Macon to NICHOLAS W. WOODFIN of Buncombe Co. NC, for $1, 100 ac. on Chattooga R., Dis. 18, near tract leading from Cashiers Valley to the Horse Cove, bd. WILSON, ELIAS NORTON, entered May 6, 1843. Mar. 15, 1844. *E.H. Phipps.* Wit: *J.W. WOODFIN.* Ack. in Mar. 1844 court. Registered June 7, 1844.

1717 EZEKIEL H. PHIPPS of Macon to NICHOLAS W. WOODFIN of Buncombe Co. NC, for $1, 640 ac. on White Water R. & Democrats Creek, Dis. 18, to stake on Rattlesnake Mtn., entered Sep. 2, 1842. Mar. 15, 1844. *E.H. Phipps.* Wit: *J.W. WOODFIN.* Ack. in Mar. 1844 court. Registered June 7, 1844.

1719 EZEKIEL H. PHIPPS of Macon to NICHOLAS W. WOODFIN of Buncombe Co. NC, for $1, 640 ac. on S. side of White Water R., Dis. 18, to Chimney Top Mtn., bd. JAMES ZACHARY, E. AMMONS, crossing public road; entered Sep. 2, 1842. Mar. 15, 1844. *E.H. Phipps.* Wit: *J.W. WOODFIN.* Ack. in Mar. 1844 court. Registered June 7, 1844.

1720 SG #573, RODERICK NORTON, ELIAS NORTON, EDWARD NORTON, for $10/100 ac., 640 ac. on Chattooga R., Dis. 18, to the Georgia line. Entered July 15, 1842; granted May 13, 1844; registered July 12, 1844.

1721 SG #531, JOHN PAINTER, for $5/100 ac., 50 ac. on Cowee Cr., Dis. 10, bd. HILEND(?). Entry Jan. 19, 1841; granted Apr. 17, 1843; registered July 12, 1844.

1722 SG #574, ALISON D. MCKENNY, for $5/100 ac., 100 ac. on Chattooga R., Dis. 18, on Publick Rd., to SC line, incl. BUCHANAN's improvement. Entry May 5, 1843; granted May 13, 1844; registered July 12, 1844.

1722 SG #530, JOHN PAINTER, for $5/100 ac., 50 ac. on Cowee Creek, Dis. 10, crossing the Camp branch. Entry Jan. 12, 1841; granted Apr. 17, 1843; registered July 12, 1844.

1723 HUGH ROGERS to WILLIAM H. BRYSON, for $150, 61+ ac., part of Sec. 44, Dis. 7, on Cullewhee Creek, on Public Rd., bd. JOHN CORN. June 11, 1844. *Hugh Rogers.* Wit: *C. MCD. PAXTON, DILLARD LOVE.* Proven by Dillard Love in June 1844 court. Reg. July 12, 1844.

1724 JAMES M. TATHAM of Cherokee Co. NC to WILLIAM TATHAM of Macon, for $100, 100 ac. on Chattooga, Dis. 18. June 10, 1844. *J.M. Tatham.* Wit: *JOHN HALL, JONATHAN FORD.* Ack. June 1844. Registered July 10, 1844.

1725 WILLIAM PRUETT to ELIJAH CLURE, both of Macon, for $225, 50 ac., Sec. 38, Dis. 10, NE bank of Tennessee R. Aug. 15, 1836. *William (his X mark) Pruitt.* Wit: *J.R. SILER, J.W. SHEARER.* Ack. June 1844 court. Registered July 12, 1844.

1726 WILLIAM KINSLAND to SAMUEL BRYSON, both of Macon, for $100, 54 ac., Sec. 117, Dis. 16 on "Wattoaga" (Watauga) Creek, the tract that AARON ROBISON purchased at the land sale. Sep. 29, 1843. *William Kinsland.* Wit: *D. MCCOY, DANEL (his X mark) GIBBY.* Ack. in June 1844 court. Registered July 12, 1844.

1727 ARON ROBINSON of Walton Co. GA, to WM. KINSLAND of Macon, for $100, 54 ac., Sec. 117, Dis. 10, on "Wattaga" (Watauga) Creek. Sep. 29, 1843. *Aaron (his X mark) Robinson.* Wit: *D. MCCOY, JOHN MASON.* Proven in June 1844 court. Registered July 12, 1844.

1728 CHARLES RIDLEY of Macon to ELIJAH CLUER, for $7, land in Sec. 43, Dis. 10, on river, on conditional line between Ridley & Clure. Oct. 18, 1839. *Charles (his X mark) Ridley.* Wit: *JOHN MASON, MARTIN HURST.* Proven by Martin Hurst in June 1844 court. Registered July 12, 1844.

1728 THOMAS M. ANGEL, Esq., High Sheriff of Macon Co., to JACOB SHOPE of Macon, property sold at public sale to satisfy judgment against JAS. FOUTS for $79.77. Sold Dec. 11, 1843, 50 ac.; Jacob Shope had high bid of $51. June 12, 1844. *Thos. M. Angel.* Wit: *J.S. GRANT, J.B. DONALDSON.* Ack. in June 1844 court. Registered July 13, 1844.

1730 THOS. M. ANGEL, Esq., High Sheriff of Macon, to JACOB SHOPE of Macon, property sold to satisfy judgment against JAS. FOUTS for $79.77. Sold at public sale on Dec. 11, 1843 was 153 ac, No. 298, for high bid of $51. June 12, 1844. *T.M. Angel.* Wit: *J.S. GRANT, N.T. TABER.* Ack. in June 1844 court. Registered July 13, 1844.

1731. THEOPHILUS JOHNSTON/JOHNSON of Cherokee Co. NC to THOS. RAYE of Macon, for $500, 151+ ac. in Dis. 15, crossing "Cartoogeechye" (Cartoogechaye) Creek. Apr. 15, 1844. *Theophilus Johnson.* Wit: *D.L. MOONEY, L.H. JOHNSON, J.H. JOHNSON.* Proven by D.L. Mooney in June 1844 court. Registered July 13, 1844.

1732 DANIEL GARLAND to JOHN HOWARD, both of Macon, for $100, 100 ac., Sec. 50, Dis. 13, bought at sale in Franklin, 1836. Apr. 3, 1843. *Daniel Garland.* Wit: *N.F. Howard* who proved in court, June 1844. Registered July 13, 1844.

1733 Gift: J.R. SILER of Macon to MATHEW RUSSELL Senr., SAMUEL READ, MATHEW N. RUSSELL, BUCKNER GUY, ARCHABALD M. RUSSELL, trustees, for affection for Methodist Denomination, 1/2 ac., incl. Meeting House they built in forks of Road leading to Franklin & Clayton on what is called the WM. ROGERS tract of land. Trustees to keep in repair a house or place of worship for use of Methodist Episcopal Church of U.S.A. May 1, 1844. *J.R. Siler.* Wit: *ROBERT A. PHILIP, J.W. DOBSON.* Proven by J.W. Dobson in June 1844 court. Registered July 13, 1844.

1736 A.C. LEDFORD to GEORGE PENLAND, for $25, 30 ac. on Tennessee R., Dis. 13, on E. AMMONS line. Sep. 12, 1843. *A.C. LEDFORD.* Wit: *JAS. RUSSEL, G.N. PENLAND.* Proven by G.N. Penland in June 1844 court. Registered July 13, 1844.

1736 GEORGE LOWDERMILK to JORSHUA AMMONS, both of Macon, for $200, Sec. 61, Dis. 11, which I purchased at Franklin sale in 1836. Jan. 30, 1843. *George (his X mark) Lowdermilk.* Wit: *JAMES FRANKS, JOHN AMMONS.* Proven by J.D. Franks in June 1844 court. Registered July 13, 1844.

1737 SAUL SMITH to ASCUE CURTIS & JOHN HOWARD, all of Macon, for $50, 50 ac. on Chattooga R., bd. WILLIAM BARNES. June 14 1844. *Saul Smith.* Wit: *WM. ANGEL.* Ack. in June 1844 court. Registered July 13, 1844.

1738 WILLIAM TATHAM to ISAAC ASH, both of Macon, for $10, land on Big Savannah, beg. at mouth of Hollow below Bridge, joins Isaac Ash's line. *W.M. Tatham.* Wit: *B.H. JAMES, A.J. BELL.* Proven by A.J. Bell in June 1844 court. Registered July 13, 1844.

1739 SG 555, E.H. PHIPPS, $10/100 ac., 640 ac. on Tomson's River, Dis. 18, beg. on Ridge div. River & Bear Camp Creek.. near a trail. Entry Sep. 2, 1842; granted Feb. 5, 1844; reg. Jul. 15, 1844.

1740 SG 557, E.H. PHIPPS, $10/100 ac., 640 ac. on White Water River, Dis. 18, crossing Democrats Creek. Entry Sep. 2, 1842; granted Feb. 5, 1844; registered Jul. 15, 1844.

1740 SG 558, E.H. PHIPPS, $10/100 ac., 640 ac. on Tomson R., Dis. 18, beg. on mtn. dividing river & "Bare" Camp Creek. Entry Sep. 2, 1842; granted Feb. 5, 1844; registered Jul. 15, 1844.

1741 SG 562, E.H. PHIPPS, $10/100 ac., 100 ac. on White Water River, Dis. 18, crossing Democrats Creek. Entry May 6, 1843; granted Feb. 5, 1844; registered Jul. 15, 1844.

1742 SG 559, E.H. PHIPPS, $10/100 ac., 640 ac. on S. side White Water River, Dis. 18.. to Chimney Top Mtn, bd. JAMES ZACHARY, E. AMMONS, crossing the Public Road. Entry Sep. 2, 1842; granted Feb. 5, 1844; registered Jul. 15, 1844.

1743 SG 561, E.H. PHIPPS, $10/100 ac., 100 ac., Chattoogah R., Dis. 18, near trail leading from "Cashes Vally" (Cashiers) to the Horse Cove, bd. ZACHARY, ELIAS NORTON. Entry May 6, 1843; granted Feb. 5, 1844; registered Jul. 15, 1844.

1744 SG 554, E.H. PHIPPS, $10/100 ac., 640 ac., White Water R., Dis. 18, bd. R. NORTON & CO., crossing Gold Run Creek to Sassafras Mtn., both sides of Public Road. Entry Sep. 2, 1842; grant Feb. 5, 1844; registered Jul. 15, 1844.

1745   SG 556, E.H. PHIPPS, $10/100 ac., 640 ac., Horse Paster fork of Toxaway (Horsepasture R.), Dis. 18, corner DOBSON'S & MILLSAP'S survey, passing ELLISON's survey, WILLIAM H. BRYSON's survey, ALEXANDER WILSON's line. Entry Sep. 2, 1842; grant Feb. 5, 1844; registered Jul. 15, 1844.

1746   SG 560, E.H. PHIPPS, $10/100 ac., 100 ac., Chattooga R., Dis. 18, SE corner of MURPHRY's lot; bd. SHELTON's line. Entry Sep. 21, 1842; grant Feb. 6, 1844; registered Jul. 15, 1844.

Next page begins section of J.R. ALLMAN, Register of Macon County

1747   SG 581, WILLIAM ALLEN Junr., assignee of ENOS SHIELDS on Sheriff's deed, for $343.90, 112 ac., Sec. 47, Dis. 10, crossing Watauga Creek of Tennesse R. Granted Nov. 28, 1840; registered Oct. 9, 1844.

1748   SG 579, ALEXANDER ZACKERRY, $5/100 ac., 25 ac. on Chattooga R., Dis. 18, N. of public road leading to S.C., bd. M. KINNEY, JOHN ZACHERRY. Entry Jun. 15, 1841; grant Jun. 8, 1844; registered Oct. 9, 1844.

1748   CHRISTOPHER C. ZACHERRY, $5/100 ac., 100 ac. on Silver Run Creek, Dis. 18. Entry Jun. 15, 1841; grant Jun. 18, 1844; registered Oct. 9, 1844.

1749   SG 580, ALEXANDER ZACHERRY, $5/100 ac., 100 ac., Silver Run Creek, Dis. 18, bd. JAMES ZACHERRY. Entry Feb. 22, 1843; grant Jun. 18, 1844; registered Oct. 9, 1844.

1750   SG 581, ALEXANDER ZACHERRY, $5/100 ac., 100 Ac. on Silver Run Creek, both sides, bd. E. AMMONS. Entry Apr. 18, 1844; grant Jun. 18, 1844; reg. Oct. 9, 1844.

1750   SG 640, NATHAN B. THOMPSON, $12.50, 50 ac., Sec. 110, Dis. 8, on NED MIL-SAPS Creek. Granted Oct. 4, 1843; registered Oct. 9, 1844.

1751   SG 644, ABRAHAM SELLARS, $17.44, 61 ac., Sec. 17, Dis. 8, on NED MILSAPS Creek. Granted Oct. 4, 1843; registered Oct. 9, 1844.

1752   SG 645, ABRAHAM SELLARS, $22.80, 80 ac., Sec. 109, Dis. 8. Granted Oct. 4, 1843; registered Oct. 9, 1844.

1753   SG 572, CARSON P. BRYSON, $5/100 ac., 100 ac. on Georges Creek, Dis. 18, beg. at fork of creek below WILLIAM H. BRYSON's camp, bd. MRS. R. MCDOWELL's line. Entry May 25, 1843; grant May 6, 1844; registered Oct. 9, 1844.

1754   SG 586, WILLIAM H. BRYSON, $5/100 ac., 100 ac. on Blue Ridge, where the Hamburg (Road?) crosses the same, both sides of road. Entry Aug. 27, 1842; grant Aug. 19, 1844; registered Oct. 9, 1844.

1754   SG 587, JOHN C. BRYSON, $10/100 ac., 200 ac. on Tuckasegee R., near Blue Ridge, on Hamburg Rd. Entry Aug. 27, 1842; grant Aug. 19, 1844; registered Oct. 9, 1844.

1755   SG 588, GEORGE W. BRYSON, $10/100 ac., 200 ac. on Tuckasegee R., W. of Hamburg Rd., on top of Blue Ridge, incl. part of "the Harricane" (Hurricane Cr.) Entry Aug. 27, 1842; grant Aug. 19, 1844; registered Oct. 9, 1844.

1757   SG 656, LETTY N. GARRETT, assignee of JAMES COCKERHAM, for $14.36, 58 ac., Sec. 76, Dis. 8. Granted Apr. 29, 1844; registered Oct. 10, 1844.

1757   SG 585, JOHN CLARK Senr., $10/100 ac., 640 ac. on Horse Pasture fork of Toxaway R., Dis. 18, incl. his improvement. Entry May 2, 1836; grant Jul. 17, 1844; registered Oct. 10, 1844.

1758   SG 527, JOHN H. WATSON, $5/100 ac., 100 ac. on W. fork of Tuckasegee R., bd. JAMES LEDFORD, incl. MAGNUS TEAGUE's improvement. Entry Nov. 26, 1842; grant Feb. 9, 1843; registered Oct. 10, 1844.

1759 Mortgage: JOHN HALL to GATHER B. JACOBS, both of Macon, 178 ac. on Wautauga Cr., known as John Hall's land and commonly called the LEARY tract. Jacobs was security to Hall in appeal in court in which Hall is plaintiff & ROBERT HALL is defendant; Hall mortgages land to hold Jacobs harmless. *John Hall.* Wit: *E. DOWDLE,* who proved deed Sep. 28, 1844. Registered Oct. 10, 1844.

1759 BENJAMIN S. BRITTAN to MICHAEL WIKLE, both of Macon, for $500, 15 ac. in Lumpkin Co., GA, part of #984 in 12th & 1st, SW of lot joining Town of Lumpkin. 12 Sep. 1839. *B.S. Brittain.* Wit: *E. DOWDLE, JAS. ROBINSON.* Proved in Sep. 1844 court by E. Dowdle. Registered Oct. 10, 1844.

1759 JAMES ROBINSON to MARY D. MOORE, for $100, 97+ ac., Sec. 94, Dis. 18. Dec. 31, 1841. *James Robinson.* Wit: *E. DOWDLE, F.T.(?) GRANT* Proven by E. Dowdle, Jun. 1844 court. Registered Oct. 10, 1844.

1760 RODERICK NORTON, ELIAS NORTON & EDWARD NORTON to JOSHUA AMMONS, all of Macon, for $500, 640 on Chattooga R., Dis. 18. July 3, 1844. *Elias Norton, Edwd. K. Norton, Roderick Norton.* Wit: *BENJAMIN P. HOLLAND, L.A. COFFEE.* Proven by Benjamin Holland in Sep. 1844 court. Registered Oct. 10, 1844. (Note: Book E, p 160-61, court authorized clerk to sign Edward K. Norton's name to deed.)

1761 State of Tennessee: THOMAS B. LOVE to EMANUEL SETSER of Macon, 146 ac., Sec. 8, Dis. 11, Macon Co., purchased at land sale 16 Oct. 1821, Waynesville. Jul. 23, 1836. *Thos. B. Love.* Wit: *THOS. LOVE, A.G. LOVE.* Witnesses' signatures proved by oath of J.R. LOVE & DILLARD LOVE. Proven by James R. Love & Dillard Love, Sep. 1844 court. Registered Oct. 10, 1844.

1762 JOHN N. DEATON to JOHN POTEET, both of Macon, for $60, 10 ac., part of lot 1, Dis. 11, on conditional line between Poteet & Deaton. Jan. 10, 1842. *John N. Deaton.* Wit: *ISAIAH COOK, WILBORN REID.* Proven by Isaiah Cook, Sep. 1844 court. Registered Oct. 10, 1844.

1762 GEORGE LOWDERMILK to JOSHUA AMMONS, both of Macon, for $100, Sec. 100, Dis. 11, bought at 1836 sale in Franklin. Jan. 30, 1843. *George (his X mark) Lowdermilk.* Wit: *JAMES D. FRANKS, JOHN AMMONS.* Proven by James D. Franks, Sep. 1844 court. Registered Oct. 10, 1844.

1763 State of Tennessee: THOS. B. LOVE to EMANUEL SETSER, 105 ac., Sec. 7, Dis. 11, purchased Oct. 16, 1821 at Waynesville sale. Jul. 25, 1836. *Thos. B. Love.* Wit: *THOS. LOVE, A.G. LOVE.* Signatures of witnesses proven by J.R. LOVE & DILLARD LOVE in Sep. 1844 court. Registered Oct. 10, 1844.

1763 JOHN BARKER of Macon to GEORGE ROWEN of Blount Co., TN for $200, 50 ac., Sec. 37, Dis. 1, on W. side of Hazlenut Creek. Sep. 7, 1844. *John Barker.* Wit: *JOHN CHAMBERS, JOSEPH WELCH.* Proven by Joseph Welch in Sep. 1844 court. Registered Oct. 10, 1844.

1764 GEORGE N. HUGHES to CURTIS SAUNDERS, both of Macon, for $75.25, 38 hogs for $25; 7 sheep for $5.25; 2 featherbeds & furniture, $5 ea.; 3 bee gums for $2; 2 pots & 2 ovens for $5; 2 tables for $1; pair of cart wheels at $2; my standing crop of corn & fodder, $25. Aug. 22, 1844. *George N. Hughes.* Wit: *JOHN HALL,* who proved in Sep. 1844 court. Registered Oct. 10, 1844.

1765 AMOS LEDFORD of Cherokee Co., NC, to JAMES M. MOFFITT "of county & state aforesaid," (Macon?) 54 ac., Sec. 110, Dis. 17. May 29, 1844. *Amos Ledford.* Wit: *A.C. LEDFORD, JOHN MCDOWELL.* Proven by John McDowell in Sep. 1844 court. Registered Oct. 10, 1844.

1765 THOMPSON WILSON to ALEXANDER ZACKERY for $15, 50 ac. on Chattooga R., Dis. 18, bd. ELIAS NORTON. May 25, 1844. *Thompson Wilson.* Wit: *JONA. ZACKERY, ALEX WILSON.* Ack. in Sep. 1844 court. Registered Oct. 10, 1844.

1766 Mortgage: ALEXANDER B. DONALDSON of 1st part, HENRY ADDINGTON of 2nd part, THOMAS J. ROANE of 3rd part, all of Macon. Donaldson, for consideration of liability incurred by T.J. Roane as security in prosecution of suit in Superior Court of Henderson Co. NC against WILLIAM STALCUP & J.R. ALLMAN, & further consideration of $1, conveys to Addington parcel where Donaldson now lives, 117 ac. on Skeener (Skeenah) Cr., also a gray mare, 5 cattle, 12 hogs, growing crop of corn & oats, household & kitchen furniture, a few farming tools. If Donaldson's suit fails & in case of failure to pay, Addington as trustee to sell the property to cover Roane's liability. Jun. 15, 1844. A.B. Donaldson, Henry Addington, T.J. Roane. Wit: JOHN MCDOWELL. Ack. Oct. 23, 1844. Registered Nov. 29, 1844.

1768 Bond: SILAS MCDOWELL, JESSE R. SILER, JAMES K. GRAY, $4,000 bond for performance of Silas McDowell, elected Clerk of Superior Court. Sep. 13, 1844. Ack. by makers Sep. 13, 1844. Registered Nov. 30, 1844.

1769 Bond: SILAS MCDOWELL, JESSE R. SILER, JAMES K. GRAY, $10,000 bond for performance of Silas McDowell as Clerk of Court. Sep. 13, 1844. Registered Nov. 30, 1844.

1769 Bond: J.K. GRAY, J.R. SILER, SILAS MCDOWELL, $10,000 bond for performance of J.K. Gray as Clerk of Court of Pleas & Qtr. Sessions. Sep. 10, 1844. Registered Nov. 30, 1844.

1770 Bond: J.K. GRAY, J.R. SILER, SILAS MCDOWELL, $2,000 bond for performance of J.K. Gray as Clerk of Court. Sep. 10 1844. Registered Nov. 30, 1844.

1771 SG 584, JAMES BUCHANON, $5/100 ac., 100 ac., E. fork of Savannah Creek. Entry Jan. 2, 1841; grant Jul. 13, 1844; registered Jun. 27, 1845.

1771 SG 638, THOMAS WEST, $5/100 ac., 50 ac., Cowee Creek, Dis. 10. Entry Mar. 27, 1840; grant Dec. 9, 1844; registered Feb. 4, 1845.

1772 SG 628, SAMUEL REED, $5/100 ac., 100 ac., White Pine Creek, bd. E. SETSER. Entry Mar. 14, 1843; grant Dec. 9, 1844; registered Feb. 4, 1845.

1773 SG 630, SAMUEL REED, $5/100 ac., 16 ac. on Tennessee River. Entry Mar. 5, 1842; grant Dec. 9, 1844; registered Feb. 4, 1845.

1774 SG 653, to ISAAC ASHE, assignee of JOHN STILES Jr., for $__, 71+ ac., Sec. 5, Dis.8, on Big Savannah. Granted Mar. 4, 1844; registered Feb. 4, 1845.

1774 SG 595, ISAAC ASHE, $5/100 ac., 50 ac., Savannah Creek, Dis. 8, on L.C. ASHE's corner. Entry Feb. 7, 1842; grant Dec. 9, 1844; registered Feb. 4, 1845.

1775 SG 594, ISAAC ASHE, $5/100 ac., 100 ac., Savannah Creek, bd. WILSON, including an improvement. Entry Jan. 11, 1844; grant Dec. 9, 1844; registered Feb. 5, 1845

1776 SG 593, MARCUS L. ASHE, $5/100 ac., 100 a., Savannah Creek. Entry Dec. 18, 1840; grant Dec. 9, 1844; registered Feb. 5, 1845.

1777 SG 569, PETER MATHIS Jr., $5/100 ac, 100 ac., Dis. 7, Cullewhee Creek, N. bank of Bryson's Mill Branch. Entry Feb. 4, 1841; grant Mar. 5, 1844; registered Feb. 5, 1845.

1777 SG 526, E.S. ALLISON, $5/100 ac., 100 ac., Dis. 18, Toxaway R., near top of Blue Ridge. Entry Oct. 30, 1840; grant Jan. 9, 1844; registered Feb. 5, 1845.

1778 SG 525, E.L. & F.P. ALISON, $5/100 ac., 100 ac., Dis. 18, on Toxaway R., top of Blue Ridge. Entry Oct. 15, 1840; grant Jan. 9, 1843; registered Feb. 6, 1845.

1779 SG 631, JAMES RUSSELL, $5/100 ac., 60 ac., Sugar town R. Entry May 2, 1837; grant Dec. 9, 1844; registered Feb. 6, 1845.

1779 Mortgage: WILLIAM B. MORGAN of Macon, for $1, to JASON H. HUNTER, one iron grey mare. Condition: Hunter is security for Morgan for an appeal from County to Superior Court in case wherein J.R. ALLMAN is plaintiff and Morgan & WM. B. CRUSE are defendants. Dec. 13, 1844. W.B. Morgan. Wit: J.K. GRAY. Ack. in Dec. 1844 court. Registered Feb. 7, 1845.

1780 Mortgage: WILLIAM B. CRUSE of Macon, for $150, convey to J.H. HUNTER, A. HESTER, R. HALL & D.R. LOWRY, all of Macon, two tracts in Dis. 6, the one on which Gnise lives & one adj.; mare & colt, 2 cows & calves, 8 stock hogs, all my household & kitchen furniture. Condition: Hunter, Hester, Hall & Lowry are security for Cruse in judgment in favor of J.R. ALLMAN against me for $52.40 and cost, obtained Jan. 5, 1841. Jan. 8, 1844. *W.B. Cruse.* Wit: *E. DOWDLE,* who proved in court, Dec. 1844. Registered Feb. 7, 1845.

1781 PETER MATHEWS to TILMAN TILLY, both of Macon, for $50, 100 ac., Dis. 7, on Culowhee Cr, N. bank of Bryson's Mill Branch. Jul. 13, 1844. *Peter (his X mark) Mathews.* Wit: *E. DOWDLE, LEWIS A. TILLEY.* Proven by E. Dowdle in Dec. 1844 court. Registered Feb. 12, 1845.

1782 Mortgage: JASON H. HUNTER of Macon to NICHOLAS W. WOODFIN of Buncombe Co., NC, for $1, 167 ac. on which Hunter lives, purchased from MICHAEL WIKLE on the Tennessee R., Sec. 38, Dis. 16; also the Sellers tract purchase of JAMES SELLERS, 174 ac., Sec. 68, Dis. 1; also 50 ac., Sec. 64, Dis. 8, purchased of BENJAMIN HYDE; also 116 ac., purch. of Hyde, Sec. 69, Dis. 8. Also, Hunter for $1 has sold to Woodfin three Negro slaves, woman of dark complexion named EMMA, 27 years, one boy child of the woman Emma, aged abt. 4 yrs, of yellow complexion, named JOHN and one other child of same woman, a female named MARGARET, aged 1 yr. Condition: Hunter indebted to Woodfin by $602 note dated Sep. 15, 1843, also following notes in hands of Woodfin as attorney for following Charleston merchants: $185.58 due firm of ROOSEVELT & BARKER, dated Oct. 26, 1843, with credit of $50; one of $144.11, same firm, dated June 4, 1844; another of $631.60, due TOWNSANDS & MENDENHALL & CO., dated Oct. 27, 1843, with credit of $140; another of $351.79, due KELSEY & DEAS, dated June 4, 1844; another of $100.12, same firm. Dec. 14, 1844. *J.H. Hunter.* Wit: *H.G. WOODFIN,* who proved Dec. 17, 1844. Registered Feb. 12, 1845.

1784 JACOB SILER, trustee, of Macon, to JESSE R. SILER of Macon and DAVID L. SWAIN of Orange Co. NC, for $1,900, all our 1/2 undivided moiety of 9 adj. tracts on "Iola" (Iotla) Creek, same conveyed by ELI MCKEE, Sheriff of Macon Co., to Jesse R. Siler and DAVID R. LOWRY Aug. 13, 1840, being same interest Lowry conveyed to Jacob Siler, trustee, to secure debts to Swain Mar. 15, 1843, same on which Lowry now lives. Sep. 16, 1843. *Jacob Siler.* Wit: *B.K. DICKEY, JON DOBSON.* Proven by B.K. Dickey, Dec. 1844 court. Registered Feb. 12, 1845.

1785 SAMUEL WIKLE of Cherokee Co. NC is bound to JACOB SIMMS of Macon for $1,600; Wikle to make Simms a good title to 390 ac., including land where Simms lives and all lands owned by Wikle on Savannah Cr. No date. *Samuel Wikle.* Wit: *WM. H. THOMAS.* Writing of Thomas proven by J.R. LOVE. "I sine this bond over to the use of JAMES JAMES." *Jacob Sims.* Wit: *WM. LIVELY, LEV YAN.* Registered Feb. 12, 1845.

1786 THOMSON WILSON of first part, JANE, BARTLY, THOMAS, JOHN, ELIXANDER & ALFRED WILSON, and ELEXANDER & ISZEBELAH ZACHERY, all of Macon except Bartley and Thomas Wilson of Georgia, counties of Gilmore and Murray, parties of other part. For $25, we the heirs of WILLIAM WILSON, dec'd, sell to Thomson Wilson our interest in 183 ac. purchased by William Wilson in Dis. 6, Sec. 35 & 26, including improvement made by William. Sep. 11, 1844. *Jane (her X mark) Wilson, Bartley Wilson, Thomas Wilson by Bartley Wilson, John (his X mark) Wilson, Alex Wilson, Alfred Wilson, Isabel Zachery.* Wit: *JOHN (his X mark) HOOPER (as to Jane), JOHN MCDOWELL, ELIAS NORTON* (as to Alexander Zachery & Isabel Zachery). Proven by witnesses, Dec. 1844 court. Registered Feb. 12, 1845.

1787 SAMUEL LAMBERT to JESSE R. SILER, for $10, "near" 2 ac., part of lot No. 19 in Franklin, adj. Baptist Church land on NE corner, incl. small portion of church grave yard. Nov. 28, 1844. *S.R. Lambert.* Wit: *WM. LAMBERT,* who proved in court, Dec. 1844. Registered Feb. 12, 1845.

1788 WILLIAM LEDFORD of Cherokee Co. NC to WILLIAM M. PENLAND of Macon, for $350, 101 ac., Sec. 55, Dis. 13. Aug. 11, 1843. *William Ledford*. Wit: *WM. S. MOORE, JAMES CRAWFORD*. Proven by William S. Moore, Dec. 1844 court. Registered Feb. 12, 1845.

1789 SG 680, UTY SHERRELL, for $__, 50 ac., Sec. 62, Dis. 8, on Chunelus-kees/Chunchukee's Creek. Granted Nov. 30, 1844. Registered Feb. 12, 1845.

1790 SG 681, UTY SHERRELL, for $__, 145 ac., Sec. 64, Dis. 8, on Chunchukee's Creek. Granted Nov. 30, 1844. Registered Feb. 12, 1845.

1791 SG 677, JOHN GIBBS, for $__, 65 ac., Sec. 107, Dis. 8, on ridge between Wesser's Creek & Cockerham's Branch. Granted Nov. 30, 1844; registered Feb. 12, 1845.

1792 SG 675, JOHN GIBBS, for $__, 85 ac., Sec. 16, Dis. 8. Granted Nov. 30, 1844; registered Feb. 12, 1845.

1793 SG 676, JOHN GIBBS, for $__, 165 ac., Sec. 103, Dis. 8. Granted Nov. 30, 1844; registered Feb. 12, 1845.

1794 SG 667, JOHN CONNELLY, $24.90, Sec. 96, Dis. 8. Granted Nov. 30, 1844; registered Feb. 12, 1845.

1795 SG 682, JOSEPH R. JOHNSTON, $27.06, Sec. 112, Dis. 10. Granted Nov. 30, 1844; registered Feb. 22, 1845.

1795 Mortgage: NOAH WYONT to ALFRED H. SLAGLE, for $70, sorrell mare & colt, 2 cows & calf, 2 beds & furniture, carry-all waggon, all my household & kitchen furniture, to secure loan due Jan. 1, 1846. No date. *Noah Wyont*. Wit: *DANIEL SLAGLE*. Ack. Feb. 22, 1845. Registered Feb. 22, 1845.

1796 SG 620, WILLIAM MOSS Sr., $5/100, 100 ac., White Pine Creek, Dis. 5. Entry Jul. 22, 1842; grant Dec. 9, 1844; registered Mar. 21, 1845.

1797 SG 589, SAMUEL SHERRILL, $5/100 ac., 99 ac., Tennessee R., Dis. 8, bd. COLBERT's old tract. Entry Oct. 16, 1837; grant Nov. 25, 1844; registered Mar. 21, 1845.

1798 SG 415, JACOB SHOPE, $5/100 ac., 50 ac. on Burningtown Cr., Dis. 17. Entry Mar. 27, 1837; grant Dec. 17, 1840; registered Mar. 21, 1845.

1799 SG 416, JACOB SHOPE, $5/100 ac., 50 ac. on Burningtown Cr., Dis. 17. Entry Mar. 31, 1837; grant Dec. 17, 1840; registered Mar. 21, 1845.

1800 LEWIS HODGINS to GEORGE W. OLLIVER, both of Macon, for $10, 24 ac., Dis. 15, assigned to Hodgins; he hereby conveys reversionary interest. Jan. 31, 1845. *Lewis Hodgins*. Wit: *A.B. DONALDSON, A.H. HODGINS*. Proven by Donaldson in Mar. 1845 court. Registered Apr. 2, 1845.

1801 DICY OLIVER to LEWIS HODGINS, both of Macon, for $10, reversionary interest in 50 ac. assigned to Oliver in Dis. 15, on Skeener (Skeenah) Cr., bd. Hodgins. Jan. 31, 1845. *Dicy (his X mark) Oliver*. Wit: *A.B. DONALDSON, A.H. HODGINS*. Proven by Donaldson, March 1845 court. Registered Apr. 2, 1845.

1802 LEWIS HODGINS to GEORGE W. OLLIVER, both of Macon, for $5, 3.5 ac. Dis. 15 and reversionary interest. Jan. 21, 1845. *Lewis Hodgins*. Wit: *A.B. DONALDSON, A.H. HODGINS*. Donaldson proved in Mar. 1845 court. RegisteredApr. 2, 1845.

1803 THOMAS AMMONS to JOHN LAMM, both of Macon, for $5, 8 ac. on Shugar town (Cullasaja) fork of Tennessee R., part of 58 ac. in Sec. 68, Dis. 12. Mar. 15, 1842. *Thomas Ammons*. Wit: THOS. M. ANGEL, S.R. LAMBERT. Ack. in Mar. 1845 court. Registered Apr. 2, 1845.

1804 WM. R. MCDOWELL to ALLEN FISHER, quitclaim title to 4 ac. of 50 ac. survey on George's Cr. of Toxaway R. May 31, 1844. *Wm. R. McDowell*. Wit: *JOHN MCDOWELL*. who proved in Mar. 1845 court. Registered Apr. 2, 1845.

1805 NICHOLAS W. WOODFIN, trustee, of Buncombe Co. NC, to SAMUEL P. RIPLEY of
Charleston SC, by virtue of a deed of trust executed to him by JAMES ROBINSON Sep.
13, 1842, and for consideration of $1,170 paid by Ripley, 2 lots in Franklin, #14 & 15
and part of #19, including house & improvements where widow of James Robinson,
dec'd, now lives, also 174 ac. and plantation where GEORGE CARSON lives, conveyed
to Robinson by JAMES POTEET about 1 mi. west of Franklin, on both sides of creek
that runs by town, and being on N. side of public road to Cherokee from Franklin; also
99 ac. originally conveyed to Robinson by J.R. SILER. All tracts were conveyed to
Woodfin as trustee by Robinson Sep. 13, 1842, to secure debts to Ripley & others trading
under firm of MILLER RIPLEY & CO. Advertised & sold town lots Mar. 11, 1845 for
$520 and lands & farm on 2nd inst. for $650 to Ripley by his agent, WILLIAM ANGEL.
Mar. 12, 1845. *N.W. Woodfin.* Wit: *THOS. HICKS, Wm. Angel.* Ack. Mar. 15, 1845.
Registered Apr. 2, 1845.

1807 EASTHER WIKLE, adm. of estate of SAMUEL WIKLE, dec'd, of Cherokee Co. NC to
JAMES JAMES of Haywood Co. NC for $500, 3 tracts on Big Savannah: Sec. 7, 137 &
145 in Dis. 8, 197 ac. in all. Mar. 5, 1844. *Esther (her X mark) Wikle.* Wit: *WM. W. PIER-
CY, G.W. HAYS.* Proven by Piercy in Mar. 1845 court. Registered Apr. 2, 1845.

1809 EASTHER WIKLE, adm. of estate of SAMUEL WIKLE, dec'd, to JAMES JAMES of
Haywood Co. NC, for $300, three tracts on Savannah Cr. of Tuckasegee R., Sec. 116,
270 and 289, containing 180 ac. in all. Mar. 5, 1844. *Esther (her X mark) Wikle.* Wit:
WM. W. PIERCY, G.W. ANGEL. Proven by Piercy in Mar. 1845 court. Registered Apr. 2,
1845.

1810 N.S. JARRETT to WILLIAM C. CONLEY, both of Macon, for $600, three tracts on
"Tasenty" (Tesentee) Cr. of Tennessee R., Dis. 13: Sec. 19 (75 ac.), Sec. 45 (77 ac.) and
a 75-ac tract. Nov. 7, 1844. *N.S. Jarrett.* Wit: *E.MCLEOD, H.N. CONNELLY.* Ack. in
Mar. 1845 court. Registered Apr. 2, 1845.

1812 Contract between CHARLES HAYS & SARAH DONALDSON, both of Macon, having
agreed to marry, agree that Charles shall reserve the property named to whatever purpose
he thinks proper and she agrees to release the property from all claims to which she may
be entitled by law as his wife: 1,200 acres worth $4,000; six slaves, ARTER, JACOB,
MARY and her 3 children, ANDREW, JANE & BETSEY, worth $2,400; 4 horses,
wagon & harness, worth $300, 30 cattle, val. $150; 25 sheep, $35; 50 hogs, $75, also
household & kitchen furniture worth $175, crop which I may have on hand at my
decease. Charles agrees to release all property Sarah may bring "into my possession," to
be applied to whatever purposes she may think proper, consisting of household & kitchen
furniture worth $80. *Charles Hays, Sarah Donaldson.* Wit: *JOHN MCDOWELL, Y.M.
DONALDSON.* Proven by John McDowell, Mar. 1845 court. Registered Apr. 2, 1845.

1813 GILBERT JONES of Haywood Co. NC, for love & affection for my dear little niece
MANDY CAROLINE JONES, dau. of HENDERSON JONES of Macon, a young horse
2 yrs. old, for her lifetime. Should she die, horse to be sold & equally divided among her
brothers and sisters. Dec. 7, 1844. *Gilbert Jones.* Wit: *WM. TATHAM, THOMAS MASH-
BURN.* Proven by Tatham in Mar. 1845 court. Registered Apr. 2, 1845.

1813 OSBURN TILLY of Lumpkin Co., GA, to LEWIS TILLEY of Macon, for $25, 50 ac. on
Cullowhee Cr., Sec. 5, Dis. 7. Feb. 14, 1845. *Osburn Tilly.* Wit: *ANDREW PRESLEY,
HENDERSON (his X mark) BRYSON.* Proven by Presley in Mar. 1845 court. Registered
Apr. 2, 1845.

1814 THOMAS AMMONS to JOHN LAMM, both of Macon, for $5, 20 ac., part of Sec. 68,
Dis. 12, on Tennessee R. Jan. 27, 1841. *Thomas Ammons.* Wit: *WILLIAM (his X mark)
EVETT, JOHN DAVIS.* Ack. in Mar. 1845 court. Registered Apr. 2, 1845.

1815 ANDREW M. BRYSON, Jr., to JOHN LAMB, both of Macon, for $230, part of Sec. 31,
Dis. 12, on the river. Apr. 3, 1841. *A.M. Bryson.* Wit: *DANIEL BRYSON, GRAY CROW.*
Proven by Crow in Mar. 1845 court. Registered Apr. 2, 1845.

1816 Z. PEEK to WILLIAM C. PEEK, both of Macon, for $100, No. 104, entered May 20,
      1836, in Dis. 11, on Elijay Cr. Mar. 11, 1844. *Zachariah Peek.* Wit: *MARTIN MCCOY,
      ISAAC M. (his X mark) PEEK.* McCoy proved in Mar. 1845 court. Registered Apr. 2,
      1845.

1817 SG 636, WILLIAM WEST, $5/100 ac., 50 ac. on Cowee Creek, bd. JOHN WEST. Entry
      Jan. 23, 1843; grant Dec. 9, 1844; registered Apr. 5, 1845.

1818 SG 571, WILLIAM R. MCDOWELL, $5/100 ac., 50 ac. on Georges Cr. of Toxaway R.
      Entry July 22, 1839; grant Apr. 29, 1844; registered Apr. 12, 1845.

1819 SG 669, JOHN CONNELLY, $25.90, 82 ac., Sec. 3, Dis. 14. Granted Nov. 30, 1844;
      registered May 7, 1845.

1830 SG 503, JOHN CONNELLY, $5/100 ac., 100 ac. on Betty's Cr., Dis. 14. Entry Mar. 10,
      1840; grant Dec. 23, 1842; registered May 7, 1845.

1820 SG 670, CORNELIUS COOPER, $14.40, 52 ac. on Wesser's Cr., Sec. 100, Dis. 8.
      Granted Nov. 31, 1844; registered May 7, 1845.

1821 SG 666, CORNELIUS COOPER, $14, 56 ac. on Wesser's Cr., Sec. 99, Dis. 8. Granted
      Nov. 30, 1844; registered May 7, 1845.

1822 SG 621, VIRGIL NORTON, $5/100 ac., 100 ac. on "Chattoogee" R., beginning at top of
      the great Chimney Top Mtn. Entry Aug. 13, 1842; grant Dec. 9, 1844; registered May 7,
      1845.

1823 SG 622, ELIAS NORTON, $5/100 ac., 100 ac. on White Water R., Dis. 18, beg. on mtn.
      dividing Whitewater & Chatooga R. Entry Jan. 24, 1842; grant Dec. 9, 1844; registered
      May 7, 1845.

1824 SG 625, ELIAS NORTON, $5/100 ac., 100 ac. on Chattooga R., Dis. 18. Entry Aug. 20,
      1842; grant Dec. 9, 1844; registered Mayi 7, 1845.

1825 SG 648, JULIUS DEAN, $5/100 ac., 50 ac. on Tennessee R. Entry Feb.22, 1843; grant
      Feb. 22, 1845; registered May 7, 1845.

1826 SG 686, ABRAM WIGGINS, $11.60, 50 ac., Sec. 63, Dis. 8, Chuncluskee's
      (Junaluskee's?) Creek. Granted Nov. 30, 1844; registered May 7, 1845.

1827 SG 685, FRANCIS WARD, $53.80, 84 ac., Sec. 152, Dis. 8. Granted Nov. 30, 1844;
      registrered May 7, 1845.

1827 SG 673, ABNER J. MOORE, assignee of MATHEW DAVIS, for $13.25, 53 ac., Sec.
      91, Dis. 11. Granted Nov. 30, 1844; registered May 7, 1845.

1828 SG 690, EBENEZER MCLEOD, assignee of MASON MCLEOD, for $29.12, 52 ac.,
      Sec. 60, Dis. 13. Granted Dec. 2, 1844; registered May 7, 1845.

1829 SG 206, NIMROD JARRETT, $5/100 ac., 25 ac. on Tesenty Cr., Dis. 13. Granted Dec.
      15, 1838; registered May 7, 1845.

1830 SG 605, JOHN DEHART, $5/100 ac., 50 ac. on "Elarke" (Alarka) Cr. Entry Jan. 16,
      1840; grant Dec. 9, 1844; registered May 7, 1845.

1831 SG 635, CHARLES WOODRING, $10/100 ac., 200 ac. on Tuckasgee R., Grassy Branch
      & Hunter Jim's Branch. Entry Aug. 5, 1841; grant Dec. 9, 1844; registered June 4, 1845.

1832 SG 687, CHARLES WOODRING, assignee of MARK BURRELL, $13.55, 55 ac., Sec.
      12, Dis. 6. Granted Nov. 30, 1844; registered June 4, 1845.

1833 SG 632, JESSE R. SILER, $5/100 ac., 30 ac. on Sugartown Fork of Tennessee R.,bd.
      THOMAS ROGERS. Entry May 15, 1841; grant Dec. 9, 1844; registered June 4, 1845.

1833 SG 698, JESSE R. SILER, $148, 113 ac., Sec. 4, Dis. 1, Tuckasegee R., first bottom
      before THE BEAR's Reserve. Granted Jan. 7, 1845; registered June 4, 1845.

1834 SG 708, JESSE R. SILER assignee of BENJAMIN BRITTAIN, for $1240, 300 ac., Sec.
      47, Dis. 16 on "I.Ollee" (Iotla) Cr. Granted Mar. 20, 1845; registered June 4, 1845.

1835 SG 709, JESSE R. SILER assignee of ROBERT HUGGINS, for $38.82, 160 ac., Sec.
      35, Dis. 16. Granted Mar. 20, 1845; registered June 4, 1845.

1836 SG 710, JESSE R. SILER assignee of GEORGE SHERRELL, for $23.955, 119 ac., Sec. 25, Dis. 12, beginning on Nantahala R., at lower end of an Indian farm. Granted Mar. 30, 1845; registered June 4, 1845.

1837 SG 711, JESSE R. SILER, $21.51, 126 ac., Sec. 79, Dis. 6. Granted Mar. 20, 1845; registered June 4, 1845.

1838 SG 712, JESSE R. SILER, $33.84, 198 ac., Sec. 81, Dis. 6. Granted Mar. 20, 1845; registered June 4, 1845.

1839 SG 713, JESSE R. SILER assignee of JOHN H. KIRKLAND, for $13.60, 68 ac., Sec. 18, Dis. 12, E. bank of Nantahala R. Granted Mar. 20, 1845; registered June 4, 1845.

1840 SG 714, JESSE R. SILER assignee of JOHN H. KIRKLAND, for $13.60, 68 ac., Sec. 17, Dis. 12, on W. bank of Nantahala R. Granted Mar. 20, 1845; registered June 4, 1845

1840 SG 715, JESSE R. SILER assignee of JOHN H. KIRKLAND, for $44, 88 ac., Sec. 20, Dis. 12, E. side Nantahala R. Granted Mar. 20, 1845; registered June 4, 1845.

1841 SG 716, JESSE R. SILER assignee of JOHN H. KIRKLAND, for $12.20, 61 ac., Sec. 21, Dis. 12. Granted Mar. 20, 1845; registered June 4, 1845.

1842 JOHN P. BREWER & JUDA BREWER, alias JUDA POINDEXTER, for $250 to me and the State of N.C., to PENDLETON CRISP, 3 tracts in Dis. 1, Sections 51, 52 & 53, on Tennessee R. Oct. 22, 1842. *John P. Brewer, Juday Brewer.* Wit: *SARAH A. POINDEXTER, JOSEPH WELCH.* Proven by Welch, Jun. 1845 court. Registered June 8, 1845.

1843 LAWRENCE BRADLEY to MILTON MCKAY, both of Macon, for $150, 55 ac. in Dis. 11, Sec. 115 on "Ellijah" (Ellijay) Cr. Oct. 12, 1838. *Lawrence Bradley.* Wit: *WILLIAM WILLIAMS, H. HAGIN.* Registered June 11, 1845.

1844 J.M. BRYSON to J.R. ALLMAN, for val. rec'd, 160 ac., Sec. 19, Dis. 11. Apr. 4, 1845. *J.M. Bryson.* Wit: *JOHN CLINE, WM. ALLMAN.* Proven by Allman in June 1845 court. Registered June 11, 1845.

1845 DAVID DAVIS to JOHN WILDS, for $159, 76 ac. on Burningtown Cr., Sec. 52, Dis. 17. Nov. 18, 1840. *David Davis.* Wit: *HENRY DEWEESE,* who proved in court, June 1845. Registered June 19, 1845.

1846 ENOS D. SHIELDS to PHILLIP GUYER, both of Macon, for $25, 50 ac. on Iola (Iotla) Cr., Dis. 16, entry 463. Sep. 4, 1838. *Enos D. Shields.* Wit: *WM. M. DEWEESE, DAVID GUYER.* Proven by David Guyer, June 1845 court. Registered June 20, 1845.

1847 JACOB B. TRAMMELL to JOHN R. ALLMAN, both of Macon, for $125, 5 ac., part of Sec. 23, Dis. 16 on W. bank of Tennessee R., upper bank of ford called the Sugartown or Phillips ford, on SE corner of Town Reservation orig. purch. by LINCOLN FULLAM, certificate 22 May 1820, surveyed by JAMES GUDGER, D. Survr. June 11, 1845. *J.C.B. Trammell.* Wit: *B.W. BELL, R.A. HALL.* Ack. in June 1845. Registered June 20, 1845.

1848 SG 429, JAMES LOVE Sr. assignee of THOS. LOVE, for $336, 78 ac., Sec. 45, Dis. 11 on Sugartown fork. Granted Jan. 7, 1839; registered Aug. 15, 1845.

1849 JOSHUA AMMONS to DAVID PEEK, both of Macon, for $200, three tracts of 66, 61 & 35 ac. in Dis. 11, on Ellijay Cr. & E. side Battle Branch, bd. Z. PEEK. Feb. 7, 1845. *Joshua Ammons.* Wit: *JOHN AMMONS, JULY AMMONS.* Acknowledged June 1845 court. Registered Aug. 15, 1845.

1851 THOMAS J. ROANE to JOHN MOORE, both of Macon, for $150, 133+ ac., Sec. 54, Dis. 16. June 14, 1843. *Thos. J. Roane.* Wit: *ELI MCKEE.* Ack. in June 1845 court. Registered Aug. 15, 1845.

1852 THOS. M. ANGEL, Esq., High Sheriff of Macon, to GABRIEL BOLICK, assignee of County of Macon, on execution from Superior Court of Macon against JOHN DAVIS, THOMAS AMMONS, JOHN LOWDERMILK & JERRY BURTON for $115.20 recovered in part of Davis, land sold at public auction to satisfy judgment: 70 ac., Dis. 1, for high bid of $1.05. June 9, 1845. *Thos. M. Angel, Sh'ff.* Wit: *WM. G. LAMBERT, J.Y. HICK.* Ack. in June 1845 court. Registered Aug. 15, 1845.

1853 DAVID LEDFORD to THOS. M. ANGEL, both of Macon, for $700, three tracts in Dis.
      15: Sec. 86, bd. HENRY ADDINTON & JOHN KIMZEY; a tract including entry 234;
      Sec. 90 and part of Sec. 95 & 86, totaling 233 ac. May 15, 1845. *David (his X mark) Led-*
      ford. Wit: *WM. LAMBERT, J.K. GRAY.* Proven by Gray in June 1845. Registered Aug.
      15, 1845.

1855 JAMES H. WATERS to MARGARET WATERS, both of Macon, for $100, 110 ac., Dis.
      17, Burningtown Cr. Sep. 2, 1844. *J.H. Waters.* Wit: *E. COLLINS, RICH'D CLAMPIT.*
      Proven by Eli Collins in June 1845 court. Registered Aug. 15, 1845.

1856 SAUL H. WATERS to MARGARET WATERS, both of Macon, for $25, 50 ac., Sec.
      345 Dis. 17, on the reservation line. Sep. 4, 1844. *S.H. Waters.* Wit: *E. COLLINS,*
      RICHARD CLAMPIT. Proven by Collins in June 1845 court. Registered Aug. 15, 1845.

1857 WILLIAM STALCUP of Macon to PETER S. STALCUP, for $25, 127+ ac. on Tuck-
      asegee R., Sec. 2, Dis. 8, also 63+ ac. on river in Dis. 8, also 3 ac. entry on river near
      State Ford, Dis. 8, beginning corner of the "Hice" tract, bd. HALL & SELLERS. Oct. 1,
      1843. *William Stalcup.* Wit: *JOEL SYMONDS, J.D. FRANKS.* Ack. in June 1845 court.
      Registered Aug. 15, 1845.

1858 WILLIAM STALCUP to PETER S. STALCUP of Macon, for $24, 55 ac. on Tuckasege
      R. Oct. 31, 1843. *Wm. Stalcup.* Wit: *JOEL SIMONDS, J.D. FRANKS.* Ack. in June 1845
      court. Registered Aug. 15, 1845.

1859 SG 627, ZACHARIAH PEEK, $5/100 ac., 50 ac. on Ellijay Cr. Entry Mar. 30, 1837;
      grant Dec. 9, 1844; registered Aug. 15, 1845.

1860 SG 722, WILLIS GUY assignee of JOHN HYDE, $59.76, 59+ ac., Sec. 19, Dis. 12.
      Granted Mar. 20, 1845; registered Aug. 16, 1845.

1860 SG 726, JACOB TRAMMELL assignee of LINCOLN FULLAM, for $591, 197 ac., Sec.
      23, Dis. 16, on W. bank Tennessee R. Granted Mar. 20, 1845; registered Aug. 16, 1845.

1861 SG 720, WILLIAM DILLS assignee of HENRY MORROW, for $15.13, 66 ac., Sec.
      150, Dis. 8, on Green's Fork. Granted Mar. 20, 1845; registered Aug. 16, 1845.

1862 SG 699, JULIUS J.W. MCCOY, $5/100 ac., 100 ac. on Tennessee R., Dis. 10. Entry
      Sep. 25, 1841; grant Dec. 9, 1844; registered Aug. 16, 1845.

1863 SG 624, DAVID NORTON, $5/100 ac., 50 ac. on Chattooga R., beginning at top of the
      great White Side Mountain. Entry Aug. 13, 1842; grant Dec. 9, 1844; registered Aug. 17,
      1845.

1864 SG 648, DAVID MCCOY, $5/100 ac., 100 ac. on Tennessee R., Dis. 10. Entry Sep. 15,
      1842; grant Dec. 9, 1844; registered Aug. 17, 1845.

1865 SG 599, NATHAN B. BUCHANNON, $5/100 ac., 75 ac. on Savannah Cr. Entry Jan. 6,
      1841; grant Dec. 7, 1844; registered Aug. 17, 1845.

1866 SG 664, EPHRAIM ASHE, $5.47, 69 ac., Sec. 25, Dis. 7. Granted Nov. 30, 1844;
      registered May 17, 1845.

1867 ROBERT LOVE of Haywood Co. NC to DILLARD LOVE, for $1,000, Negro SUKY
      and her four children, two boys & two girls. July 2, 1824. *Ro. Love.* Wit: *B. CHAM-*
      BERS, THOS. LOVE. At Macon, the handwriting of the witness, Thos. Love, being dead,
      as well as handwriting of bargainer of within proven before me by oath of J.R. LOVE &
      JOSEPH KEANER, Sep. 17, 1845. *J.L. BAILEY,* J.S.Ct. Registered Sep. 19, 1845.

1867 SG 697, MOSES ADDINGTON, $__, 52 ac., Sec. 157, Dis. 15. Granted Jan. 2, 1845;
      registered Oct. 27, 1845.

1868 SG 671, JOHN COCKERHAM, $11, 52 ac. on west fork of Cowee Cr. Granted Nov. 30,
      1844; registered Oct. 27, 1845.

1868 SG 672, JOHN COCKERHAM, $15.29, 51 ac., Sec. 65, Dis. 10. Granted Nov. 30, 1844;
      registered Oct. 27, 1845.

1869 SG 634, DAVID SHELTON, $5/100 ac., 50 ac. on Trout Cr. Entry Aug. 27, 1842; grant
      Dec. 9, 1844; registered Oct. 27, 1845.

1870 SG 641, MOSES WATSON, $5/100 ac., 25 ac. on Tuckaseege R., near a trail. Entry Jan. 23, 1843; grant Dec. 9, 1844; registered Oct. 27, 1845.

1870 SG 664, UTE HYATTE, $5/100 ac., 10 ac. on Tuckaseege R., at upper end of an Island, including all the Island. Entry Dec. 19, 1840; grant Mar. 5, 1845; registered Oct. 27, 1845.

1871 SG 665, AMOS ASHE, $__, 54 ac., Sec. 32, Dis. 7. Granted Nov. 30, 1844; registered Oct. 27, 1845.

1872 SG 612, WILLIAM H. HIGDON, $5/100 ac., 50 ac. on Savannah Cr., bd. R. JONES, LUKE WILLSON. Entry Jan. 6, 1842; grant Dec. 9, 1844; registered Oct. 28, 1845.

1872 SG 655, LUKE WILLSON, $5/100 ac., 50 ac. on Savannah Cr. Entry Apr. 11, 1837; grant Jan. 2, 1845; registered Oct. 28, 1845.

1873 SG 637 DANIEL WEST, $5/100 ac., 50 ac. on "Elarkey" (Alarka) Cr. Entry Oct. 2, 1842; grant Dec. 9, 1844; registered Oct. 28, 1845.

1873 SG 664, EPHRAIM ASHE, $15.47, 69 ac., Sec. 25, Dis. 7. Granted Nov. 30, 1844; registered Oct. 28, 1845.

1874 SG 598, GEORGE H. BARNS, $5/100 ac., 100 ac. on Chattooga R., Dis. 18, bd. SAMUEL SMITH, ELIZABETH NORTON, D.L. MCDOWELL, including an improvement. Entry Jan. 6, 1842; grant Dec. 9, 1844; registered Oct. 28, 1845.

1875 SG 615, JOSHUA HALL, $5/100 ac., 50 ac. Savannah Cr. & "Lorrell" (Laurel) Branch, bd. JESSE HALL. Entry Apr. 17, 1841; grant Dec. 9, 1844; registered Oct. 28, 1845.

1876 SG 665, CLARK GUYE, $5/100 ac., 50 ac. on Sugar town R., passing 2 fords. Entry Mar. 16, 1844; grant Mar. 22, 1845; registered Oct. 28, 1845.

1876 SG 649, THOMAS C. FORD, $5/100 ac., 10 ac. on "Elijay" Cr., Dis. 11. Entry May 3, 1838; grant Jan. 2, 1845; registered Oct. 28, 1845.

1877 SG 679, JAMES M. MOFFITT assignee of AMOS LEDFORD, for $12.24, 44 ac., Sec. 110, Dis. 15. Granted Nov. 30, 1844; registered Oct. 28, 1845.

1878 SG 541, JOHN MCGEE, $5/100 ac., 50 ac., Dis. 15, "Skeener" (Skeenah) Cr., bd. JAMES MOFFITT. Entry Dec. 14, 1841; grant Aug. 18, 1843; registered Oct. 29, 1845.

1878 JOHN CLARK, Senr. of Henderson Co. NC, to ALEXANDER ENGLAND, WALTER H. CLARK, WILLIAM CLARK & JOHN CLARK, Jr., all of Henderson, for $50, undiv. one-half of 640 ac., Dis. 18, on Horsepasture fork of Toxaway R., bd. HYATT. Aug. 22, 1844. *John Clark.* Wit: *ANDERSON TRULL,* who proved before WILL. H. BATTLE, J.S.C., Sep. 24, 1844. Registered Oct. 29, 1845.

1880 JOHN CLARK, Sr. of Macon, to JOSHUA ROBERTS of Buncombe Co. NC, for $200, one undiv. half of 640 ac. tract on Horse pasture fork of Toxaway R., Dis. 18. Aug. 9, 1844. *John Clark, Sr.* Wit: *JAS. HAMBLEN, MARTH(A) (her X mark) LOWS.* Proven by Hamblen before (WILL) H. BATTLE, Sep. 24, 1844. Registered Oct. 29, 1845.

1881 Mortgage: JOHN HALL to MARY F. HALL, both of Macon, 134 ac. known as the BATES tract. Condition: Mary was security for John for something more than $100. No date. *John Hall.* Wit: *D.R. LOWRY, S.R. LAMBERT.* Registered Oct. 29, 1845.

1882 Mortgage: JOHN HALL to SILAS MCDOWELL & GATHER B. JACOBS of Macon, with THOMAS W.P. POINDEXTER & TYRA DAVIS collateral security, in case pending in Sup. Ct. of Macon, Hall as plaintiff, JAMES WHITAKER Sr. of Cherokee Co. N.C. as defendant. Hall mortgages 178 ac. tract, Sec. 40, Dis. 16. Sep. 20, 1845. *John Hall.* Registered Oct. 30, 1845.

1882 Mortgage: ALFRED HESTER of 1st part, to JOHN INGRAM of 2nd part, JAMES K.
GRAY of 3rd part. Hester is indebted to Gray for $65; to ALLISON & MORROW for
$24.71; to G.N. PENLAND for $55.57; to THOS. M. ANGEL for $300; to JOAB L.
MOORE for $24. He now conveys to Ingram lots 1, 2, 3, 4, 6, 10 and 11 in Franklin and
personal property 5 horses, a road wagon, a small ox wagon, one yoke of oxen, cow &
calf, 7 head of stock hogs, all my stock in my Tanyard of all kinds, leather, hides, bark,
lime, tools, etc.; abt. 100 bu. of corn; all my household & kitchen furniture beds,
bedclothes, besteads, chairs, tables, bureaus, pots, pails, etc. in trust to apply to debts not
paid off by Mar. 10, 1846. Gray is to sell property at public auction. Oct. 25, 1845. *A.
Hester, John Ingram, J.K. Gray*. Wit: *E. DOWDLE*, who proved before J.K. Gray, clerk.
Registered Oct. 31, 1845.

1884 JOSEPH HICKS to WILLIAM MCDOWELL, both of Macon, for $200, 126 ac. on
Crow's Fork of "Coweter" (Coweeta) Cr., Sec. 39, Dis. 14. Feb. 18, 1844. *Joseph Hicks*.
Wit: *J. HOWARD, JACOB HICKS*. Proven by Howard in Sep. 1845 court. Registered
Nov. 3, 1845.

1885 JAMES POINDEXTER of Macon to TYRA H. DAVIS for $1,200, 217+ ac. on
"Chunuluskies" (Junaluskee's) Cr. of Alarka Cr. Jan. 3, 1844. *James (his X mark) Poin-
dexter*. Wit: THOS. W.P. POINDEXTER, who proved in Sep. 1845 court. Registered
Nov. 3, 1845.

1885 WILLIAM E. MULL of Macon to FELIX KILLPATRICK, 4 tracts in Dis. 12, Sec. 85
(54 ac.), 80 (54 ac.), 87 (71 ac.) & 47 (50 ac.). Feb. 15, 1843. *Wm. E. Mull*. Wit: *M. RUS-
SELL, A.M. RUSSELL*. Proven by A.M. Russell in Sep. 1845 court. Registered Nov. 3,
1845.

1887 DAVID L. SWAIN of Chapel Hill & JESSE R. SILER of Macon, to GEORGE F.
CAILOR of Macon, for $90, 2 tracts on "Iola" (Iotla) Cr., 1st, six acres bd. B. BRIT-
TAIN, J.R. PACE, NOAH HILL, 2nd, 23 ac. bd. Hill. June 27, 1844. *D.L. Swain, J.R.
Siler*. Wit: *D.R. LOWRY*, who proved in Sep. 1845 court. Registered Nov. 3, 1845.

1888 ALEXANDER WILLSON to WILLIAM H. BRYSON, both of Macon, for $60, 100 ac.
on Chattooga R., Dis. 18, bd. TRAMMELL. Feb. 28, 1844. *Alex Wilson*. Wit: *C.McD.
PAXTON, PETER (his X mark) MATHES*. Paxton proved in Sep. 1845 court. Registered
Oct. 4, 1845.

1889 RICHARD WILLSON of Macon to RACHEL HICE of Walker Co. GA, for $50, 70 ac.
in Dis. 8, bd. LEVI WILLSON. Apr. 26, 1844. *Richard (his X mark) Wilson*. Wit: *W.R.
BUCKHANNON, JAMES WILLSON*. Proven by James Willson in Sep. 1845 court.
Registered Oct. 4, 1845.

1889 RICHARD WILLSON of Macon to RACHEL HEISE of Walker Co. GA, 90 ac. on
Savannah Cr., Dis. 8, beginning above sd. Willson's farm. Apr. 26, 1844. *Richard (his
mark) Willson*. Wit: *W.R. BUCKHANNON, JAMES WILLSON*. Proven by James Willson
in Sep. 1845 court. Registered Oct. 4, 1845.

1890 DAVID MOSES to DAVID SUTTON, both of Macon, for $100, 2 tracts in Dis. 8, Sec.
123 (67 ac.) & Sec. 124 (80 ac.). Sep. 18, 1844. *David (his X mark) Moses*. Wit: *WM.
PARTIN*, who proved in Sep. 1845 court. Registered Oct. 4, 1845.

1890 LEWIS VANDYKE to JOHN HOWARD for $290, 56 ac., part of Sec. 5, Dis. 14 on
Coweta Cr. & Vandyke's Cr., also another tract in Dis. 14. Dec. 20, 1843. *L. Vandyke*.
Wit: *JOHN MCDOWELL*. Ack. in Sep. 1845 court. Registered Oct. 4, 1845.

1891 W.H. HIGDON to LUKE WILLSON, both of Macon, for $20, 50 ac. on Savannah Cr.,
bd. RICHARD JONES. Mar. 15, 1845. *W.H. Higdon*. Wit: *CHARLES JONES*. Ack. in
Sep. 1845 court. Registered Nov. 4, 1845.

1892 ISAAC MAUNY to JESSE R. SILER, both of Macon, for $3,000, three tracts totaling
611+ ac.: Sec. 2, Dis. 15 on "Cautoogajay" (Cartoogechaye) Cr.; Sec. 3, Dis. 16; and Sec.
4, Dis. 16, on Cartoogejay, on Dis. 15 line. Feb. 13, 1843. *Isaac Mauney*. Wit: *JAS.
ROBINSON, A. HESTER*. Proven by Hester in Sep. 1845 court. Registered Nov. 5, 1845.

1893 MARY MURY of Union Co., Ga., to ELIJAH KIMZEY for $80, all (my) right in estate
of WILLIAM BRYSON, dec'd, on "Shoogar fork", Dis. 12. Jan. 26, 1843. *Mary (her X
mark) Murry.* Wit: *JOHN BROWN, EBENEZER FAIN, J.P.* Proven by Fain in Sep. 1845
court. Registered Nov. 5, 1845.

1894 WILLIAM MORRISON to JESSE R. SILER, both of Macon, for $1, a small parcel, part
of Sec. 46, Dis. 15, orig. owned by GEORGE N. HUGHES near road leading from the
mill to Franklin, abt. 4 ac. Feb. 25, 1843. *Wm. Morrison.* Wit: *B.K. DICKY, A. HALL.*
Proven by A. Hall in Sep. 1845 court. Registered Nov. 5, 1845.

1894 JOHN DOBSON to JOSEPH DOBSON, both of Macon, for $100, 2.6 parts of undivided
100-ac. tract in Fairfield on Toxaway R., Dis. 18, granted to BERRICK NORTON,
THOMAS MILLSAPS, DAVID MILLSAPS, W. BRYSON, John Dobson, also 1/5 of
undiv. tract on Whitewater Cr. Dis. 18, known as the Soapstone quarry tract, 100 ac. Oct.
31, 1842. *Jno. Dobson.* Wit: *J.R. SILER, WM. HICKS.* Siler proved in Sep. 1845 court.
Registered in Sep. 1845 court. Registered Nov. 5, 1845.

1895 SETH W. HYATT to J.W. DOBSON, for $50, 640 ac. on Horsepasture fork of Toxaway
R., Dis. 18, also 1/3 of 200-ac. tract on Horsepasture, bd. JOHN CLARK. Sep. 17, 1845.
S.W. Hyatt, J.L. HYATT by S.W. Hyatt. Wit: *S. MCDOWELL.* Proven by Silas McDowell
in Sep. 1845 court. Registered Nov. 5, 1845.

1896 Mortgage: ALFRED HESTER of 1st part to WILLIAM HICKS of 2nd part, both of
Macon, and THOMAS M. ANGEL of 3rd part. Hester owes Angel debts of $301 and
$62; to secure payment, he conveys to Hicks 5 horses, one common road waggon, yoke
of oxen, 2-horse waggon, set of tanner's tools, with all stock of leather, hides, bark, lime,
etc. in my tanyard, 7 head of hogs, all household & kitchen furniture, standing crop of
corn on farm where I live, six town lots, all in trust. Hester to pay Angel by Oct. 12,
1845, or Hicks to sell property. Sep. 20, 1845. *A. Hester, Thos. M. Angel, Wm. Hicks.*
Wit: *JOHN GRAY.* Ack. Nov. 7, 1845. Registered Nov. 15, 1845.

1898 DAVID MILLSAPS to JOSEPH W. DOBSON, bor $25, undiv. 1/6 part of 100 ac. on
Toxaway R. in Fairfield, Dis. 18. Mar. 25, 1842. *David Millsaps.* Wit: *W.R. BUCKHAN-
NON, WM. H. HIGDON.* Proven by Higdon in Sep. 1845 court. Registered Nov. 15,
1845.

1899 THOMAS MILLSAPS to JOSEPH W. DOBSON, for $25, undiv. 1/6 part of 100 ac. on
Toxaway in Fairfield, Dis. 18. Dec. 17, 1842. *Thomas Millsaps.* Wit: *JOHN WATSON,
ISAAC MILLSAPS.* Proven by John D. Watson in Sep. 1845 court. Registered Nov. 15,
1845.

1899 JOHN DOBSON to JOSEPH DOBSON & JASON HYATT, for $100, Sec. 33, Dis. 18,
79 ac. Oct. 31, 1842. *Jno. Dobson.* Wit: *J.R. SILER, B.K. DICKEY.* Registered Nov. 15,
1845.

1900 JOHN SUTTON, WM. PARTON (PARTIN), 50 ac. on Savannah Cr., Dis. 8, bd. CAR-
PENTER. Mar. 24, 1844. *John Sutton.* Wit: *WM. SUTTON, JOSEPH (his X mark) SUT-
TON.* Proven by Wm. Sutton in Sep. 1845 court. Registered Nov. 15, 1845.

End of Volume D

Macon County Deed Book E

J.R. ALLMAN, Register,

1 DANIEL WEST to THOMAS WEST, both of Macon, for $5, 50 ac. on "Alarky" Cr. Sep. 17, 1845. *Daniel West.* Wit: *J. HOWARD, MADISON COCKERHAM.* Proven by Howard in Sep. 1845 court.

1 SG 590, JOHN ZACKERY, $5/100 ac., 100 ac. on Chattooga R., Dis. 18. Entry Sep. 13, 1842; grant Dec. 2, 1844; registered Nov. 17, 1845.

2 SG 591, JOHN ZACHERY,$5/100 ac., 100 ac. on Chattooga R., Dis. 18. Entry Oct. 31, 1840; grant Dec. 2, 1844; registered Nov. 17, 1845.

2 SG 592, ROBERT ASHLY/ASHLEY, $5/100 ac., 100 ac. on Toxaway R., bd. WIL- LIAM SLOAN. Entry Jan. 24, 1840; grant Dec. 2, 1844; registered Nov. 17, 1845.

3 JESSE SAUNDERS is bound to BRYANT GIBBS in sum of $250, to make good deed for 61+ ac., Dis. 15, part of Sec. 104, on line of land that Saunders lives on. Feb. 22, 1839. *Jesse Saunders.* Wit: *JOHN MCDOWELL,* who proved in Sep. 1845 court. Registered Nov. 17, 1845.

4 ELIZABETH BRYSON, MARY MURRY, JEFFERSON BRYSON, JOHN T. BRYSON, JOHN PHILLIPS & wife ELIZABETH, WILLIAM BRYSON & JOSEPH BRYSON, to ELIJAH KIMZEY, for $850, certain tracts that belonged to WM. BRYSON, dec'd, on Sugarfork R. between "Elajay" (Ellijay) and Nickajack, Dis. 12: Sec. 23 (50 ac.) on both sides of river; Sec. 49 (48 ac.), below the big rocks up river with line of 23, which lot includes the widow's dowry. Feb. 1, 1844. *Elizabeth Bryson, Joseph Bryson, William (his X mark) Bryson, Mary (her X mark) Murry, John T. Bryson, Jeffer- son Bryson, John Phillips, Elizabeth Phillips.* Wit: *PETER MCLURE, HENRY BAR- RONY* as to J.T. Bryson, *GEORGE MCCLURE* as to Joseph Bryson, *J.R. SILER* as to Phillips & wife. Proven in Sep. 1845 court by Henry Barrony as to John T. Bryson, Elijah Kimzy as to Joseph, William and Jefferson. John Phillips & wife Elizabeth ack. before WILLIAM H. BATTLE, judge of Sup. Ct. on Sep. 10, 1844. Reg. Nov. 17, 1845.

5 CLARK GUY to JOHN H. LEDFORD, for $10, 50 ac. on S. side "Shugatown" R., adj. MARGERETT BRYSON, down meanders of river, passing 2 fords, with WIDOW BRYSON's line. Sep. 17, 1845. *Clark (his X mark) Guy.* Wit: *J.K. GRAY.* Ack. in Sep. 1845. Registered Nov. 18, 1845.

6 DAVID MOSES to WM. PARTIN, for $205, 150 ac. on Savanna Cr. of Tuckasiegah R., Dis. 8, also all appurtenances belonging to Moses. Mar. 16, 1844. *David (his X mark) Moses.* Wit: *JOSEPH (his mark) SUTTON, WM. B. (his X mark) PARTIN.* Ack. in Sep. 1845 court. Registered Nov. 18, 1845.

7 JESSE ASH of Haywood Co. NC to AMOS ASH of Macon, for $300, 52+ ac. on SW bank of Tuckasegee R., the tract on which Amos Ash now lives, orig. purch. from state by WILLIAM H. BRYSON. Aug. 25, 1842. *Jesse (his X mark) Ash.* Wit: *J.B. ALLISON, THOMAS MONTEITH.* Proven by Allison in Sep. 1845 court. Registered Nov. 18, 1845.

8 SG 613, WILLIAM H. HIGDON, $5/100 ac., 25 ac. on Savannah Cr., incl. an inprove- ment. Entered Jan. 6, 1842; granted Dec. 9, 1844; registered Nov. 18, 1845.

8 SG 614, JOSEPH HIGDON, $5/100 ac., 50 ac. on Savannah Cr., incl. an improvement. Entered Jan. 6, 1842; granted Dec. 9, 1844; registered Nov. 18, 1845.

9 THOS. M. ANGEL, Esq., High Sh'ff of Macon Co., to HENRY WILLSON, high bidder, property sold to satisfy judgment of $35.72 against HIRAM DODGINS: 100 ac. on Cul- lowhee Cr., Dis.7. At sale Jun 12, 1843, Willson had high bid of $35.75. June 12, 1843. *Thos. M. Angel.* Wit: *J.K. GRAY,* who proved in Sep. 1845 court.

11 Mortgage: JOHN SHULER of Macon to MARK COLEMAN of Macon of 2nd part and DILLARD LOVE of 3rd part. Shuler for $1 conveys to Love 230 ac. on Deep Cr. bd. by GEORGE SHULER's land on which George now lives & by land of DAVID SHULER & THE BIG BEAR's reservation. Condition: Shuler was bound over to Superior Ct. on charge of perjury, on $1,000 bond secured by Coleman; if he appear in court when due, then deed void. Nov. 24, 1845. *John (his mark) Shuler, Mark Coleman, Dillard Love.* Wit: *WM. LAMBERT.* Registered Dec. 1, 1845.

12 SG 659, ELI WALDROP, $15.50, 72 ac., Sec. 133, Dis. 15. Granted Nov. 18, 1844; registered Dec. 1, 1845.

13 SG 660, ELI WALDROP, $15.50, 50 ac., Sec. 137, Dis. 15. Granted Jan. 18, 1844; registered Dec. 1, 1845.

14 SG 639, ALEXANDER WILSON, $5/100 ac., 100 ac. on Tuckasegee R., near the Hamburg Rd. & Bridge Rd., incl. the Flat Rock. Entry Aug. 3, 1842; grant Ddec. 9, 1844; registered Dec. 2, 1845.

15 Bond: DAVID R. LOWRY, J.R. SILER, JOHN HOWARD, B.K. DICKY, $4,000 bond for Lowry, duly elected Clerk of Superior Ct. of Law for Macon County. Sep. 16, 1845. Registered Dec. 12, 1845.

16 Bond: J.K. GRAY, J.R. SILER, SILAS MCDOWELL, $4,000 bond for Gray, duly elected Clerk of Court of Pleas & Qtr. Sessions. Sep. 16, 1845. Registered Dec. 12, 1845.

17 SG 607, TRAVIS ELMORE, $5/100 ac., 100 ac. on White Pine Creek. Entry Feb. 28, 1842; grant Dec. 9, 1844; registered Dec. 12, 1845.

18 SG 645, HENRY DEWEESE, $5/100 ac., 50 ac. on Burningtown Creek, Dis. 17, incl. an improvement. Entry June 15, 1851; grant Dec. 27, 1844; registered Dec. 12, 1845.

18 SG 724, THOMAS KIMZEY, $101, 62 ac., Sec. 88, Dis. 15. Granted Mar. 20, 1845; registered Dec.13, 1845.

19 SG 678, THOMAS KIMZEY, $9.08, 158 ac., Sec. 75, Dis. 15. Granted Nov. 30, 1844; registered Dec. 13, 1845.

20 SG 616, RICHARD JONES, $5/100, 50 ac. on Savannah Cr., bd. LUKE WILSON, incl. an improvement. Entry Dec. 19, 1840; grant Dec. 9, 1844; registered Dec. 23, 1845.

20 Mortgage: JOHN SHERRELL of Macon to SAMUEL SHERRELL of Haywood Co., NC, for $1,000 or thereabouts due the Asheville Branch of the Bank of Cape Fear which sd. John Sherrell owes by bond; to secure Samuel from harm, John conveys to him a Negro girl named MANDY, abt. 5 years old and one other Negro girl named HANNAH, abt. 3 years old. Oct. 27, 1845. *John Sherrell.* Wit: *SAMUEL P. SHERRELL, NATH'L BLACKBURN.* Proven by Samuel P. Sherrell Dec. 29, 1845. Registered Jan. 6, 1846.

22 JAMES W. GUINN to B.G. JACOBS, for $30, 100 ac. on John Hall's Mill Creek, Dis. 15, bd. JAMES ROBINSON & CREUS (CRUSE); also 50 ac. Oct. 27, 1845. *James W. Guinn.* Wit: *W.B. CREUS,* who proved in Dec. 1845 court. Registered Jan. 6, 1846.

23 JAMES W. GUINN to JOHN R. ALLMAN for $100, 95 ac. on Sugartown R., Dis. 11, also 28 ac., part of Sec. 42, Dis. 11. Oct. 27, 1845. *James W. Guinn.* Wit: *W.B. CRUES,* who proved in Dec. 1845 court. Registered June 6, 1846.

24 JOHN HALL to THOMAS P. MOORE, both of Macon, for $246, Hall's interest in 164 ac., Sec. 42, Dis. 16. The purchase price paid as follows: Thomas P. Moore, THOMAS M. MOORE & B.G. JACOBS on last Sep. 9 endorsed a bond due state in consideration of Hall's purchase of Sec. 42 & other tracts in Dis. 16; Thomas P. Moore, $49.50; Thomas M. Moore, $78.75; Jacobs, $117.65. Nov. 5, 1845. *John Hall.* Wit: *J.L. MOORE, WM. ALLMAN.* J.L. Moore proved in Dec. 1845 court. Registered Jan. 6, 1846.

25 JAMES K. GRAY to JOHN R. ALLMAN, both of Macon, for $10, land in Town of Franklin, 25 poles on S. side Main Street, S. end Lott 6, at Cross Street. Dec. 9, 1845. *James K. Gray.* Ack. in Dec. 1845 court. Registered Jan. 7, 1846.

26 DANIEL MASHBURN of Polk Co. TN to JACOB SILER of Macon, for $200, 65+ ac., Sec. 16, Dis. 17, on Burningtown Creek. Oct. 22, 1845. *Daniel Mashburtn.* Wit: *D.W. SILER, WILLIAM GARRETT, LEWIS GREENLEE.* Proven by D.W. Siler in Dec. 1845 court. Registered Jan. 7, 1846.

27 WILLIAM MASHBURN of Polk Co. TN to JACOB SILER of Macon for $50, 53 ac., Sec. 17, Dis. 17, on Burningtown Cr. Oct. 22, 1845. *Wm. Mashburn,* Wit: *WILLIAM GARRETT, LEWIS GREENLEE, D.W. SILER.* Proven by D.W. Siler in Dec. 1845 court. Registered Jan. 7, 1846.

27 JEREMIAH MASHBURN of Polk Co. TN to JACOB SILER of Macon, for $300, 80 ac., Sec. 14, Dis. 17, on Burning Town Cr., also 87 ac., Sec. 15, Dis. 17. Oct. 22, 1845. *Jeremiah Mashburn.* Wit: *WILLIAM GARRETT, LEWIS GREENLEE, D.W. SILER.* Proven by D.W. Siler in Dec. 1845 court. Registered Jan. 7, 1846.

28 ANDREW HOOPER to WILSON PICKLESIMER, both of Macon, 50 ac., Sec. 11, Dis. 5, on condition Picklsimer pay amount due state. Jan. 23, 1844. *Andrew Hooper.* Wit: *BENSON (his X mark) PICKLESIMER, JOHNSON (his X mark) MCCALL.* Ack. in Dec. 1845 court. Registered Jan. 7, 1846.

29 WARREN BARKER of Macon to RUSSELL SUTTON for $125, 120 ac. on Secatoway Cr., Sec. 120, Dis. 8. Nov. 12, 1845. *Warren Barker.* Wit: *JOHN WILLSON, RICHARD K. ROBERTS.* Willson proved in Dec. 1845 court. Registered Jan. 7, 1846.

29 WARREN BARKER of Macon to RUSSELL SUTTON for $100, 84 ac. on Sicatowey Cr., Sec. 119, Dis. 8. Nov. 12, 1845. *Warren Barker.* Wit: *JOHN WILLSON, RICHARD K. ROBERTS.* Registered Jan. 7, 1846.

30 WILLIAM H. THOMAS of Haywood Co. NC to DILLARD LOVE of Macon, for $490.36 3/4, Negro slaves: SUD, TAMER, ISAM, WILEY and the increase of Tamer. Dec. 14, 1840. *Wm. H. Thomas.* Wit: *JOSEPH WELCH,* who proved in court, Dec. 1845. Registered Jan. 7, 1846.

30 SAMUEL KELLY to LABUN H. STILES, both of Macon, for $150, 112 ac. on "hick-rinole" (Hickory Knoll) Cr. *Samuel Kelly.* No witnesses. Ack. Dec. 1845 court. Registered Jan. 7, 1846.

31 BRANTLY BARKER of Macon, for $60 paid by NATHAN B. THOMPSON, sells to RUSH SUTTON 148 ac., Sec. 121, Dis. 8. Nov. 24, 1845. *Brantly (his X mark) Barker.* Wit: *JAS. CONNELLY, CALEB (his mark) NORTON.* Connelly proved in Dec. 1845 court. Registered Jan. 7, 1846.

32 SG 737, to JOHN R. ALLMAN, assignee of JONATHAN M. BRYSON, for $21.80, 160 ac., Sec. 19, Dis. 11, crossing county road. Granted Dec. 30, 1845; reg. Jan. 7, 1846.

33 SG 717, NIMROD S. JARRETT, $42, 56 ac., Sec. 44, Dis. 13. Granted Mar. 20; registered Jan. 19, 1846.

34 Mortgage: ABRIHAM PICKLESIMER to WILSON PICKLESIMER, both of Macon, for $15.75 to be paid within the year with interes: a red & white cow and calf, 15 hogs, 4 sheep, 150 bu. corn. Jan. 12, 1846. *A. Pickklesimer.* Wit: *BENSON (his X mark) PICKEL-SIMER, JOHNSON (his X mark) MCCALL.* Benson Pickelsimer proved Jan. 19, 1846 before J.K. GRAY. Registered Jan. 19, 1846.

35 Mortgage: DEMPSEY RABY of the 1st part, E. DOWDLE of the 2nd part, STEPHEN MUNDAY of 3rd part, all of Macon. Raby owes WILLIAM TATHAM, Adm., $107, with Munday as security; he conveys to Dowdle for $1 further consideration, a certain Jack ass Don Gizard, with rents, issues, etc. of same, for payment on debt. Feb. 11, 1846. *Demps Raby, E. Dowdle, Stephen Munday.* Ack. by parties in Feb. 1846 court. Registered Feb. 22, 1846.

36 Mortgage: DEMPSY RABY of 1st part, JAS. K. GRAY of 2nd part, JOAB L. MOORE of 3rd part, all of Macon. Raby owes $60 to Moore, $48.25 to FREDERICK RABY Senr., $60 to FREDERICK RABY Jr. To secure payment, Dempsy Raby conveys to Gray for $1 further consideration a road waggon & gearing, complete for 4 horses; 7 horses, incl. Bony, a Stallion; 35 stock cattle, 26 sheep, 40 hogs of all kinds. Feb. 21, 1846. *Demps Raby, J.K. Gray, J.L. Moore.* Wit: *A.J. PATTON,* who proved Feb. 26 before County Clerk. Registered Feb. 27, 1846.

38 SG 604, JOHN A. CLURE, $5/100 ac., 100 ac. on Lowry Fork of Cartoogechaye Cr., Dis. 15. Entry Jan. 23, 1843; grant Dec. 9, 1844; registered Feb. 27, 1846.

39 SG 661 to E.V. AMMONS, assignee of JOHN BROWN, for $15.92 1/2, 55 ac., Sec. 126, Dis. 10, on NE side of Brown's fork of Watauga Cr. Granted Nov. 25, 1844; registered Feb. 27, 1846.

39 SG 603, JOHN CLURE, $5/100 ac., 50 ac. on Lowry fork of "Cautoogahage" (Cartoogechaye) Cr. Entry Aug. 8, 1844; grant Dec. 9, 1844; registered Feb. 27, 1840.

40 SG 667, BRYANT CONLEY, $5/100 ac., 50 ac. on Tesentee Cr. Entry Jun. 13, 1845; grant Oct. 11, 1945; registered Feb. 27, 1846.

41 JESSE KIRBY of Cherokee Co. NC, to THOMAS M. ANGEL of Macon, for $200, 57 ac., Sec. 37, Dis. 11, on E. side "Elyage" (Ellijay) Cr., on N. side of public road. Feb. 10, 1846. *Jesse Kirby.* Wit: *WALLACE A. MOORE, BENJAMIN STILES.* Stiles proved in Mar. 1846 court. Registered Mar. 19, 1846.

42 SG 565, WILLIAM B. QUEEN, $5/100 ac., 100 ac., Dis. 18, Chattooga R., incl. improvement. Entry Dec. 15, 1840; grant Mar. 1, 1844; registered Mar. 19, 1846.

43 JOHN HANNES (Hanner?) of Polk Co. TN to RUBIN B. CAILOR of Macon, for $49, 2 tracts purch. at 1836 sale, 120 ac. in all, Sec. 62 & 63 in Dis. 17, on Burningtown Cr. Jan. 15, 1846. *John Hannes (Hanner?)* Wit: *GEORGE F. CALER.* Proven by George F. Cailer in Mar. 1846 court. Registered Mar. 20, 1846.

44 SG 753, NATHAN TABER, $20.41, 67+ ac., Sec. 34, Dis. 9 on left fork of Mill Cr. Granted Apr. 2, 1846; registered Apr. 2, 1846.

45 SG 738, ABRAHAM WIGGINS, $10.60, 53 ac., Sec. 1, Dis. 8, on N. fork of Junaluskah's or Elarka (Alarka) Cr. Granted Dec. 30, 1845; registered Apr. 20, 1846.

45 SG 609, WILLIAM HENDERSON, $5/100 ac., 100 ac. on Culowhee Cr., Dis. 7. Entry Nov. 7, 1840; grant Dec. 9, 1844; registered Apr. 20, 1846.

46 SG 611, JAMES HENDERSON, $5/100 ac., 100 ac. on Cullowhee Cr., bd. HENRY WILSON. Entry Dec. 3, 1842; grant Dec. 9, 1844; registered Apr. 20, 1846.

47 SG 610, WILLIAM HENDERSON, $5/100 ac., 100 ac., Cullowhee Cr., E. of Hamburg Rd., incl. his improvement. Entry Dec. 3, 1842; grant Dec. 9, 1844; reg. Apr. 20, 1846.

48 SG 669, WILLIAM DUCKWORTH, $5/100 ac., 100 ac. on Flat Creek of Toxaway R., incl. an improvement. Entry Oct. 28, 1842; grant Nov. 15, 1845; registered Apr. 20, 1846.

49 SG 433, WILLIAM DUCKWORTH, $5/100 ac., 100 ac. on Flat Cr. of Toxaway R., Dis. 18, incl. Duckworth's improvement. Grant May 2, 1836; grant Feb. 18, 1841; registered Apr. 20, 1846.

50 SG 663, EMANUEL SETSER, $5/100 ac., 100 ac. on White Pine Cr., on Cowee Mtn., incl. a cabin & big spring. Entry Feb. 28, 1842; grant Dec. 9, 1844; reg. Apr. 20, 1846.

50 SG 718, EMANUEL SETSER, assignee of THOMAS LOVE Junr., for $315.96, 146 ac., Sec. 8, Dis. 11. Granted Mar. 20, 1845; registered Apr. 20, 1846.

51 SG 719, EMANUEL SETSER, assignee of THOMAS LOVE Junr., for $165.11, 105 ac., Sec. 7, Dis. 11. Granted Mar. 20, 1845; registered Apr. 20, 1846.

52 Mortgage: ELI MCKEE of 1st part, JOAB L. MOORE, of 2nd part, N.S. JARRETT, of 3rd part, all of Macon: whereas McKee owes Jarrett $166 on a note, he now conveys (to Moore) a negro boy named MARTIN, 12 years old, to be sold at public auction if debt not satisfied. Mar. 20, 1846. *Eli McKee, J.S. Moore, N.S. Jarrett.* Wit: *E. DOWDLE,* who proved in court. Registered Apr. 20, 1846.

53 Mortgage: MILES POTTS to ALFRED HALL, both of Macon, for $1, all my crop of oats & corn that I am making in year 1846, also a roan mare. Condition is that Potts is to pay note of $15, payable to JOHN QUEEN with Hall as security. Apr. 14, 1846. *Milas Potts.* Wit: *WILLIAM DRENON, J.H.(A?) POTTS.* Ack. Apr. 6, 1846. Registered Apr. 20, 1846.

54 Sheriff's sale: EZEKIEL DOWDLE, Esq., High Sheriff of Macon Co., to SAMUEL BRYSON of Macon, to satisfy judgment against JOHN FOSTER for $35, 82 ac., Sec. 90, Dis. 10. At public sale, Bryson had high bid of $50.50. Mar. 14, 1845. *E. Dowdle.* Ack. Mar. 1846 court. Registered Apr. 21, 1846.

56 RICHARD WILSON, administrator for DAVID WILLSON of Macon, for $150, to JOHN WILLSON & JAMES WILLSON, jointly, of Macon, 50 ac. on Big Savannah Cr. Oct. 6, 1846. *Richard (his mark) Wilson.* Wit: *W.R. BUCHANAN, THOMAS R. CABE.* Buchanan proved in Mar. 1846 court. Registered Apr. 21, 1846.

57 RICHARD WILLSON to JOHN WILLSON & JAMES WILLSON, all of Macon, for $300, 72+ ac. on Sec. 11, Dis. 8 on Big Savannah. Oct. 6, 1845. *Richard (his X mark) Willson.* Wit: *WM. R. BUCHANAN, THOMAS R. CABE.* Buchanan proved in Mar. 1846 court. Registered Apr. 21, 1846.

58 RICHARD WILLSON to JOHN WILLSON & JAMES WILLSON, all of Macon, for $50, 99 ac. near Savannah Cr. Oct. 6, 1845. *Richard (his X mark) Willson.* Wit: *W.R. BUCHANAN, THOMAS R. CABE.* Buchanan proved in Mar. 1846 court. Registered Apr. 21, 1846.

58 RICHARD WILLSON to JOHN WILLSON & JAMES WILLSON, all of Macon, for $100, 100 ac. on Savannah Cr., Dis. 8. Oct. 6, 1845. *Richard (his X mark) Willson.* Wit: *W.R. BUCHANAN, THOMAS R. CABE.* Buchanan proved in Mar. 1846 court. Registered Apr. 21, 1846.

59 RICHARD WILLSON to JOHN WILLSON & JAMES WILLSON, all of Macon, 99 ac. on Savanah Cr., bd. BUCHANAN. Oct. 6, 1845. *Richard (his X mark) Wilson.* Wit: *W.R. BUCHANAN, THOMAS R. CABE.* Buchanan proved in Mar. 1846 court. Registered Apr 21, 1846.

60 RICHARD WILLSON to JOHN WILLSON & JAMES WILLSON, all of Macon, 100 ac. on Savannah Cr. Oct. 6, 1845. *Richard (his X mark) Willson.* Wit: *W.R. BUCHANAN, THOMAS R. CABE.* Buchanan proved in Mar. 1846 court. Registered Apr. 21, 1846.

61 RICHARD WILLSON to JOHN WILLSON for $300, Negro boy named ALFRED, age abt. 16 years old. Oct. 6, 1845. *Richard (his X mark) Willson.* Wit: *W.R. BUCHANAN, THOMAS R. CABE.* Buchanan proved in Mar. 1846 court. Registered Apr. 21, 1846.

61 RICHARD WILLSON to JAMES WILLSON, for $300, Negro girl HARRIETT, age 14. Oct. 6, 1845. *Richard (his X mark) Willson.* Wit: *W.R. BUCHANAN, THOMAS R. CABE.* Buchanan proved in Mar. 1846 court. Registered Apr. 21, 1846.

62 Haywood Co. NC: MARGARIT DAVIDSON to ZEBULON THOMAS of Macon, for $500, Negro girl ADELINE. Jan. 15, 1846. *Margarit (her X mark) Davidson.* Wit: *A.L. DAVIDSON, H.L. POTTS.* Potts proved in Mar. 1846 court. Registered Apr. 21, 1846.

63 Sheriff's sale: THOS. M. ANGEL, Esq., High Sheriff of Macon Co., to TRAVIS EL-
    MORE of Macon, to satisfy judgment against JOHN DAVIS, THOS. AMMONS, JOHN
    LOWDERMILK & JERRY BARTON/BERTON for $115.23 3/4, a tract of land of sd.
    Thomas Ammons' on Sugar town fork. At public sale Feb. 12, 1844, Elmore had high
    bid of $10.15. Aug. 18, 1845. *Thos. M. Angel.* Wit: *LEM'L BIRD, E. BIRD.* Ack. in
    court. Registered Apr. 21, 1846.

64 LETTY N. GARRETT to MATHEW GARRETT, both of Macon, for $125, 58 ac., same
    granted to Letty N. Garrett, assignee of JAMES COCKERHAM by SG 655. Aug. 21,
    1845. *Letty N. Garrett.* Wit: *A.B. (his X mark) GARRETT, MONTGOMERY MCLEIR.*
    A.B. Garrett proved in Mar. 1846 court. Registered Apr. 22, 1846.

66 Heirs of WILLIAM MCCONNELL, dec'd, of one part, of Macon, to DAVID MCCON-
    NELL, one of the heirs, also of Macon, of the other part, for $250, part of Sec. 3, Dis. 15
    on W. side of Tennessee R. Feb. 27, 1837. Signed: *MILAS (his X mark) MCCONNELL,
    MARTHA (her X mark) MCCONNELL, ENOS SCROGGS, JANE SCROGGS, JOHN
    SCROGGS, MARY (her X mark) SCROGGS, WM. CABE, ELIZABETH CABE, J.D.
    DRYMAN, RACHEL (her X mark) DRYMAN, SARAH (her X mark) MCCONNELL, MAR-
    GARET (her X mark) CARPENTER, JONATHAN DENTON, AGNES (her X mark) DEN-
    TON, SANFORD CARPENTER, PATIENCE (her X mark) CARPENTER, JOHN
    MCCONNELL, MARY (her X mark) MCCONNELL, WILLIAM MCCONNELL, SARAH
    (her X mark) MCCONNELL, CHARLES STILES, KESIAH (her X mark) STILES.* Wit:
    MILAS (his X mark) MCCONNELL, who proved in Mar. 1846 court. Registered Apr. 22,
    1846.

67 WILLIAM PRUITT of Macon to ABNER MOORE of Cherokee Co. NC, 355 ac., Sec.
    131, Dis. 2, on Shooting Cr., now Cherokee Co, purchased at 1838 sale. Mar. 18, 1846.
    William (his X mark) Pruitt. Wit: *A.J. PATTON, J.R. ALLMAN* Patton proved in Mar.
    1846 court. Registered Apr.22, 1846.

67 THOMAS KIMZEY to DAVID MCCONNELL, both of Macon, for $9.87 1/2, reversion-
    ary interest Kimzey has in 158 ac., Sec. 75, Dis. 15. Aug. 20, 1845. *Thomas Kimsey.* Wit:
    WILLIAM DONALDSON, ELISHA KIMZEY. Donaldson proved in Mar. 1846 court.
    Registered Apr. 22, 1846.

69 JESSE SAUNDERS is bound to JAMES KIMZY for $16, for part of Sec. 104, Dis. 15.
    Feb. 22, 1839. *Jesse (his X mark) Saunders.* Wit: *JOHN MCDOWELL,* who proved in
    Mar. 1846 court. Registered Apr. 22, 1846.

69 REBECCA WOODFIN to GEORGE W. PARTON, both of Macon, for $5.62 1/2, 50 ac.
    purchased by JAMES BELK, dec'd, in 1820 sale, Sec. 46, Dis. 17, on Burningtown Cr.
    Mar. 14, 1846. *Rebecca Woodfin.* Wit: *THOS. WELCH, D.H. ALLEN.* Welch proved in
    Mar. 1846 court. Registered Apr. 22, 1846.

70 MARTIN MCCOY to JOHN A. WILLSON, both of Macon, for $50, 58 ac. in Dis. 11,
    W. side of Ellijay Cr. Jan. 4, 1845. *Martin McCoy.* Wit: *JOHN A. WILLIAMS, A.J.
    MOORE.* Ack. in Mar. 1846 court. Registered Apr. 22, 1846.

71 Gift: JOHN COCKERHAM of Macon, for natural love & affection for beloved son-in-
    law MATISON COCKERHAM of Macon, all my goods and chattels, 3 horses, 7 cattle,
    50 hogs, 100 bu. corn, all household & kitchen furniture. Jan. 10, 1846. *John (his X
    mark) Cockerham.* Wit: *URIAH C. BURNS, N. BURCHFIELD.* Proven by Burchfield in
    Mar. 1846 court. Registered Apr. 22, 1846.

72 ABRAHAM WIGGINS of Macon to JOHN WEST, Senr., for $50, 53 ac., S. bank of N.
    fork of Junaluskas or Elarka (Alarka) Cr., Dis. 5. Mar. 18, 1846. *Abraham (his X mark)
    Wiggins.* Wit: *D. MCCOY.* Ack. in Mar. 1846 court. Registered Apr. 22, 1846.

72 ABRAHAM WIGGINS to JOHN WEST Junr., for $25, 50 ac. on east side of Junaluska
    Cr. Mar. 12, 1845. *Abram (his X mark) Wiggins.* Wit: *D. MCCOY, DANIEL WEST.*
    Proven by McCoy in Mar. 1846 court. Registered Apr. 22, 1846.

73 DANIEL WEST to JOHN WEST Jr. for $300, 50 ac. on Alarka Cr., Dis. 8. Mar. 17, 1846. *Daniel West.* Wit: *D. MCCOY.* Ack. in Mar. 1846 court. Registered Apr. 22, 1846.

74 Gift: JOHN COCKERHAM to MATISON COCKERHAM, son-in-law of John, both of Macon, for natural love, etc., also for better maintenance & preferments of Matison, 50 ac. where John now lives, also 100 ac. adjoining tract, also another 50 ac, all in Dis. 10: No. 672, 671 & 36. Jan. 10, 1846. *John (his X mark) Cockerham.* Wit: *URIAH C. BURNS, N. BIRCHFIELD.* Birchfield proved in Mar. 1846 court. Registered Apr. 22, 1846.

76 WILLIAM WILLIAMS of Macon to JOHN WILSON for $50, 68 ac., Sec. 110, Dis. 11, on "Ellijha" (Ellijay) Cr. Sep. 1, 1841. *William Williams.* Wit: *N.H. PALMER, JAMES D. FRANKS.* Franks proved in Mar. 1846 court. Registered Apr. 22, 1846.

77 JOAB L. MOORE of Cherokee Co. NC to ABNER MOORE of Macon, for $100, 80 ac., Sec. 133, Dis. 2, Cherokee County, Muskrat's Fork of Shooting Creek. Apr. 15, 1842. *J.L. Moore.* Wit: *J.R. SILER, JCB TRAMMELL.* Ack. in Mar. 1846 court. Registered Apr. 24, 1846.

77 JOHN H. AMMONS of Cherokee Co. NC to ABNER MOORE of Macon, for $450, 176 ac., Sec. 135, Dis. 2. Mar. 15, 1842. *John H. Ammons.* Wit: *JAMES PEEK, H.R. KIMZEY.* Peek proved in Mar. 1846 court. Registered Apr. 24, 1846.

78 Mortgage: DAVID RAIDER of the 1st part, JOEL SAWYERS of the 2nd part, JESSE R. SILER of 3rd part, all of Macon, whereas Siler holds several debts on Raider totaling $150, Raider conveys to Sawyers as security, for $1, 52 ac., Sec. 132, Dis. 8, also 3 horse beasts, 15 cattle, 5 milk cows, 2 oxen, 8 cattle, 40 hogs, 24 sheep, household & kitchen furniture. If Raider shall not pay debts as they come due, Sawyer to sell property to highest bidder. Mar. 18, 1846. *David (his mark) Raider, Joel Sawyers.* Wit: *JOSHUA ROBERTS, E.M. HALL.* Hall proved in Mar. 1846 court. Registered Apr. 8, 1846.

80 SARAH ENLOE to W.W. DOBSON for $300, 40 ac., Sec. 78, Dis. 15, near the old still house... on branch near the meeting house, bd. JOHN MCDOWELL; also one other tract, being dower assigned me as widow of ASAPH ENLOE, dec'd, 70 ac. on Tennessee River, Sec. 70, Dis. 15, near the still house, the first tract forever and the last my life estate as widow. Aug. 13, 1839. *Sarah Enloe.* Wit: *J.W. GUINN, WM. M. ENLOE.* Guinn proved in Mar. 1846 court. REgistered Apr. 24, 1846.

81 JONATHAN PHILLIPS, Ch'man of the Court of Pleas & Qtr. Sessions of Macon, to JAMES W. GUINN of Macon, for several sums, lots in Franklin: for $125, No. 29 on Main St. (1 ac.); $20, No. 25 (1 ac.); $26, No. 24, on Main St. (1 ac.); $20, No. 41 (150 poles); $20, No. 42 (150 poles); $21, No. 43 (150 poles). Jan. 22, 1839. *J. Phillips, Ch.* Wit: *JASON L. HYATT.* Signature proved by J.R. ALLMAN & E. DOWDLE, Mar. 1846 court. Registered Apr. 24, 1846.

83 JAMES ROBINSON to JAMES W. GUINN, both of Macon, for $600, 2 parcels in Franklin, one bd. Guinn & JOAB L. MOORE on Main St., No. 11 (1 ac.), 2nd, part of lot adj. No. 19, bd. Methodist church lands on S., bd. line of Seminary land (91 poles). Sep. 14, 1839. *Jas. Robinson.* Wit: *J. PHILLIPS, E. DOWDLE.* Dowdle proved in Mar. 1846 court. Registered Apr. 24, 1846.

84 JOHN PHILLIPS to JOHN R. ALLMAN, both of Macon, for $8, 4 ac. on Sugartown fork of Tennessee R. Dec. 13, 1845. *John Phillips.* Wit: *E. PHIPPS, HENRY MILLER.* Ack. in Mar. 1846 court. Registered Apr. 24, 1846.

85 JAMES CONLY to WILLIAM HYDE, both of Macon, for $5, 100 ac. on Tuckasegee R. Nov. 22, 1845. *James Conly.* Wit: *J.W. HYDE, WM. ANGEL.* Ack. in Mar. 1846 court. Registered Apr. 24, 1846.

86 THOMAS M. ANGEL of Macon to JESSEY KIRBY of Cherokee Co. NC, for $25, 4 ac. on Ellijay Cr., part of Sec. 56, Dis. 11, on public road, incl. house where Kirby formerly lived. Feb. 10, 1846. *Jesse Kirby.* Wit: *WALLACE A. MOORE, BENJAMIN STILES.* Stiles proved in Mar. 1846 court. Registered Apr. 24, 1846.

87 JOHN P. MOORE to THOMAS M. ANGEL, both of Macon, for $200, 36 ac., Sec. 55,
    Dis. 11, Ellijay Cr., on conditional corner between me & Angel, made by HENRY
    HAGAN.. to side of mill pond. Mar. 2, 1846. *John (his X mark) P. Moore*. Wit:
    ABRAHAM MOORE, ANDREW J. MOORE. Abraham Moore proved in Mar. 1846 court.
    Registered Apr. 24, 1846.

88 Mortgage: JOHN HALL to THOMAS M. MOORE, both of Macon, 178 ac., Sec. 40,
    Dis. 16. Condition: Moore endorsed note in favor of North Carolina and signed by
    THOS. W.P. POINDEXTER as principal for $25. Land is security. Jan. 24, 1846. *John
    Hall*. Wit: *SOLOMON T. CLAYTON*. Ack. in Mar. 1846 court. Registered Apr. 25, 1846.

89 WILLIAM HOOD, executor of estate of JOHN HOOD, dec'd, of Macon, to JOHN
    GALASPY of Macon, for $70, 80 ac., Sec. 37, Dis. 15, crossing Wolf (Wayah) Creek.
    Mar. 19, 1846. *William Hood*. Wit: *THOS. M. ANGEL, MOSES ADDINGTON*. Ack. in
    Mar. 1846 court. Registered Apr. 25, 1846.

90 Sheriff's sale: THOS. M. ANGEL, Esq. High Sheriff of Macon, to TRAVIS ELMORE,
    to satisfy judgment against property of JOHN DAVIS, THOMAS AMMONS, J. LOW-
    DERMILK & JERRYMIAH BARTON FOR $115.23 1/2, 59 AC., Sec. 54, Dis. 12. At
    public sale Feb. 12, 1844, Elmore had high bid of $10.05. Mar. 17, 1846. *Thos. M.
    Angel*. Wit: *LEM'L BIRD, C. BIRD*. Ack. in Mar. 1846 court. Registered Apr. 27, 1846.

91 Sheriff's sale: THOS. M. ANGEL, Esq., High Sheriff of Macon, to TRAVIS ELMORE
    of Macon, to satisfy judgment against JOHN DAVIS, T. AMMONS, J. LOWDERMILK,
    J. BARTON/BURTON for $115.23 1/2, recovered in part of JEREMIAH BURTON, 100
    ac. on Ellijay Cr, Dis. 11, incl. the Hickory Flats. At sale Feb. 12, 1844, Elmore had high
    bid of $7.20. Feb. 12, 1844. *Thos. M. Angel*. Wit: *J. R. LAMBERT, JAS. RUSSELL*. Ack.
    Mar. 1846 court. Registered Apr. 27, 1846.

93 Sheriff's sale: same case as above; THOS. M. ANGEL, Esq., High Sheriff of Macon, to
    TRAVIS ELMORE, the court commanding Angel to seize propery of JOHN DAVIS, 50
    ac. on mouth of Watauga Cr. Elmore had high bid of 75 cents. Feb. 12, 1844. *Thos. M.
    Angel*. Wit: *J.R. LAMBERT, JAS. RUSSELL*. Ack. in Mar. 1846 court. Registered Apr.
    27, 1846.

95 JAMES W. GUINN of Randolph Co., Ala. to JOHN R. ALLMAN of Macon, for $2,000,
    140 ac., corner of town lot 5, on Tennessee River. Mar. 17, 1846. *James W. Guinn*. Wit:
    SAUL SMITH, W. BRYSON. Ack. in Mar. 1846 court. Registered Apr. 27, 1846.

96 Sheriff's sale: ELI MCKEE, Esq., High Sheriff of Macon, to W.W. DOBSON of Macon,
    to satisfy 2 executions against real estate descending to ROBERT H. ENLOE, SARAH
    ANN ENLOE, WM. B. ENLOE, A.H. ENLOE, ASAPH T. ENLOE, ALFRED P.
    ENLOE, CHRISTOPHER C. ENLOE, minor heirs at law of ASAPH ENLOE, for
    $1,002.89 and $1,101.89 recovered by state against heirs. The property was on Ten-
    nessee R., Sec. 70, Dis. 15, crossing "Ruches" (Rush's) Branch, 185 ac., excepting life es-
    tate of SARAH ENLOE as laid off by jury as her dower of Asaph, dec'd. At public sale,
    Dobson had high bid of $400. Aug. 12, 1839. *Eli McKee, Sh'ff*. Wit: *J.W. GUINN, RIS-
    DON COOPER*. Guinn proved in Mar. 1846 court. Registered Apr. 27, 1846.

98 SG 746, JULIAS DEAN, $10.50, 50 ac., Sec. 22, Dis. 9, NE bank of Tennessee R.
    Granted Apr. 2, 1846; registered June 8, 1846.

99 SG 747, JULIAS DEAN, $11.49, 54+ ac., Sec. 23, Dis. 9. Granted Apr. 2, 1846;
    registered June 8, 1846.

100 SG 748, JULIAS DEAN, $8.42, 58+ ac., Sec. 24, Dis. 9, Tennessee R. Granted Apr. 2,
    1946; June 8, 1846.

100 SG 749, E.M. KILPATRICK, $13.21, 59 ac., Sec. 2 of JENNY's Reservation. Granted
    Apr. 2, 1846; registered June 8, 1846.

101 SG 305, DEMPSY RABY, $10.23, 52 ac., Sec. 30, Dis. 10 on Cane Cr. Granted Dec. 12,
    1836; registered June 8, 1846.

102 SG 306, DEMPSY RABY, $11.75, 57 ac., Sec. 31, Dis. 10, Cox Creek. Granted Dec. 12, 1836; registered June 8, 1846.

103 SG 629, A.M. RUSSELL, $5/100 ac., 6+ ac., Sugartown R. Entry Jan. 30, 1843; grant Dec. 9, 1844; registered June 8, 1846.

104 SG 677, WILLIAM WEST, $5/100 ac., 100 ac. on Tennessee R., bd. SHEPHERD. Entry Jan. 2, 1846; grant apr. 2, 1846; registered June 19, 1846.

105 SG 672, DAVID NORTON, $5/100 ac., 100 ac. on Chattooga R., incl. the Bull pen improvements. Entry Jun. 1, 1843; grant Dec. 10, 1845; registered June 19, 1846.

105 SG 608, THOMAS B. GRANT, $5/100 ac., 100 ac. on Tennessee R. Entry Jan. 1, 1841; grant Dec. 9, 1844; registered June 19, 1846.

106 T.J. ROANE to JOHN Y. HICKS, both of Macon, for $10, 50 ac. in Dis. 15, on Thompson's fork of "Cartoogahee". Jan. 29, 1844. *T.J. Roane.* Wit: *THOMAS M. MOORE.* Ack. in June 1846 court. Registered Aug. 1, 1846.

107 T.J. ROANE to JOHN Y. HICKS, both of Macon, for $10, 100+ ac., Sec. 63, Dis. 15, on Thompson's fork of "Cartoogahee". Jan. 29, 1844. *T.J. Roane.* Wit: *THOMAS M. MOORE.* Ack. in June 1846 court. Registered Aug. 1, 1846.

108 DAVID GRIFFITH to SAMUEL JACKSON, both of Macon, for $100, 50 ac., Dis. 15. Feb. 12, 1845. *David Griffith.* Wit: *A.B. DONALDSON, JOHN A. LONG.* Donaldson proved in June 1846 court. Registered Aug. 1, 1846.

109 JOSEPH J. LOWDERMILK of Morgan Co. GA to JACOB SHOAP of Macon, for $150, land in Cherokee Co. NC, Dis. 4, Sec. 13, on Notley R. Apr. 29, 1846. *Joseph J. Lowdermilk.* Wit: *DAVID ALLEN,* who proved in June 1846 court. Registered Aug. 1, 1846.

109 ELI GILBERT WATSON to JOHN H. WATSON, both of Macon, for $5, 50 ac. in Dis. 7. June 9, 1844. *E.G. Watson.* Wit: *S. MCDOWELL.* Ack. in June 1846 court. Registered Aug. 1, 1846.

110 JAMES WITHROW to CURTIS SAUNDERS, both of Macon, for $50, 65 ac., No. 1168 Dis. 10, bd. WILLIAM G. WATTS. Jan. 2, 1846. *James Withrow.* Wit: *WILBORNE SAUNDERS, JOHN (his X mark) BAYNS.* Proven by Wilborne Saunders in June 1846. Registered Aug. 1, 1846.

111 JAMES WITHROW of Macon to HENRY SAUNDERS for $100, 63 ac., Sec. 116, Dis. 10, on Watauga Cr. Dec. 27, 1845. *James Withrow.* Wit: *BARNETT WILSON, CURTIS SANDERS.* Proven by Curtis Sanders in June 1846 court. Registered Aug. 1, 1846.

112 JAMES WITHROW to CURTIS SAUNDERS for $500, 105+ ac., Sec. 50, Dis. 10. Dec. 26, 1845. *James Withrow.* Wit: *MADISON SAUNDERS, WILBORN SAUNDERS.* Proven by Wilborn Sanders in June 1846 court. Registered Aug. 1, 1846.

112 SG 642, HENSON QUEEN, $22.20, 78+ ac., Sec. 28, Dis. 17 on Tennessee R. Granted Aug. 18, 1843; registered Aug. 1, 1846.

113 SG 752, WILLIAM BIRD, $21.30, 160 ac., Sec. 16, Dis. 11. Granted Apr. 2, 1846; registered Aug. 1, 1846.

114 SG 661, GILBERT WATSON, $5/100 ac., 50 ac., Dis. 7, on Cullewhee Cr., bd. PETER LONG. Entry Jan. 22, 1841; grant Jan. 28, 1845; registered Aug. 1, 1846.

114 SG 678, BRYANT CONLEY, $5/100 ac., 100 ac. on Tessentee Cr., incl. a saw mill. Entry Jan. 27, 1845; grant Apr. 7, 1846; registered Aug. 1, 1846.

115 SG 751, THOMAS M. ANGEL, assignee of JESSE KIRBY, for $121, 57 ac., Sec. 37, Dis. 11, incl. an Indian improvement. Granted Apr. 2, 1846; registered Oct. 31, 1846.

116 JOHN AMMONS to WILLIAM HOLLBROOK for $175, 86 ac. on Cats Cr., Dis. 11. Jan. 30, 1843. *John Ammons.* Wit: *E. SETSER, M.B. STARR(?)* Setser proved in Sep. 1846 court. Registered Oct. 31, 1846.

117 SG 734, WILLIS GUY, assignee of JOHN HYDE, for $186.46, 117 ac., Sec. 20, Dis. 12. Granted Aug. 16, 1845; registered Oct. 31, 1846.

118 JACOB B. TRAMMELL to ALISON D. MCKINNEY for $500, Entry 100 on Chattooga
R., 500 ac., reserving to use of EPHRAIM AMMONS one-half of minerals. Sep. 17,
1845. *J.C.B. Trammell.* Wit: *E.L. ALLISON, WM. R. MCDOWELL.* Ack. in Sep. 1846
court. Registered Nov. 4, 1846.

119 AARON SMITH of Cherokee Co. NC to JOHN HOWARD of Macon, for $25, 54 ac. on
Middle Cr., Sec. 26, Dis. 13, bought at 1836 sale. Sep. 22, 1846. *A. Smith.* Wit: *SAUL
SMITH.* Ack. in Sep. 1846 court. Registered Nov. 4, 1846.

119 JAMES WILSON of Macon to D. LOVE, for $400, a certain Molatto or negro man
named ISAM, age abt. 40 years. Sep. 21, 1846. *James Willson.* Wit: *J.R. SILER.* Ack. in
Sep. 1846 court. Registered Nov. 4, 1846.

120 ALLEN SHEARER to WILLIAM D. HART (DEHART), both of Macon, for $165, 2
tracts in Dis. 17: Sec. 81 (62 ac.), Sec. 80, crossing Lick Log Cr. (50 ac.). Aug. 1, 1846.
Allen Sherer. Wit: *ELI MCKEE,* who proved in Sep. 1846 court. Registered Nov. 4, 1846.

121 JOHN BRYSON, Senr. to WILLIAM H. BRYSON, both of Macon, John's part of a
grant for 76 ac., Sec. 8, Dis. 7, which they obtained together. Oct. 15, 1841. *W.H.
Bryson.* Wit: *THOS. M. ANGEL, J.B. ALLISON.* Allison proved in Sep. 1846 court.
Registered Nov. 5, 1846.

122 JOHN WILLSON to WILLIAM TATHAM, both of Macon, for $30, his part in 100-ac.
parcel held jointly on Savannah Cr., entered Mar. 29, 1846, except 10 ac. marked off for
a mill site. Aug. 15, 1846. *John Willson.* Wit: *WM. H. HIGDIN, W.R. BUCHANAN.* Higdin proved in Sep. 1846 court. Registered Nov. 9, 1846.

123 JONATHAN BIRD of Burke Co. NC to LEMUEL BIRD of Macon, for $600, 142 ac. on
"Iolee" (Iotla) Cr., Sec. 56, Dis. 16, where Lemuel now lives. Aug. 13, 1845. *Jonathan
Bird.* Wit: *B.J. BIRD, J.A. CURTIS.* Curtis proved in Sep. 1846 court. Registered Nov.
10, 1846.

124 CURTIS SAUNDERS of Macon to SAMUEL REID, JOSEPH BRANDLE and
THOMAS MASHBURN, school committeemen for 11th school dis. of Macon, land on
W. side of Branch from School house, line of No. 48, with the wind of fence through
school house yard to a stake a few rods above chimney of school house; in trust for
school and meeting house in 11th dis. Jan. 19, 1846. *Curtis Saunders.* Wit: *D. MCCOY,
MADISON SAUNDERS.* McCoy proved in Sep. 1846 court. Registered Nov. 10, 1846.

125 ALEXANDER WILLSON to WM. H. BRYSON, both of Macon, for $65, 100 ac. on
Chattooga R., Dis. 18, bd. MCKINNEY. Dec. 22, 1845. *Alex Wilson.* Wit: *WM. W. LOW-
DERMILK, JNO. C. BRYSON.* Proven by John C. Bryson, Sep. 1846 court. Registered
Nov. 10, 1846.

126 RICHD. WILSON, late of Macon, for $400, to JAMES WILSON of Macon, Negro man,
ISAM, abt. 37 yrs. Aug. 12, 1843. *Richard (his X mark) Wilson.* Wit: *J.M. ANGEL,
JOHN W. DILLS.* Angel proved in Sep. 1846 court. Registered Nov. 10, 1846.

126 JOSEPH CLEMENTS to JOHN W. QUEEN Jr., for $500, 2 tracts on Tennessee R., Dis.
17: 79+ ac., Sec. 30; also 100 ac. Nov. 17, 1842. *Joseph Clements.* Wit: *ALFRED HALL,
RILEY MARTIN.* Hall proved in Sep. 1846 court. Registered Nov. 11, 1846.

127 JOHN BRYSON to WILLIAM H. BRYSON, for $50, 10+ ac. on Cullowhee Cr., river
road. Sep. 10, 1846. *John Bryson.* Wit: *J.B. ALLISON, MILTON M. BRYSON.* Allison
proved in Sep. 1846 court. Registered Nov. 11, 1846.

128 RODERICK NORTON, ELIAS NORTON & EDWARD NORTON to JOSHUA AM-
MONS & EPHRAIM OSBOURN, all of Macon, for $200, 640 ac. on Chattooga R., on
Georgia line, near "Elliot's" (Ellicott's) Rock on S.C. and Ga. lines. Aug. 12, 1845.
Roderick Norton, Elias Norton, Edward Norton. Wit: *E. DOWDLE, TRAVES (his X
mark) ELMORE, JAMES (his X mark) LEDFORD.* Dowdle proved in Sep. 1846 court.
Registered Nov. 12, 1846.

130 NATHAN PILKINGTON before DANIEL MCCOY, both of Macon; he purchased land on W. side of Nantahala R., Sec. 38, Dis. 12, in Cherokee land sale, 1838, but certificate was lost. Aug. 29, 1846. Acknowledged, *N. Pilkington*. Wit: *J.K. GRAY*. This day before Daniel McCoy, one of the acting justices of the peace of Macon County, JAMES LED-BETTER swore he purchased land of Nathan Pilkington, W. side Nantahala R., Sec. 38, Dis. 12, in 1838, and certificate was lost. *James Ledbetter*. Wit: *Daniel McCoy*. Ack. in Sep. 1846 court. Registered Nov. 12, 1846.

131 TRAVIS ELMORE and THOMAS AMMONS to JAMES HENSTON, all of Macon, for $300, 4 tracts: 50 ac. on Walnut Cr. of Sugartown fork; 59 ac., Sec. 64, Dis. 12; 100 ac. on Walnut Cr., Sec. 151, Dis. 12; 20 ac. adjoining these. Mar. 17, 1846. *Travis (his X mark) Elmore*. Wit: *STEPHEN MONDAY, THOS. M. ANGEL*. Monday proved in Sep. 1846 court. Registered Nov. 12, 1846.

132 CLARK GUY to ISAAC MOORE, both of Macon, for $8.50, 50 ac. entered Sep. 27, 1841, on Sugartown R., bd. WIDOW BRYSON. Mar. 20, 1846. *Clark Guy*. Wit: *ISAAC N. KEENER, M.N. RUSSEL*. Ack. in Sep. 1846 court. Registered Nov. 12, 1846.

133 CHRISTOPHER SETSER to JAMES D. FRANKS, both of Macon, for $100, 146 ac., Sec. 12, Dis. 11, purchased at 1836 sale. Sep. 30, 1840. *C. Setser*. Wit: *U. KEENER, HIRAM LEDFORD*. Ack. in Sep. 1846 court. Registered Nov. 12, 1846.

143 JOEL SIMONDS to BYNUM W. BELL, both of Macon, for $31.25, 70 ac. on Tuck-asegee R., line of DICK's reservation. Sep. 22, 1846. *Joel Simonds*. Wit: *J.Y. HICK, E.M. HALL*. Ack. in Sep. 1846 court. Registered Nov. 12, 1846.

135 Bond: DAVID R. LOWRY, B.W. BELL, JESSE R. SILER, BURTON K. DICKEY, JOHN HOWARD, SILAS MCDOWELL, WILLIAM TATHAM, post $4,000 bond for Lowry, duly elected clerk of Superior Court. Registered Nov. 23, 1846.

135 Bond: Second bond for DAVID R. LOWRY, duly elected clerk of Superior Court; amount of $10,000; same principals as previous.

136 Bond: J.K. GRAY, J.R. SILER, SILAS MCDOWELL post $4,000 bond for Gray, duly elected clerk of Court of Pleas and Quarter Sessions. Sep. 22, 1846. Registered Nov. 23, 1846.

137 Bond: Second bond for J.K. GRAY, duly elected clerk of Court of Pleas and Quarter Sessions; amount of $10,000; same principals as previous.

137 Mortgage: JOHN HALL of Macon to MATHEW MASHBURN, 178 ac., Sec. __, Dis. 16, or so much as will amount to $100, to secure SILAS MCDOWELL & GATHER B. JACOBS, who went bond for Hall for prosecution of suit in which he is plaintiff & __ WHITAKER is defendant. Oct. 10, 1846. *John Hall*. Wit: *J.R. ALLMAN, JAS. (his X mark) CUNNINGHAM*. Proven by Allman Nov. 21, 1846 before J.K. GRAY, clerk. Registered Nov. 23, 1846.

138 Mortgage: ELI MCKEE of 1st part, JOAB L. MORE of 2nd part; THOMAS J. ROANE & JOHN HOWARD of 3rd part, all of Macon. McKee for $100 paid by Moore conveys to him the following Negro slaves: MARY ANA, a woman of dark complexion aged abt. 26, her female child, MILLY, also of dark complexion, abt. 10 years, also her other female child, VIOLET, of dark complexion, age abt. 8, all sound & healthy. Condition: Howard & Roane are security for McKee to the Bank of Cape Fear for $300; the property is conveyed to Moore in trust as security. Sep. 24, 1846. Signed: *Eli McKee, J.L. Moore, J. Howard, T.J. Roane*. Wit: *J.H. HUNTER*, who proved in Sep. 1846 court. Registered Dec. 31, 1846.

140 Mortgage: ELI MCKEE of 1st part, JOAB L. MOORE of 2nd part, N.S. JARRETT & JOHN SILER of 3rd part. McKee is indebted to Jarrett & Siler in amount of $137.45. To secure loan, he mortgages to Moore a certain Negro girl, ADELINE, aged __ years. Sep. 25, 1846. Signed: *Eli McKee, Joab L. Moore, N.S. Jarrett, John Siler*. Wit: *G.W.J. MOORE*, who proved in Sep. 1846 court. Registered Dec. 3, 1846.

141 Mortgage: JOHN SHERRELL of Macon to SAMUEL SHERRELL of Haywood Co.
NC, the listed property for $1,000 due to Asheville branch of Bank of Cape Fear by loans
- one of $500 with Samuel as security, one of $500 with Samuel as principal but in fact
for John: one sorrel mare with bold face, one claybank stud colt, one bay stud in hands of
ASAPH SHERRELL, 4 cattle, all my stock hogs, crop of corn & crop of tobacco, also 50
ac. where R. BLACKBURN lives - all my assets except my house. Oct. 7, 1846. *John
Sherrell*. Wit: *NATH'L BLACKBUN, GEORGE (his X mark) SHULER*. Proven by Shuler
in Oct. 1846, in clerk's office. Registered Dec. 3, 1846.

143 Mortgage: JOHN HALL to THOMAS M. MOORE, both of Macon, my part of crop of
corn now standing on land occupied by Mr. SOLOMON CLAYTON, being 1/3 part of
corn & fodder, also my interest in corn & fodder growing in what is known by name of
the MASSEY field and crop of tobacco standing near house in which I live. Condition:
Moore is security for sum of $100 due by Moore & Hall to THOMAS WELCH; this
mortgages secures him against harm should Hall fail in suit he has instituted against
Welch in Macon Superior Court, or fail to pay costs & charges. June 15, 1846. *John
Hall*. Wit: *EDWARD (his X mark) A. HORTON*. Ack. Sep. 21, 1846 before clerk.
Registered Dec. 3, 1846.

144 WILLIAM H. THOMAS of Haywood Co. NC to Capt. N.J. JARRETT of Macon, for
$122, 122 ac. on Nantahala R., purchased of state by HENRY GRADY, Sec. 2, Dis. 12.
June 15, 1846. *Wm. H. Thomas*. Wit: *J.R. ALLMAN, J.M. BRYSON*. Proven by Allman in
Dec. 1846 court. Registered Dec. 17, 1846.

144 ELISHA THOMAS of "Raburn" (Rabun) Co. GA to ARON THOMAS of Macon, for
$40, 100 ac. on Flats of Middle Cr. where Aron Thomas now lives, granted by state to
Elisha. Mar. 5, 1845. *Elisah Thomas*. Wit: *JOHN __ (illeg), J. HOWARD*. Proven by
Howard in Dec. 1846 court. Registered Jan. 9, 1847.

145 JOHN STEPHENSON to J.R. SILER for $900, 235 ac. on "Cartoogajaya" (Car-
toogechaye) Cr., Dis. 16. Jun. 13, 1843. *John Stevenson*. Wit: *GEORGE MCCLURE,*
who proved in Dec. 1846 court. Registered Jan. 9, 1847.

146 JOHN STEPHENSON of Union Co. GA to WILLIAM ANGEL of Macon, for $181, 64
ac., Sec. 4, Dis. 16, S. side of "Cartoogajay" Cr. Jun. 24, 1843. *John Stevenson*. Wit:
GEORGE MCCLURE, who proved in Dec. 1846 court. Registered Jan. 9, 1847.

147 Gift: WILLIAM COCKERHAM of Macon for natural love & affection for SARAH
COCKERHAM, WILLIAM COCKERHAM, JOHN C. COCKERHAM, DAN'L COCK-
ERHAM, CHARITY COCKERHAM, ELIZABETH A. COCKERHAM, DAVID
COCKERHAM & the infant or youngest child, name not known, all children of DAN'L
S. & CELIA COCKERHAM: one new green painted waggon & Gearing, bay horse, sor-
rel horse, bay steed, gray mare, brown mare, black mare, also 7 beds & furniture, 150
yds. of domestic cloth & all the cooking utensils at Dan'l S. Cockerham's. Dec. 16, 1846.
Wm. Cockerham. Wit: *E. DOWDLE*. Ack. in Dec. 1846 court. Registered Jan. 9, 1847.

148 JOHN ZACHARY to JONATHAN ZACHARY, MORDECAI ZACKERY, & WOOD-
FORD ZACKERY, all of Macon, for $800, three tracts: 640 ac. on Chattooga R., Dis.
18, bd. T.J. ZACHARY; 100 ac. on Chattooga R., Dis. 18; another 100 ac. tract on Chattooga, Dis. 18. Nov. 14, 1846. *Jno. Zachary*. Wit: *ELIAS NORTON,* who proved in Dec.
1846 court. Registered Jan. 9, 1847.

150 Mortgage: THOMAS M. MOORE to JESSE R. SILER, both of Macon, whereas Moore
owes DAVID L. SWAIN of Chapel Hill $650, due Jan. next, he conveys to Siler as
security three Negro slaves: JACKSON, 12 years, LIZZY, 8 years and LEA, 7 years.
Dec. 9, 1846. *Thos. M. Moore*. Wit: *SAMUEL ROBINSON, D.E. HEAD*. Proven by
Robinson in Dec. 1846 court. Registered Jan. 9, 1847.

151 BARNETT WILLSON to WILLIAM SILER, both of Macon, for $200, 127+ ac., Sec.
32, Dis. 15, on Cartoogechaye Cr. Oct. 2, 1846. *Barnett Willson*. Wit: *JACOB SILER,*
who proved in Dec. 1846 court. Registered Jan. 9, 1847.

151 WILLIAM ANGEL, Ch'man of the Court of Pleas & Qtr. Sessions of Macon Co. to S.R.
& W. LAMBERTS of Macon, assignees of BENJAMIN S. BRITTAIN, lots 13 & 14,
which Brittain purchased of commissioners JESSE R. SILER & JOHN HALL on Apr.
21, 1835: lot 13 (4 ac.) on NW corner of Seminary lands; lot 14 (5 ac.)—Dis. 16 of
Macon County. Aug. 7, 1846. *Wm. Angel, Ch.* Wit: *THOS. WELCH.* Ack. in Dec. 1846
court. Registered Jan. 9, 1847.

153 ROBERT LOVE of Haywood Co. NC, property in Washington Co. TN to D. LOVE, all
of the upper Farm formerly owned by THOS. DILLARD dec'd, beg. near small bridge
below Mill Creek, bd. the Block house tract... to Nolachusky R.; the heirs of THOS. D.
LOVE to have balance of property, value to be determined by two disinterested men
chosen by D. Love & R. Love, & whoever gets greatest share is to pay the other the dif-
ference... as this is the land that I intend them by my will. Sep. 8, 1835. *R. Love.* Wit:
JOHN CLINE, J.R. LOVE. Proven by Cline in Dec. 1846 court. Registered Jan. 9, 1847.

153 TERRELL FULCHER of Macon to CHARLES HAYS, a certain Negro Boy named
JACK, 16 yrs. old, healthy & sensible, for $450. June 16, 1846. *T.(his X mark) Fulcher.*
Wit: *JAS. RUSSELL,* who proved in Dec. 1846 court. Registered Jan. 9, 1847.

154 GARRETT HEADIN (HEADY) of Macon to DYER TALLEY of Pickins Co. SC, for
$100, tract in Dis. 18, beg. on top of Elicut Mt., incl. what is known by Heady's moun-
tain field. Aug. 2, 1840. *Garrett Heddin.* Wit: *JNO. ZACHARY,* who proved in Dec. 1846
court. Registered Jan. 9, 1847.

155 SG 651, ELIAS NORTON, $5/100 ac., 100 ac. on White Water R., near Public Road,
above HEDDY's on top of mtn. Entry Dec. 10, 1845; grant Oct., 1, 1846; registered Jan.
9, 1847.

155 SG 680, MARK BURRELL, $5/100 ac., 100 ac. on Chattooga R., incl. several old im-
provements. Entry Dec. 12, 1843; grant Oct. 1, 1846; registered Jan. 9, 1847.

156 SG 676, ANDREW YOUNCE, $5/100 ac., 100 ac. on Tuckasegee R., Dis. 6, incl. his im-
provement. Entry Aug. 30, 1844; grant Mar. 12, 1846; registered Jan. 9, 1847.

157 Sheriff's sale: EZEKIEL DOWDLE, Esq., High Sheriff of Macon County, to JOHN IN-
GRAM, assignee of WILLIAM LAMBERT, to satisfy judgment against ALFRED
HESTER with others for $51.52 recovered by JOSEPH WELCH, town lots 10 & 11 on
river, 10 ac. in all. At sale Mar. 15, 1846, Ingram had high bid of $21.62 1/2. Dec. 14,
1846. *E. Dowdle, Sh'ff.* Ack. in Dec. 1846 court. Registered Jan. 9, 1847.

159 Mortgage: JOHN HALL of Macon to MATHEW MASHBURN, 178 ac., Sec. __, Dis.
16, to secure SILAS MCDOWELL & GATHER B. JACOBS, who entered with Hall into
bond for prosecution of a suit in Supreme Court at Raleigh, JAMES WHITAKER, defendant, Hall, plaintiff. Oct. 10, 1846. *John Hall.* Wit: *J.R. ALLMAN, J.S. (his X mark) CUN-*
NINGHAM, SAUL SMITH. Registered Jan. 9, 1847.

160 Mortgage: J.H. ALLEY to WILLIAM NORTON, both of Macon, a grey horse and black
cow & calf for $30. Jan. 15, 1847. *J.H. Alley.* Wit: *E.R. NORTON,* who proved before
county clerk J.R. ALLMAN Jan. 15, 1847. Registered Jan. 28, 1847.

160 RODERICK NORTON, ELIAS NORTON & EDWARD NORTON to JOSHUA AM-
MONS, all of Macon, for $500, 640 ac. on Chattooga R., Dis. 18, on Georgia line. July 3,
1844. *Elias Norton, Roderick Norton, Edward R. Norton.* Wit: *BENJAMIN P. HOL-*
LAND, E. DOWDLE, L.A. COFFEE. Proven by Holland in Sep. 1844 court. Registered
Jan. 28, 1847.

161 SG 767 JOHN DEHART, $10.08, 50 ac., Sec. 2 in JACK's Reservation, Dis. 8, bd.
JOSEPH SHERRELL's old tract, on N. side of Tessenty on Elarkey Cr. Granted Nov.
25, 1846; registered Feb. 10, 1847.

162 SG 768, to JOHN DEHART, assignee of JOSEPH SHERRELL, for $2.02, 100 ac., Sec.
Dis. 8. Granted Nov. 25, 1846; registered Feb. 10, 1847.

163 SG 769, to JOHN DEHART, assignee of JOSEPH SHERRELL, for $15.60, 100 ac., Sec.
58, Dis. 8, on Chunaluskey's Cr. Granted Nov. 25, 1846; registered Feb. 10, 1847

164 SG 713, JOHN C. ALLMAN, $5/100 ac., 100 ac. on "Shugartown" R. Entry Dec. 9, 1845; grant Jan. 28, 1847; registered Feb. 10, 1847.

164 JOHN HALL to ROBERT HALL, both of Macon: John having been appointed guardian of Robert and others, minor heirs of CAROLINE HALL, dec'd, and Robert having become of age of 21 years, and John having failed to pay him the amount to which he is entitled, John hereby releases to Robert 43 ac., part of Sec. 43, originally purchased by the Rev. HUMPHREY POSEY and sold by him to John Hall. June 3, 1843. *John Hall.* Wit: *JAMES W. CARSON, A. HESTER.* Ack. in Mar. 1847 court. Registered Mar. 15, 1847.

165 Cherokee Co. NC: SETH W. HYATT appoints ANDREW PATTON of Macon my lawful agent & attorney in all things pertaining to my business in Macon. Mar. 22, 1847. *S.W. Hyatt.* Ack. Mar. 23, 1847 before JNO. M. DICK. Registered Mar. 27, 1847.

166 SG 705, ELIAS NORTON, $5/100 ac., 100 ac. on White Water & Chattooga R. Entry Dec. 10, 1845; grant Dec. 26, 1846; registered Apr. 28, 1847.

167 SG 674, _____, $5/100 ac., 50 ac. on Sugartown fork of Tennessee R. Entry Mar. 13, 1845; grant Jan. 13, 1846; registered Apr. 28, 1847.

167 SG 696, CHARLES WOODRING, $5/100 ac., 25 ac. on Tuckasegee R., bd. HUGH BROWN. Entry Feb. 22, 1843; grant Dec. 3, 1846; registered Apr. 28, 1847.

168 SG 695, CHARLES WOODRING, $5/100 ac., 75 ac. on Tuckasegee R. Entry Dec. 9, 1844; grant Dec. 3, 1846; registered Apr. 28, 1847.

169 SG 643, JONAS JENKINS, $5/100 ac., 25 ac. on Tuckasegee R. Entry Sep. 27, 1841; grant Dec. 19, 1844; registered Apr. 28, 1847.

170 SG 697, BURTON K. DICKEY, $5/100 ac., 50 ac. on "Elarkey" (Alarka or Yalaka) Cr. Entry May 13, 1843; grant Dec. 10, 1846; registered Apr. 28, 1847.

170 SG 698, GEORGE W. DICKEY, $5/100 ac., 100 ac. on "Elarkey" (Alarka or Yalaka) Cr. Entry May 13, 1843; grant Dec. 10, 1846; registered Apr. 29, 1847.

171 SG 694, THOMAS WEST, $5/100 ac., 50 ac. on Cowee Cr. Entry Oct. 19, 1844; grant Dec. 3, 1846; registered Apr. 29, 1847.

172 SG 730, to THOMPSON WILSON, assignee of WILLIAM WILLSON, for $31.17 1/2, 133 ac., Sec. 26, Dis. 6 on Tuckasegee R., E. fork of river. Granted Mar. 22, 1845; registered Apr. 29, 1847.

173 SG 793, ABRAHAM WIGGINS, $__, 50 ac., Sec. 1 of TOM's Reservation, on E. bank of Junaluskee's or "Elarkey" (Alarka or Yalaka) Cr. Granted Jan. 14, 1847; reg. Apr. 29, 1847.

174 SG 790, UTA SHERRELL, $__, 60+ ac., Sec. 31, Dis. 8, on E. bank of Chunaluska's Cr, incl. the improvement on which INDIAN TOM now lives, issued by resolve of General Assembly of 1846-7. Granted Jan. 9, 1847; registered Apr. 30, 1847.

175 SG 766, ADAM CORN, $6.86, 50 ac., Sec. 50, Dis. 7. Granted Nov. 25, 1846; registered Apr. 30, 1847.

175 SG 772, HENDERSON SANDERS, $5.39, 75 ac., Sec. 109, Dis. 15. Granted Nov. 25, 1846; registered May 1, 1847.

176 SG 770, WILLIAM HOLLBROOKS, assignee of JOHN AMMONS, for $28.40, 86 ac., Sec. 68, Dis. 11. Granted Nov. 25, 1846; registered May 1, 1847.

177 SG 786, WILLIAM TATHAM, $32.62, 122 ac., Sec. 158, Dis. 8. Granted Jan. 6, 1847; registered May 5, 1847.

178 SG 725, to HOWELL MOSS, assignee of JOHN MURRAY, for $150, 100 ac., Sec. 26, Dis. 11. Granted Mar. 20, 1845; registered May 5, 1847.

179 SG 715, WILLIAM WEST, $5/100 ac., 100 ac. on "Elarkey" (Alarka or Yalaka) Cr., incl. a mill shoal. Entry Mar. 17, 1846; grant Apr. 5, 1847; registered May 5, 1847.

179 Mortgage: SAMUEL JACKSON to HENRY JACKSON, 100 ac. on "Skeener" (Skeenah) Cr., 2 tracts: Sec. 124 & 107 in Dis. 15, as security for $125 loan. Mar. 13, 1847. *Samuel Jackson.* Wit: *A.B. DONALDSON,* who proved in Mar. 1847 court. Registered May 5, 1847.

180 RICHARD WILSON of Macon to JOHN WILSON & JAMES WILSON, all my
household & kitchen furniture, farming utensils, livestock incl. 2 mares, cattle, hogs &
sheep. John & James are bound to support & maintain sd. Richard & his wife RACHEL,
which support they are to have out of the property or some other source. Richard also
makes over to John & James one still and vessels with all necessaries. Oct. 13, 1845.
Richard (his X mark) Wilson. Wit: *W.R. BUCKHANNON, THOMAS B. CABE.* Proven by
Buckhannon in Mar. 1847 court. Registered May 5, 1847.

181 RICHARD WILSON to JOHN & JAMES WILLSON jointly for $50, a Negro woman by
name CLO, age 75 years. Oct. 13, 1845. *Richard (his X mark) Willson.* Wit: *W.R.
BUCHANAN, THOMAS B. CABE.* Proven by Buchanan in Mar. 1847 court. Registered
May 6, 1847.

181 ANDREW JUSTICE to SAMUEL KELLY, both of Macon, for $50, 83 ac., Sec. 47, Dis.
13, on Tennessee R., Tessentee Cr. Mar. 9, 1844. *Andrew (his X mark) Justice.* Wit:
LEANDER(?) B. SELL. Ack. in Mar. 1847 court. Registered May 6, 1847.

182 B.K. DICKEY to THOMAS WEST, both of Macon, for $5, 10 ac. on "Elarkey" (Alarka
or Yalaka) Cr., incl. the BEAR MEAT's improvement. Mar. 10, 1847. *B.K. Dicky.* Wit:
G.W. DICKEY, who proved in Mar. 1847 court. Registered May 6, 1847.

183 GEORGE W. DICKY to THOMAS WEST, both of Macon, for $25, 100 ac. on "Elarky"
(Alarka or Yalaka) Cr. Mar. 10, 1847. *George W. Dickey.* Wit: *JAS. (his X mark)
MCGAHEY.* Ack. in Mar. 1847. Registered May 6, 1847.

184 JOHN DAVIS to HENRY DEWEESE, both of Macon, for $25, 50 ac. in Dis. 17, begin-
ning at N. end of SIX KILLER's Reservation. Feb. 10, 1846. *John Davis.* Wit: *JOHN
WILDE, D._. SHIELD.* Ack. in Mar. 1847 court. Registered May 6, 1847.

184 JOHN DAVIS to HENRY DEWEESE, both of Macon, for $50, Sec. 1728, Dis. 17. Feb.
10, 1846. *John Davis.* Wit: *JOHN WILDE, D._. SHIELDS.* Ack. in Mar. 1847 court.
Registered May 8, 1847.

185 JOHN DAVIS to HENRY DEWEESE, both of Macon, for $100, 109 ac., Dis. 17, on
Burningtown Cr. Feb. 10, 1846. *John Davis.* Wit: *JOHN WILDE, D._. SHIELDS.* Ack. in
Mar.1847 court. Registered May 8, 1847.

186 WILLIAM BIRD to DILLARD LOVE, both of Macon, for $600, 110ac., part of Sec.
10, Dis. 11, bd. WILLIAM K. MORGAN. Feb. 15, 1847. *William (his X mark) Bird.*
Wit: *J.Y. HICKS, L.S. ROBINSON.* Proven by Hicks in Mar. 1847 court. Registered May
8, 1847.

186 WILLIAM ALLMAN to PETER S. STALLCUP, both of Macon, for $2,000, lots in
Franklin he purchased from J.W. GUIN: No. 11 (1 ac.) on N. side of Main St.; part of
No. 19 (91 poles), adj. No. 11 & adj. NE corner of Methodist Church land, S. boundary
of seminary land; No. 29 (1 ac.) on Main St.; No. 25 (2/3 ac.); No. 24 (1 ac.) on S. side of
Main St.; part of No. 26 running with conditional fence between J.R. ALLMAN & Wil-
liam Allman, & with conditional fence between WASHINGTON DOBSON & William
Allman. Also, a part of the town 400 ac., called the Rabit patch, on the big road leading
from Franklin to the Tennessee R., containing 4+ ac., including parts of No. 38, 42 & 43,
which Allman purchased of J.R. SILER. Apr. 3, 1846. *W. Allman.* Wit: *J.Y. HICKS.*
Ack. in Mar. 1847 court. Registered May 8, 1847.

188 RICHARD WILLSON of Macon to JOHN GATHER WILLSON for $20, land entered
Feb. 15, 1846, on Savannah Cr. Aug. 22, 1846. *Richard (his X mark) Wilson.* Wit:
JAMES ANGEL, W.H. HIGDON. Proven by Angel, Mar. 1847 court. Reg. May 8, 1847.

189 PETERS S. STALLCUP to WILLIAM ALLMAN, both of Macon, for $2,000, several
tracts: 127+ ac. on Tuckasegee R., Sec. 9, Dis. 8; 63+ ac. on Tuckasegee, Dis. 8; also 3+
ac. entered May 22, 1836, on the river near the State ford in Dis. 8, bd. HALL &
SELLERS. Apr. 3, 1846. *Peter S. (his X mark) Stallcup.* Wit: *JOHN Y. HICKS.* Ack. in
Mar. 1847 court. Registered May 10, 1847.

190 RICHARD WILLSON to JOHN GATHER WILLSON, for $80, 73 ac., part of Entry No.
494 on Savannah Cr. Aug. 22, 1846. *Richard Willson.* Wit: *JAMES ANGEL, W.H. HIG-
DON.* Proven by Angel, Mar. 1847 court. Registered May 10, 1847.

190 ABRAHAM WIGGINS of Cherokee Co. NC to DANIEL WEST of Macon for $25, 50
ac., Sec. 1, Dis. 8, on E. bank of Junaluskee's or "Elarky" (Alarka or Yalaka) Cr. Mar.
18, 1847. *Abraham (his X mark) Wiggins.* Wit: *JOHN HALL, J.R. ALLMAN.* Ack. in
Mar. 1847 court. Registered May 10, 1847.

191 THOMAS CANTRELL to JOHN FISHER, 100 ac. Oct. 20, 1846. *Thomas Cantrell.* Wit:
JOHN W. BREEDLOVE, JAMES (his X mark) FISHER. Proven by Fisher in Mar. 1847
court. Registered May 11, 1847.

191 WILLIAM STALLCUP to WILLIAM ALLMAN, both of Macon, for $100, 72 ac. on
Savanna Cr., Sec. 132, Dis. 8. Apr. 3, 1846. *Wm. Stallcup.* Wit: *JOHN Y. HICKS.* Ack. in
Mar. 1847 court. Registered May 11, 1847.

192 WILLIAM STALLCUP to WILLIAM ALLMAN, both of Macon, for $50, a 50-ac. tract
purchased at land sales of 1836, Sec. 128, Dis. 8, on W. bank of Tuckasegee R., mouth of
Big Savanna. Apr. 3, 1846. *Wm. Stallcup.* Wit: *JOHN Y. HICKS.* Ack. in Mar. 1847
court. Registered May 11, 1847.

193 PHILLIP GUYER Senr. to DAVID GUYER, both of Macon, for $400, 94 ac. on "Iola "
(Iotla) Cr., part of Sec. 58, No. 1 Reserved, also 58 ac., No. 89, running with line of
LEACH's Reserve. Jul. 20, 1846. *Phillip (his X mark) Guyer.* Wit: *JOHN WILDE,
THOMAS P. MOORE.* Ack. in Mar. 1847 court. Registered May 11, 1847.

194 PHILLIP GUYER Senr. to DAVID GUYER for $200, 62 ac, Sec. 1 of Reservation land,
Dis. 16 and 58 ac., Sec. 89. Jul. _, 1846. *Phillip (his X mark) Guyer.* Wit: *JOHN
MCDOWELL, THOMAS P MOORE.* Ack. in Mar. 1847 court. Registered May 11, 1847.

195 PHILLIP GUYER Senr. to GEORGE H. GUYER, both of Macon, for $400, 150 ac. on
"Iola" (Iotla) Cr., Sec. 58 and No. 2 & No. 1 Reservations, also Entry No. 566 on both
sides of Iola. Jul. 30, 1846. *Phillip (his X mark) Guyer.* Wit: *JOHN WILDE, THOMAS P.
MOORE.* Ack. in Mar. 1847. Registered May 11, 1847.

195 PHILLIP GUYER Senr. to PHILLIP GUYER Junr. for $200, 2 tracts, 150 ac. on "Iola"
(Iotla) Cr., Dis. 16. Jul. 30, 1846. *Phillip (his X mark) Guyer.* Wit: *JOHN MCDOWELL,
THOMAS P. MOORE.* Ack. in Mar. 1847 court. Registered May 11, 1847.

196 EPHRAIM ASH of Haywood Co. NC to AMOS ASHE of Macon, for $275, Sec. 25,
Dis. 7. Jan. 7, 1847. *Ephraim Ash.* Wit: *ELY SHULER, J.(I?) KEENER.* Proven by
Keener in Mar. 1847 court. Registered May 11, 1847.

197 EPHRAIM E. AMMONS of Cherokee Co. NC to T. FULCHER of Macon, for $600, the
following tracts: 130+ ac.; 57 ac.; 56 ac; 100 ac. bd. DOBSON; 48 ac. bd. Dobson's
fence, near JOHN LEDFORD. Jul. 6, 1846. *E. Ammons.* Wit: *JAS. RUSSELL, JNO. C.
(his X mark) FULCHER.* Russell proved in Mar. 1847 court. Registered May 11, 1847.

198 ROBERT BRYSON to LEWIS TILLEY, both of Macon, for $100, 50 ac. on Cullowhee
Cr. Nov. 20, 1846. *Robert Bryson.* Wit: *ANDREW PRESLEY, GEORGE W. BRYSON.*
Proven by Presley in Mar. 1847 court. Registered May 11, 1847.

199 JOHN N. MATTHIS to LEWIS TILLY, both of Macon, for $100, 50 ac. on Tuckasegee
R. & Cullowhee Cr. Nov. 20, 1846. *John N. Matthis.* Wit: *ANDREW PRESLEY,
GEROGE W. BRYSON.* Proven by Presley in Mar. 1847 court. Registered May 11, 1847.

200 JAMES BUCHANON Senr. to MARGARET BUCHANON, both of Macon, for $50, 50
ac. in Dis. 8 on Savannah Cr., bd. W.R. BUCHANON & others. Jan. 13, 1844. *James
Buchanon.* Wit: *JOSEPH BUCHANON, W.R. Buchanon.* Proven by Joseph Buchanon in
Mar. 1847 court. Registered May 11, 1847.

201 DAVID MORGAN of Macon to PHILAMON CRAIN of Pickens Dis. SC, for $150, 56 ac. tract bought at Franklin, 1836, on Big Creek, Sec. 5, Dis. 18. ___ 1845. *David Morgan*. Wit: *JONA. ZACHARY, RODERICK NORTON*. Proven by Norton in Mar. 1847 court. Registered May 11, 1847.

202 GEORGE F. CALER to JOHN PANTHER, both of Macon, 215 ac., Dis.10, Sec. 23, 71 & 105. Dec. 2, 1843. *George F. Caler*. Wit: *ROBERT CALER, LARKIN LINDSEY*. Ack. Mar. 1847. Registered May 11, 1847.

203 JOHN J. ROSE of Cherokee Co. NC to JOHN PANTHER of Macon, for $200, 78 ac., Sec. 33, Dis. 7. Dec. 12, 1845. *John J. Rose*. Wit: *LENARD (his X mark) PANTHER, RILY MARTIN*. Proven by Lenard Panther in Mar. 1847 court. Registered May 11, 1847.

203 ARCHIBALD VAUGHN to ABRAHAM MORE, both of Macon, 297 ac. purchased in Oct. 1836, Sec. 107, Dis. 11. Jan. ___ 1840. *Archibald Vaughn*. Wit: *HIRAM LEDFORD, JOHN H. LEDFORD*. Proven by John H. Ledford, Mar. 1847 court. Reg. May 11, 1847.

204 ANTHONY HOLLAND to JAMES D. FRANKS, both of Macon, for $10, 50 ac., part of No. 144, Dis.11, on top of ridge leading towards JOHN STRAIN's Mill pond, near WIDOW STUMAN's house. Mar. 13, 1848. *Anthony Holland*. Wit: *JOSHUA AMONS, JOHN D. FRANKS*. Ack. in Mar. 1847 court. Registered May 11, 1847.

205 JAMES PEEK to ANTHONY HOLLAND, both of Macon, for $150, land entered May 2, 1836, in Dis. 11. Jan. 24, 1846. *James Peek*. Wit: *T.R. TRAMMELL, WILLIAM PEEK*. Ack. in Mar. 1847 court. Registered May 11, 1847.

206 N.S. JARRETT to JOSEPH ROLAND, both of Macon, for $40, 101 ac. on "Nantayala" R. purchased in lands sales of 1836, Dis. 13, Sec. 14, E. side of river above a Shut-in, crossing the Burningtown trail. Mar. 17, 1846. *N.S. Jarrett*. Wit: *S.H. WATERS, J.R. LOVE*. Ack. in Mar. 1847 court. Registered May 11, 1847.

207 SAMUEL BRYSON, N.S. JARRETT & GEORGE F. CALER to JOHN ROLAND/ROWLAND, all of Macon, for $50, 187 ac. on Nantahala R. known as Cherokee lands, purchased at sales of 1838, Dis. 13, tract 14. Mar. 18, 1846. *Samuel (his X mark) Bryson, N.S. Jarrett, George F. Caler*. Wit: *S.H. WATERS, J.R. LOVE*. Ack. in Mar. 1847 court. Registered May 11, 1847.

208 WILLIAM F. PASSMORE of Macon to WILLIAM DEALE, for value rec'd, 82 ac., Sec. 60, Dis. 11. Feb. 18, 1846. *William F. Passmore*. Wit: *HIRAM LEDFORD, JOHN R. LEDFORD*. Ack. in Mar. 1847 court. Registered May 11, 1847.

208 MATTHEW RUSSELL to DAVID H. RUSSELL, both of Macon, for $50, 50 ac. on "Shugartown" R., part of Sec. 47, Dis. 11, opposite WIDOW FULTON's house. Apr. 25, 1846. *Matthew (his X mark) Russell*. Wit: *ALFRED ANGEL, JOHN MCDOWELL*. Proven by McDowell in Mar. 1847 court. Registered May 11, 1847.

209 HIRAM LEDFORD to WILLIAM DEALE, both of Macon, for value received, 58 ac. which I purchased in 1838, Sec. 53, Dis. 11. ___ 24, 1845. *Hiram Ledford*. Wit: *J.D. FRANKS*, who proved in Mar. 1847 court. Registered May 11, 1847.

210 JOHN GIBBS & SAM'L SHERRELL, administrators of UTE SHERRELL, dec'd, convey to JOHN WEST, in compliance with a bond given by Ute Sherrell for a title, Sec. 31 Dis. 8 on "Elarkey" (Alarka or Yalaka) Cr. Mar. 17, 1847. *John Gibbs, Samuel Sherrell*. Wit: *JOHN MCDOWELL, S. MCDOWELL*. Ack. in Mar. 1847. Registered May 11, 1847.

210 Mortgage: WILLIAM MCKIMSEY/MCKINSEY to E.T. LONG & WILLIAM R. MCDOWELL a black mare, two year-old colts, 13 hogs, waggon & 4 cattle, for $37. Condition is that Long & McDowell stand security for McKinsey to SAUL SMITH, administrator of JOHN CONLY, dec'd, for $29 due before Jan. next. Mar. 17, 1847. *William (his X mark) McKinsey*. Wit: *B.K. DICKEY*, who proved in Mar 1847 court. Registered May 11, 1847

211 MARGARET WATERS to PETER S. STALLCUP, both of Macon, for $200, 110 ac. in
Dis. 11, on Burningtown Cr., on NE corner of SIX KILLER's Reservation. Nov. 4, 1846.
Margrat (her X mark) Waters. Wit: *JOEL SIMONS, S. WATERS.* Proven by Simons in
Mar. 1847 court. Registered May 11, 1847.

212 MARGRET WATERS to P.S. STALLCUP, both of Macon, for $50, 50 ac. in Dis. 17,
Sec. 345, on the Reservation line. Nov. 4, 1846. *Margret (her X mark) Waters.* Wit:
JOEL SIMONDS, S.H. WATERS. Proven by Simonds in Mar. 1847 court. Registered
May 11, 1847.

212 WILLIAM ALLEN of Haywood Co. NC to SAMUEL REID of Macon, for $900, 112
ac., Sec. 47, Dis. 10, on Watauga Cr. & Tennessee R., also in Dis. 10, part of entry made
by WM. POTEET & ISAIAH COOK on corner of JOHNSTON's entry. Jan. 30, 1847.
Wm. Allen. Wit: *JOHN HALL, JOHN REID.* Proven by Hall in Mar. 1847. Registered
May 11, 1847.

213 CURTIS SAUNDERS to SAMUEL REID, both of Macon, for $10, 30 ac., part of Sec.
112, Dis. 16, bd. JOSEPH R. JOHNSTON & WILLIAM ALLEN. Jan. 30, 1847. *Curtiss
Saunders.* Wit: *JOHN HALL, JOHN REID.* Proven by Hall in Mar. 1847 court.
Registered May 11, 1847.

214 WILLIAM ALLMAN and wife MARY ALLMAN to PETER S. STALLCUP, all of
Macon, for $500, 181 ac. Apr. 3, 1846. *W. Allman, Mary (her X mark) Allman.* Wit:
JOHN Y. HICKS. Acknowledged before JNO. M. DICK, JSCL&E, who examined Mary
apart from her husband, Mar. 20, 1847. Registered May 11, 1847.

215 Mortgage: B.G. JACOBS to JAS. K. GRAY & JOAB L. MOORE, all of Macon. Jacobs
owes Moore $150, $80 on judgment to J.R. SILER & J.K. Gray as trustees of D.R.
LOWRY, DILLARD LOVE as security; $35 to WILLIAM WEST, Moore as security.
To pay debts, Jacobs mortgages 100-ac. tract on John Hall's Mill Creek, Dis. 16; 50 ac.
on ridge dividing "Iola" (Iotla) & "Cartoogajay" creeks, Dis. 16; 50-60 hogs, 15 stock
cattle, one road waggon & gearing, all my corn, abt. 150-200 bu., household & kitchin
furniture, beds, bedclothes, Chears, tables, one clock, pots, pails, my still & vessels, etc. Jar. 22, 1847. *B.G. (his X mark) Jacobs, James K. Gray, J.L. Moore.* Wit:
JOHN INGRAM. Ack. Mar. 22, 1847. Registered May 11, 1847.

217 SG 683, JILES(GILES?) NORTON, $5/100 ac., 100 ac. on Chattooga R., bd. ELIAS
NORTON. Entry Oct. 19, 1844; grant Nov. 11, 1846; registered May 11, 1847.

218 Mortgage: DAVID MALONEE & THOMAS MALONEE of Macon, of the 1st part;
WILLIAM ANGEL of Macon, of the 2nd part; AUGUSTUS A. BRIDLEMAN, VALEN-
TINE BRIDLEMAN & JAMES W. CURETON of Sulavan Co. TN, parties of the 3rd
part. David & Thomas owe $700 to parties of the 3rd part in several notes. To secure the
notes, they convey to Angel a wool carding machine now in operation on sd. William
Angel's land on Cartoogachaye Creek. May 14, 1847. *David Malonee, Thomas Malonee,
Wm. Angel.* Wit: *J.K. GRAY.* Ack. June 3, 1847. Registered May 1847.

220 Mortgage: THOMAS LONG to L. VANDYKE & JOHN HOWARD, all of Macon, for
$100, a bay horse, 3 cattle, bed & furniture, small colt, as security for a debt of $15 Long
owes JOHN QUEEN. May 25, 1847. *Thos. Long.* Wit: *E.T. LONG.* Reg. Jun. 7, 1847.

220 SG 701, WILLIAM QUILLIAMS, $5/100 ac., 50 ac. on Savannah Cr. Entry Jan. 25,
1844; grant Dec. 24, 1846; registered Jun. 26, 1847.

221 SG 702, WILLIAM QUILLIAMS, $5/100 ac., 50 ac. on Savannah Cr. Entry Jan. 25,
1844; grant Dec. 24, 1846; registered Jun. 26, 1847.

222 SG 690, DAVID HALL, $5/100 ac., 50 ac. on Savannah Cr. Entry Nov. 30, 1845; grant
Dec. 3, 1846; registered Jun. 26, 1847.

222 AARON THOMAS to JOHN HOWARD, both of Macon, for $100, 200 ac. in flats of Middle Cr. where Aaron now lives, made up of 3 tracts: two 50-ac. tracts granted to Aaron and one of 100 ac. granted to ELISHA THOMAS & conveyed to Aaron, all joining. Also, a tract on N. fork of Middle Cr. above Thomas's mill and another on SW corner of mill tract. Mar. 25, 1847. *Aaron (his X mark) Thomas*. Wit: *JESSE (his X mark) THOMAS, LAFAETT HOWARD*. Proven by Jesse Thomas in Jun. 1847 court. Registered Jun. 26, 1847.

224 JOHN R. ALLMAN to W.G. STANFIELD, both of Macon, for $200, 92+ ac. in three tracts: 1st, 59+ ac., Sec. 26, Dis. 12, on the river, originally granted SAM'L D. FINLEY in Dec. 1835; 2nd, 4 ac. on river, Dis. 12; 3rd, 28 ac., part of Entry 713 on Sugartown fork of Tennessee River. Jun. 16, 1847. *J.R. Allman*. Wit: *JOHN HALL, SAUL SMITH*. Ack. in June 1847 court. Registered June 29, 1847.

225 JOSHUA HALL to DAVID HALL, both of Macon, for $250, 50 ac. on Savannah Cr., beginning on top of the River Hill. Jan. 11, 1847. *Joshua Hall*. Wit: *W.R. BUCHANNON, M.M. HALL*. Proven by Buchannon in June 1847 court. Registered Jun. 29, 1847.

225 Sheriff's sale: EZEKIEL DOWDLE, Esq, High Sheriff of Macon Co. to WILLIAM NORTON of Macon, to satisfy judgment against WILLIAM B. QUEEN of $14.85 recovered by JOHN H. ALLEY: 50 ac., Dis. 18, No. 566, on Chattooga R. in which Queen owned 1/2 an undivided interest. At public sale, Sep. 21, Norton had high bid of $10.20. Jun. 15, 1847. *Ezekiel Dowdle, Sheriff*. Ack. in June 1847 court. Registered Jun. 29, 1847.

227 Sheriff's sale: EZEKIEL DOWDLE, Esq., High Sheriff of Macon Co. to JOHN C. BRYSON of Haywood Co. NC and JOHN WILD of Macon, to satisfy judgment against WILLIAM B. QUEEN of $14.85, 100 ac. on Beed or Bad Cr., Dis. 18, No. 567, on SC line, incl. part of an improvement. At public sale at courthouse in Franklin, Sep. 21, Bryson & Wild had high bid of $1.05. Jun. 16, 1847. *E. Dowdle*. Ack. in June 1847 court. Registered Jun. 30, 1847.

228 Sheriff's sale: EZEKIEL DOWDLE, Esq., High Sheriff of Macon, to JOHN C. BRYSON of Haywood Co. NC and JOHN WILD of Macon, land sold to satisfy judgment against WILLIAM B. QUEEN of $14.85: 100 ac. on Beed or Bad Cr., Dis. 18, No. 567. At public sale on Dec. 21, 1846, Bryson & Wild had high bid of $1. Jun. 16, 1847. *E. Dowdle*. Ack. in June 1847 court. Registered Jun. 30, 1847.

230 SG 750, FREDERICK RABY, $125.56, 81 ac., Sec. 10, Dis. 10. Granted Apr. 2, 1846; registered Jun. 30, 1847.

231 SG 694, FREDERICK RABY, $20.42, 87 ac., Sec. 99, Dis. 10. Granted Dec. 28, 1844; registered Jun. 30, 1847.

231 B.W. BELL to J.R. SILER for $250, 122 ac., Sec. 57, Dis. 15, purchased in 1836 at $91.50 with 1/8 down, balance in 1, 2, 3 and 4 years. The 4th payment is due in fall 1840. Bell sells tract & premises, incl. the sawmill & all appurtenances. Mar. 31, 1840. *B.W. Bell*. Wit: *JOHN MCDOWELL*. Ack. in Jun. 1847 court. Registered Sep. 30, 1847.

232 WESTLY JOHNSTON of Cherokee Co. NC to JESSE R. SILER of Macon, for $30, 61 ac., Sec. 59, Dis. 15. Jan. 20, 1840. *Westly (his X mark) Johnston*. Wit: *JOHN INGRAM, T.P. SILER*. Proven by T.P. Silr in June 1847 court. Registered Jul. 2, 1847.

233 FREDERICK RABY Senr. to ELIJAH RABY, both of Macon, for $500, 106 ac., Sec. 92, Dis. 10, on Cowee Cr.; 87 ac., Sec. 99, Dis. 10; 81 ac., Sec. 100, Dis. 10; 82 ac., Sec. 90, Dis. 10. May 10, 1847. *Frederick (his X mark) Raby*. Wit: *E. DOWDLE*, who proved in Jun. 1847 court. Registered Jul. 2, 1847.

234 B.K. DICKY to JAMES RABY, both of Macon, for $46.26, land on right-hand fork of Cowee Cr., 52 ac., Sec. 30, Dis. 10; 57 ac., Sec. 31, Dis. 10. Also, 40 ac. tract, Sec. 29 & 32 in Dis. 10, on conditional corner between D. RABY & JACOB GIBSON, and on conditional corner with JACOB CAILOR. Jan. 7, 1847. *B.K. Dicky*. Wit: *J.K. GRAY*, who proved in Jun. 1847 court. Registered Jul. 2, 1847.

235 JESSE HALL, ELBERT HALL, JAMES HALL, M.M. HALL, GEMASON HALL & DAVID HALL, to JOHN WILLSON, for $550, Negro woman MANERVA, 28 or 29 years, and child LEUSENDA. Jun. 12, 1847. *Jesse Hall, Elbert Hall, James A. Hall, M.M. Hall, Jemmison Hall, David (his X mark) Hall.* Wit: *JEREMIAH STILLWELL, JACOB STILLWELL.* Proven by Jeremiah Stillwell in Jun. 1847 court. Registered Jul. 2, 1847.

235 DANIEL BREWER of Macon to SAMUEL CABEL, 60 ac., Dis. 1, on Tennessee R., Cable to pay state amount due. Jan.(?) 17, 1846. *Daniel Brewer.* Wit: *THOS. W.P. POINDEXTER, WM. (his X mark) DONASON.* Proven by Poindexter in Jun. 1847 court. Registered Jul. 2, 1847.

236 DANIEL NICHOLS to J.R. SILER for $50, 60 ac., Sec. 62, Dis. 15. Oct. 7, 1839. *Daniel Nickels.* Wit: *J. HOWARD.* Ack. in Jun. 1847 court. Registered Jul. 2, 1847.

236 SILAS MCDOWELL of Macon to ELIZABETH MCDOWELL, for $975, 108+ ac., Sec. 27, Dis. 12, crossing the river; 80 ac., Sec. 28, Dis. 12, on Sugartown fork of Tennesse R.; 69+ ac., Sec. 29, Dis. 12, on Sugartown fork. Feb. 4, 1847. *S. McDowell.* Wit: *J.Y. HICKS, J.K. GRAY.* Ack. in Jun. 1847 court. Registered Jul. 3, 1847.

237 SAMUEL REID to DRURY W. MASHBURN, both of Macon, for $200, 90 ac., part of Sec. 2 & 4 in Dis. 11. Jan. 19, 1847. *Samuel Reid.* Wit: *N.H. PALMER,* who proved in Jun. 1847 court. Registered Jul. 3, 1847.

238 SAMUEL BRYSON to FREDERICK RABY Senr., both of Macon, for $50.50, 82 ac. on Cowee Cr., Sec. 90, Dis. 10. Ju. 26, 1846. *Samuel (his X mark) Bryson.* Wit: *GEO. W. DICKEY,* who proved in Jun. 1847 court. Registered Jul. 3, 1847.

239 J.R. STALLCUP of Cherokee Co. NC to FREDERICK RABY Senr. of Macon, for $65, 106 ac. on Cowee Cr., Sec. 92, Dis. 10. Aug. 12, 1846. *J.R. Stallcup.* Wit: *J.K. GRAY, PETER S. (his X mark) STALLCUP.* Proven by Gray in Jun. 1847 court. Registered Jul. 3, 1847.

240 Sheriff's sale: EZEKIEL DOWDLE, Esq., High Sheriff of Macon, to BURTON K. DICKEY of Macon, property sold to satisfy judgment of the county court against DEMPSEY RABY for $36.26, recovered by FREDERICK RABY Jr. & JOAB L. MOORE. Sold to satisfy FREDERICK RABY Senr., Frederick Jr. & Moore were 3 tracts, 52 ac., Sec. 30, Dis. 10; 57 ac., Sec. 31, Dis. 10 on Cowee Cr.; and 40 ac., part of Sec. 27 & 32, Dis. 10, on corner of D. RABY & JACOB GIBSON, line of JACOB CALER. At sale on Sep. 21, 1846, Dickey had high bid of $17. Dec. 14, 1846. *E. Dowdle.* Wit: *CURTIS SANDERS.* Ack. in Jun. 1847 court. Registered Jul. 3, 1847.

242 SG 642, JOHN YOUNG, $5/100, 50 ac. on Savannah Cr., incl. REDICK's cabin. Entry Mar. 3, 1843; grant Dec. 9, 1844; registered Ju. 20, 1847.

243 SG 411, JOSEPH YOUNG, $5/100 ac., 50 ac. on Watauga Cr., Dis. 10, on edge of the old road. Entry May 2, 1836; grant Nov. 24, 1840; registered Jul. 20, 1847.

244 SG 150, YOUNG AMMONS, $5/100 ac., 75 ac. on Wattauga Cr., Dis. 10. Entry May 2, 1836; grant Dec. 10, 1838; registered Jul. 20, 1847.

244 Mortgage: ISOM LAGLE to E.M. HALL, both of Macon, standing crop of corn & present crop of rye, to secure debt of $60 by book acct. Aug. 16, 1847. *Isom (his X mark) Lagle.* Wit: *ALFRED HALL.* Ack. Aug. 21, 1847.

245 SG 773, MICHAEL LONG, $12, 51 ac., Sec. 38, Dis. 7. Granted Dec. 3, 1846; registered Sep. 6, 1847.

246 SG 686, WILSON PICKLESIMER, $5/100 ac., 50 ac. on Tuckasegee R., Dis. 5, on ABM. PICKLESIMER's line. Entry Sep. 15, 1845; grant Dec. 3, 1846; registered Sep. 21, 1847.

247 SG 640, ANDREW J. WOOD, $5/100 ac., 100 ac. on Culowhee Cr., Dis. 7, incl. improvement where WILLIAM DOGGINS lives. Entry Feb. 7, 1843; grant Dec. 9, 1844; registered Sep. 22, 1847.

247 SG 718, JOHN R. ALLMAN, $5/100 ac., 32+ ac., Sugartown R., including all that is vacant land at this place. Entry Feb. 24, 1846; grant Jul. 5, 1847; registered Sep. 22, 1847.

248 SG 717, JOHN R. ALLMAN, $5/100 ac., 58 ac. on Sugartown R. Granted Jul. 5, 1847; registered Sep. 22, 1847.

249 SG 691, MARTIN HUCK, $5/100 ac., 100 ac. on Cowee Cr. Entry Sep. 12, 1843; grant Dec. 3, 1846; registered Sep. 22, 1847.

250 JOHN HALL to E. DOWDLE, both of Macon, for $50, two town lots, part of tract around Franklin or the Town Commons, No. 3 (5+ ac.) and No. 4 (5+ ac.). Feb. 9, 1847. *John Hall.* Wit: *STEPHEN MONDAY,* who proved in court. Registered Sep. 23, 1847.

251 Performance Bond: DAVID R. LOWRY, JOHN HOWARD, J.R. SILER, B.K. DICKEY, B.W. BELL, WILLIAM TATHAM, post $5,000 bond for David R. Lowry, duly elected clerk of Superior Court of Law for Macon County. Sep. 23, 1847. Wit: *JOHN BAXTER,* who proved in fall court, 1847. Registered Oct. 2, 1847.

251 Performance Bond: DAVID R. LOWRY, JOHN HOWARD, J.R. SILER, B.W. BELL, WILLIAM TATHAM post $10,000 bond for Lowry, elected clerk of Superior Court. Registered Oct. 2, 1847.

252 Performance Bond: J.K. GRAY, J.R. SILER, SILAS MCDOWELL post $4,000 bond for J.K. Gray, duly elected cler of Court of Pleas & Qtr. Sessions. Sep. 21, 1847. Wit: *WM. ANGEL.* Registered Oct. 2, 1847.

252 Performance Bond of $10,000, details same as previous entry.

253 SG 791, THOMAS MONTEITH, $15.20 1/2, 58 ac. on Tuckasegee R., Sec. 26, Dis. 7. Granted Jan. 13, 1847; registered Oct. 2, 1847.

254 SG 398, MERRIT B. STRAIN, $5/100 ac., 50 ac. on Cat's & Wattauga Creeks. Entry Mar. 29, 1837; grant Nov. 24, 1840; registered Oct. 2, 1847.

254 SAMUEL P. RIPLEY of Charleston, SC, by att'y in fact N.W. WOODFIN of Buncombe Co. NC, to STEPHEN MUNDAY of Macon, for $1,200, 99-ac. tract on which Munday lives, one mile W. of Franklin, both sides of creek that runs by town, on N. side of road; tract originally conveyed to JAMES ROBINSON & JAMES POTEET, and by J.R. SILER to Robinson; conveyed to Ripley Mar. 12, 1845 by Woodfin as trustee. Sep. 25, 1847. *N.W. Woodfin.* Wit: *H.G. WOODFIN, SAUL SMITH.* Proven by Smith in Sep. 1847 court. Registered Oct. 4, 1847.

256 SG 689, WILLIAM DILLS, $5/100 ac., 50 ac. on Savannah Cr., on MASON's corner. Entry Sep. 10,. 1844; grant Dec. 3, 1846; registered Nov. 10, 1847.

256 JACOB SILER of Macon to NOAH MILLER, for $300, four tracts on Burningtown Cr., Dis. 17: Sec. 14 (80 ac.); Sec. 15 (87+ ac.); Sec. 16 (65+ ac.); Sec. 17 (53 ac.). Sep. 22, 1846. *Jacob Siler.* Wit: *WM. MORISON,* who proved in Sep. 1847 court. Registered Nov. 10, 1847.

257 JOHN DILLS to THOMAS MONTEITH, both of Macon, for $8, 16 ac., Sec. 30, Dis. 7. Jul. 26, 1845. *John Dills.* Wit: *WM. CARSON, JACOB DEITZ.* Ack. in Sep. 1847 court. Registered Nov. 10, 1847.

258 ZACHARIAH CABE to WILLIAM M. PENLAND, both of Macon, for $1,000, 199 ac. on E. side Tennessee R., Sec. 5, Dis. 12, except the 1 ac. 40 poles deeded to the Trustees of the Meeting house & land including the meeting house & grave yard for use of M.E. Church. Sep. 21, 1847. *Z. Cabe.* Wit: *JOHN MCDOWELL, J.A. CURTIS.* Ack. in Sep. 1847 court. Registered Nov. 10, 1847.

259 WILLIAM PEEK to JOHN SETSER, both of Macon, for $250, 72 ac. on Rabbit's Cr., Sec. 65, Dis. 11. Feb. 25, 1842. *Wm. Peeke.* Wit: *J.K. GRAY, LEMUEL BIRD.* Proven by Gray in Sep. 1847 court. Registered Nov. 10, 1847.

259 DAVID PEEK to GABRIL BOLOCK, both of Macon, for $12, 10ac. on Battle Branch
     of Tennessee R., transferred by JOSHUA AMMONS to Peek. Nov. 12, 1846. *David
     Peek* Wit: *JOHN YOUNG, JAMES M. PEEKE.* Ack. in Sep. 1847 court. Registered Nov.
     10, 1847.

260 MASON MCLEOD of Union Co. GA to JOHN HOWARD of Macon, for $25, 50 ac. on
     Middle Cr. Mar. 5, 1847. *Mason McCleod.* Wit: *GEORGE WIKLE, J.A. BELL.* Proven
     by Wikle in Sep. 1847 court. Registered Nov. 10, 1847.

261 JOSHUA HALL to WILLIAM ALLMAN, both of Macon, for $100, 66 ac. on Savannah
     Cr., purchased by sd. Joshua Hall Jr. at 1836 sale. Apr. 2, 1847. *Joshua (his X mark) Hall
     Junr.* Wit: *WM. R. BUCHANON, JEMMISON HALL.* Buchanon proved in Sep. 1847
     court. Registered Nov. 10, 1847.

261 THOMAS LONG to JOHN HOWARD, both of Macon, for $150, 109 ac. on Crow's
     Mill Creek waters of Coweta, Sec. 56 & 55, Dis. 14. Sep. 21, 1843. *Thos. Long.* Wit: *D.
     GARLAND.* Ack. in Sep. 1847 court. Registered Nov. 10, 1847.

262 MICAJAH M. HALL to WILLIAM ALLMAN, both of Macon, for $250, 50 ac. on Big
     Savannah on River Hill, on State Rd. Also, for $300, 50 ac. on W. side of Savannah Cr.,
     JOSHUA HALL's corner. Apr. 2, 1847. *M.M. Hall.* Wit: *WM. R. BUCHANAN, JEM-
     MISON HALL.* Buchanon proved in Sep. 1847 court. Registered Nov. 10, 1847.

263 SAMUEL LOVINGOOD of Union Co. GA to THOMAS J. ROLLINS of Spartenburg
     Dis. SC, for $300, 284+ (288?) ac. on Burningtown Cr., Dis. 17: Nov. 56 on corner of
     SIX KILLER's Reservation; No. 59; No. 61. Dec. 4, 1846. *Samuel Lovingood.* Wit:
     HENRY DEWESE, JOHN WILDE. Proven by Wilde in Sep. 1847 court. Registered Nov.
     10, 1847.

264 PETER S. STALLCUP to JOHN INGRAM, both of Macon, for $230, 151 ac. Apr. 17,
     1847. *Peter S. (his X mark) Stallcup.* Wit: *A. HESTER, WM. STALLCUP.* Ack. in Sep.
     1847 court. Registered Nov. 10, 1847.

265 JILES (GILES) NORTON to ELIAS NORTON, both of Macon, for $200, 100 ac. on
     Chattooga R., bd. Elias. Jan. 19, 1847. *Jiles (his X mark) Norton.* Wit: *J.H. ALLEY,* who
     proved in Sep. 1847 court. Registered Nov. 15, 1847.

266 JOHN DILLS to WILLIAM FRADY (FRANDY), both of Macon, 62 ac., Sec. 31, Dis.
     7. Sep. 20, 1847. *John Dills.* Wit: *J.Y. HICKS.* Ack. in Sep. 1847 court. Registered Nov.
     15, 1847.

266 GEORGE FOX to ROBERT FOX, 50 ac. on W. side Tennessee R., Dis. 6, near
     WEBSTER's improvement, above Fox's improvement. Jan. 1, 1847. *George (his X
     mark) Fox.* Wit: *E.B. ERWIN, PHILIP WIKE.* Proven by Erwin in Sep. 1847 court.
     Registered Nov. 15, 1847.

267 JESSE HALL to JOSHUAH HALL, both of Macon, for $5, 25 ac. on little Savannah Cr.,
     part of an entry, beginning at mouth of a hollow below a still house. Jan. 14, 1847. *Jesse
     Hall.* Wit: *WM. R. BUCHANAN, JACOB MASON.* Proven by Buchanan in Sep. 1847
     court. Registered Nov. 15, 1847.

267 DAVID SUTTON TO WILLIAM PARTON, both of Macon, for $164.64, 50 ac. on
     Tuckasegee R., Dis. 8. Sep. 9, 1845. *David (his X mark) Sutton.* Wit: *SOLOMON
     MESSER, WILLIAM MCMAHAN.* Messer proved in Sep. 1847 court. Registered Nov.
     15, 1847.

268 WILLIAM M. PENLAND to R.C. PENLAND, both of Macon, for $4.50, 50 ac. joining
     Sec. 58, Dis. 13. Jul. 7, 1847. *W.M. Penland.* Wit: none. Ack. in Sep. 1847 court.
     Registered Nov. 15, 1847.

269 W.M. PENLAND to ROBERT C. PENLAND, both of Macon, for $350, 101 ac., Sec.
     58, Dis. 13. Jul. 7, 1847. *W.M. Penland.* Ack. in Sep. 1847. Registered Nov. 15, 1847.

269 ELIAS NORTON of Macon to JOHN HOLDEN of Pickens Dis. SC, for $100, 50 ac. on White Water Cr., Dis. 18, near Terepin Mtn. Jun. 8, 1847. *Elias Norton.* Wit: *J.H. ALLEY, R. NORTON.* Alley proved in Sep. 1847 court. Registered Nov. 15, 1847.

270 WILLIAM R. MCDOWELL to JOHN HOWARD, both of Macon, for $5, 41-ac tract, Dis. 14, on Crows Mill Cr. Feb. 19, 1845. *Wm. R. McDowell.* Wit: *JOHN MCDOWELL*, who proved in Sep. 1847 court. Registered Nov. 15, 1847.

271 JOHN LEATHERWOOD of Haywood Co. NC to GEORGE WIKLE of Macon, for $830, 167+ ac. on Tennessee R., Sec. 3, Dis. 14. Oct. 3, 1832. *John Leatherwood.* Wit: *WM. H. THOMAS, J.B. TRAMMELL.* Proven by JCB Trammell in Sep. 1847 court. Registered Nov. 15, 1847.

272 ASCUE CURTIS to JOHN HOWARD, both of Macon, for $50, one-half of the 50-ac. tract we bought jointly from SAUL SMITH, on the Chattooga R., bd. WILLIAM BARNS. Jul. 31, 1845. *Askew Curtis.* Wit: *A.J. CONLEY, L. HOWARD.* Proven by Conley in Sep. 1847 court. Registered Nov. 15, 1847.

273 MERIT B. STRAIN to JOHN YOUNG for $10, 50 ac. Sep. 23, 1847. *M.B. Strain.* Wit: none. Ack. in Sep. 1847 court. Registered Nov. 15, 1847.

273 WILLIAM M. PENLAND to R.C. PENLAND, both of Macon, for $4.50, 50 ac. adj. Sec. 58, Dis. 13. Jul. 7, 1847. *W.M. Penland.* Wit: none. Ack. in Sep. 1847 court. Registered Nov. 15, 1847.

274 ELIAS NORTON of Macon to JOHN HOLDEN of Pickens Dis. SC, for $100, 50 ac. on White Water R., near Terepin Mtn. Dis. 18. Jun. 8, 1847. *Elias Norton.* Wit: *J.H. ALLEY, R. NORTON.* Proven by John H. Alley, Sep. 1847. Registered Nov. 15, 1847.

275 ELIAS NORTON to EVAN PEARSON (PERSON), both of Macon, for $100, 100 ac. on White Water R., above HEDDY's on top of mountain. Jun. 8, 1847. *Elias Norton.* Wit: *J.H. ALLEY Junr., R. NORTON.* Proven by Alley in Sep. 1847 court. Registered Nov. 15, 1847.

276 THOMAS J. ROANE, Trustee of State of N.C., County of Macon, to NICHOLAS WOODFIN of Buncombe Co. NC, land which H.G. WOODFIN conveyed to JAMES ROBINSON, since dec'd, in trust. On Mar. 14, 1843, Robinson offered lands at court-house door to highest bidder. Agreeable to deed of trust, N.W. Woodfin bought land with high bid of $350. Court of Equity, Macon Co. appointed Roane trustee in Fall 1843 session. Now Roane conveys to Nicholas Woodfin the following property in Dis. 15: No. 60, 55 ac. on Thompson's fork of Cartoogachaye Cr.; No. ___, 55 ac; two entries, 225 ac.; tract Nos. 123 (76 ac.), 57 (122 ac.), 62 (60 ac.); 59 (61 ac.), 58 (65 ac.)—being 788 ac. in all; land conveyed by JESSE R. SILER to H.G. Woodfin on which is situated the saw mill, known as the ROBT. JOHNSON Saw Mill. Sep. 24, 1847. *T.J. Roane, trustee.* Wit: *B.K. DICKEY*, who proved in Sep. 1847 court. Registered Nov. 15, 1847.

277 ABRAHAM HOOPER to JOHN HOOPER, both of Macon, for $30, 10 ac. granted me as assignee of MILTON BROWN, 1837, on Tuckasegee R., Dis. 6. Sep. 13, 1837. *Abraham (his X mark) Hooper.* Wit: *JOHN A. HOOPER, HENSON QUEEN.* Proven by John A. Hooper in Sep. 1847 court. Registered Nov. 15, 1847.

278 JACOB B. TRAMMELL to CAROLINA GRAHAM & WILLIAM K. TRAMMELL, for $1,000, 192 ac. on Tennessee R., Sec. 23, Dis. 16. Mar. 24, 1847. *J.B. Trammell.* Wit: *J. PHILLIP, MAHALA BATEMAN.* Ack. in Sep. 1847 court. Registered Nov. 15, 1847.

279 ENOS SCROGGS to SAMUEL W. DOWDLE, both of Macon, for value rec'd, 131 ac. Jan. 22, 1839. *Enos Scroggs.* Wit: *J. PHILLIPS, J.W. DOWDLE.* Phillips proved in Sep. 1847 court. Registered Nov. 15, 1847.

279 JACOB B. TRAMMELL to CAROLINA GRAHAM & WILLIAM K. TRAMMELL, for $600, 171 ac., Sec. 2, Dis. 16 on N. side of Cartoogachayee Cr., on the river. Mar. 24, 1847. *J.B. Trammell.* Wit: *J. PHILLIPS, MAHALA BATEMAN.* Ack. in Sep. 1847 court. Registered Nov. 15, 1847.

280 EPHRAIM AMONS to JACOB TRAMMELL for $64, 640 ac. on Chatooga R., Dis. 18.
     Mar. 24, 1841. *E. Amons*. Wit: *JOHN MCDOWELL, JAS. ROBINSON*. Proven by Mc-
     Dowell in Sep. 1847 court. Registered Nov. 15, 1847.

281 SARAH E. HOWARD by her next friend JOHN HOWARD to ASCUE CURTIS, for
     $50, 100 ac. on Tessenty Cr., incl. JACK NATION's improvement. If any of described
     tract should cover any part of land of WILLIAM CONLEY that he bought of N.S. JAR-
     RETT, that part is null and void. Jul. 21, 1845. *Sarah E. Howard by her next friend J.
     Howard.* Wit: *L. HOWARD, A.J. CONLEY.* Proven by Conley in Sep. 1847 court.
     Registered Nov. 15, 1847.

282 SG 716, BERT LEDFORD, $5/100, 50 ac. on White Pine Cr. Entry Apr. 2, 1845; grant
     May 10, 1847; registered Dec. 12, 1847.

283 SG 709, EDMUN DALRYMPLE, $5/100 ac., 50 ac. on Walnut Cr., Dis. 15, bd. the
     HOOD tract. Entry Feb. 44; grant Jan. 2, 1847; registered Dec. 15, 1847.

283 SG 700, WOREN BARKER, $5/100 ac., 60 ac. on Savannah Cr. Entry Oct. 11, 1842;
     grant Dec. 21, 1846; registered Dec. 14, 1847.

284 SG 712, JOHN A. WILLSON, $5/100 ac., 75 ac. on Elijay Cr. Entry Jan. 7, 1844; grant
     Jan. 22, 1847; registered Jan. 15, 1848.

285 SG 707, W.W. JONES, $5/100 ac., 25 ac. on Savannah Cr., bd. LUKE WILLSON &
     WESLEY ASHE, incl. HESEKIAH JONES' improvement. Entry Mar. 5, 1846; grant
     Dec. 28, 1846; registered Jan. 15, 1848.

286 SG 602, H.N. CONLEY, $5/100 ac. on Tesenty Cr., Dis. 13. Entry Nov. 1, 1841; grant
     Dec. 9, 1844; registered Jan. 15, 1848.

286 SG 721, ELIAS NORTON,$5/100 ac., 100 ac. on White Water R., bd. JOHN HOLDEN.
     Entry Jun. 9, 1846; grant Oct. 6, 1847; registered Jan. 15, 1848.

287 B.W. BELL & JACOB B. TRAMMELL to ALEX. ZACKARY, all of Macon, for $50,
     56 ac. on headwaters of Chatooga R., Sec. 82, Dis. 18. Dec. 14, 1847. *JCB Trammell,
     B.W. Bell,* Wit: none. Ack. in Dec. 1847 court. Registered Jan. 15, 1848.

288 Power of Attorney: Shelby Co. TN, I, JULIAS N. GARRETT of Shelby Co. appoint
     MATTHEW GARRETT of Macon, or, if he fail to act, L.N. GARRETT of Macon, my
     lawful attorney to act for me in N.C. Oct. 13, 1846. *Julias N. Garrett.* Garrett appeared
     before me, D.M. SHORT, deputy Co. Clerk of Shelby & ack. same Oct. 12, 1846. A.
     MCLAMORE by D.M. Short. Registered in Macon Jan. 15, 1848.

288 I sold to Miss JANE KINSLAND one sorrell Horse named John, two years old last
     spring, at $50; he used to suck the stump before I purchased him, but I have never seen
     him sucking the Stump since I git him. Oct. 5, 1847. *W.H. THOMAS per SAM'L P.
     SHERRELL.* Wit: *WILLIAM KINSLAND,* who proved in Dec. 1847 court. Registered
     Jan. 15, 1848.

289 SG 710, MARTIN ADAMS, $5/100 ac., 50 ac. on Cullewhee Cr. Entry Aug. 25, 1844;
     grant Jan. 7, 1847; registered Jan. 15, 1848.

289 SAMUEL H. WATERS to JACOB FOUTS, both of Macon, for $100, 57+ ac., Sec. 26,
     Dis. 17. Sep. 9, 1844. *S.H. Waters.* Wit: *RICHARD CLAMPITT, GEORGE ROWLAND.*
     Proven by Clampitt in Dec. 1847 court. Registered Jan. 15, 1848.

290 SILAS MCDOWELL of Macon to SAMUEL R. LAMBERT, for $600, 1-ac. town lot,
     No. 20, on Main Street. Jan. 26, 1839. *S. McDowell.* Wit: *J.W. GUINN.* Ack. in Dec.
     1847 court. Registered Jan. 15, 1848.

291 SG 613, WILLIAM YOUNG, assignee of WALTER SORRELLS, for $__, 50 ac, Sec.
     125, Dis. 10. Granted Dec. 30, 1840; registered Mar. 13, 1848.

292 SG 729, JOSEPH YOUNG, $210, 160 ac., Sec. 17, Dis. 11. Granted Mar. 20, 1845;
     registered Mar. 13, 1848.

292 SG 583, JAMES ANGEL $101, 148 ac., Sec. 123, Dis. 10. Granted Dec. 17, 1840;
     registered Mar. 13, 1848.

293 Sheriff's sale: EZEKIEL DOWDLE, Esq., High Sheriff of Macon, to ALEXANDER ZACHARY, property sold to satisfy judgment of the Superior Court of N.C. at Raleigh against JACOB B. TRAMMELL &B.W. BELL of $637.25, recovered by G.W. CANSLER & T.L. CLINGMAN of Trammell & Bell. Sold at public auction was 140-ac. tract, part of 640 ac. entry originally granted EPHRAIM AMMONS in Dis. 18, taken as property of Trammell. At public sale Dec. 13, 1847, at courthouse in Franklin, Zachary had high bid of $3.50. Dec. 13, 1847. *E. Dowdle.* Ack. in Sep. 1847 court. Registered Mar. 13, 1848.

295 SG 675, to JOHN SHERRIL & JOSEPH SHERRILL, $10/100, 600 ac. on W. side Tuckaseege R., bd. ARMSTRONG survey, crossing Deep Cr. Entry Sep. 29, 1843; grant Mar. 4, 1846; registered Mar. 27, 1848.

End of section of J.R. ALLMAN, R.M.C.

This begins section of ISAAC N. KEENER Register of Macon County.

296 Power of attorney: SUSAN CLAYTON of Macon appoints JOHN CLAYTON of Person Co. NC my true & lawful agent & att'y to sue for any persons indebted to me, etc., to selll & make title to my land willed me by my husband SOLOMON CLAYTON, dec'd, in Person Co. Mar. 23, 1848. *Susan (her X mark) Clayton.* Wit: *STEPHEN HAYS,* who swore before WILLIAM H. BATTLE, judge of Superior Court of Law & Equity on Mar. 23, 1848. Registered Mar. 3, 1848.

296 SG 687, THOMAS M. ANGEL, $5/100 ac., 50 ac. on Brushy Cr. near the Yellow mtn. Entry Aug. 21, 1841; grant Dec. 2, 1846; registered Apr. 25, 1848.

297 CLARK GUY of Macon to JAMES H. BRYSON of Cherokee Co. NC, for $80, Sec. 42, Dis. 12, purchased at 1836 sale. Nov. 19, 1847. *Clark Guy.* Wit: *JOHN KERBY, Y.W. HAYES.* Proven by Kerby in Mar. 1848 court. Registered May 8, 1848.

298 SG 731, ALEXANDER ZACHARY, $5/100 ac., 100 ac. on the Blue Ridge, headwaters of the Tuckasegee R. Entry Oct. 19, 1845; grant Dec. 14, 1847; registered May 5, 1848.

299 SG 815, NATHAN TABER, $14.74 1/2, 73 ac, Sec. 36, Dis. 9. Granted Apr. 17, 1848; registered May 8, 1848.

300 SG 739, WILLIAM C. CONLEY, $5/100 ac., 50 ac. on N. side of Tesenty Cr. Entry Jan. 27, 1845; grant Jan. 10, 1848; registered May 10, 1848.

301 SG 738, WILLIAM C. CONLEY, $5/100 ac., 50 ac. on Tesenty Cr. Entry Jan. 27, 1845; grant Jan. 10, 1848; registered May 10, 1848.

302 SG 732, ANDREW J. CONLEY, $5/100 ac., 100 ac. on Tesenty Cr., bd. NICKLES survey, crossing Nickles Branch. Entry Oct. 30, 1845; grant Dec. 14, 1847; registered May 12, 1848.

303 THOMAS M. MOORE of Macon to A.J. CONLEY, $675 for a Negro man, ABRAM, about 28 years old, sound, healthy, serviceable. Jan. 1, 1848. *Thomas M. Moore.* Wit: *J.R. SILER, E. DOWDLE.* Proven by Dowdle in Mar. 1848. Registered May 12, 1848.

303 JAMES H. BRYSON of Cherokee Co. NC to JOHN H. LEDFORD of Macon, for $530, 95 ac., Dis. 12, part of Sec. 21 on the Sugartown fork of the Tennessee River. Feb. 2, 1848. *Jas. H. Bryson.* Wit: *JOHN MCDOWELL, ULRICK KEENER.* Proven by McDowell in Mar. 1848 court. Registered May 13, 1848.

304 JAMES H. BRYSON of Cherokee Co. NC to GEORGE T. LEDFORD of Macon, for $600, 87 ac. on Sugartown fork of Tennessee R., Dis. 12, part of Sec. 21. Feb. 3, 1848. *Jas. H. Bryson.* Wit: *JOHN MCDOWELL, ULRICK KEENER.* Proven by McDowell in Mar. 1848. Registered May 13, 1848.

305 JAMES H. BRYSON of Cherokee Co. NC to JOHN H. LEDFORD of Macon, for $80, 63 ac., Sec. 42, Dis. 12 pruchased as 1836 sale by MARGARET BRYSON, transferred by her to CLARK GUY and by him to me. Feb. 2, 1848. *J.H. Bryson.* Wit: *JOHN MCDOWELL, ULRICK KEENER.* Proven by McDowell in Mar. 1848. Registered May 14, 1848.

306 JAMES H. BRYSON of Cherokee Co. NC to JOHN H. LEDFORD, for $70, 55 ac. on Sugartown fork of Tennessee R., purchased at 1836 sale by MARGARET BRYSON & transferred from her to me. Feb. 2, 1848. *Jas. H. Bryson.* Wit: *JOHN MCDOWELL, ULRICK KEENER.* Proven by McDowell in Mar. 1848 court. Registered May 14, 1848.

307 MARGARET BRYSON of Cherokee Co. NC to JAS. H. BRYSON, for $20, quitclaim to him Tract 46, Dis. 12, purchased by me at 1836 sale. Jan. 28, 1848. *Margaret (her X mark) Bryson.* Wit: *J.H.(K?) COLLETT, A.T. DAVIDSON.* Proven by Davidson in Mar. 1848 court. Registered May 14, 1848.

307 MARGARET BRYSON of Cherokee Co. NC to JAMES H. BRYSON, for $100, Sec. 21, Dis. 12, which I hold as tenant in dower for & during my natural life as widow of ANDREW BRYSON, dec'd; to James H., all my right etc. in the estate of said Andrew, it being 1/3 of said tract, including dwelling house & outhouses, the late dwelling of said Andrew. Jan. 21, 1848. *Margaret (her X mark) Bryson.* Wit: A.T. DAVIDSON, J.H. COLLETT.

308 JAMES H. BRYSON of Cherokee Co. NC to GEORGE T. LEDFORD, for $10, 50 ac. on Shugartown R., Dis. 12. Feb. 2, 1848. *Jas. H. Bryson.* Wit: *JOHN MCDOWELL, JOHN H. LEDFORD.* Proven by McDowell in Mar. 1848. Registered May 24, 1848.

309 ISAAC MORE of Cherokee Co. NC to JAMES H. BRYSON for $10, 50 ac. on Sugartown fork of Tennessee R., corner WIDOW BRYSON's land, corner CLARK GUY's land. Jan. 8, 1848. *Isaac Moor.* Wit: *A.T. DAVIDSON, J.H. COLLETT* Proven by Davidson in Mar. 1848 court. Registered May 25, 1848.

310 CLARK GUY of Macon to JAMES H. BRYSON of Cherokee Co. NC, for $20, 50 ac. on Sugartown fork of Tennessee R., on top of ridge dividing where Guy and HIRAM GIPSON live. Feb. 2, 1848. *Clark Guy.* Wit: *JOHN MCDOWELL, JOHN H. LEDFORD* Proven by Ledford in Mar. 1848 court. Registered May 24, 1848.

311 JAMES H. BRYSON of Cherokee Co. NC to JAMES H. LEDFORD of Macon for $20, 50 ac. on Sugartown fork of Tennessee River. Feb. 2, 1848. *Jas. H. Bryson.* Wit: *JOHN MCDOWELL, ULRICK KEENER.* Proven by McDowell in Mar. 1848 court. Registered May 29, 1848.

311 SG 728; granted to THOMAS WELCH by sheriff's deed, for $134.34 paid by THOMAS W.P. POINDEXTER, 50+ ac., Sec. 38, Dis. 8, where Tennessee & Tuckasegee rivers intersect. Granted Mar. 20, 1845; registered May 29, 1948.

312 SG 301, THOMAS WELCH, $5/100 ac., 100 ac. on E. side Burningtown Creek. Entry May 2, 1836; grant Dec. 24, 1838; registered May 29, 1848.

313 SG 658, WILLIAM H. BRYSON, $5/100 ac., 50 ac. on Cullewhee Creek. Entry Mar. 18, 1841; grant Jan. 9, 1845; registered May 29, 1848.

314 SG 727, granted to THOMAS WELCH by sheriff's deed, for $105.48 paid by WILLIAM WELCH Senr., 54 ac., Sec. 1, Dis. 1, on N. bank of Tennessee R., lower end of an old Indian field, on Tuckasegee River. Granted Mar. 20, 1845; registered May 29, 1848.

315 ANDR. WOOD to WILLIAM DODGEN, both of Macon, for $7, 100 ac. on Culowhee Cr., Dis. 7, including improvement where Dodgeen lives. Jan. 1, 1847. *A.J. Woods.* Wit: *S.A. DAVIS, DANIEL WOOD, JOHN WILSON.* Proven by Wilson in Mar. 1848. Registered May 29, 1848.

316 ANTHONY HOLLAND to LOGAN BERRY, both of Macon, for $150, 50 ac., Dis. 11, bd. FRANKS. Oct. 6, 1847. *Anthony Holland.* Wit: *J.D. FRANKS, M.B. STRAIN.* Ack. in Mar. 1848 court. Registered May 29, 1848.

316 SG 725, PHILLIP GUYER Junr., $5/100 ac., 100 ac. on "Iola" (Iotla) Cr., on Coal pitt Branch, to a stake in LEACHE's Reservation line. Entry Nov. 30, 1845; grant Oct. 22, 1847; registered May 29, 1848.

317 SG 723, DAVID GUYER, $5/100 ac., 50 ac. on Burningtown Cr., bd. PHILLIP GUYER. Entry Nov. 30, 1845; grant Oct. 22, 1847; registered May 29, 1848.

318 SG 421, ROBERT FOX, $___, 50 ac., Sec. 2, Dis. 6, on SW side of Tuckasegee R. Granted Jan. 7, 1839; registered June 1, 1848.

319 SG 724, PHILLIP GUYER, $5/100 ac., 50 ac. on N. side Burningtown Cr., near a trail. Entry Nov. 30, 1845; grant Oct. 22, 1847; registered Jun. 3, 1848.

319 SG 736, PHILLIP GUYER, $5/100 ac., 52+ ac. on "Iola" (Iotla) Cr., SW corner of LEMUEL BIRD's land. Entry Nov. 30, 1845; grant Dec. 27, 1847; registered Jun. 4, 1848.

320 LOGAN BERRY to ANTHONY HOLLAND, both of Macon, for $150, 56 ac., Sec. 70, Dis. 11. Oct. 6, 1847. *Logan (his X mark) Berry*. Wit: *J.B. STRAIN, M.B. STRAIN*. Ack. in Mar. 1848. Registered Jun. 5, 1848.

321 WILLIAM H. THOMAS of Haywood Co. NC to JOHN R. ALMAN of Athens, GA, for $200, 200 ac. in Cherokee Co., Tract 136, Dis. 5. Mar. 25, 1848. *William H. Thomas*. Wit: *JNO. ANGEL*. Ack. in Mar. 1848 court. Registered Jun. 10, 1848.

321 WILLIAM H. THOMAS of Haywood Co. NC to WILLIAM ALLMAN of Macon, for $50 to be paid by SHADE STALLCUP, 50 ac. adj. lands occupied by Allman in Dis. 8, tract 134. Mar. 24, 1848. *William (his X mark) Thomas*. Wit: *MARK COLEMAN*. Ack. in Mar. 1848 court. Registered Jun. 10, 1848.

322 JCB TRAMMELL to WM. K. TRAMMELL, for $120, 76 ac., Sec. 40, Dis. 11. Mar. 7, 1848. *JCB Trammell*. Wit: ALVIS CHEEK, M. CAROLINE (her X mark) GRAHAM. Ack. in Mar. 1848. Registered Jun. 12, 1848.

322 WILLIAM D. TROTTER to DANIEL WEST, for $300, Negro girl FRANCIS, aged 4 years, sound in body & mind. Sep. 30, 1847. *William D. Trotter*. Wit: *WM. WEST*, who proved in Mar. 1842 court. Registered Jun. 13, 1848.

323 WILLIAM D. TROTTER to WILLIAM WEST, for $212.50, Negro girl LYDIA, age about 9 years, sound in body & mind. Oct. 1, 1847. *William D. Trotter*. Wit: *WM. TROT-TER Senr.*, who proved in Mar. 1848 court. Registered Jun. 13, 1848.

323 ARON SMITH to ZACHARIAH CABE, for $100, 88 ac., Sec. 66, Dis. 13, purchased at 1836 land sale in Franklin. Dec. 17, 1847. *A. Smith*. Wit: *SAUL SMITH, SILAS LED-FORD*. Proven by Saul Smith in Mar. 1848 court. Registered Jun. 17, 1848.

324 SAMUEL BRYSON, ISAAC MOORE & wife RACHEL, and STEPHEN BRYSON, all of Cherokee Co. NC, to JAMES H. BRYSON of Cherokee Co., for $1,000, their interest in 147 ac., Sec. 21, Dis. 12, purchased by ANDREW BRYSON, dec'd, on Sugar Town Fork of Tennessee R., where sd. Andrew resided & which descended to the heirs, Samuel Bryson, Isaac Moore & Rachel, Stephen Bryson and James H. Bryson. Jan. 21, 1848. *Samuel Bryson, Isaac Moore, Rachel (her X mark) Moore, Stephen Bryson*. Wit: *S.W. DAVIDSON, JOHN J. ROSE*. Proven by Davidson before WILLIAM H. BATTLE, judge of Superior Court of Law & Equity, Mar. 13, 1848. Isaac Moore & wife Rachel acknowledged deed and Rachel was examined separately before Battle. Registered Jun. 17, 1848.

325 SG 735, JONATHAN FORD, $5/100 ac., 100 ac. on "Eliyaye" (Ellijay) Cr., beginning at THOMAS FORD's old corner. Entry Oct. 15, 1845; grant Dec. 27, 1847; registered Jun. 17, 1848.

326 SAMUEL REID to CURTIS SAUNDERS, both of Macon, for $2.50, 2 ac., part of Sec. 48, Dis. 10, on S. bank of Watauga Cr., bd. JOSEPH R. JOHNSTON's entry. Sep. 23, 1847. *Samuel Reid*. Wit: *JOHN HALL, JOHN REID*. Ack. in Mar. 1848 court. Registered Jul. 5, 1848.

327 ARON SMITH to ZACHARIAH CABE, for $100, 90 ac., Sec. 64, Dis. 13, on E. side of
Tennessee River. Dec. 17, 1847. *A. Smith*. Wit: *SAUL SMITH, SILAS LEDFORD*.
Proven by Saul Smith in Mar. 1848. Registered Aug. 4, 1848.

328 PHEBE PRICHARD of Macon to WILLIAM HOOD of Habersham Co., GA, for $400,
87+ ac., part of Sec. 36, Dis. 16. Jan. 16, 1845. *Phebe Prichard*. Wit: *J.M. ANGEL, N.H.
PALMER*. Proven by Angel in Mar. 1848 court. Registered Aug. 4, 1848.

328 JAMES W. GUINN to Z.J. THOMAS, both of Macon, for $900, 165 ac., Sec. 78, Dis.
15 on Tennessee R., near the meeting house, running w. top of ridge dividing line between JOHN MCDOWELL & SARAH ENLOE. Jul. 25, 1840. *J.W. Guinn*. Wit: *J.R.
ALLMAN*, who proved in Mar. 1848 court. Registered Aug. 22, 1848.

329 SARAH ENLOE to E. DOWDLE, both of Macon, for $800, 60 ac., Sec. 70, Dis. 15, on
W. bank of Tennessee R. at the old still; 80 ac., Sec. 71, Dis. 15 on W. bank of Ten-
nessee R.; 61 ac. on Sec. 12, Dis. 15, on W. bank of Tennessee R., including mill seat on
"Skenah" (Skeenah) or Standridges Cr. Nov. 8, 1847. *Sarah Enloe*. Wit: *JOHN N.
GIBBS, JOHN SELLERS, BRYANT GIBBS*. Proven by Sellars in Mar. 1848 court.
Registered Aug. 23, 1848.

Original book has no page 330-339

340 MICHAEL LONG of Haywood Co. NC to JAMES M. & EDWARD HOOPER, for $50,
51 ac., Sec. 38, Dis. 7. No date. *Michael (his X mark) Long*. Wit: *L.C. HOOPER, M.
LONG*. Proven by L.C. Hooper in Mar. 1848. Registered Aug. 23, 1848.

341 SG 688, ANDREW BRYSON, $5/100 ac., 50 ac. on Culowhee Cr. Entry Nov. 30, 1840;
grant Dec. 3, 1846; registered Aug. 23, 1848.

342 Sheriff's sale: THOMAS M. ANGEL, Esq., High Sheriff of Macon, to DAVID L.
SWAIN of Orange Co., NC, property sold to satisfy judgment of county court against
JOHN HALL for $300.02 recovered by J.B. BETTS to use of HYATT & CO. Sold was
50 ac., No. 260, on N. bank of Tennessee R & bank of Turkey Cr.; 50 ac., No. 261, on
Turkey Cr.; 60 ac., No. 262, on Turkey Cr.; 72 ac., No. 263; 71 ac., No. 264, on E. bank
of Tennessee R.; 59 ac., No. 265, on fork of Turkey Cr. At public sale Jun. 14, 1843,
Swain had high bid of $50. Mar. 24, 1840. *Thos. M. Angel*. Wit: *SAUL SMITH, A.B.
DONALDSON, J.K. GRAY*. Proven by Gray, Mar. 24, 1848 before WILLIAM H. BAT-
TLE, judge of Superior Ct. Registered Aug. 24, 1848.

344 Sheriff's sale: EZEKIEL DOWDLE, Esq., High Sheriff of Macon, to ALEXANDER
ZACHARY, property sold to satisfy judgment of Supreme Ct. at Raleigh against JACOB
B. TRAMMELL & BYNAM W. BELL for $137.25 + cost, recovered by G.W.
CANSLER & T.L. CLINGMON of Trammell & Bell. Property sold was 56 ac. on Chattooga R., Sec. 82, Dis. 18. At public sale, Dec. 13, 1847, Zachary had high bid of 50
cents. Mar. 22, 1848. *E. Dowdle, Sh'ff*. Ack. in Mar. 1845 court. Registered Aug. 24,
1848.

346 Mortgage: T.H. OWENS to N.G. ALLMAN, JOHN INGRAM & J.L. MOORE, all of
Macon, for $40.89, paid as follows—$13.06 by Allman, $11.51 by Moore, $16.32 by Ingram, conveys following property: 3 cattle, 2 horses, 13 hogs, 8 sheep, crop of oats,
household & kitchen furniture. Jul. 24, 1848. *T.H. Owens*. Wit: *ELI TIPPETT*. Ack. in
Jul. 24, 1848 in clerk's office. Registered Aug. 24, 1848.

347 SAMUEL SMITH to SAUL SMITH for $150, 75 ac., Sec. 36, Dis. 13, on N. bank of
Middle Cr. Mar. 28, 1839. *Samuel Smith*. Wit: *JOHN MCDOWELL, BRYANT CONLEY*.
Proven by McDowell in Mar. 1848 court. Registered Aug. 27, 1848.

348 SG 745, ALEXANDER DOWNS, $5/100 ac., 50 ac. on Tennessee R., bd. E.M. HALL.
Entry Sep. 18, 1846; grant May 15, 1848; registered Aug. 27, 1848.

348 JOHN BREWER of Macon to JOHN R. SILER, for $65, 50 ac. on Tuckasegee R., what
is called Brewer's mine on the fall branch. Jan. 15, 1848. *John Brewer*. Wit: *M.
HEDGECOCK*, who proved in Mar. 1848 court. Registered Sep. 12, 1848.

349 Sheriff's sale: THOS. M. ANGEL, Esq., High Sheriff of Macon to J.R. SILER, assignee of N.W. WOODFIN, property sold to satisfy judgment of county court of Macon for $300.52 against JOHN HALL, recovered by J.B. BETTS to use of HYATT, MCBURNEY & CO., 1-ac town lot on Main St. At public sale Jun. 14, 1843, Siler, assignee of Woodfin had high bid of $45. Mar. 24, 1848. *Thos. M. Angel.* Wit: *J. HOWARD, SAUL SMITH.* Ack. in Mar. 1848. Registered Sep. 12, 1848.

350 ROBERT FOX to JAMES HOOPER, both of Macon, for $100, 50 ac., Sec. 2, Dis. 8, SE side of Tuckasegee River. Oct. 8, 1846. *Robert (his X mark) Fox.* Wit: *E.K. ERWIN, ANDREW WIKE.* Proven by Wike in Mar. 1848 court. Registered Sep. 12, 1848.

351 MARK BURREL of Macon to A.T. EDWARDS of Cherokee Co. NC, for $40, 100 ac., Dis. 18 on Chattooga R., on both sides of trail leading from the Horse Cove to Georgia. *Mark (his X mark) Burrel.* Wit: *W.A. EDWARDS, BUTLER BURREL.* Ack. in Mar. 1848. Registered Sep. 13, 1848.

352 WM. STALLCUP to MARGARET AMANDA STALLCUP for $325, Negro girl Tilda, age 10. Apr. 8, 1843. *Wm. Stallcup.* Wit: *JOHN GOOME(?)Ack. in Jun. 1848 court. Registered Sep. 14, 1848.*

352 Mortgage/guardianship bond: SAUL SMITH to JOHN HOWARD, both of Macon, for $1, 100 ac. in Dis. 13, on Middle Creek; 50 ac. in Dis. 18, on Chattooga R., beginning on the GA line, on Buzard Rock Mtn., bd. DAN'L S. MACDOWELL; 50 ac. on Chattooga R., beginning on top of ridge near the Horse Cove; 40 ac., Sec. 36, Dis. 13, on Middle Cr.; 50 ac. on Middle Cr.; 30 ac. in Dis. 16 adj. preceding and No. 59, Dis. 16, on Middle Cr.; 30 ac. in Dis. 13, E. side of Middle Cr.; 40 ac. in Dis. 13, Middle Cr.; 40 ac. in Dis. 13, Middle Cr.; 104 ac., Sec. 59, on Middle Cr.; 58 ac., adj. No. 36 & 59. Condition: Saul Smith has been appointed by the Court of Pleas & Qtr. Sessions for Macon, at late spring term, the guardian of the 4 youngest heirs of WILLIAM CARPENTER, dec'd - HUMPHREY, HENRY, BENJAMIN & JACKSON CARPENTER. Howard entered guardian bond with Smith. Now, if Smith discreetly manages legacy of 4 sd. minors, deed is void. Jun. 14, 1848. *Saul Smith.* Wit: *SILAS MCDOWELL* Ack. before clerk of court, Jun. 16, 1848. Registered Sep. 14, 1848.

355 JAMES HOOPER to ANDREW WIKE, both of Macon, for $45, 45 ac., West end of Sec. 2, Dis. 6, what is known as the pounding mill branch. Feb. 26, 1848. *James (his X mark) Hooper.* Wit: *JACOB WIKE, J. KEENER.* Proven by Jacob Wike in Mar. 1848 court. Registered Sep. 15, 1848.

355 THOMAS MONTEITH of N.C. to AMOS ASH of Macon, for $150, 58 ac., Sec. 26, Dis. 7, on Tuckasegee River. Mar. 18, 1848. *Thomas Monteeth.* Wit: *THOMAS GRIBBLE, JOHN MONTEETH.* Proven by Gribble in Mar. 1848 court. Registered Sep. 15, 1848.

356 SAUL SMITH, Clerk and Master in Equity for Macon, to NICHOLAS W. WOODFIN, for $400, property sold on decree of Court of Equity, Sep. 1846, in case of GEORGE H. KELSEY & others against JASON H. HUNTER. Woodfin had high bid of $400 at public sale for 167 ac. tract on Tennessee R., Sec. 38, Dis. 16. Mar. 25, 1848. *Saul Smith, CME* Wit: LEONIDAS W. SILER Ack. in Mar. 1848 court. Registered Sep. 18, 1848.

357 I certify that JOHN HANNER was purchaser of Sec. 62, Dis. 17, containing 64 ac. I certify that Hanner was purchaser of Sec. 63, Dis. 17, 56 ac. Oct. 29, 1836. J.K. GRAY, Clerk, Macon County Court of Pleas & Qtr. Sessions. Registered Sep. 20, 1848.

358 SG 804, to REUBEN B. CALER, assignee of JOHN HANER, for $29.69, 64 ac., Sec. 62, Dis. 17. Granted Oct. 9, 1847; registered Sep. 20,. 1848.

359 SG 805 to REUBEN B. CALER, assignee of JOHN HANNER, for $19, 50 ac., Sec. 63, Dis. 17, W. bank of Buyner's Cr. Granted Oct. 9, 1847; registered Sep. 20, 1848.

359 SG 708, HENRY THOMAS, $5/100 ac., 100 ac. on Indian Creek. Entry May 7, 1844; grant Dec. 31, 1846; registered Sep. 6, 1848.

Original book has two pages numbered "359".

359 SG 662, JOHN STEWART, $5/100 ac., 50 ac. on White Pine Cr. Entry Sep. 9, 1842; grant Jan. 28, 1845; registered Sep. 6, 1848.

360 ELI WALDROUP to FRANCIS NICKLES, both of Macon, for $20, No. 1908 in Dis. 15, on Lowry's fork of "Cattoogaja" (Cartoogechaye) Cr. Sep. 20, 1843. *Eli (his X mark) Waldroup.* Wit: *WM. G. WATS, W. (his X mark) E. CARTER, MILES H. (his X mark) PENDERGREISS.* Proven by WM. GUFFEY (sic) in Mar. 1848 court. Reg. Sep. 7, 1848.

361 SG 733, JOSEPH M. DONALDSON, $5/100 ac., 100 ac. on "Skeener" (Skeenah) Cr., bd. ELI MCKEE. Entry Feb. 22, 1843; grant Jan. 27, 1847; registered Sep. 7, 1848.

361 Deed of Gift: SILAS MCDOWELL of Macon, in consideration of the last will of my mother, ELIZABETH MCDOWELL, which was made void through informality of being executed in presence of but one witness, in which will she left my eldest son WILLIAM E. MCDOWELL all her estate. Because of informality of the will, all descended to me as her only heir at law. Wishing to have carried into effect the last will etc. of my mother, and in consideration of love I have for William, I shall therefore pursue the letter and tenor of said will and make the following bequests to him: 3 tracts on Sugar town fork of Tennessee R., the lower tract 108+ ac.; 2nd, 80 ac. on E. side of river; 3rd, 69+ ac. on NE side; also all the household furniture which was Elizabeth's, beds and bedsteads and stock of cattle - 10 cattle, 2 horses (mares), one known as the Marblieu filly and the other Buzzard. Mar. 22, 1848. *S. McDowell.* Wit: *JOHN HALL,* who proved in Mar. 1848 court. Registered Oct. 7, 1848.

363 SG 737, JAMES REED, $5/100 ac., 100 ac. on Bear Wallow Creek. Entry Jan. 4, 1845; grant Jan. 10, 1848; registered Oct. 10, 1848.

364 Mortgage: SILAS BLAIN & WILSON BLAIN to JOHN HOWARD, all of Macon. Silas has bargained to Howard a gray horse, standing crop of corn, stack of oats at L. VANDYKE's, 16 sheep, all his household furniture, 3 cows & last spring's calves. Wilson conveys to Howard a black cow & calf, 2 sheep, 10 hogs. Condition: Wilson to pay a court judgment obtained against them in State vs. WILLIAM BLAIN, Sep. 1848, with Howard as security; also Howard stands surety for a suit obtained in Sep. court in State vs. JAMES BLAIN, minor son of Silas, which debt Silas has bound himself to see paid. Silas gives Howard his note for $15.81 1/4. If Silas pay the 2 court costs & note, this deed is void. Sep. 30, 1848. *S. Blain.* Wit: *L. Vandyke,* who proved Oct. 3, 1848 before J.K. GRAY, clerk. Registered Oct. 11, 1848.

366 RABUN MASHBURN to SAMUEL WOODS, both of Macon, whereas Woods is security for Mashburn in stay of judgment in W. HESTER vs. R. Mashburn for $29.62 1/2, which stay is about out, with interest & cost; he enters surety this day for 2 notes to CHARLES THOMAS(?) for 100 bu. of corn to be paid at common gathering time, the other for $15 to be paid at Christmas next. To make Woods harmless, Mashburn conveys all his standing crop of corn, one horse, yellowish culler, and one sorrel mare pony. Sep. 11, 1848. *R. Mashburn.* Wit: *J. HOWARD.* Ack. Sep. 2, 1848 before J.K. Gray, Clk. Registered Oct. 12, 1848.

366 JOHN DOBSON to CHARLES HAYES, both of Macon, for $1,000, 239+ ac., No. 9, Dis. 12 on Tennessee River. Mar. 17, 1842. *John Dobson.* Wit: *JOHN MCDOWELL,* who proved in Sep. 1848 court. Registered Oct. 12, 1848.

367 Performance bond: DAVID R. LOWRY, JESSE R. SILER, BURTON K. DICKEY, B.W. BELL, WILLIAM TATHAM, JOHN HOWARD post $4,000 for David R. Lowry, duly elected clerk of Superior Court. Sep. 22, 1848. Wit: *THAD P. SILER*, who proved Sep. 23, 1848 before M.E. MANLEY, JSCL&E. Registered Oct. 17, 1848.

368 Performance bond: $10,000 bond for DAVID R. LOWRY; details same as previous entry.

368 Performance bond: J.K. GRAY, J.R. SILER, SILAS MCDOWELL post $10,000 bond for Gray, duly elected clerk of Court of Pleas and Qtr. Sessions. Ack. by makers before WM. ANGEL, Ch'man, Sep. 19, 1848. Registered Oct. 18, 1848.

369 Performance bond: $4,000 bond for J.K. GRAY; details same as previous entry.

369 SG 730, WILLIAM NORTON, $5/100 ac., 100 ac. on Chattooga R., S. side of road leading to Pickens court house. Entry sep. 15, 1848; grant Dec. 14, 1847; registered Oct. 18, 1848.

370 Union Co. GA. WILLIAM J. HUNTER of Union Co. to JOHN A. HUNTER of Macon, nephew of said William, for natural love & affection, a Negro boy slave, SAMUEL, 20 years old; also one waggon & yoke of steers. Oct. 20, 1848. *William J. Hunter*. Wit: J.W. HUNTER, THOS. BOLING. Proven by J.W. Hunter before county clerk, Oct. 23, 1848. Registered Oct. 24, 1848.

370 Mortgage: THOS. W. OWENS of 1st part, E. DOWDLE of 2nd part, STEPHEN MONDAY of 3rd part. Owens owes Monday $50 on bond or note; also to JOHN INGRAM $16, to J.L. MOORE $11.51 and to N.G. ALLMAN $12.50, with Monday as security on all these notes. To secure Monday, Owens conveys to Dowdle 3 horses, 5 cattle, 21 hogs, 8 sheep, 200 doz. of oats in the sheaf, growing crop of corn & tobacco, a quantity of wheat threshed & to thresh, say 25 bu., in trust. Dowdle is to use same to pay off debts if Owens does not pay by dates due. Sep. 21, 1848. *T.W. Owens, E. Dowdle, Stephen Monday*. Wit: *D.R. LOWRY*. Registered Oct. 24, 1848.

372 THOMAS C. FORD to JONATHAN FORD, both of Macon, for $50, 50 ac. on "Elijah" (Ellijay) Cr., Dis. 11. Jun. 29, 1846. *Thomas C. Ford*. Wit: *N.H. PALMER, MOSES FORD*. Ack. in Sep. 1848 court. Registered Oct. 12, 1848.

373 Mortgage: SAMUEL SELLERS to Z.J. THOMAS, both of Macon, for $100, sorrel mare, bay mare called Pigeon, 12 sheep, 14 hogs, household & kitchen furniture, all my farming tools, standing crop of corn, 2 oats stacks, one hay stack, 5 fodder stacks. Condition: Sellers to pay sum to Thomas in 2 years. Oct. 7, 1848. *Samuel Sellers*. Wit: *J. HOWARD*. Ack. Oct. 7, 1848. Registered Nov. 7, 1848.

373 JESSE M. SMILEY to JANE KINSLAND, both of Macon, for $2, one sorrel calf, six mos. old. Sep. 19, 1848 *Jesse M. Smiley*. Wit: *JOHN HALL, WILLIAM KINSLAND*. Proven by William Kinsland in Sep. 1848 court. Registered Nov. 8, 1848.

374 Mortgage: JOHN STRAIN of 1st part, MERRIT B. STRAIN of 2nd part, JONATHAN PHILLIPS of 3rd part. John Strain owes Phillips $142.97 by note. To secure payment, John sells to Merrit for further consideration of $1, 105 ac, Sec. 11, Dis. 11. John is entitled to live on lands, premises & take use & apply rents, issues & profits to own use until Apr. 13, 1850. If debt is not paid by then, Merrit is to sell land and apply proceeds. Apr. 13, 1848. *John Strain, M.B. Strain, J. Phillips*. Wit: DILLARD LOVE, who proved deed before clerk, Oct. 28, 1848. Registered Nov. 8, 1848.

375 THOMAS C. FORD & JAMES HOLLAND to JOHN A. MCCALL for $25, 100 ac. in Dis. 18, on "Chattoogy" (Chattooga) R. & Scotchman's Branch, adj. WILLIAM NORTON's survey. Sep. 20, 1848. *Thomas Ford, James (his X mark) Holland*. Wit: *JOHN REID, J. FORD*. Proven by Reid in Sep. 1848 court. Registered Nov. 8, 1848.

376 C.R. HARDIN to JAMES KIRKLAND, both of Macon, for $100, land W. of JOHN COCKERHAM's creek, Sec. 80, Dis. 82 (sic). May 31, 1842. *C.R. (his X mark) Hardin*. Wit: *N. BURCHFIELD, M.C. BERRY*. Proven by Burchfield in Sep. 1848. Registered Nov. 18, 1848.

377 MICHAEL CLINE Senr. to LEVI CLINE, both of Macon, for $100, 100 ac. in Dis. 1, on
     Bets Branch, below REDMAN's improvement. Feb. 2, 1847. *Michael (his X mark)*
     Cline. Wit: *J.H. HUNTER, JAMES A. THOMPSON*. Proven by Thompson in Sep. 1848
     court. Registered Nov. 18, 1848.

378 LEGRAN S. ROBINSON to SAMUEL ELLIOTT, both of Macon, for $250, 85 ac., Sec.
     11, Dis. 62 (sic), purchased at 1836 sale. Nov. 9, 1846. *L.S. Robinson*. Wit: *J.R. SILER,
     JAMES JENNINGS*. Ack. in Sep. 1848 court. Registered Nov. 18, 1848.

379 LEGRAN S. ROBINSON to SAMUEL ELLIOTT,both of Macon, for $50, 42 ac. pur-
     chased at sheriff's sale Sep. 15, 1842, on corner of No. 62. Nov. 9, 1846. *L.S. Robinson*.
     Wit: *J.R. SILER, JAMES JENNINGS*. Ack. in Sep. 1848 court. Registered Nov. 18, 1848.

379 DYER TALLEY of Pickens Dis. SC to DAVIS/DAVID MCKINNEY for $100, tract in
     Dis. 18, on top of Elicut Mtn., including Headee's mountain field. Aug. 16, 1845. *Dyer
     Talley*. Wit: *JAMES R. MCKINNEY, JAMES SMAWLEY*. Proven by James R. McKinney
     in Sep. 1848 court. Registered Nov. 23, 1848.

381 SG 758, JONATHAN PHILLIPS, $38.27, 92 ac., Sec. 37, Dis. 11, at jcn. of Tennessee
     R. & Sugar town fork. Granted Nov. 23, 1846; registered Jan. 24, 1849.

381 SG 757, JONATHAN PHILLIPS, $155.52, 126 ac., Sec. 1, Dis. 12, at jcn. of Tennessee
     R. & Sugar town fork. Granted Nov. 23, 1846; registered Jan. 24, 1849.

382 SG 797, to NIMROD S. JARRETT, assignee of HENRY GRADY, for $63.44, 122 ac.,
     Sec. 2, Dis. 13, on NW corner of DOBSON's camp crossing Wolf Cr. Granted Feb. 23,
     1847; registered Jan. 24, 1849.

383 JOHN SHULER to G.W. HAYES, for $1450, five Negroes: a boy named BILL abt. 20
     years old; woman, VILET, abt. 24 yrs.; boy child MARION, abt. 6; girl child (no name)
     abt. 4; girl child (no name) abt. 2 years old. Feb. 6, 1847. *John (his X mark) Shuler*. Wit:
     JAS. WIGINS, DAVID SHULER. Proven by David Shuler in Dec. 1848 court. Registered
     Jan. 24, 1849.

384 J.Y. HICKS to HUGH WALSTENHOME/WALSTENHOLME for $75, 300 ac. on War-
     rior (Wayah) Cr. at the foot of Nantahala mtn. granted Apr. 8 last, also $45 for No. 5,
     Dis. 17, taken up by me as assignee of ___ Fouts on Feb. 7 last. May 29, 1848. *J.Y.
     Hicks*. Wit: *W.E. MCDOWELL* Proven by Wm. McDowell in Dec. 1848 court.
     Registered Jan. 27, 1849.

385 WILLIAM H. THOMAS, by my agent, N.W. WOODFIN, to N.S. JARRETT, for $400,
     my interest in the Cowee turnpike road or company, being 1/2 interest, it belonging to me
     & said Jarrett equally. Mar. 21, 1846. *William H. Thomas by N.W. Woodfin, agent*. Wit:
     J.L. MOORE, who proved in Dec. 1848 court. Registered Jan. 28, 1849.

385 LEWIS VANDIKE to JOHN HOWARD, B.W. BELL & SAUL SMITH, all of Macon,
     for debts where the three stand surety for Vandike: one in the Bank at Asheville, $207
     renewing this month, Howard & Bell security; in bank, $200 note, Saul Smith principal,
     Howard & Vandike surety, of which Vandike got $53, to be renewed this month; one
     note of $260 given to SILAS LEDFORD by Lewis Vandyke, Smith & Howard surety,
     and one of the same, having been on interest 14 years or more, on which note we are now
     bil(l)ed and stand for trial at March term; one note given JOSEPH HODGENS of $104 or
     $105, given Vandyke with Howard as security, having been on interest for several years
     with some small credit. Now Vandyke conveys to Howard, Bell & Smith to secure the
     notes the following property: 6 beds furniture, one day clock, 7 cattle, viz cows, one road
     waggon, 1 fifth chain, 2 pare streachers, 6 pare of waggon gearing, 5 riding saddles, 5
     riding bridals, 4 horse beasts, 3 trunks, 1 looking glass, all my kitchen furniture. Also, 2
     notes on CHARLES W. THOMAS, one of which is for $200 due Dec. 1, 1850, other
     $100 due Dec. 1, 1851, with credit on same. Feb. 2, 1849. *L. Vandyke*. Wit: *E.
     DOWDLE*. Ack. Feb. 3, 1849 before clerk. Registered Feb. 6, 1849.

387 ANDREW M. BRYSON to CANADA/CANADAY HENDERSON, both of Macon, 100 ac. in Dis. 12, on Sugartown fork of Tennessee R., incl. place where YAM MORGAN formerly lived. Nov. 23, 1846. *Andrew M. Bryson.* Wit: *GRAY CROW, WM. PEEK.* Proven by Peek in Dec. 1848 court. Registered Feb. 3, 1849.

388 SG 781, JACOB W. SETSER, $5/100 ac., 100 ac. on Watauga Cr. Entry Feb. 22, 1847; grant Jan. 4, 1849; registered Feb. 19, 1849.

389 SG 782, WILLIAM HOLBROOK, $5/100 ac., 50 ac. on Rabbits Creek. Entry Mar. 16, 1847; grant Jan. 4, 1849; registered Mar. 8, 1849.

390 SG 787, JACOB DEETS, $5/100 ac., 100 ac. on Tuckasegee River. Entry Mar. 6, 1847; grant Jan. 20, 1849; registered Mar. 19, 1849.

391 SG 728, JOHN C. GALLOWAY, $5/100 ac., 100 ac. on Flat Cr. of Toxaway River. Entry Mar. 11, 1845; grant Dec. 3, 1847; registered Mar. 20, 1849.

392 SG 766, GEORGE N. HUGHS, $5/100 ac., 50 ac. on Tennessee River. Entry Oct. 24, 1846; grant Dec. 30, 1848; registered Mar. 22, 1849.

393 SG 852, to DANIEL MCCOY, assignee of NATHAN PILKINTON, for $46, 92 ac., Sec. 38, Dis. 12, on Nantahala R., up main sluice of river. Granted Dec. 13, 1848; registered Apr. 16, 1849.

394 SG 375, to ASAPH ENLOE, assignee of BENJAMIN HOWARD, for $1441(?), 185 ac., Sec. 70, Dis. 15, on Tennessee R., crossing Roache's (Rush's?) Branch. Granted Mar. 1, 1838; registered Apr. 19, 1849.

395 SG 878, JULIUS DEAN, assignee of E.M. KILPATRICK, for $__, 195 ac., Sec. 1 of QUNY's(?) reservation, N. side Tennese River. Granted Oct. 25, 1848; registered Apr. 20, 1849.

395 WILLIAM COCKERHAM of Macon, for natural love & affection for beloved daughter-in-law DELPHA COCKERHAM, wife of my son, JOHN COCKERHAM, the use of a Negro girl named ANN, aged 8 years, with her increase, during her natural life, & at her death, to the children of Delpha which she now has or may subsequently have. Apr. 26, 1848. *Wm. Cocerham.* Wit: *WM. H. THOMAS.* Ack. in Mar. 1849 court. Registered Apr. 21, 1849.

396 Bond: THOMAS B. GRANT binds self to JOSHUA TETHEROW for $300. Condition, Grant is to give a good deed to 100 ac., Dis. 9, Sec. 1 when Tetherow pays last payment. Nov. 17, 1845. *Thomas B. Grant.* Wit: *J.B. LAKEY,* who proved in Mar. 1849 court. Registered Apr. 21, 1849.

397 Performance Bond: SILAS MCDOWELL, J.R. SILER, JAMES K. GRAY post $4,000 bond for McDowell, appointed Clerk & Master in Equity. Mar. 23, 1849. Ack. by principals before J.L. BAILEY, judge of Superior Ct. of Law & Equity, Mar. 29, 1849. Registered Apr. 23, 1849.

397 Performance bond, 2nd for SILAS MCDOWELL, for $10,000; other details same as previous entry.

398 JOSEPH WELCH to JOSHUA HALL, both of Macon, for $200, quitclaim deed date 1830, Sec. 37, Dis. 17. Dec. 19, 1848. *Joseph Welch.* Wit: *DANIEL WEST, ALFRED HALL.* Proven by Alfred Hall in Mar. 1849 court. Registered Apr. 24, 1849.

398 JAMES PEEK to LOGAN BERRY, both of Macon, 70 ac., Sec. 72, Dis. 17. Jan. 18, 1849. *James Peek.* Wit: *E. DOWDLE, JOHN STRAIN.* Acknowledged. Registered Apr. 24, 1849.

399 SG 803, THOMAS J. ROAN, assignee of JESSE GRIGGS, for $26.91, 50 ac., Sec. 127, Dis. 17. Granted Oct. 6, 1847; registered Apr. 26, 1849.

400 SG 874, ELIAS M. KILPATRICK, $__, 82+ ac., NE bank of Tennessee River. Granted Dec. 25, 1848; registered Apr. 24, 1849.

401 S.G. 875, E.M. KILPATRICK, $___, 93 ac., Sec. 13, Dis. 9, N. bank of Tennessee R., below a large island. Granted Dec. 25, 1848; registered Apr. 26, 1849.

401 SG 876, JACOB FOUTS, $__, 50 ac., Sec. 90, Dis. 16. Granted 1848; registered May 2, 1849.

402 SG 894, JOHN CONLEY, $86.25, 115 ac., Sec. 50, Dis. 14, on N. fork of Betty's Cr., on state line. Granted Jan. 22, 1849; registered May 4, 1849.

403 SG 699, ANDREW J. WOODS, $5/100 ac., 100 ac. on headwaters of Cullowhee Cr., Dis. 7, near the Beech Cove. Entry Sep. 27, 1842; grant Dec. 231, 1846; registered May 7, 1849.

404 SG 877, JACOB FOUTS, $__, 66 ac., Sec. 84, Dis. 16. Granted Dec. 25, 1848; registered May 8, 1849.

405 Sheriff's sale: EZEKIEL DOWDLE, Esq., High Sh'ff of Macon, to JOHN B. ALLISON of Haywood Co. NC, property sold to satisfy judgment against ARCHIBALD HENDERSON of Macon, for $18.24 & $2.65 cost, recovered by Allison. Property was 100 ac. on Cullowhee Cr., Dis. 7, originally granted to WM. HENDERSON & since transferred to Archibald. At sale, Dec. 13 at courthouse in Franklin, Allison had high bid of 75 cents. Dec. 13, 1847. *E. Dowdle.* Wit: *J.R. SILER.* Ack. in Mar. 1849 court. Reg. May 15, 1849.

406 JESSE R. SILER to G.H. GUYER, for $8, 61 ac., Sec. 21, Dis. 12, on Nantahala River. Feb. 10, 1849. *J.R. Siler.* Wit: *L. LONG, PHILLIP GUYER.* Proven by Phillip Guyer in Mar. 1849 court. Registered May 18, 1849.

407 JESSE R. SILER to PHILLIP GUYER Junr. for $90, 88 ac. on Nantahala R., Sec. 20, Dis. 12. Feb. 10, 1849. *J.R. Siler.* Wit: *L. LONG, GEORGE H. GUYER.* Proven by George H. Guyer in Mar. 1849 court. Registered May 18, 1849.

408 SAMUEL H. ROPER to ALFRED HALL, both of Macon, for $125, 80 ac., Sec. 31, Dis. 17, on Tennessee R. Aug. 6, 1846. *Samuel H. (his X mark) Roper.* Wit: *NOAH MILLER, THOMAS J. SHEPHERD Sr.* Proven by Shepherd, Mar. 1849 court. Reg. May 1849.

408 GEORGE HUGHS to NATHAN D. HART (DEHART), both of Macon, for $600,103 ac., Sec. 39, Dis. 8, on Tennessee River. Nov. 15, 1848. *Geo. N. Huges.* Wit: *JOHN (his X mark) D.HART, JOHN P. (DE)HART.* Nathan D.Heart is bound to pay the state the am't req. & stand between Hughs & all damage for same. Nov. 15, 1848. *Nathan D.Hart.* Wit: *DILLEN A. HUGHS(?), JOHN P. D.HART.* Proven by John P. D.Hart in Mar. 1849 court. Registered Jun. 5, 1849.

409 JOHN B. ALLISON of Haywood Co. NC to JAMES H. BRYSON of Macon, for $100, land on Cullowhee, sold by E. DOWDLE, Sh'ff of Macon, on writ against ARCHIBALD HENERSON. Oct. 19, 1848. *J.B. Allison.* Wit: *A. BUMGARNER, MICHAEL (his X mark) LONG.* Ack. in Mar. 1849 court. Registered Jun. 5, 1849.

410 WM. C. PEEK to JOHN AMMONS Senr., both of Macon, for $162.50, 100 ac. on "Elijak" (Ellijay) Cr., Dis. 11. Mar. 8, 1849. *William C. Peek.* Wit: *THOS. M. ANGEL, A.L. RUSSELL.* Proven by Angel in Mar. 1849 court. Registered Jun. 5, 1849.

411 SG 752, ELEANA/ELEANY ASH, $5/100 ac., 50 ac. on Savannah Creek. Entry Feb. 13, 1847; grant Dec. 20, 1848; registered Jun. 6, 1849.

412 SG 792, JAMES M. ZACKERY, $5/100 ac., 100 ac. on Tuckasegee R., top of Blue Ridge. Entry Feb. 2, 1847; grant Jan. 30, 1849; registered Jun. 11, 1849.

413 SG 733, MARTHA J. ZACHERY, $5/100 ac., 100 ac. on Tuckasegee R., Blue Ridge. Entry Feb. 2, 1847; grant Jan. 30, 1849; registered Jun. 11, 1849.

414 SG 794, CHRISTOPHER C. ZACKERY, $5/100 ac., 100 ac. on Tuckasegee R. near the Grassy Camp. Entry Jan. 2, 1847; grant Jan. 30, 1849; registered Jun. 11, 1849.

415 SG 796, D.E. ZACKERY, $5/100 ac., 100 ac. on Tuckasegee near the Grassy Camp. Entry Feb. 2, 1847; grant Jan. 30, 1849; registered Jun. 11, 1849.

416 SG 795, ALEXANDER W. ZACKERY, $5/100 ac., 100 ac. on Tuckasegee R. near the Grassy Camp. Entry Feb. 2, 1847; grant Jan. 30, 1849; registered Jun. 11, 1849.

416 SG 797, ALEXANDER ZACKERY, $5/100 ac., 100 ac. on Tuckasegee River. Granted (no date); registered Jun. 12, 1849.

417 GEORGE SHULER to G.W. HAYES for $700, 80 ac. on Deep Creek, Sec. 161, Dis. 17.
     Feb. 4, 1846. *George (his X mark) Shuler.* Wit: *MARK COLEMAN, N. BURCHFIELD.*
     Ack. in Jun. 1848 court. Registered Jun. 12, 1849.

418 SG 771, JOSEPH OLIVER, $5/100 ac., 50 ac. on "Cottoogeejah" (Cartoogechaye) near
     the road by ELI MCKEE's farm. Entry Sep. 22, 1846; grant Dec. 30, 1848; registered
     Jun. 13, 1849.

419 SG 787, to HORATIO N. CONLEY, assignee of JACOB PALMER, for $16.16, 66 ac.,
     Sec. 46, Dis. 13. Granted Jan. 8, 1847; registered Jun. 13, 1849.

419 SG 788, to HORATIO N. CONLEY, assignee of JACOB PALMER, 63 ac., Sec. 48, Dis.
     13. Granted Jan. 8, 1847; registered Jun. 13, 1849.

420 DAVID B. LEDFORD to WM. H. BRYSON, both of Macon, for $100, 56 ac., my inter-
     est in Sec. 22, Dis. 5, transferred to me by WILLIAM DODGEN of Macon, purchased by
     Dodgen in 1836 sale. Feb. 13, 1849. *David B. (his X mark) Ledford.* Wit: *JNO. C.
     BRYSON, J.F. PARKS.* Proven by J.C. Bryson. Registered Aug. 13, 1849.

421 SG 878, HIRAM GIPSON, $14.04, 50 ac., Sec. 39, Dis. 12. Granted Dec. 25, 1845;
     registered Aug. 16, 1849.

422 DAVID PEEK to WILLIAM PEEK, both of Macon, for $100, two tracts, one of 66 ac.
     and one of 35 ac. in Dis. 11, top of mountain between Battle Branch & Elijay Cr., bd. Z.
     PEEK. Mar. 16, 1849. *David Peek.* Wit: *JOHN AMMONS Senr., THOMAS (his X mark)
     AMMONS.* Proven by John Ammons Sr., Jun. 1849 court. Registered Aug. 24, 1849.

423 DAVID PEEK to JAMES PEEK & DAVID L. PEEK, all of Macon, for $100, 61 ac.,
     Dis. 11, on Elijay Creek. Mar. 20, 1849. *David Peek.* Wit: *ABRAHAM MOORE, A.J.
     MOORE.* Proven by Abraham Moore in Jun. 1849 court. Registered Aug. 29, 1849.

424 In suit of WILLIAM KLINE vs. JOHN SHULER & W.H. THOMAS, judgment of
     Supreme Court at Morganton was in favor of Kline for $3 cost & $15.20. E. DOWDLE,
     Sh'ff of Macon sold to B.K. DICKEY for $369, at public sale at courthouse, Negro
     woman BABARY & her child JOI as property of John Shuler at suit of Kline. Sep. 20,
     1848. *E. Dowdle.* Ack. in Jun. 1849 court. Registered Aug. 29, 1849.

42   JOHN SHULER of Macon to DICKY & TABOR for $500, Negro man slave PETER
     about 33 years old. Dec. 26, 1848. *John (his X mark) Shuler.* Wit: *J.L. MOORE,* who
     proved in Jun. 1849 court. Registered Aug. 29, 1849.

425 DAVID B. LEDFORD to WILLIAM H. BRYSON, both of Macon, for $50, 50 ac. on
     Tuckasegee R., Dis. 6. Feb. 15, 1848. *David B. (his X mark) Ledford.* Wit: *JOHN C.
     BRYSON, J.F. PARKS.* Proven by Bryson in Jun. 1849 court. Registered Aug. 29, 1849.

426 THOMAS LONG to JOHN HOWARD, both of Macon, for $200, 100 ac. on Curvens?
     Mill Creek. Dec. 12, 1848. *Thos. Long.* Wit: *DAVID ALLEN, WM. ALLEN.* Proven by
     William Allen in Jun. 1849 court. Registered Aug. 30, 1849.

427 SG 772, HUGH ROGERS, $5/100 ac., 100 ac on Ellijays Creek. Entry Aug. 18, 1845;
     grant Dec. 20, 1848; registered Sep. 3, 1849.

428 SG 750, WILLIAM H. BRYSON, $5/100 ac., 100 ac. on Tuckasegee R., incl. the high
     falls of river. Entry Sep. 24, 184_; grant Dec. __, 1848; registered Aug. 3, 1849.

429 SG 726, $5/100 ac., A.D. MCKINEY, 100 ac. on Chattooga R., bd. GARRETT
     HEDDY's survey. Entry Feb. 1, 1846; grant Oct. 22, 1847; registered Sep. 3, 1849.

429 SG 757, WILLIAM BEASLEY, $5/100 ac., 50 ac. on Cowee Creek. Entry Jun. 9, 1846;
     grant Dec. 30, 1848; registered Sep. 4, 1849.

430 SG 778, POLASKIE HOWARD, $5/100 ac., 100 ac. on Coweta Creek, bd. WILLIAM
     MCDOWELL. Entry Mar. 16, 1844; grant Dec. 30, 1848; registered Sep. 4, 1849.

End of Volume E

FULL NAME INDEX

PLACE INDEX